Middle School 2-1

기말고사 완벽대비

KB100515

적중 100

영어 기출 문제집

중2

동아 | 윤정미

Best Collection

구성과 특징

교과서의 주요 학습 내용을 중심으로 학습 영역별 특성에 맞춰 단계별로 다양한 학습 기회를 제공하여 단원별 학습능력 평가는 물론 중간 및 기말고사 시험 등에 완벽하게 대비할 수 있도록 내용을 구성

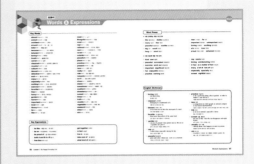

Words & Expressions

Step1
Key Words 단원별 핵심 단어 설명 및 풀이
Key Expression 단원별 핵심 숙어 및 관용어 설명
Word Power 반대 또는 비슷한 뜻 단어 배우기
English Dictionary 영어로 배우는 영어 단어

Step2 실력평가 단원별 수시평가 대비 주관식, 객관식 문제풀이

Step3 서술형 대비 학업성취도 및 수행능력평가 대비 서술형 문제풀이

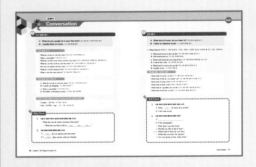

Conversation

Step1
핵심 의사소통 의사소통에 필요한 주요 표현 방법 요약
핵심 Check 기본적인 표현 방법 및 활용능력 확인

Step2 대화문 익히기 상황에 따른 대화문 활용 및 연습

Step3 기본평가 시험대비 기초 학습 능력 평가

Step4 실력평가 단원별 수시평가 대비 주관식, 객관식 문제풀이

Step5 서술형 대비 학업성취도 및 수행능력평가 대비 서술형 문제풀이

Grammar

Step1
주요 문법 단원별 주요 문법 사항과 예문을 알기 쉽게 설명

핵심 Check 기본 문법사항에 대한 이해 여부 확인

Step2 기본평가 시험대비 기초 학습 능력 평가

Step3 실력평가 단원별 수시평가 대비 주관식, 객관식 문제풀이

Step4 서술형 대비 학업성취도 및 수행능력평가 대비 서술형 문제풀이

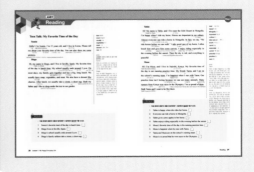

Reading

Step1 구문 분석 단원별로 제시된 문장에 대한 구문별 분석과 내용 설명
확인문제 문장에 대한 기본적인 이해와 인지능력 확인

Step2 확인학습A 빈칸 채우기를 통한 문장 완성 능력 확인

Step3 확인학습B 제시된 우리말을 영어로 완성하여 작문 능력 키우기

Step4 실력평가 단원별 수시평가 대비 주관식, 객관식 문제풀이

Step5 서술형 대비 학업성취도 및 수행능력평가 대비 서술형 문제풀이
교과서 구석구석 교과서에 나오는 기타 문장까지 완벽 학습

Composition

  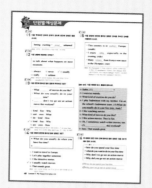 

|영역별 핵심문제|

단어 및 어휘, 대화문, 문법, 독해 등 각 영역별 기출문제의 출제 유형을 분석하여 실전에 대비하고 연습할 수 있도록 문제를 배열

|서술형 실전 및 창의사고력 문제|

학교 시험에서 점차 늘어나는 서술형 시험에 집중 대비하고 고득점을 취득하는데 만전을 기하기 위한 학습 코너

|단원별 예상문제|

기출문제를 분석한 후 새로운 시험 출제 경향을 더하여 새롭게 출제될 수 있는 문제를 포함하여 시험에 완벽하게 대비할 수 있도록 준비

|단원별 모의고사|

영역별, 단계별 학습을 모두 마친 후 실전 연습을 위한 모의고사

INSIGHT
on the textbook

교과서 파헤치기

- **단어Test1~2** 영어 단어 우리말 쓰기와 우리말을 영어 단어로 쓰기
- **대화문Test1~2** 대화문 빈칸 완성 및 전체 대화문 쓰기
- **본문Test1~5** 빈칸 완성, 우리말 쓰기, 문장 배열연습, 영어 작문하기 복습 등 단계별 반복 학습을 통해 교과서 지문에 대한 완벽한 습득
- **구석구석지문Test1~2** 지문 빈칸 완성 및 전문 영어로 쓰기

Ideas for Saving the Earth

의사소통 기능

- 물건 사기 1
  A: How much is this soccer ball?
  B: It's 6 dollars.

- 물건 사기 2
  A: Can I get a discount?
  B: OK. I'll take 1 dollar off.

언어 형식

- 수동태
  This **was made by** Hajun.

- 목적격보어로 to부정사를 취하는 동사
  I **want you to understand** the meaning of "upcycling."

교과서
Words & Expressions

Key Words

- **afraid**[əfréid] 혱 두려워하는, 걱정하는
- **almost**[ɔ́ːlmoust] 뷔 거의
- **anyone**[éniwʌn] 떼 누군가, 누가
- **backpack**[bǽkpæk] 몡 가방
- **better**[bétər] 혱 (good의 비교급) 더 나은
- **blue jeans** 청바지
- **bottom**[bɑ́təm] 몡 아래 부분, 바닥
- **bucket**[bʌ́kit] 몡 양동이
- **clock**[klɑk] 몡 (벽에 걸거나 실내에 두는) 시계
- **clothes**[klouz] 몡 옷, 의복
- **club**[klʌb] 몡 동아리, 동호회, 클럽
- **combination**[kɑ̀mbənéiʃən] 몡 조합, 결합
- **condition**[kəndíʃən] 몡 상태, 조건
- **creative**[kriéitiv] 혱 창의적인
- **decorate**[dékərèit] 동 장식하다
- **discount**[dískaunt] 몡 할인
- **each**[iːtʃ] 혱 각각의 떼 각각
- **environment**[inváiərnmənt] 몡 환경
- **event**[ivént] 몡 행사
- **expensive**[ikspénsiv] 혱 비싼
- **explain**[ikspléin] 동 설명하다
- **glasses**[glǽsiz] 몡 안경
- **glove**[glʌv] 몡 장갑, 글러브
- **help**[help] 동 돕다, 도와주다
- **hold**[hould] 동 개최하다, 열다
- **instrument**[ínstrəmənt] 몡 악기
- **interesting**[íntərəstiŋ] 혱 흥미로운
- **kit**[kit] 몡 (도구·장비) 세트, 용구 한 벌

- **knife**[naif] 몡 칼
- **large**[lɑːrdʒ] 혱 큰
- **lastly**[lǽstli] 뷔 마지막으로
- **like**[laik] 전 ~처럼, ~와 같이
- **meaning**[míːniŋ] 몡 의미
- **musical**[mjúːzikəl] 혱 음악의
- **number**[nʌ́mbər] 몡 숫자
- **nursing home** 양로원
- **price**[prais] 몡 가격
- **purple**[pə́ːrpl] 혱 자주색의 몡 자주색
- **recycling**[riːsaikəliŋ] 몡 재활용
- **round**[raund] 혱 둥근
- **rubber band** 고무 밴드, 고무줄
- **sew**[sou] 동 바느질하다
- **sewing**[sóuiŋ] 몡 바느질
- **shoulder**[ʃóuldər] 몡 어깨
- **soccer ball** 축구공
- **strap**[stræp] 몡 가죽 끈
- **thing**[θiŋ] 몡 물건
- **through**[θruː] 전 ~를 통해
- **throw**[θrou] 동 던지다
- **trash**[træʃ] 몡 쓰레기
- **T-shirt** 몡 티셔츠
- **understand**[ʌndərstǽnd] 동 이해하다
- **upcycle**[ʌ́psaikl] 동 업사이클하다
- **upcycling**[ʌ́psaikliŋ] 몡 업사이클링
- **upgrade**[əpgréid] 몡 향상, 개선 동 개선하다
- **used**[juːzd] 혱 중고의

Key Expressions

- **be about** ~에 관한 것이다
- **become interested in** ~에 관심을 가지다
- **be good for** ~에 좋다
- **be made by** ~에 의해 만들어지다
- **cut off** ~을 자르다
- **for example** 예를 들어
- **get a discount** 할인을 받다
- **hear from** ~로부터 이야기[소식]를 듣다
- **How much+동사+주어 ~?** ~은 얼마예요?
- **I'll take it**. 그것을 살게요.

- **let me think** 잠깐 생각해 볼게
- **let's+동사원형** ~하자
- **look for** ~을 찾다
- **plan to+동사원형** ~할 계획이다
- **sound like+명사** ~처럼 들리다
- **take ~(돈) off** ~을 할인하다, 깎다
- **talk about** ~에 관해 말하다
- **throw away** 버리다
- **want+목적어+to+동사원형** ~가 …하기를 원하다
- **What[How] about+명사 ~?** ~은 어때?

Word Power

※ 서로 반대되는 뜻을 가진 단어

□ **much** (많은) ↔ **little** (적은)

□ **afraid** (두려워하는) ↔ **unafraid** (두려워하지 않는)

□ **expensive** (비싼) ↔ **cheap** (값싼)

□ **good** (좋은) ↔ **bad** (나쁜)

□ **used** (중고의) ↔ **new** (새로운)

□ **interesting** (흥미로운) ↔ **uninteresting** (재미없는)

□ **large** (큰) ↔ **small** (작은)

□ **give** (주다) ↔ **take** (받다)

□ **better** (더 좋은) ↔ **worse** (더 나쁜)

□ **like** (~와 같이) ↔ **unlike** (~와 달리)

□ **before** (~ 전에) ↔ **after** (~ 후에)

□ **upgrade** (개선하다) ↔ **downgrade** (격하시키다)

※ 서로 비슷한 뜻을 가진 단어

□ **discount** : **reduction** (할인)

□ **afraid** : **scared** (무서워하는)

□ **used** : **second-hand** (중고의)

□ **condition** : **state** (상태)

□ **understand** : **comprehend** (이해하다)

□ **trash** : **garbage** (쓰레기)

□ **fun** : **enjoyable** (재미있는)

□ **use** : **utilize** (이용하다)

□ **creative** : **original** (독창적인, 창의적인)

□ **bucket** : **pail** (양동이)

English Dictionary

□ **clothes** 옷
→ the things that people wear, such as shirts, coats, trousers, and dresses
셔츠, 코트, 바지, 드레스와 같은 사람들이 입는 것들

□ **combination** 조합
→ two or more different things that exist together or put together
둘 또는 그 이상의 다른 것이 함께 존재하거나 결합되어 있는 것

□ **creative** 창의적인
→ involving the use of imagination to produce new ideas or things
새로운 생각이나 물건을 만들기 위해 상상력을 사용하는 것을 포함하는

□ **decorate** 장식하다
→ to make something look more attractive by putting something pretty on it
어떤 예쁜 것을 위에 놓음으로써 물건을 더 매력적으로 보이게 만들다

□ **discount** 할인
→ a reduction in the usual price of something
어떤 물건의 보통 가격보다 싸진 가격

□ **environment** 환경
→ the air, water, and land on Earth, which is affected by man's activities
인간의 활동에 의해 영향을 받는 지구상의 공기, 물과 땅

□ **explain** 설명하다
→ to tell someone about something in a way that is clear or easy to understand
이해하기 쉽거나 분명한 방식으로 어떤 것을 말해주다

□ **instrument** 악기
→ an object used for producing music
음악을 만들어 내기 위해 사용되는 물건

□ **interested** 관심 있는
→ giving a lot of attention to something because you want to find out more about it
더 많이 알고 싶기 때문에 어떤 것에 더 많은 관심을 가지는

□ **meaning** 의미
→ a particular idea that a word, expression, or sign represents
어떤 단어나 표현 또는 표시가 나타내는 특정한 생각

□ **recycling** 재활용
→ the process of treating things that have already been used so that they can be used again
이미 사용된 것을 다시 사용할 수 있도록 처리하는 과정

□ **trash** 쓰레기
→ things that you throw away because you no longer want or need them
당신이 더 이상 원하지 않거나 필요하지 않기 때문에 버리는 것

서답형

01 다음 짝지어진 두 단어가 관계가 같도록 빈칸에 알맞은 단어를 쓰시오.

> discount : reduction = _____ : state

02 다음 빈칸에 공통으로 들어갈 말은?

> • How do I _____ to the police station?
> • Can I _____ a discount?

① take   ② get
③ go   ④ make
⑤ look

03 다음 중 밑줄 친 단어의 우리말 뜻이 잘못된 것은?

① I'll take 2 dollars off. 2달러 할인하다
② How about this hat? ~은 어때?
③ I want you to understand the meaning of this word. 의미
④ Students became interested in upcycling. ~에 관심을 가졌다
⑤ We're going to give all the money to a nursing home. 탁아소

[04~05] 다음 영영풀이에 해당하는 단어로 알맞은 것을 고르시오.

04

> an object used for producing music

① meaning   ② combination
③ instrument   ④ trash
⑤ creative

05

> to make something look more attractive by putting something pretty on it

① sell   ② paint
③ sew   ④ decorate
⑤ produce

서답형

06 다음 우리말에 맞게 빈칸에 알맞은 단어를 쓰시오.

> 이곳의 모든 것은 오래되었거나 중고다.
> ➡ Everything here is old or _____.

07 다음 빈칸에 들어갈 말로 알맞게 짝지어진 것은?

> • _____ recycling, upcycling is good for the environment.
> • I'm looking _____ a baseball glove.

① Like – for   ② Likely – for
③ Unlike – at   ④ Unlike – for
⑤ Unlikely – on

08 다음 빈칸에 들어갈 말로 알맞은 것은?

> "Trashion" is a(n) _____ of "trash" and "fashion."

① instrument   ② upcycling
③ combination   ④ idea
⑤ meaning

01 다음 빈칸에 들어갈 말을 〈보기〉에서 찾아 쓰시오. (필요하면 변형하여 쓰시오.)

┤ 보기 ├

discount   kit   interest   instruments

(1) Students became _____ in upcycling.

(2) Do you have a sewing _____?

(3) We plan to play the _____ in a concert.

(4) Can I get a _____?

02 다음 제시된 밑줄 친 단어의 철자를 재배열하여 문장의 의미에 맞게 단어를 만든 후, 단어의 뜻을 쓰시오.

(1) My group wants to dohl a trashion show.

➡ _____

(2) How chum are the round glasses?

➡ _____

(3) Can anyone plainex the meaning of upcycling?

➡ _____

(4) Your ideas are so reactive.

➡ _____

03 다음 우리말과 같은 표현이 되도록 문장의 빈칸을 채우시오.

(1) 청바지 다리 부분을 잘라라.

➡ _____ the legs of the blue jeans.

(2) 트래션 쇼는 재미있을 것 같은데.

➡ A trashion show _____ _____ fun!

(3) 나를 버리지 말아줘.

➡ Don't _____ me _____!

(4) 그것을 살게요.

➡ I'll _____ it.

04 다음 빈칸에 들어갈 말을 〈보기〉에서 골라 알맞은 형태로 고쳐 쓰시오.

┤ 보기 ├

mean   music   take   combine

(1) My group is going to make _____ instruments from old things.

(2) I want you to understand the _____ of "upcycling."

(3) The word "upcycling" is a _____ of "upgrade" and "recycling."

(4) A: Can I get a discount?
B: OK. I'll _____ 1 dollar _____.

05 다음 영영풀이에 해당하는 단어를 주어진 철자로 시작하여 쓰시오.

- t_____ : things that you throw away because you no longer want or need them

- c_____ : two or more different things that exist together or put together

06 다음에 제시된 우리말에 맞는 영어를 쓰고, 각 단어의 첫 글자를 이용하여 단어를 완성하고 그 뜻을 쓰시오.

(1) 다른: _____

(2) 환경: _____

(3) 창의적인: _____

(4) 한 번: _____

(5) 고무: _____

(6) 거의: _____

(7) ~을 통해: _____

(8) 비싼: _____

➡ _____

Conversation

1 물건 사기 1

A How much is this soccer ball? 이 축구공은 얼마입니까?
B It's 6 dollars. 6달러예요.

■ **가격 묻고 말하기**
"How much is[are] ～?"는 '～은 얼마입니까?'라는 뜻으로, 물건의 가격을 물을 때 사용하는 표현이다. 대답은 "It is[They are] 10 dollars."처럼 구체적인 가격을 넣어 답한다. 가격을 묻는 다른 표현은 How much does it cost?, What's the price?, I want to know the price., Can you tell me the price? 등이 있다.

상점에서 점원이 손님에게 도움이 필요한지 물을 때

• May[Can] I help you? 도와 드릴까요?
  = How may I help you? 도와 드릴까요?
  = What can I do for you? 무엇을 도와 드릴까요?

상점에서 점원이 손님에게 물건을 추천할 때

• How about this[that] one? 이건[저건] 어떠세요?

상점에서 손님이 점원에게 찾는 물건을 말할 때

• I'm looking for ～. 저는 ～을 찾고 있어요. • I'd like to buy ～. 저는 ～을 사고 싶어요.

상점에서 손님이 점원에게 가격을 물어볼 때

• How much is it[are they]? 그것은 얼마입니까?
• What's the price (of it[them])? (그것의) 가격은 얼마입니까?

상점에서 손님이 물건의 구입 의사를 말할 때

• I'll take it[them]. 그것을 살게요.

핵심 Check

1. 다음 대화의 빈칸에 알맞은 말을 쓰시오.

   A: _____ _____ is this blue T-shirt?

   B: It's 10 dollars.

2. 다음 주어진 문장과 같은 의미가 되도록 빈칸에 알맞은 말을 쓰시오.

   How much does it cost? = What's the _____ of it?

② 물건 사기 2

> **A** Can I get a discount? 할인을 받을 수 있나요?
>
> **B** OK. I'll take 1 dollar off. 네. 1 달러 깎아 드릴게요.

■ 물건을 사면서 할인을 원할 때 사용하는 표현으로 Is[Are] ~ on sale?(~은 할인 판매 중인가요?)을 사용할 수 있다. 또 어느 정도 할인이 되는지에 대해 언급할 때는 '~달러 할인하여'라는 의미의 ~dollar[dollars] off라는 표현을 쓴다.

손님이 점원에게 할 수 있는 표현

- Is this computer on sale? 이 컴퓨터는 할인 판매 중인가요?
- 40% off? 40% 할인하나요?
- (That's) Great! I'll take[buy] it. 좋아요. 그것을 살게요.

점원이 손님에게 할 수 있는 표현

- I'll take 15 dollars off. 15달러 할인해 드릴게요.
- They're 30% off. 그것들은 30% 할인 판매 중입니다.
- It's 40% off the regular price. 정상 가격에서 40% 할인해 드려요.
- It was 100 dollars before, but now it's only 60 dollars. 전에 100달러였는데 지금은 단지 60달러입니다.
- The regular price is 100 dollars, so it's 50 dollars now. 정상 가격이 100달러이니까 지금은 50달러입니다.

핵심 Check

3. 다음 우리말에 맞게 빈칸에 들어갈 알맞은 말은?

이 가방은 할인 판매 중입니다.

= This backpack is _____.

① on sale   ② for sale   ③ sale   ④ to sell   ⑤ selling

4. 다음 빈칸에 들어갈 알맞은 것은?

This red shirt is 50% _____. The regular price is 100 dollars, so it's 50 dollars now.

① up   ② at   ③ out   ④ on   ⑤ off

A. Listen and Talk A-1

G: Excuse me. ❶How much are the round glasses?

M: ❷They're 18 dollars.

G: Hmm. ❸Can I get a discount?

M: No, ❹I'm afraid not. Sorry.

G: ❺That's OK. ❻I'll take them.

G: 실례합니다. 저 동그란 안경은 얼만가요?

M: 그것은 18달러예요.

G: 음. 할인을 받을 수 있을까요?

M: 아니요, 안 될 것 같아요. 미안합니다.

G: 괜찮아요. 그것을 살게요.

❶ How much are ~?는 가격을 물어볼 때 사용하는 표현으로 '~은 얼마입니까?'라는 뜻이다.

❷ They는 복수형 대명사로 the round glasses를 가리킨다.

❸ Can I ~?는 '~할 수 있을까?'라는 뜻이고, get a discount는 '할인을 받다'는 뜻이다.

❹ 상대방에게 정중하게 미안함을 나타낼 때 사용하는 표현이다.

❺ Sorry에 대한 대답으로 '괜찮아요.'라는 뜻이다. It's okay.를 사용할 수 있다.

❻ take는 '선택하다, 사다'라는 의미다.

Check(√) True or False

(1) The girl is able to get a discount. T ☐ F ☐

(2) The girl will buy the round glasses. T ☐ F ☐

B. Listen and Talk C

B: Wow! There are so many interesting things here.

W: ❶Everything here is old or used. What are you looking for?

B: ❷I'm looking for a clock.

W How about this red clock?

B: How much is it?

W: It's 15 dollars.

B: That's too expensive for me. Can I get a discount?

W: No, ❸I'm afraid not. It's only one year old. It's ❹almost new.

B: Then, how much is this blue clock with the large numbers?

W: It's 10 dollars.

B: Then, I'll take the blue one. Thank you.

B: 와. 여기에는 흥미로운 것들이 많이 있네요.

W: 여기 있는 모든 물건들은 오래되었거나 이미 사용한 물건들입니다. 무엇을 찾고 있나요?

B: 시계를 찾고 있어요.

W: 이 빨간색 시계는 어때요?

B: 얼마예요?

W: 15달러예요.

B: 저에게 너무 비싸군요. 깎아주실 수 있어요?

W: 미안하지만 안 돼요. 그건 일년밖에 안된 거예요. 거의 새 것입니다.

B: 그럼 숫자가 큰 이 파란 시계는 얼마예요?

W: 10달러예요.

B: 그럼 파란색을 살게요. 감사합니다.

❶ Everything은 단수 취급한다. used는 '중고의'란 뜻으로 second-hand로 바꾸어 쓸 수 있다.

❷ look for ~: '~을 찾다'는 의미로 be동사와 함께 사용되어 현재진행형 구문이다.

❸ 상대방에게 정중하게 미안함을 나타낼 때 사용하는 표현으로 '유감스럽지만 안 됩니다.'란 의미다.

❹ almost는 부사로 '거의'란 뜻이며 형용사 new를 꾸며주고 있다.

Check(√) True or False

(3) The boy can buy the red clock at a discount. T ☐ F ☐

(4) The boy will take the blue clock. T ☐ F ☐

Listen and Talk A-2

M: Hello. ❶May I help you?

G: Yes. ❷I'm looking for a backpack for school.

M: ❸What about this red one? ❹It's 12 dollars.

G: Can I get a discount?

M: OK. ❺I'll take 2 dollars off.

G: ❻That sounds good. I'll take it.

❶ 매장에 손님이 들어올 때 점원이 사용하는 말이다. Can I help you?, What can I do for you?, Do you need any help? 등의 표현이 있다.

❷ '~을 찾고 있다'는 표현으로 'I'm looking for ~'를 사용한다.

❸ 'What about ~?'은 '~은 어떤가요?'라는 표현이고, one은 a backpack을 받는 부정대명사이다.

❹ 가격을 말할 때 사용하는 표현으로 It은 this red backpack을 가리킨다.

❺ take off는 '할인하다'는 뜻이다.

❻ 'sound+형용사'는 '~처럼 들리다'라는 의미로 대화에서 '좋아요', '좋은 생각이야'의 의미로 사용된다.

Listen and Talk A-3

G: Excuse me. ❶How much is this purple T-shirt?

M: ❷It's 10 dollars.

G: That's expensive. Can I get a discount?

M: OK. ❸I'll take 1 dollar off. That'll be 9 dollars.

G: I'll take it, then. Thank you!

❶ How much is[are] ~?는 가격을 물어볼 때 사용하는 표현으로 '~은 얼마입니까?'라는 뜻이다.

❷ It은 this purple T-shirt를 가리킨다.

❸ take off는 '할인하다'는 뜻이다.

Listen and Talk A-4

M: Hello. ❶May I help you?

G: I'm looking for a baseball glove.

M: ❷This one is 15 dollars and it's in good condition.

G: Can I get a discount?

M: OK. I'll take 2 dollars off.

G: Then it's 13 dollars. I'll take it.

❶ Can I help you?, What can I do for you?, Do you need any help? 등의 표현으로 바꾸어 쓸 수 있다.

❷ one은 a baseball glove를 가리키는 부정대명사다. in good condition은 '상태가 좋은'의 의미다.

Listen and Talk B

A: May I help you?

B: Yes. How much is this soccer ball?

A: It's 6 dollars.

B: ❶Can I get a discount?

A: OK. ❷I'll take 1 dollar off.

B: Then that'll be 5 dollars. ❸I'll take it.

❶ '할인해 주시겠습니까?'라는 뜻이다.

❷ take off는 '할인하다'는 뜻이다.

❸ take는 '선택하다, 사다'는 의미다.

Review 1

G: Excuse me. How much is this yellow backpack?

M: It's 18 dollars.

G: Hmm. ❶That's expensive for me. ❷How about this red one?

M: It's 15 dollars.

G: That's a good price. I'll take it.

❶ '그것은 나에게 비싸다'는 뜻이다.

❷ 'How about+명사 ~?'는 '~은 어때요?'라는 뜻이다.

Review 2

W: May I help you?

B: Yes. How much is this blue T-shirt?

W: It's 10 dollars.

B: Can I get a discount?

W: OK. ❶I'll take 2 dollars off.

B: That sounds good. I'll take it.

❶ take off는 '할인하다'는 뜻으로, '2달러 할인해 드리겠습니다.'는 의미다.

Review 3

M: Hello. May I help you?

G: I'm looking for a clock.

M: ❶This one is 15 dollars and it's in good condition.

G: Can I get a discount?

M: OK. I'll take 2 dollars off.

G: Then it's 13 dollars. I'll take it.

❶ one은 a clock을 가리키는 부정대명사다.

● 다음 우리말과 일치하도록 빈칸에 알맞은 말을 쓰시오.

Listen and Talk A-1

G: Excuse me. _____ _____ are the round glasses?

M: They're 18 dollars.

G: Hmm. Can I _____ _____ _____?

M: No, _____ _____ _____. Sorry.

G: That's OK. I'll _____ them.

G: 실례합니다. 저 동그란 안경은 얼만가
요?
M: 그것은 18달러예요.
G: 음. 할인을 받을 수 있을까요?
M: 아니요, 안 될 것 같아요. 미안합니다.
G: 괜찮아요. 그것을 살게요.

Listen and Talk A-2

M: Hello. May I help you?

G: Yes. I'm _____ _____ a backpack for school.

M: _____ _____ this red _____? It's 12 dollars.

G: Can I _____ a discount?

M: OK. I'll _____ 2 dollars _____.

G: That sounds good. I'll _____ it.

M: 안녕하세요. 도와드릴까요?
G: 네. 저는 학교 갈 때 쓸 배낭을 찾고
있어요.
M: 이 빨간색은 어때요? 12달러입니다.
G: 할인을 받을 수 있을까요?
M: 네. 2달러 깎아 드릴게요.
G: 좋군요. 그것을 살게요.

Listen and Talk A-3

G: Excuse me. _____ _____ _____ this purple T-shirt?

M: It's 10 dollars.

G: That's _____. Can I get a _____?

M: OK. I'll _____ 1 dollar _____. That'll be 9 dollars.

G: I'll _____ _____, then. Thank you!

G: 실례합니다. 이 보라색 티셔츠는 얼마
인가요?
M: 10달러예요.
G: 비싸군요. 할인을 받을 수 있을까요?
M: 네. 1달러 깎아 드릴게요. 9달러예요.
G: 그럼 그것을 살게요. 감사해요.

Listen and Talk A-4

M: Hello. _____ I help you?

G: I'_____ _____ _____ a baseball glove.

M: This _____ is 15 dollars and it's _____ good _____.

G: Can I get a discount?

M: OK. I'll _____ _____ _____ _____.

G: Then it's 13 dollars. I'll take it.

M: 안녕하세요. 도와드릴까요?
G: 저는 야구 글러브를 찾고 있어요.
M: 이건 15달러고, 상태가 좋아요.
G: 할인을 받을 수 있을까요?
M: 네. 2달러 깎아드릴게요.
G: 그럼 13달러네요. 그것을 살게요.

Listen & Talk B

A: May I help you?

B: Yes. _____ _____ is this soccer ball?

A: It's 6 dollars.

B: Can I _____ _____ _____?

A: OK. I'll _____ 1 dollar _____.

B: Then that'll be 5 dollars. I'll _____ _____.

A: 도와드릴까요?
B: 네. 이 축구공은 얼마인가요?
A: 6달러예요.
B: 할인을 받을 수 있을까요?
A: 네. 1달러 깎아 드릴게요.
B: 그러면 5달러겠네요. 그것을 살게요.

Listen and Talk C

B: Wow! There are so many _____ things here.

W: Everything here is old or _____. What are you _____ _____ ?

B: I'm looking for a clock.

W: _____ _____ this red clock?

B: How much is it?

W: It's 15 dollars.

B: That's _____ _____ _____ me. Can I get a discount?

W: No, I'm _____ not. It's only one year old. It's almost new.

B: Then, how much is this blue clock _____ the large numbers?

W: It's 10 dollars.

B: Then, I'll _____ the blue _____. Thank you.

Review 1

G: Excuse me. _____ _____ is this yellow backpack?

M: It's 18 dollars.

G: Hmm. That's _____ _____ me. _____ _____ this red _____ ?

M: It's 15 dollars.

G: That's a good _____. I'll take _____.

Review 2

W: May I help you?

B: Yes. _____ _____ is this blue T-shirt?

W: It's 10 dollars.

B: Can I _____ a discount?

W: OK. I'll _____ 2 dollars _____.

B: That sounds good. I'll take it.

Review 3

M: Hello. May I help you?

G: I'm _____ _____ a clock.

M: This _____ is 15 dollars and it's _____ _____ _____ _____.

G: Can I _____ a discount?

M: OK. I'll _____ 2 dollars _____.

G: Then it's 13 dollars. I'll _____ it.

01 다음 우리말에 맞도록 빈칸에 들어갈 알맞은 말을 쓰시오.

시계를 하나 사려고 합니다.
➡ I'm _____ _____ a clock.

02 다음 대화의 밑줄 친 부분과 의미가 같은 것은?

A: How much are these shoes?
B: They're 13 dollars.

① What are your favorite shoes?
② What is the size of these shoes?
③ What color are these shoes?
④ Which shoes are the best?
⑤ What is the price of these shoes?

03 다음 대화의 빈칸에 들어갈 말로 가장 적절한 것은?

W: May I help you?
B: Yes. How much is this blue T-shirt?
W: It's 10 dollars.
B: Can I get a discount?
W: OK. I'll take 2 dollars off.
B: That sounds good. _____

① Show me another.   ② I'll take it.
③ Hurry up.   ④ Here you are.
⑤ It's too expensive.

04 다음 우리말에 해당하는 표현에 맞게 주어진 문장의 빈칸을 채워 쓰시오.

깎아 줄 수 있어요?
➡ Can I _____ a discount?

[01~02] 다음 대화를 읽고, 물음에 답하시오.

G: Excuse me. _____(A)_____ the round glasses?
M: They're 18 dollars.
G: Hmm. Can I get a discount?
M: No, _____(B)_____ Sorry.
G: That's OK. I'll take them.

01 위 대화의 빈칸 (A)에 들어갈 말로 알맞은 것은?

① How much is
② What are for
③ How much are
④ Why are there
⑤ Where are

02 위 대화의 빈칸 (B)에 들어갈 말로 알맞은 것은?

① I want to know the price.
② That's too expensive.
③ You can get a discount.
④ You should buy them.
⑤ I'm afraid not.

03 다음 대답이 나올 수 있는 질문으로 알맞지 <u>않은</u> 것은?

> It's 5,000 won.

① How much does this book cost?
② How much is this book?
③ I want to know the price of this book.
④ Is this book on sale?
⑤ What's the price of this book?

[04~05] 다음 대화를 읽고, 물음에 답하시오.

M: Hello. May I help you?
G: Yes. (A)I'm looking for a backpack for school.
M: What about this red one? It's 12 dollars.
G: Can I get a discount?
M: OK. I'll take 2 dollars ___(B)___.
G: That sounds good. I'll take it.

04 위 대화의 밑줄 친 (A)와 바꾸어 쓸 수 <u>없는</u> 말은?

① I want to buy a backpack for school.
② Where can I get a backpack for school?
③ I'm trying to find a backpack for school.
④ I'd like to buy a backpack for school.
⑤ Do you have any backpacks for school?

05 위 대화의 빈칸 (B)에 들어갈 말로 알맞은 것은?

① in   ② of   ③ about
④ for   ⑤ off

06 다음 주어진 문장에 이어질 대화의 순서로 알맞은 것은?

> May I help you?

(A) They're 13 dollars.
(B) Can I get a discount?
(C) OK. I'll take 2 dollars off.
(D) Yes. How much are these shoes?

① (A) – (B) – (C) – (D)
② (B) – (A) – (C) – (D)
③ (B) – (C) – (A) – (D)
④ (D) – (A) – (B) – (C)
⑤ (D) – (B) – (A) – (C)

[07~08] 다음 대화를 읽고, 물음에 답하시오.

G: Excuse me. How much is this yellow backpack?
M: It's 18 dollars.
G: Hmm. (A)저에게는 비싸네요. How about this red (B)one?
M: It's 15 dollars.
G: That's a good price. I'll take it.

07 위 대화의 밑줄 친 (A)의 우리말에 맞게 주어진 단어를 이용하여 영어로 쓰시오.

> that / expensive / for

➡ _____

08 위 대화의 밑줄 친 (B)의 one이 가리키는 것을 찾아 쓰시오.

➡ _____

09 다음 중 짝지어진 대화가 <u>어색한</u> 것을 고르시오.

① A: How much is it?
　 B: It's 15 dollars.
② A: Can I get a discount?
　 B: OK. I'll take 1 dollar off.
③ A: Hello. May I help you?
　 B: Yes. I'm looking for a backpack.
④ A: Excuse me. How much are these sneakers?
　 B: They are $15.
⑤ A: What are you looking for?
　 B: I'm looking at a clock.

[10~12] 다음 대화를 읽고, 물음에 답하시오.

B: Wow! There are so many interesting things here.
W: Everything here is old or ___(A)___. What are you looking for?

B: I'm looking for a clock.
W: How about this red clock?
B: How much is it?
W: It's 15 dollars.
B: That's too expensive for me. Can I get a discount?
W: _____(B)_____ It's only one year old. It's almost new.
B: Then, how much is this blue clock with the large numbers?
W: It's 10 dollars.
B: Then, I'll take the blue one. Thank you.

10 위 대화의 빈칸 (A)에 들어갈 단어에 대한 영어 설명을 보고 알맞은 단어를 쓰시오.

> dirty or not in good condition any longer as a result of being used

➡ _____

11 위 대화의 빈칸 (B)에 들어갈 말로 알맞은 것은?

① That sounds good.
② No, I'm afraid not.
③ Of course.
④ How about this one?
⑤ This is on sale.

12 위 대화의 내용과 일치하지 <u>않는</u> 것은?

① 두 사람은 중고가게에서 대화중이다.
② B는 시계를 사려고 한다.
③ 15달러는 B가 사기에 비싼 가격이다.
④ 가게 주인은 5달러를 깎아주었다.
⑤ B는 파란색 시계를 10달러에 구입했다.

[01~02] 다음 대화를 읽고, 물음에 답하시오.

Man: Hello. May I help you?
Girl: Yes. I'm looking for a backpack for school.
Man: What about this red one? It's 12 dollars.
Girl: (A)깎아 줄 수 있어요? (can, I)
Man: OK. I'll take 2 dollars off.
Girl: That sounds good. I'll take it.

01 위 대화의 밑줄 친 (A)의 우리말에 맞게 주어진 단어를 이용하여 영어로 쓰시오.

➡ _____

02 Q: How much will the girl pay? (Write a full sentence in English.)

➡ _____

03 다음 대화의 밑줄 친 우리말에 맞게 주어진 단어를 이용하여 빈칸을 채우시오.

G: Excuse me. (A)이 노란색 배낭은 얼마인가요? (how)
M: It's 18 dollars.
G: Hmm. That's expensive for me. (B)이 빨간색은 어떤가요? (about, one)
M: It's 15 dollars.
G: That's a good price. (C)그걸로 살게요. (take)

(A) _____
(B) _____
(C) _____

04 다음 그림을 참고하여 두 사람이 나누는 대화의 빈칸을 완성하시오.

B: Wow! There are so many interesting things here.
W: Everything here is old or _____. What are you looking for?
B: I'm looking for a clock.
W: How about this red clock?
B: _____ _____ _____ _____?
W: It's 15 dollars.
B: That's too expensive for me. Can I _____ _____ _____?
W: No, I'm _____ not. It's only one year old. It's almost new.
B: Then, how much is this blue clock with the _____ _____?
W: It's 10 dollars.
B: Then, I'll take the blue one. Thank you.

05 다음 대화의 밑줄 친 우리말에 맞게 영어로 쓰시오.

G: Can I get a discount?
M: OK. 3달러를 깎아줄게요.
G: Then it's 13 dollars. I'll take it.

➡ _____

Grammar

1 목적격보어로 to부정사를 취하는 동사

> • Sue wants her father **to come** home early. Sue는 아빠가 집에 일찍 오기를 원한다.
> • She asked me **to wait** for her. 그녀는 내게 그녀를 기다리라고 요청했다.

■ 동사(want) 다음에 목적어와 to부정사가 쓰여 '~가 …하는 것을 (원)한다'라는 의미를 나타낸다. 이때 목적어 다음의 to부정사를 목적격보어라고 하고 이런 문장 유형을 5형식이라고 한다.

■ to부정사를 목적격보어로 취하는 동사에는 advise, allow, ask, cause, enable, encourage, expect, force, get, help, order, persuade, teach, tell, want, would like 등이 있다.

　• Mom wants Jane **to study** harder. 엄마는 Jane이 더 열심히 공부하기를 원한다.

　• Mom asked me **to wash** the dishes. 엄마는 내게 설거지를 부탁하셨다.

■ 목적격보어로 쓰인 to부정사의 부정형은 'not to+동사원형'으로 쓴다.

　• I told him **not to go**. 나는 그에게 가지 말라고 말했다.

핵심 Check

1. 다음 괄호 안에서 알맞은 것을 고르시오.

　(1) She wanted me (to buy / buy) her a bag.

　(2) I expected him (to be / being) a soccer player.

　(3) He asked them (to be / be) quiet.

2. 다음 우리말에 맞게 빈칸에 알맞은 말을 쓰시오.

　그는 자기 아이들에게 천천히 걸으라고 말했다.

　➡ He told his children ＿＿＿＿＿ ＿＿＿＿＿ slowly.

2 수동태

> • People planted many trees. 사람들이 많은 나무를 심었습니다. 〈능동태〉
> • Many trees **were planted** by people. 많은 나무가 사람들에 의해 심겨졌습니다. 〈수동태〉

■ 수동태는 '주어+be동사+동사의 과거분사+by+행위자'의 형식을 가지며 수동태 문장의 주어 자리에는 능동태 문장의 목적어가 오고, by 다음에는 능동태 문장의 주어를 쓴다. 누가 그 동작을 했는지 중요하지 않거나 잘 모를 때, 수동태 문장으로 표현한다. 수동태는 현재, 과거, 미래 시제로 쓸 수 있고, 'be동사+동사의 과거분사'에서 be동사로 시제를 표현한다.

  • The pizza **was cooked** by my mother. 그 피자는 우리 엄마에 의해 요리되었다.

■ 4형식 문장의 수동태는 간접목적어와 직접목적어 각각을 주어로 하는 수동태가 가능하다. 직접목적어를 주어로 한 수동태에서는 간접목적어 앞에 특정한 전치사를 써야 한다. 전치사 to를 쓰는 동사는 'give, send, tell, teach, show, bring' 등이고, 전치사 for를 쓰는 동사는 'buy, make, choose, cook, get' 등이며, 전치사 of를 쓰는 동사는 'ask, inquire' 등이 있다. 또한 make, buy, read, write 등은 직접목적어를 주어로 하는 수동태만 가능하다.

  • Stella **was given** a book by me. Stella는 나에게서 책 한 권을 받았다.

  • A book **was given** to Stella by me. 책 한 권이 나에 의해 Stella에게 주어졌다.

■ 조동사가 있는 문장의 수동태는 '조동사+be+p.p.' 형식을 갖는다.

  • A flower pot **can be made** by us. 화분이 우리에 의해 만들어질 수 있다.

■ 목적격보어가 원형부정사인 경우, 수동태 문장에서는 to부정사로 바뀐다.

  • He **was made** to do the dishes by his mom. 그는 엄마에 의해 설거지를 하도록 시켜졌다.

■ by 이외의 전치사를 사용하는 수동태

  • be interested in ~에 흥미가 있다   be filled with ~로 가득 차다

  • be covered with ~로 덮여 있다   be surprised at ~에 놀라다

  • be made of ~로 만들어지다(물리적 변화)   be made from ~로 만들어지다(화학적 변화)

  • be satisfied with ~에 만족하다   be pleased with ~에 기뻐하다

핵심 Check

3. 다음 우리말에 맞게 빈칸에 알맞은 말을 쓰시오.

  (1) 그 건물은 10년 전에 지어졌다.

   ➡ The building ＿＿＿＿ ＿＿＿＿ 10 years ago.

  (2) 이메일이 Andrew에 의해 나에게 보내졌다.

   ➡ An email ＿＿＿＿ ＿＿＿＿ ＿＿＿＿ me by Andrew.

01 다음 문장에서 어법상 <u>어색한</u> 부분을 바르게 고쳐 쓰시오.

(1) The floor cleans once a week.

_____ ➡ _____

(2) A letter is sent to me yesterday.

_____ ➡ _____

(3) They asked everyone sit down.

_____ ➡ _____

(4) Mom told me to not play computer games.

_____ ➡ _____

02 다음 빈칸에 알맞은 것은?

The book _____ by Roald Dahl.

① writes ② writing

③ to write ④ was writing

⑤ was written

03 다음 괄호 안의 동사를 어법에 맞게 빈칸에 쓰시오.

(1) They _____ _____ in a car accident. (injure)

(2) The vase _____ _____ by Bill. (break)

(3) I want you _____ _____ happy. (be)

(4) He advised me _____ _____ regularly. (exercise)

04 다음 우리말에 맞게 빈칸에 알맞은 말을 쓰시오.

(1) 나는 엄마가 그것에 관해 아시는 것을 원하지 않아.

➡ I don't want my mom _____ _____ about it.

(2) 그 방은 Jenny에 의해 청소되었다.

➡ The room _____ _____ by Jenny.

⭐ 중요
01 다음 중 어법상 <u>어색한</u> 문장은?

① Two parrots were bought by Jane.
② The picture was taken by Morris.
③ The old building was build about 200 years ago.
④ *Romeo and Juliet* was written by Shakespeare.
⑤ The letter was sent to her yesterday.

02 다음 우리말을 바르게 영작한 것은?

> 그는 Christine에게 집에 조금 일찍 도착하라고 요청했다.

① He asked Christine arrive home a little early.
② He asked Christine arrives home a little early.
③ He asked Christine arrived home a little early.
④ He asked Christine to arrive home a little early.
⑤ He asked Christine arriving home a little early.

서답형
03 다음 괄호 안에서 알맞은 것을 고르시오.

(1) Math was taught (to / for) them by Mr. Lee.
(2) A beautiful dress was bought (to / for) me by my mom.
(3) Some interesting questions were asked (to / of) me by Sally.

04 다음 빈칸에 알맞은 것은?

> She told me _____ careful when I crossed the road.

① be   ② was   ③ is
④ being   ⑤ to be

05 다음 중 수동태로의 전환이 <u>어색한</u> 것은?

① Roald Dahl wrote the book, *Charlie and the Chocolate Factory.*
  → The book, *Charlie and the Chocolate Factory,* was written by Roald Dahl.
② They make a lot of wonderful smartphones in Korea.
  → A lot of wonderful smartphones are made in Korea.
③ He made her a pizza while she was studying.
  → A pizza was made for her by him while she was studying.
④ Mary showed me her pictures taken at the party.
  → Her pictures shown to me were taken at the party by Mary.
⑤ Thomas Edison invented the light bulb.
  → The light bulb was invented by Thomas Edison.

⭐ 중요
06 다음 문장의 빈칸에 알맞지 <u>않은</u> 것은?

> Yuna _____ him to follow her advice.

① made   ② wanted
③ asked   ④ expected
⑤ advised

[07~08] 다음 중 어법상 옳은 것을 고르시오.

07 ① A difficult question was asked to her by them.
② Who built this bridge hundreds years ago?
③ These books was sent to you tomorrow morning.
④ The window will be broken by Mike yesterday.
⑤ The telephone invented Alexander Bell in 1876.

08 ① I asked my friend to help me.
② The coach told us did our best in the game.
③ His father advised him join the science club.
④ My mom wanted me reading many books.
⑤ I expected him goes there with me as it was getting dark.

09 다음 중 두 문장의 의미가 <u>다른</u> 것은?

① Amy told me that I must not forget to bring some sandwiches.
→ Amy told me not to forget to bring some sandwiches.
② Her parents expected that she would study English very hard.
→ Her parents expected her to study English very hard.
③ Dan asked that he should come over at once.
→ Dan asked him to come over at once.
④ Mom advised me that I should be cautious when driving.
→ Mom advised me to be cautious when driving.
⑤ The doctor hoped that Harry would get well soon.
→ Harry wanted the doctor to get well soon.

10 다음 빈칸에 공통으로 들어갈 말로 가장 적절한 것은?

• His shoes were covered _____ dust.
• He was pleased _____ the result.

① by   ② for   ③ in
④ with   ⑤ of

서답형

11 다음 우리말을 주어진 단어를 이용하여 영어로 쓰시오.

(1) *The Mona Lisa*는 Leonardo da Vinci에 의해 그려졌다. (paint)
➡ _____

(2) 그 유명한 선수는 그녀의 움직임에 깜짝 놀랐다. (famous, surprise, movements)
➡ _____

(3) 그 집은 토네이도에 의해 부서지지 않았다. (break, the tornado)
➡ _____

(4) Ms. Jackson은 Tom에게 창문을 청소하라고 말했다. (clean the windows)
➡ _____

(5) 그 선생님은 그의 학생들이 최선을 다하길 기대했다. (expect, do)
➡ _____

12 다음 문장을 수동태로 바르게 바꾼 것은?

Jane turned on the TV.

① The TV turned Jane.
② The TV turned on by Jane.
③ The TV was turned on Jane.
④ The TV was turned by Jane.
⑤ The TV was turned on by Jane.

서답형

13 다음 괄호 안에 주어진 동사를 어법에 맞게 빈칸에 쓰시오.

> • Jane wants Tom _____ _____ a computer club. (join)
> • Computers allow him _____ the work quickly. (do)

16 다음 중 어법상 <u>어색한</u> 부분을 찾아 바르게 고친 것은?

> Mom wants Tom come home by 5:30.

① wants → want   ② Tom → Tom's
③ come → to come   ④ home → to home
⑤ by → to

[14~15] 다음 두 문장이 같은 의미가 되도록 빈칸에 알맞은 말을 고르시오.

중요

14

> Cinderella made her daughter a doll.
> = A doll _____ her daughter by Cinderella.

① was making
② was made
③ was made for
④ was made to
⑤ made to

중요

17 다음 빈칸에 들어갈 괄호 안에 주어진 동사의 형태가 <u>다른</u> 하나는?

① I want you _____ the dishes. (wash)
② Mom made me _____ playing the computer games. (stop)
③ They got him _____ a new contract. (sign)
④ She asked him _____ to the movies together. (go)
⑤ My parents didn't allow me _____ camping. (go)

서답형

18 다음 문장을 수동태는 능동태로, 능동태는 수동태로 고치시오.

(1) The picture was painted by Sujin.
　　➡ _____

(2) Antonio Gaudi built Casa Mila.
　　➡ _____

(3) My father made me a model plane.
　　➡ _____

(4) Kate will finish her homework by the end of this week.
　　➡ _____

15

> Chuck saw Wendy flying high above the sky.
> = Wendy _____ high above the sky by Chuck.

① was seen flying
② was seen fly
③ was seen to fly
④ is seen fly
⑤ is seen flying

(5) Who built the house?
　　➡ _____

01 다음 문장을 수동태로 바꿔 쓰시오. (두 가지로 쓸 것.)

> Williams taught Angelina English last year.

(1) _____

(2) _____

02 다음 두 문장이 비슷한 의미를 갖도록 빈칸을 알맞은 말로 채우시오.

(1) The teacher said to her, "Draw pictures. You can do it!"
➡ The teacher encouraged her _____ _____ pictures.

(2) His daughter said to him, "Please read me a story book."
➡ His daughter told him _____ _____ her a story book.

(3) My dad ordered that I should solve the math problems.
➡ My dad ordered me _____ _____ the math problems.

(4) Vivian said to her son, "Don't drive too fast."
➡ Vivian warned her son _____ _____ _____ too fast.

(5) Mom asked that I should clean my room every Sunday.
➡ Mom asked me _____ _____ my room every Sunday.

03 다음 우리말을 괄호 안에 주어진 어휘를 이용하여 영작하시오.

(1) 그 마루는 아름다운 카펫으로 덮여 있었다. (floor, cover, a carpet)
➡ _____

(2) 그 책은 한글로 쓰여져 있지 않았다. (write)
➡ _____

(3) 그곳의 동물들은 사람들에 의해 잘 돌보아지고 있었다. (there, good care, take)
➡ _____

(4) 그 시계는 이년 전에 아버지에 의해 나에게 주어진 것이다. (watch, give)
➡ _____
_____

(5) 그녀는 나에게 책 한 권을 사주었다. (buy) (수동태로 쓸 것.)
➡ _____

04 다음 문장을 수동태는 능동태로, 능동태는 수동태로 고치시오.

(1) A basket was made by me.
➡ _____

(2) Marc Chagall painted *I and the Village* in 1911.
➡ _____
_____

(3) The dentist pulled out a rotten tooth.
➡ _____

(4) The way to the National Museum was kindly shown to me by Matthew.
➡ _____
_____

(5) He was covered with dust while he was walking along the road.
➡ _____
_____

05 다음 문장에서 어법상 어색한 부분을 찾아 바르게 고쳐 다시 쓰시오.

(1) She wants Steve coming home early.

　➡ _____

(2) He believed his students be diligent.

　➡ _____

(3) He asked me drive a car very carefully.

　➡ _____

(4) My boss forced me signed the agreement.

　➡ _____

(5) The doctor told me to not do exercise too much.

　➡ _____

06 다음 문장에서 어법상 어색한 부분을 찾아 바르게 고쳐 다시 쓰시오.

(1) The airplane invented the Wright brothers.

　➡ _____

(2) The house was build by him in 1963.

　➡ _____

(3) Handerson is not interested by playing the guitar.

　➡ _____

(4) He is told of the news by his sister tomorrow.

　➡ _____

(5) Soup was cooked to Christina by John.

　➡ _____

07 괄호 안에 주어진 단어를 사용해 다음을 영작하시오.

(1) 그 여자는 그 남자에게 그녀의 가방을 들어달라고 요청했다. (ask, carry)

　➡ _____

(2) Emma는 나에게 내일까지 기다리라고 충고했다. (advise, till)

　➡ _____

(3) Peter는 Sylvia에게 그와 함께 춤을 추자고 말했다. (tell, dance)

　➡ _____

(4) 그들은 그가 축제에 참가할 것으로 기대했다. (expect, participate, the festival)

　➡ _____

(5) 좋은 건강이 그가 그 계획을 마칠 수 있도록 했다. (good, enable, finish)

　➡ _____

08 다음 괄호 안에 주어진 동사를 어법에 맞게 빈칸에 쓰시오.

(1) Linda had her son _____ science. (study)

(2) I would like you _____ _____ me when you arrive there. (call)

Reading

Let's Talk about Upcycling

Mr. Brown: Hello, club members. As you know, this year's Environment
동아리   ~인 것처럼(접속사)

Day is about upcycling. Before we talk about each group's
~에 관하여   ~하기 전에(접속사)

event idea for that day, I want you to understand the meaning of
= Environment Day   5형식 문장(want+목적어+to부정사)   의미

"upcycling." Can anyone explain upcycling?
누구라도(의문문)

Sumi: Yes. The word "upcycling" is a combination of "upgrade" and

"recycling."

Eric: Like recycling, upcycling is good for the environment. When you
~처럼   be good for: ~에 좋다   ~할 때(접속사)

upcycle, you make new and better things from old things.
good의 비교급(더 나은)   ~에서

Mr. Brown: Good. Now, let's talk about each group's idea for the event.
let's+동사원형: ~하자

Let's start with Pei's group.

Pei: My group wants to hold a trashion show. "Trashion" is a
열다(= have)

combination of "trash" and "fashion." We'll use trash to make
~의 (전치사)   목적을 나타내는 to부정사

clothes. We want other students to become interested in upcycling
5형식 문장(want+목적어+to부정사)   ~에 관심이 있는

through the show.
~을 통해서 (전치사)

Mr. Brown: A trashion show sounds like fun! What about your group,
sound like: ~처럼 들리다   What about ~?: ~은 어떠니? (= How about ~?)

Eric?

environment 환경
upcycling 업사이클링
event 행사
meaning 뜻
explain 설명하다, 알려주다
upgrade 개선하다
recycling 재활용
trash 쓰레기
through ~을 통해

확인문제

● 다음 문장이 본문의 내용과 일치하면 T, 일치하지 않으면 F를 쓰시오.

1 Mr. Brown wants the club members to understand the meaning of "upcycling." ☐

2 Sumi says the word "upcycling" is a combination of "upgrade" and "reusing." ☐

3 Mr. Brown says upcycling is good for the environment. ☐

4 When you upcycle, you make old things into new and better things. ☐

5 Pei's group wants to hold a trashion show. ☐

6 Other students became interested in upcycling through the trashion show. ☐

Eric: My group is going to make musical instruments from old things.
be going to: ~할 예정이다 · 악기
We'll make drums from old plastic buckets. We'll also make a
플라스틱(으로 만들어진) 양동이
guitar from old boxes and rubber bands. We plan to play the
plan to+동사원형: ~할 계획이다
instruments in a mini-concert.
작은, 소규모의

Mr. Brown: Thank you, Eric. Now, let's hear from Sumi's group.

Sumi: My group will make bags from old clothes. For example, we'll
예를 들면
use blue jeans. Look at this bag. This was made by Hajun, one of
수동태(be동사+과거분사 ~+by+행위자)
our group members. Isn't it nice? We'll make more bags and sell
= the bag made by Hajun
them on Environment Day. We're going to give all the money to
= bags · = give a nursing home all the money(4형식 문장)
a nursing home.

Mr. Brown: That's a great idea. Your ideas are all so creative. I want
5형식 문장(want+
everyone to work hard for Environment Day.
목적어+to부정사)

Blue Jeans Bag

You Need: old blue jeans, sewing kit, scissors, pins and buttons

Step: 1 Cut off the legs of the blue jeans. 2 Sew the bottom together.
자르다
3 Make shoulder straps from one of the legs. 4 Sew the straps to
the top of the jeans. 5 Decorate the bag with pins and buttons.
청바지의 위쪽 · ~을 사용하여(도구) · 단추

instrument 기구, 악기
bucket 양동이
rubber band 고무 밴드, 고무줄
example 예
sell 팔다
nursing home 양로원
creative 창의적인
kit 도구 세트
bottom 맨 아래
strap 끈, 줄
decorate 장식하다, 꾸미다
button 단추

확인문제

● 다음 문장이 본문의 내용과 일치하면 T, 일치하지 않으면 F를 쓰시오.

1. Eric's group will make drums from old boxes and rubber bands. ☐

2. Eric's group plans to play the instruments in a mini-concert. ☐

3. Sumi's group will make bags from old clothes. ☐

4. Hajun made blue jeans from old bags. ☐

5. Sumi's group will make more bags and send them to a nursing home on Environment Day. ☐

6. Sumi's group is going to give all the money to a nursing home. ☐

● 우리말을 참고하여 빈칸에 알맞은 말을 쓰시오.

1 Let's Talk ＿＿＿＿ ＿＿＿＿

2 Hello, ＿＿＿＿ ＿＿＿＿.

3 ＿＿＿＿ ＿＿＿＿ ＿＿＿＿, this year's Environment Day is about upcycling.

4 Before we talk about ＿＿＿ ＿＿＿ ＿＿＿ ＿＿＿ for that day, I want ＿＿＿ ＿＿＿ ＿＿＿ the meaning of "upcycling."

5 Can anyone ＿＿＿ ＿＿＿?

6 Yes. The word "upcycling" is ＿＿＿ ＿＿＿ ＿＿＿ "upgrade" and "recycling."

7 ＿＿＿ ＿＿＿, upcycling ＿＿＿ ＿＿＿ ＿＿＿ the environment.

8 When you upcycle, you make new and better things ＿＿＿ ＿＿＿ ＿＿＿.

9 Good. Now, let's talk about each group's idea ＿＿＿ ＿＿＿ ＿＿＿.

10 ＿＿＿ ＿＿＿ ＿＿＿ Pei's group.

11 My group wants ＿＿＿ ＿＿＿ ＿＿＿ ＿＿＿ ＿＿＿.

12 "Trashion" is ＿＿＿ ＿＿＿ ＿＿＿ "trash" and "fashion."

13 ＿＿＿ ＿＿＿ ＿＿＿ to make clothes.

14 We want other students to ＿＿＿ ＿＿＿ upcycling through the show.

15 A trashion show ＿＿＿ ＿＿＿ ＿＿＿!

16 ＿＿＿ ＿＿＿ your group, Eric?

17 My group is going to ＿＿＿ ＿＿＿ ＿＿＿ from old things.

---

1 업사이클링에 대해 이야기해 봅시다

2 동아리 회원 여러분, 안녕하세요.

3 여러분도 알다시피 올해의 환경의 날은 업사이클링에 관한 것입니다.

4 각 그룹이 그날에 할 행사 아이디어를 이야기하기 전에 여러분이 '업사이클링'의 의미를 이해하기를 바랍니다.

5 누가 업사이클링의 뜻을 설명해 줄 수 있나요?

6 네. '업사이클링'이란 단어는 "upgrade"와 "recycling"이 결합한 것입니다.

7 재활용과 마찬가지로 업사이클링도 환경에 좋아요.

8 업사이클링을 하면, 여러분은 오래된 것들로 새롭고 더 좋은 것을 만들어요.

9 좋아요. 이제 각 그룹의 행사 아이디어에 대해 이야기해 봅시다.

10 Pei의 그룹부터 시작하죠.

11 저희 그룹은 트래션 쇼를 하고 싶습니다.

12 "트래션(Trashion)"은 "trash"와 "fashion"이 결합한 말입니다.

13 저희는 옷을 만들기 위해 쓰레기를 이용할 것입니다.

14 저희는 이 쇼를 통해서 다른 학생들이 업사이클링에 관심을 갖게 되기를 바랍니다.

15 트래션 쇼라니 멋지겠구나!

16 너희 그룹은 어떠니, Eric?

17 저희 그룹은 낡은 물건으로 악기를 만들려고 합니다.

18 We'll _____ drums _____ old plastic buckets.

19 We'll also make a guitar _____ _____ _____ and _____
   _____.

20 We _____ _____ _____ _____ _____ in a mini-
   concert.

21 Thank you, Eric. Now, _____ _____ _____ Sumi's
   group.

22 My group will _____ _____ _____ old clothes.

23 _____ _____, we'll use blue jeans.

24 _____ _____ this bag.

25 This _____ _____ _____ Hajun, one of our group members.

26 _____ _____ nice?

27 We'll make more bags and _____ _____ _____ _____ _____
   _____.

28 We're going to give all the money _____ _____ _____
   _____.

29 That's _____ _____ _____.

30 Your ideas are _____ _____ _____.

31 I want everyone _____ _____ _____ for Environment
   Day.

32 _____ _____ the legs of the blue jeans.

33 _____ the bottom _____.

34 _____ _____ _____ from one of the legs.

35 Sew the straps _____ _____ _____ _____ the jeans.

36 _____ the bag _____ pins and buttons.

18 낡은 플라스틱 양동이로 드럼을
   만들 겁니다.

19 또한 저희는 낡은 상자와 고무
   줄로 기타를 만들 겁니다.

20 저희는 소규모 음악회를 열어
   그 악기들로 연주할 계획입니다.

21 고맙다, Eric. 그럼 이제 수미의
   그룹 의견을 들어 보자.

22 저희 그룹은 낡은 옷으로 가방
   을 만들 거예요.

23 예를 들어 청바지를 이용할 거
   예요.

24 이 가방을 보세요.

25 이것은 저희 모둠원 중 한 명인
   하준이가 만들었어요.

26 멋지지 않나요?

27 우리는 가방을 더 많이 만들어
   서 환경의 날에 팔 거예요.

28 번 돈을 모두 양로원에 줄 예정
   이에요.

29 훌륭한 생각이구나.

30 너희들의 발상은 모두 아주 창
   의적이구나.

31 너희들 모두 환경의 날을 위해
   열심히 노력하길 바란다.

32 청바지의 다리 부분을 잘라낸다.

33 아래쪽을 붙여서 바느질한다.

34 다리 한 짝으로 어깨끈을 만든다.

35 청바지의 윗부분에 어깨끈을 바
   느질한다.

36 핀이나 단추로 가방을 장식한다.

● 우리말을 참고하여 본문을 영작하시오.

1 업사이클링에 대해 이야기해 봅시다
➡ _____

2 동아리 회원 여러분, 안녕하세요.
➡ _____

3 여러분도 알다시피 올해의 환경의 날은 업사이클링에 관한 것입니다.
➡ _____

4 각 그룹이 그날에 할 행사 아이디어를 이야기하기 전에 여러분이 '업사이클링'의 의미를 이해하기를 바랍니다.
➡ _____
_____

5 누가 업사이클링의 뜻을 설명해 줄 수 있나요?
➡ _____

6 네. '업사이클링'이란 단어는 "upgrade"와 "recycling"이 결합한 것입니다.
➡ _____

7 재활용과 마찬가지로 업사이클링도 환경에 좋아요.
➡ _____

8 업사이클링을 하면, 여러분은 오래된 것들로 새롭고 더 좋은 것을 만들어요.
➡ _____

9 좋아요. 이제 각 그룹의 행사 아이디어에 대해 이야기해 봅시다.
➡ _____

10 Pei의 그룹부터 시작하죠.
➡ _____

11 저희 그룹은 트래션 쇼를 하고 싶습니다.
➡ _____

12 "트래션(Trashion)"은 "trash"와 "fashion"이 결합한 말입니다.
➡ _____

13 저희는 옷을 만들기 위해 쓰레기를 이용할 것입니다.
➡ _____

14 저희는 이 쇼를 통해서 다른 학생들이 업사이클링에 관심을 갖게 되기를 바랍니다.
➡ _____

15 트래션 쇼라니 멋지겠구나!
➡ _____

16 너희 그룹은 어떠니, Eric?
➡ _____

17 저희 그룹은 낡은 물건으로 악기를 만들려고 합니다.
➡ _____

18 낡은 플라스틱 양동이로 드럼을 만들 겁니다.

➡ _____

19 또한 저희는 낡은 상자와 고무줄로 기타를 만들 겁니다.

➡ _____

20 저희는 소규모 음악회를 열어 그 악기들로 연주할 계획입니다.

➡ _____

21 고맙다, Eric. 그럼 이제 수미의 그룹 의견을 들어 보자.

➡ _____

22 저희 그룹은 낡은 옷으로 가방을 만들 거예요.

➡ _____

23 예를 들어 청바지를 이용할 거예요.

➡ _____

24 이 가방을 보세요.

➡ _____

25 이것은 저희 모둠원 중 한 명인 하준이가 만들었어요.

➡ _____

26 멋지지 않나요?

➡ _____

27 우리는 가방을 더 많이 만들어서 환경의 날에 팔 거예요.

➡ _____

28 번 돈을 모두 양로원에 줄 예정이에요.

➡ _____

29 훌륭한 생각이구나.

➡ _____

30 너희들의 발상은 모두 아주 창의적이구나.

➡ _____

31 너희들 모두 환경의 날을 위해 열심히 노력하길 바란다.

➡ _____

32 청바지의 다리 부분을 잘라낸다.

➡ _____

33 아래쪽을 붙여서 바느질한다.

➡ _____

34 다리 한 짝으로 어깨끈을 만든다.

➡ _____

35 청바지의 윗부분에 어깨끈을 바느질한다.

➡ _____

36 핀이나 단추로 가방을 장식한다.

➡ _____

[01~03] 다음 글을 읽고, 물음에 답하시오.

Mr. Brown: Hello, club members. As you know, this year's Environment Day is about upcycling. Before we talk about each group's event idea for that day, I want you ⓐto understand the meaning of "upcycling." Can anyone explain upcycling?

Sumi: Yes. The word "upcycling" is a combination of "upgrade" and "recycling."

Eric: Like recycling, upcycling is good for the environment. When you upcycle, you make new and better things ____ⓑ____ old things.

Mr. Brown: Good. Now, let's talk about each group's idea for the event. Let's start with Pei's group.

01 위 글의 내용과 일치하지 <u>않는</u> 것은?

① 올해의 환경의 날은 업사이클링에 관한 것이다.
② '업사이클링'이란 단어는 "upgrade"와 "recycling"이 결합한 것이다.
③ recycling과는 달리 upcycling은 환경에 좋다.
④ 업사이클을 하면 오래된 것들로 새롭고 더 좋은 것들을 만들게 된다.
⑤ Brown 선생님은 각 그룹의 행사 아이디어에 대해 이야기해 보자고 한다.

02 위 글의 밑줄 친 ⓐto understand와 용법이 같은 것을 고르시오.

① He worked hard to pass the test.
② I want a chair to sit on.
③ She went out to buy some snacks.
④ Show me the way to go to the park.
⑤ Mom told me to wash the dishes.

03 위 글의 빈칸 ⓑ에 들어갈 알맞은 전치사를 고르시오.

① for   ② from   ③ by
④ to   ⑤ on

[04~06] 다음 글을 읽고, 물음에 답하시오.

Pei: My group wants to hold a trashion show. "Trashion" is a combination of "trash" and "fashion." We'll use trash to make clothes. We want (A)[another / other] students to become interested in upcycling (B)[though / through] the show.

Mr. Brown: A trashion show sounds (C)[like / alike] fun! What about your group, Eric?

Eric: My group is going to make musical instruments from old things. We'll make drums from old plastic buckets. We'll also make a guitar from old boxes and rubber bands. We plan to play the instruments in a mini-concert.

서답형

04 위 글의 괄호 (A)~(C)에서 문맥이나 어법상 알맞은 낱말을 골라 쓰시오.

(A)_____ (B)_____ (C)_____

05 위 글을 읽고 알 수 <u>없는</u> 것을 고르시오.

① "Trashion"의 뜻
② 트래션 쇼에 출품되는 옷의 재료
③ 트래션 쇼를 통해 Pei의 그룹이 바라는 것
④ Eric의 그룹이 만드는 악기들의 재료
⑤ Eric의 그룹이 소규모 음악회를 여는 장소

06 위 글의 제목으로 알맞은 것을 고르시오.

① How to Hold a Trashion Show
② Use Trash to Make Clothes
③ Event Ideas of Two Groups
④ Musical Instruments from Old Things
⑤ Play the Instruments in a Mini-concert

[07~09] 다음 글을 읽고, 물음에 답하시오.

Sumi: My group will make bags from old clothes. ____ⓐ____, we'll use blue jeans. Look at this bag. This was made by Hajun, one of our group members. Isn't it nice? We'll make more bags and sell ⓑthem on Environment Day. We're going to give all the money to a nursing home.

중요

07 위 글의 빈칸 ⓐ에 들어갈 알맞은 말을 고르시오.

① However   ② For example
③ Therefore   ④ In addition
⑤ As a result

서답형

08 위 글의 밑줄 친 ⓑthem이 가리키는 것을 본문에서 찾아 쓰시오.

➡ _____

서답형

09 다음 문장에서 위 글의 내용과 <u>다른</u> 부분을 찾아서 고치시오.

Sumi's group will make bags from old clothes and sell them. They will give the bags to a nursing home.

_____ ➡ _____

[10~12] 다음 글을 읽고, 물음에 답하시오.

Step: 1 Sew the bottom together.
2 Decorate the bag ____ⓐ____ pins and buttons.
3 Make shoulder straps from one of the legs.
4 Cut off the legs of the blue jeans.
5 Sew the straps ____ⓑ____ the top of the jeans.

서답형

10 위 글은 Blue Jeans Bag을 만드는 법을 설명하는 글이다. 알맞은 순서대로 배열하시오.

➡ _____

서답형

11 위 글의 빈칸 ⓐ와 ⓑ에 들어갈 알맞은 전치사를 쓰시오.

ⓐ _____   ⓑ _____

서답형

12 위 글을 읽고, 다음 질문에 대한 대답을 완성하시오.

Q: What do you need to make shoulder straps of the Blue Jeans Bag?
➡ We need _____ _____ _____
_____ of the blue jeans.

[13~15] 다음 글을 읽고, 물음에 답하시오.

Mr. Brown: ①Hello, club members. ②As you know, this year's Environment Day is about upcycling. ③Before we talk about each group's event idea for that day, I want you to understand the meaning of "upcycling." ④"Upcycling" is the use of waste materials to make new things. ⑤Can anyone explain upcycling?

Sumi: Yes. The word "upcycling" is a combination of "__ⓐ__" and "__ⓑ__."

Eric: ⓒLike recycling, upcycling is good at the environment. When you upcycle, you make new and better things from old things.

13 위 글의 ①~⑤ 중에서 전체 흐름과 관계 없는 문장은?

① ② ③ ④ ⑤

14 위 글의 빈칸 ⓐ와 ⓑ에 들어갈 알맞은 말을 고르시오.

① recycling – reusing
② update – reducing
③ upgrade – recycling
④ repairing – update
⑤ upgrade – repairing

서답형

15 위 글의 밑줄 친 ⓒ에서 흐름상 어색한 부분을 찾아 고치시오.

_____ ➡ _____

[16~19] 다음 글을 읽고, 물음에 답하시오.

Pei: My group wants ⓐto hold a trashion show. "Trashion" is a combination of "trash" and "fashion." We'll use trash to make clothes. We want other students to become interested __①__ upcycling through the show.

Mr. Brown: A trashion show sounds __ⓑ__ fun! What about your group, Eric?

Eric: My group is going to make musical instruments __②__ old things. We'll make drums __③__ old plastic buckets. We'll also make a guitar __④__ old boxes and rubber bands. We plan to play the instruments in a mini-concert.

Mr. Brown: Thank you, Eric. Now, let's hear __⑤__ Sumi's group.

16 위 글의 밑줄 친 ⓐto hold와 to부정사의 용법이 다른 것을 고르시오.

① To know oneself is important.
② My goal is to become a scientist.
③ It isn't easy for me to learn English.
④ She awoke to find herself famous.
⑤ He continued to solve the problem.

서답형

17 위 글의 빈칸 ①~⑤ 중에서 들어갈 전치사가 나머지 넷과 다른 것을 고른 후, 그곳에 들어 갈 전치사를 쓰시오.

_____번, 들어갈 전치사: _____

18 위 글에서 알 수 있는 'Mr. Brown'의 심경으로 가장 알맞은 것을 고르시오.

① bored   ② satisfied
③ depressed   ④ ashamed
⑤ disappointed

서답형

19 위 글의 빈칸 ⓑ에 들어갈 알맞은 말을 쓰시오.

➡ _____

[20~22] 다음 글을 읽고, 물음에 답하시오.

Sumi: My group will make bags from old clothes. (①) For example, we'll use blue jeans. (②) This was made by Hajun, one of our group members. (③) Isn't it nice? (④) We'll make more bags and sell them on Environment Day. (⑤) We're going to give all the money to a nursing home.

Mr. Brown: That's a great idea. Your ideas are all so creative. ⓐ너희들 모두 환경의 날을 위해 열심히 노력하길 바란다.

20 위 글의 흐름으로 보아, 주어진 문장이 들어가기에 가장 적절한 곳은?

> Look at this bag.

①   ②   ③   ④   ⑤

서답형

21 위 글의 밑줄 친 ⓐ의 우리말에 맞게 주어진 어휘를 이용하여 9단어로 영작하시오.

> want / hard

➡ _____

서답형

22 다음 빈칸 (A)와 (B)에 알맞은 단어를 넣어 upcycling을 위한 수미의 아이디어 노트를 완성하시오.

> Sumi's Group: For Environment Day
> • make bags from ____(A)____
> • sell the bags on ____(B)____ and give a nursing home ____(C)____

(A)_____
(B)_____
(C)_____

[23~25] 다음 글을 읽고, 물음에 답하시오.

Creative Upcycling Idea: Blue Jeans Basket

There are many great upcycling ideas. Here is ___ⓐ___ example. I made a basket from my old blue jeans. Do you want to make ___ⓑ___, too? Then I want you to follow these ___ⓒ___.

You Need: old blue jeans, sewing kit, scissors, and pins and buttons

First, ① _____.
Second, ② _____.
Third, ③ _____.
Lastly, ④ _____.

Upcycling is good for the environment. I want you to become interested in upcycling.

서답형

23 위 글의 빈칸 ⓐ와 ⓑ에 공통으로 들어갈 알맞은 단어를 쓰시오.

➡ _____

서답형

24 주어진 영영풀이를 참고하여 빈칸 ⓒ에 철자 d로 시작하는 단어를 쓰시오.

> instructions that tell you what to do, how to do something, or how to get somewhere

➡ _____

서답형
25 위 글의 빈칸 ①~④에 들어갈 알맞은 말을 〈보기〉에서 골라 쓰시오.

┌─ 보기 ┐
- cut out a piece to make the bottom of the basket
- decorate with pins and buttons
- cut off a leg of the old blue jeans
- sew the bottom to the leg

① _____ .
② _____ .
③ _____ .
④ _____ .

26 주어진 글 다음에 이어질 글의 순서로 가장 적절한 것은?

My group is going to make musical instruments from old things.

(A) We'll make drums from old plastic buckets.
(B) We plan to play the instruments in a mini-concert.
(C) We'll also make a guitar from old boxes and rubber bands.

① (A) – (C) – (B)   ② (B) – (A) – (C)
③ (B) – (C) – (A)   ④ (C) – (A) – (B)
⑤ (C) – (B) – (A)

[27~30] 다음 글을 읽고, 물음에 답하시오.

Sumi: My group will make bags from old clothes. ⓐFor example, we'll use blue jeans. Look ⓑ this bag. ⓒThis was made by Hajun, one of our group members. Isn't it nice? We'll make more bags and sell them ⓓ Environment Day. ⓔWe're going to give all the money for a nursing home.

서답형
27 위 글의 밑줄 친 ⓐ와 바꿔 쓸 수 있는 말을 쓰시오.

➡ _____

28 위 글의 빈칸 ⓑ와 ⓓ에 알맞은 말이 바르게 짝지어진 것은?

① at – in   ② for – at
③ in – at   ④ at – on
⑤ for – during

서답형
29 위 글의 밑줄 친 ⓒ를 능동태로 고치시오.

➡ _____

서답형
30 위 글의 밑줄 친 ⓔ에서 어법상 틀린 부분을 찾아 바르게 고쳐 쓰시오.

_____ ➡ _____

[31~33] 다음 글을 읽고, 물음에 답하시오.

How can we make a bag from old blue jeans? First, cut off the legs of the blue jeans. Second, sew the bottom together. Third, make shoulder straps from one of the legs. Fourth, sew the straps to the top of the jeans. ___ⓐ___, decorate the bag with pins and buttons.

서답형

31 위 글의 빈칸 ⓐ에 들어갈 알맞은 말을 ㄴ로 시작하여 쓰시오.

➡ _____

서답형

32 위 글에서 다음 영영풀이에 해당하는 단어를 찾아 쓰시오.

> to make something look more attractive by putting things on it

➡ _____

서답형

33 다음 질문에 대한 알맞은 대답을 영어로 쓰시오. (6 단어)

> Q: After making shoulder straps, where do you have to sew them?

➡ _____

[34~37] 다음 글을 읽고, 물음에 답하시오.

Pei: My group wants to ___ⓐ___ a trashion show. "Trashion" is a ①combination of "trash" and "fashion." We'll use ②trash to make clothes. We want other students ⓑ become interested in ③upgrading through the show.

Mr. Brown: A trashion show sounds like fun! What about your group, Eric?

Eric: My group is going to make ④musical instruments from old things. We'll make drums from old plastic buckets. We'll also make a ⑤guitar from old boxes and rubber bands. We plan to play the instruments in a mini-concert.

중요

34 위 글의 빈칸 ⓐ에 알맞은 것을 모두 고르시오. (정답 2개)

① hold   ② take
③ have   ④ bring
⑤ catch

35 위 글의 밑줄 친 ①~⑤ 중 문맥상 쓰임이 어색한 것은?

①   ②   ③   ④   ⑤

서답형

36 위 글의 밑줄 친 ⓑ를 알맞은 형태로 고쳐 쓰시오.

➡ _____

서답형

37 What kind of musical instrument will Eric's group make from old things? Answer in English.

➡ _____

[01~03] 다음 글을 읽고, 물음에 답하시오.

Mr. Brown: Hello, club members. As you know, this year's Environment Day is about upcycling. Before we talk about each group's event idea for that day, I want you ___ⓐ___ the meaning of "upcycling." Can anyone explain upcycling?

Sumi: Yes. ⓑ'업사이클링'이란 단어는 "upgrade" 와 "recycling"이 결합한 것입니다.

Eric: Like recycling, upcycling is good for the environment. ⓒWhen you upcycle, you make old and better things from new things.

01 위 글의 빈칸 ⓐ에 understand를 알맞은 형태로 쓰시오.

➡ _____

02 위 글의 밑줄 친 ⓑ의 우리말에 맞게 주어진 어구를 이용하여 10 단어로 영작하시오.

The word / combination

➡ _____
_____

03 위 글의 밑줄 친 ⓒ에서 흐름상 어색한 부분을 찾아 고치시오.

_____ ➡ _____
_____ ➡ _____

[04~06] 다음 글을 읽고, 물음에 답하시오.

Pei: My group wants to hold a trashion show. "Trashion" is a combination of " ___ⓐ___ " and "fashion." We'll use ___ⓐ___ to make clothes. We want other students to become interested in upcycling through the show.

Mr. Brown: A trashion show sounds like fun! ⓑWhat about your group, Eric?

Eric: My group is going to make ⓒmusical instruments from old things. We'll make drums from old plastic buckets. We'll also make a guitar from old boxes and rubber bands. We plan to play the instruments in a mini-concert.

04 주어진 영영풀이를 참고하여 빈칸 ⓐ에 철자 t로 시작하는 단어를 쓰시오.

unwanted things or waste material such as used paper, empty bottles, and waste food

➡ _____

05 위 글의 밑줄 친 ⓑ와 바꿔 쓸 수 있는 말을 쓰시오.

➡ _____

06 위 글의 밑줄 친 ⓒ의 재료를 악기별로 각각 우리말로 쓰시오.

드럼: _____

기타: _____

[07~08] 다음 글을 읽고, 물음에 답하시오.

> Sumi: My group will make bags from old clothes. For example, we'll use blue jeans. Look at this bag. This was made by Hajun, one of our group members. Isn't it nice? We'll make more bags and sell them on Environment Day. ⓐ We're going to give all the money to a nursing home.
>
> Mr. Brown: That's a great idea. Your ideas are all so creative. ⓑI want everyone to work hardly for Environment Day.

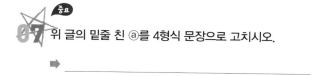

07 위 글의 밑줄 친 ⓐ를 4형식 문장으로 고치시오.

➡ _____

08 위 글의 밑줄 친 ⓑ에서 문맥상 낱말의 쓰임이 적절하지 않은 것을 찾아 알맞게 고치시오.

_____ ➡ _____

[09~10] 다음 글을 읽고, 물음에 답하시오.

> Mr. Brown: Hello, club members. As you know, this year's Environment Day is about upcycling. ⓐBefore we talk about each groups' event idea for that day, I want you to understand the meaning of "upcycling." Can anyone explain upcycling?

09 다음 문장에서 위 글의 내용과 다른 부분을 찾아 고치시오.

> Mr. Brown wants to understand the meaning of "upcycling."

_____ ➡ _____

10 위 글의 밑줄 친 ⓐ에서 어법상 틀린 것을 찾아 고치시오.

_____ ➡ _____

[11~12] 다음 글을 읽고, 물음에 답하시오.

> Pei: My group wants to hold a trashion show. "Trashion" is a combination of "trash" and "fashion." We'll use trash to make clothes. We want other students to become interested in upcycling through the show.
>
> Mr. Brown: A trashion show sounds like fun! What about your group, Eric?
>
> Eric: My group is going to make musical instruments from old things. We'll make drums from old plastic buckets. We'll also make a guitar from old boxes and rubber bands. We plan to play the instruments in a mini-concert.

11 다음 빈칸 (A)와 (B)에 알맞은 단어를 넣어 upcycling을 위한 Pei 그룹의 아이디어 노트를 완성하시오.

> Pei's Group: For Environment Day
> • use trash to _____(A)
> • hold a _____(B)

(A)_____ (B)_____

12 다음 빈칸 (A)와 (B)에 알맞은 단어를 넣어 Eric의 그룹이 만들 악기들에 대한 소개를 완성하시오.

> Eric's group is going to make _____(A) from old plastic buckets and _____(B) from old boxes and rubber bands.

(A)_____ (B)_____

교과서 구석구석

Talk and play

A: May I help you?
손님을 맞이할 때 '어서 오세요'라는 표현이다.

B: Yes. How much is this T-shirt?
가격을 묻는 표현으로 How much is[are] ~?를 사용한다.

A: It's 20 dollars.

B: Can I get a discount?
할인을 받다

A: OK. I'll take 3 dollars off.
할인 금액을 말할 때 사용한다.

B: Great. I'll take it.

구문해설 • discount: 할인 • take off: 할인하다 • take: 사다, 선택하다

Around the World

Kids, I want to give music lessons to you. But we don't have any musical instruments. I can help you. I have a good idea. Oh, thank you! I can make musical instruments from trash. The world sends us trash. We send back music. This is the power of upcycling.

구문해설 • give lessons: 수업하다 • musical instrument: 악기 • send back: 되돌려주다

Think and Write

Creative Upcycling Idea: Blue Jeans Basket

You Need: old blue jeans, sewing kit, scissors, buttons and pins

Step:

1 Cut off a leg of the old blue jeans.
자르다

2 Cut out a piece to make the bottom of the basket.
바구니의 바닥

3 Sew the bottom to the leg.

4 Decorate with buttons and pins.

구문해설 • creative: 창의적인 • sewing kit: 바느질 도구 세트 • bottom: 밑부분, 바닥
• decorate: 장식하다

해석

A: 도와 드릴까요?
B: 이 티셔츠는 얼마인가요?
A: 20달러예요.
B: 할인을 받을 수 있을까요?
A: 네. 3달러 깎아 드릴게요.
B: 좋아요. 그걸 살게요.

얘들아, 너희에게 음악 수업을 해주고 싶구나. 하지만 우리는 악기가 하나도 없어. 내가 도와줄 수 있어. 나에게 좋은 생각이 있어. 오, 고마워! 나는 쓰레기로 악기를 만들 수 있어. 세상은 우리에게 쓰레기를 보내줬어. 우리는 음악으로 되돌려준다. 이것이 업사이클링의 힘이란다.

창의적인 업사이클링 아이디어: 청바지 바구니

준비물: 낡은 청바지, 바느질 도구 세트, 가위, 단추와 장식 핀
단계
1. 낡은 청바지의 다리를 자른다.
2. 바구니의 바닥을 만들기 위해 한 조각을 자른다.
3. 바닥을 다리 부분과 꿰맨다.
4. 단추와 핀으로 장식한다.

[24~26] 다음 글을 읽고, 물음에 답하시오.

Pei: My group wants to hold a trashion show. "Trashion" is a combination of "trash" and "fashion." We'll use trash to make clothes. We want other students to become interested in upcycling through the show.

Mr. Brown: A trashion show sounds like fun! What about your group, Eric?

Eric: My group is going to make ____ⓐ____ from old things. We'll make drums from old plastic buckets. We'll also make a guitar from old boxes and rubber bands. We plan to play the instruments in a mini-concert.

Mr. Brown: Thank you, Eric. Now, let's hear from Sumi's group.

24 위 글의 내용과 일치하지 <u>않는</u> 것은?

① Pei의 그룹은 트래션 쇼를 열 것이다.
② Pei의 그룹은 옷을 만들기 위해 쓰레기를 사용할 것이다.
③ Eric의 그룹은 낡은 양철 양동이로 드럼을 만들 것이다.
④ Eric의 그룹은 낡은 상자와 고무줄로 기타를 만들 것이다.
⑤ Eric의 그룹은 소규모 음악회를 열 것이다.

25 위 글의 빈칸 ⓐ에 들어갈 알맞은 말을 고르시오.

① experiment equipment
② motor vehicles
③ communication instruments
④ construction equipment
⑤ musical instruments

26 위 글을 읽고, 다음 질문에 대한 대답을 완성하시오.

Q: Where will Eric's group play the musical instruments?
➡ They will play them _____.

[27~28] 다음 글을 읽고, 물음에 답하시오.

Sumi: My group will make bags ①<u>from</u> old clothes. For example, we'll use blue jeans. Look ②<u>at</u> this bag. This was made ③<u>of</u> Hajun, one of our group members. Isn't it nice? We'll make more bags and sell them ④<u>on</u> Environment Day. We're going to give all the money to a nursing home.

Mr. Brown: That's a great idea. Your ideas are all so ____ⓐ____. I want everyone to work hard ⑤<u>for</u> Environment Day.

27 위 글의 밑줄 친 ①～⑤에서 전치사의 쓰임이 적절하지 <u>않</u>은 것을 찾아 알맞게 고치시오.

➡ _____

28 위 글의 빈칸 ⓐ에 들어갈 알맞은 말을 고르시오.

① dull   ② creative
③ common   ④ boring
⑤ old-fashioned

출제율 90%

01 다음 짝지어진 두 단어의 관계가 같도록 빈칸에 철자 c로 시작하는 단어를 쓰시오.

> trash : garbage = original : _____

출제율 95%

02 다음 영영풀이에 해당하는 단어는?

> particular idea that a word, expression, or sign represents

① instrument
② discount
③ meaning
④ condition
⑤ combination

출제율 90%

03 다음 빈칸에 우리말에 맞게 알맞은 단어를 쓰시오.

> • 아래쪽을 붙여서 바느질해라.
> _____(A)_____ the bottom together.
> • 핀과 단추로 가방을 장식해라.
> _____(B)_____ the bag with pins and buttons.

(A)_____ (B)_____

출제율 100%

04 다음의 Upcycling에 관한 글을 읽고, 괄호 (A)~(C)에 알맞은 단어가 바르게 짝지어진 것을 고르시오.

> The word "upcycling" is a (A)[combination / meaning] of "upgrade" and "recycling." (B)[Unlike / Like] recycling, upcycling is good for the environment. When you upcycle, you make new and better things from (C)[old / new] things.

① combination – Like – new
② combination – Unlike – old
③ meaning – Like – new
④ combination – Like – old
⑤ meaning – Unlike – new

[05~06] 다음 대화를 읽고, 물음에 답하시오.

M: Hello. May I help you?
G: _____(A)_____
M: This one is 15 dollars and it's in good condition.
G: Can I get a discount?
M: OK. I'll take 2 dollars off.
G: Then it's 13 dollars. (B)그것을 살게요.

출제율 85%

05 위 대화의 빈칸 (A)에 들어갈 말로 알맞은 것은?

① Is this clock on sale?
② I'm looking for a baseball glove.
③ How much money do you have?
④ How much are these shoes?
⑤ That's good.

출제율 95%

06 위 대화의 (B)의 우리말에 맞게 영어로 쓰시오.

➡ _____

[07~09] 다음 대화를 읽고, 물음에 답하시오.

B: Wow! There are so ⓐmany interesting things here.
W: Everything here ⓑare old or used. What are you looking for?
B: I'm looking for a clock.
W: _____(A)_____
B: How much is it?
W: It's 15 dollars.
B: That's ⓒtoo expensive for me.
_____(B)_____
W: No, I'm afraid not. It's only one year old. It's ⓓalmost new.
B: Then, 숫자가 큰 이 파란색 시계는 얼마예요?
W: It's 10 dollars.
B: Then, I'll take the blue ⓔone. Thank you.

07 위 대화의 빈칸 (A)와 (B)에 들어갈 말로 알맞은 것을 〈보기〉에서 찾아 쓰시오.

┌─ 보기 ─┐
- Where can I find them?
- How about this red clock?
- What can I do for you?
- Can I get a discount?
- How much is it?

(A) _____

(B) _____

08 위 대화의 밑줄 친 우리말에 맞게 주어진 단어를 이용하여 영어로 쓰시오.

how / this blue / with / numbers

➡ _____

09 위 대화의 밑줄 친 부분 중 어법상 어색한 것은?

① ⓐ　② ⓑ　③ ⓒ　④ ⓓ　⑤ ⓔ

10 다음 대화의 빈칸에 들어갈 말로 알맞은 것은?

A: May I help you?
B: Yes. How much is this scarf?
A: It's 6 dollars.
B: Can I get a discount?
A: _____
B: Then, I don't think I'll take it.

① OK. I'll take 2 dollars off.
② Sounds good.
③ No, I'm afraid not. Sorry.
④ It is on sale.
⑤ I got it.

11 다음 중 어법상 올바른 것은?

① The key was stole by Bill.
② Presents were given for all the children.
③ The pictures were taken by Jerry.
④ Did her homework finished by her?
⑤ The spaghetti made my dad.

12 다음 중 어법상 올바르지 <u>않은</u> 것은?

① They asked me to stay longer.
② Sujin, do you want me to dance?
③ I made her clean her room.
④ Tell them coming to my birthday party.
⑤ Mom didn't allow me to go camping.

13 다음 문장을 수동태로 고쳐 쓰시오.

(1) Did Emma teach the students English?
　　(두 가지로)

➡ _____

➡ _____

(2) We can send a lot of data through the Internet.

➡ _____

(3) Edgar Degas painted *The Dance Class*.

➡ _____

14 다음 문장에서 어법상 잘못된 것을 고치시오.

(1) They asked him give a speech.

_____ ➡ _____

(2) Clara made him to wait for her for an hour outside.

_____ ➡ _____

15 다음 질문에 맞는 답을 빈칸을 알맞게 채워 완성하시오.

(1) Who painted *The Walk*?

➡ *The Walk* _____ Marc Chagall.

(2) Who invented Hangeul?

➡ Hangeul _____ King Sejong.

(3) Who was pleased to hear the news?

➡ Jake _____ the news.

[16~18] 다음 글을 읽고, 물음에 답하시오.

Mr. Brown: Hello, club members. ⓐAs you know, this year's Environment Day is about upcycling. Before we talk ⓑ each group's event idea ⓒ that day, I want you to understand the meaning of "upcycling." Can anyone explain upcycling?

Sumi: Yes. The word "upcycling" is a combination of "upgrade" and "recycling."

Eric: Like recycling, upcycling is good for the ⓓ . When you upcycle, you make new and better things from old things.

16 위 글의 밑줄 친 ⓐAs와 같은 의미로 쓰인 것을 고르시오.

① I respect him as a doctor.

② As you can see, I have no money.

③ She doesn't play as well as her sister.

④ As he was busy, he couldn't go there.

⑤ As he grew older, he became faster.

17 위 글의 빈칸 ⓑ와 ⓒ에 들어갈 전치사가 바르게 짝지어진 것은?

① about – to
② for – from
③ to – for
④ with – by
⑤ about – for

18 위 글의 빈칸 ⓓ에 들어갈 알맞은 말을 본문에서 찾아 쓰시오.

➡ _____

[19~21] 다음 글을 읽고, 물음에 답하시오.

Pei: My group wants to ⓐ a trashion show. "Trashion" is a combination of "trash" and "fashion." We'll use trash ⓑ to make clothes. We want other students to become interested in upcycling through the show.

19 위 글의 빈칸 ⓐ에 들어갈 알맞은 말을 고르시오.

① bring
② hold
③ find
④ take
⑤ get

20 위 글의 밑줄 친 ⓑto make와 to부정사의 용법이 다른 것을 고르시오.

① This river is dangerous to swim in.

② I was sad to lose the game.

③ He ran fast to catch the bus.

④ She must be careless to do so.

⑤ Pei's group plans to make clothes.

21 본문의 내용과 일치하도록 다음 빈칸 (A)~(C)에 알맞은 단어를 쓰시오.

> Pei's group will make   (A)   by using trash and prepare a   (B)   . They want other students to become interested in   (C)   through the show.

(A)_____ (B)_____ (C)_____

[22~24] 다음 글을 읽고, 물음에 답하시오.

Sumi: My group will make bags from old clothes. For example, we'll use blue jeans. Look at this bag. ⓐThis was made by Hajun, one of our group members. Isn't it nice? We'll make more bags and sell them on Environment Day. We're going to give all the money to a nursing home.

Mr. Brown: That's a great idea. Your ideas are all so creative. I want everyone to work hard for Environment Day.

22 위 글을 읽고 대답할 수 <u>없는</u> 질문은?

① What will Sumi's group make?
② When will Sumi's group sell more bags?
③ How much money does Sumi's group expect to earn?
④ How will Sumi's group use the money from the sale?
⑤ What does Mr. Brown want everyone to do?

23 위 글의 밑줄 친 ⓐThis가 가리키는 것을 본문에서 찾아 쓰시오.

➡ _____

24 위 글을 읽고, 다음 빈칸에 들어갈 말로 가장 적절한 것을 고르시오.

> Sumi's group will sell more bags and _____ all the money to a nursing home.

① save
② donate
③ keep
④ store
⑤ recycle

[25~26] 다음 그림을 보고, 물음에 답하시오.

25 위 그림의 Step 1~5의 빈칸에 들어갈 알맞은 단어를 쓰시오.

(1)_____ (2)_____ (3)_____
(4)_____ (5)_____

26 위 글의 Blue Jeans Bag을 만드는 데 필요한 재료가 <u>아닌</u> 것을 고르시오.

① 낡은 청바지
② 바느질 도구 세트
③ 가위
④ 지퍼
⑤ 핀과 단추들

01 다음 대화를 읽고, 아래 문장의 빈칸을 채우고 질문에 영어로 답하시오.

> B: Wow! There are so many interesting things here.
> W: Everything here is old or used. What are you looking for?
> B: I'm looking for a clock.
> W: How about this red clock?
> B: How much is it?
> W: It's 15 dollars.
> B: That's too expensive for me. Can I get a discount?
> W: No, I'm afraid not. It's only one year old. It's almost new.
> B: Then, how much is this blue clock with the large numbers?
> W: It's 10 dollars.
> B: Then, I'll take the blue one. Thank you.

 Price: _____
It's only _____ old.

 Price: _____
It has _____.

Q: What is the boy going to buy?
➡ _____

02 다음 그림을 보고 대화를 완성하시오.

 black bag
$15 → $13

A: (A)_____
B: It's 15 dollars.
A: Can I get a discount?
B: OK. (B)_____
A: Then it's 13 dollars. I'll take it.

03 다음 그림을 보고, Jenny가 점원과 나누는 대화의 빈칸을 완성하시오.

 $18

> Jenny: Excuse me. How much are the _____ _____?
> Man: They're _____ _____.
> Jenny: Hmm. Can I get a discount?
> Man: No, _____ _____ _____. Sorry.
> Jenny: That's OK. I'll take them.

04 다음 주어진 문장을 같은 뜻을 갖는 문장으로 바꾸어 쓰시오.

(1) Ms. Brown asked that the students should clean the classroom.
➡ _____

(2) His parents expected that he would win the contest.
➡ _____

(3) The boss warned that the driver should drive very carefully.
➡ _____

05 다음 우리말을 영작하시오.

> 그 책은 한국어로 쓰이지 않았다.

➡ _____

06 다음 상황에 알맞은 말을 어법에 맞게 빈칸에 쓰시오.

(1) This morning he was late for school. The teacher said to him, "Don't be late."
➡ The teacher told him _____ _____ _____ _____ for school.

(2) Mr. White said to me, "Don't give up."
➡ Mr. White encouraged me _____ _____ _____ _____.

Pei: My group wants to hold a trashion show. "Trashion" is a combination of "trash" and "fashion." We'll use trash to make clothes. ⓐWe want other students to become interesting in upcycling through the show.

Mr. Brown: ⓑ트래션 쇼라니 멋지겠구나! What about your group, Eric?

Eric: My group is going to make musical instruments from old things. We'll make drums from old plastic buckets. We'll also make a guitar from old boxes and rubber bands. We plan to play the instruments in a mini-concert.

중요

07 위 글의 밑줄 친 ⓐ에서 어법상 틀린 부분을 찾아 고치시오.

_____ ➡ _____

08 위 글의 밑줄 친 ⓑ의 우리말에 맞게 주어진 어휘를 이용하여 6 단어로 영작하시오.

like / fun

➡ _____

09 다음 빈칸 (A)~(D)에 알맞은 단어를 넣어 upcycling을 위한 Eric의 아이디어를 완성하시오.

Eric's Group: For Environment Day
- make (A)_____ _____ from old things
- make drums from (B)_____ _____
- make a guitar (C)_____ old boxes and rubber bands
- play (D)_____ _____ in a mini-concert

Sumi: My group will make bags from old (A)[cloths / clothes]. For example, we'll use blue jeans. Look at this bag. This was made by Hajun, one of our group members. (B)[Is / Isn't] it nice? We'll make more bags and sell them on Environment Day. We're going to give all the money (C)[for / to] a nursing home.

Mr. Brown: ⓐThat's a great idea. Your ideas are all so creative. I want everyone to work hard for Environment Day.

중요

10 위 글의 괄호 (A)~(C)에서 문맥이나 어법상 알맞은 낱말을 골라 쓰시오.

(A)_____ (B)_____ (C)_____

11 위 글의 밑줄 친 ⓐThat이 가리키는 내용을 우리말로 쓰시오.

➡ _____

_____

중요

12 다음 문장에서 위 글의 내용과 다른 부분을 찾아서 고치시오.

Mr. Brown wants to work hard for Environment Day.

_____ ➡ _____

창의사고력 서술형 문제

01 다음 연결된 말을 보고 두 개의 대화를 완성하시오. (할인을 받는 경우는 I'll take it.으로, 할인을 받지 못하는 경우는 Then, I don't think I'll take it.으로 대화를 끝내시오.)

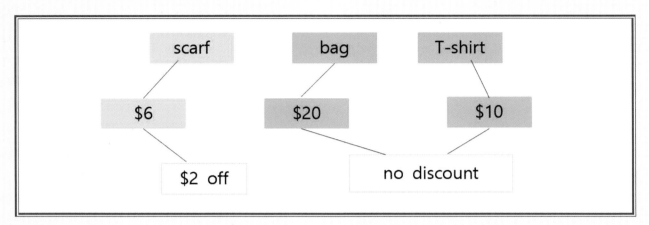

02 다음 메모 내용과 일치하도록 want를 이용하여 어법에 맞게 쓰시오.

> To-do List
> (1) Minsu – clean your room
> (2) Mina – do the dishes
> (3) me – walk the dog
>   - Mom -

(1) _____
(2) _____
(3) _____

03 다음 빈칸 (A)~(D)에 알맞은 단어를 넣어 낡은 청바지를 이용하여 바구니를 만드는 방법을 설명하는 글을 완성하시오.

> **Creative Upcycling Idea: Blue Jeans Basket**
>
>   There are many great upcycling ideas. Here is one example. I made a basket from my old blue jeans. Do you want to make one, too? Then I want you to follow these (A)_____.
>   You Need: old blue jeans, sewing kit, scissors, and pins and buttons
> First, (B)_____ off a leg of the old blue jeans.
> (C)_____, cut out a piece to make the bottom of the basket.
> Third, sew the bottom to the leg.
> Lastly, (D)_____ with pins and buttons.
> Upcycling is good for the environment. I want you to become interested in upcycling.

단원별 모의고사

01 다음 단어에 대한 영어 설명이 <u>어색한</u> 것은?

① decorate: to make something look nice by adding pretty things to it
② environment: the natural world, including water, air, land, and plants
③ discount: the amount of money that you have to pay in order to buy something
④ bucket: a deep round container with a handle on the top
⑤ instrument: something such as a piano, guitar, or drum that you play in order to make music

02 다음 짝지어진 두 단어의 관계가 같도록 빈칸에 알맞은 말을 쓰시오.

> expensive : cheap = downgrade : _____

03 다음 영영풀이에 해당하는 단어를 고르시오.

> to tell someone about something in a way that is clear or easy to understand

① explain
② sell
③ know
④ understand
⑤ throw

04 다음 대화의 빈칸에 공통으로 들어갈 말은?

> M: This backpack is 15 dollars.
> G: Can I get a discount?
> M: OK. I'll _____ 2 dollars off. So it'll be 13 dollars.
> G: I'll _____ it, then.

① get
② buy
③ make
④ turn
⑤ take

05 다음 그림을 보고, 대화의 빈칸을 완성하시오.

> W: May I help you?
> B: Yes. (A)_____ _____ is this blue T-shirt?
> W: (B)_____ _____.
> B: Can I get a discount?
> W: OK. I'll (C)_____ _____ _____.
> B: That sounds good. I'll take it.

06 다음 그림을 참고하여 대화의 빈칸에 들어갈 알맞은 말을 쓰시오.

clock
$15
$3 off

> M: Hello. May I help you?
> G: I _____ _____ _____ a clock.
> M: This one is 15 dollars and it's in good condition.
> G: Can I _____ _____ _____?
> M: OK. I'll _____ 3 dollars _____.
> G: Then it's _____ dollars. I'll take it.

07 다음 그림을 보고, 대화의 빈칸을 완성하시오.

pink skirt
$10 → $9

A: (1)_____
B: It's 10 dollars.
A: Can I get a discount?
B: OK. (2)_____

08 다음 밑줄 친 ⓐ와 ⓑ가 가리키는 것으로 알맞게 짝지어진 것은?

G: Excuse me. How much is this yellow backpack?
M: It's 18 dollars.
G: Hmm. That's expensive for me. How about this red ⓐone?
M: It's 15 dollars.
G: That's a good price. I'll take ⓑit.

① yellow backpack – the red backpack
② red backpack – the red backpack
③ backpack – the yellow backpack
④ backpack – the red backpack
⑤ yellow backpack – the backpack

09 다음 두 사람의 대화가 어색한 것은?

① A: What are you looking for?
   B: I'm looking for a clock.
② A: How much is this red clock?
   B: It's 15 dollars.
③ A: What's the price of this hat?
   B: It's 15 dollars.
④ A: Can I get a discount?
   B: No, I'm afraid not.
⑤ A: May I help you?
   B: That sounds good. I'll take it.

10 다음 대화의 밑줄 친 ⓐ와 쓰임이 같은 것은?

M: Hello. May I help you?
G: I'm looking for a clock.
M: This ⓐone is 15 dollars and it's in good condition.

① Do you want one biscuit or two?
② There's only one thing we can do
③ He has only one dollar in his wallet.
④ It cost one hundred and fifty pounds.
⑤ I don't like this color. Do you have a red one?

[11~12] 다음 대화를 읽고, 물음에 답하시오.

Ben: Wow! There are so many interesting things here.
Woman: Everything here is old or used. What are you looking for?
Ben: I'm looking for a clock.
Woman: How about this red clock?
Ben: How much is it?
Woman: It's 15 dollars.
Ben: That's too expensive for me. Can I get a discount?
Woman: No, I'm afraid not. It's only one year old. It's almost new.
Ben: Then, how much is this blue clock with the large numbers?
Woman: It's 10 dollars.
Ben: Then, 그 파란색을 살게요(take, one). Thank you.

11 위 대화를 읽고 답할 수 없는 질문은?

① Where does the conversation probably take place?
② How much is the red clock?
③ How old is the blue clock?
④ Did Ben get a discount?
⑤ What is Ben going to buy?

12 위 대화의 밑줄 친 우리말에 맞게 주어진 단어를 이용하여 영어로 쓰시오.

➡ _____

13 다음 능동태는 수동태로, 수동태는 능동태로 바꾸어 쓰시오.

(1) This flower pot was made from an ice cream bowl.

➡ _____

(2) The Beatles wrote the song, *Yesterday*.

➡ _____

(3) She cooked us some cookies.

➡ _____

(4) People laughed at Picasso at first.

➡ _____

14 다음 중 밑줄 친 부분의 쓰임이 바르지 못한 것은?

① Jack wants Jane to water the plants.
② He asked her teach math to his son.
③ He made her do her work right now.
④ We saw him singing in the rain.
⑤ He advised me not to smoke.

15 다음 문장과 같은 의미가 되도록 빈칸에 알맞은 말을 쓰시오.

I heard her open the window.

➡ She _____ .

16 다음 문장에서 어법상 어색한 것을 찾아 고치시오.

Tom asked him close the window.

_____ ➡ _____

17 다음 우리말을 to부정사를 써서 영작하시오.

나는 그녀가 친절하다고 믿는다.

➡ _____

[18~20] 다음 글을 읽고, 물음에 답하시오.

Mr. Brown: Hello, club members. As you know, this year's Environment Day is about upcycling. Before we talk about each group's event idea for ⓐthat day, I want you to understand the meaning of "upcycling." Can anyone explain upcycling?

Sumi: Yes. The word "upcycling" is a combination of "upgrade" and "recycling."

Eric: Like recycling, upcycling is good for the environment. When you upcycle, you make new and better things from old things.

Mr. Brown: Good. Now, let's talk about each group's idea for the event. Let's start ___ⓑ___ Pei's group.

18 위 글의 밑줄 친 ⓐthat day가 가리키는 것을 본문에서 찾아 쓰시오.

➡ _____

19 위 글의 빈칸 ⓑ에 들어갈 알맞은 전치사를 고르시오.

① with ② by ③ in
④ for ⑤ on

20 다음 빈칸 (A)와 (B)에 알맞은 단어를 넣어 위 글의 다음에 올 내용을 완성하시오.

> (A)_____ _____ will talk about the event idea for (B)_____ _____.

(A) _____ (B) _____

[21~22] 다음 글을 읽고, 물음에 답하시오.

Pei: My group wants to hold a trashion show. "Trashion" is a combination of "trash" and "fashion." We'll use trash to make clothes. We want other students to become interested in upcycling through the show.

Mr. Brown: A trashion show sounds ⓐlike fun! What about your group, Eric?

Eric: My group is going to make musical instruments from old things. We'll make drums from old plastic buckets. We'll also make a guitar from old boxes and rubber bands. We plan to play the instruments in a mini-concert.

Mr. Brown: Thank you, Eric. Now, let's hear from Sumi's group.

21 위 글을 읽고 대답할 수 <u>없는</u> 질문은?

① Who wants to hold a trashion show?
② How many students are interested in upcycling?
③ What does Mr. Brown think about Pei's idea?
④ From what is Eric's group going to make musical instruments?
⑤ Who will talk about the idea for the event after Eric?

22 위 글의 밑줄 친 ⓐlike와 쓰임이 <u>다른</u> 것을 고르시오.

① She looks like a serious person.
② It smells like coffee.
③ I don't like the way he talks to me.
④ It tastes like tomato juice.
⑤ That sounds like a good plan.

[23~25] 다음 글을 읽고, 물음에 답하시오.

Sumi: My group will make bags from old clothes. For example, we'll use blue jeans. Look at this bag. ⓐThis was made by Hajun, one of our group member. Isn't it nice? We'll make more bags and sell them on Environment Day. We're going to give all the money to a nursing home.

Mr. Brown: That's a great idea. ⓑ너희들의 아이디어들은 모두 아주 창의적이다. I want everyone to work hard for Environment Day.

23 위 글의 내용과 일치하지 <u>않는</u> 것은?

① 수미의 그룹은 낡은 옷으로 가방을 만들 예정이다.
② 하준이는 수미의 그룹에 속해 있다.
③ 수미의 그룹은 더 많은 가방을 만들어 그것들을 환경의 날에 팔 것이다.
④ 수미의 그룹은 모든 돈을 양로원에 드릴 것이다.
⑤ Mr. Brown은 환경의 날을 위해 열심히 일하고 싶어 한다.

24 위 글의 밑줄 친 ⓐ에서 어법상 틀린 부분을 찾아 고치시오.

_____ ➡ _____

25 위 글의 밑줄 친 ⓑ의 우리말에 맞게 주어진 어휘를 이용하여 6 단어로 영작하시오.

so

➡ _____

Lesson

4

The Amazing World of Animals

 의사소통 기능

- 외모 묘사하기

  A: What does your cat look like?

  B: It's small and it has grey hair.

- 정보 묻기

  A: Can you tell me more about it?

  B: It has a long tail.

 언어 형식

- 주격 관계대명사

  Scientists **who** were studying crows did an experiment.

- 접속사 if

  If you think this bird is special, you are wrong.

Words & Expressions

Key Words

- **also**[ɔ́ːlsou] 부 또한
- **announcement**[ənáunsmənt] 명 발표, 소식
- **carry**[kǽri] 동 휴대하다
- **coconut**[kóukənʌt] 명 코코넛 열매
- **coin purse** 동전 지갑
- **cotton**[kátn] 명 면
- **crow**[krou] 명 까마귀
- **drop**[drap] 동 떨어뜨리다
- **else**[els] 부 또 다른
- **example**[igzǽmpl] 명 예, 예제
- **experiment**[ikspérəmənt] 명 실험, 시험
- **fable**[féibl] 명 우화, 동화
- **female**[fíːmeil] 형 여성의, 암컷의
- **float**[flout] 동 [물체가] (액체 면에) 뜨다, 떠다니다
- **floss**[flɔːs] 동 치실질을 하다 명 치실
- **gorilla**[gərílə] 명 고릴라
- **hide**[haid] 동 숨다, 감추다
- **imagine**[imǽdʒin] 동 상상하다
- **jar**[dʒaːr] 명 병, 단지
- **leave**[liːv] 동 ~을 두고 가다, 떠나다
- **level**[lévəl] 명 높이, 정도, 수준
- **lucky**[lʌ́ki] 형 운이 좋은
- **male**[meil] 형 남자의, 수컷의
- **navy**[néivi] 명 남색
- **octopus**[áktəpəs] 명 문어
- **once**[wʌns] 부 한때, 한동안
- **parrot**[pǽrət] 명 앵무새
- **pattern**[pǽtərn] 명 무늬, 도안
- **photograph**[fóutəgræf] 명 사진
- **pile**[pail] 동 쌓다, 포개다
- **protection**[prətékʃən] 명 보호
- **record**[rikɔ́ːrd] 동 기록하다, 등록하다 명 기록
- **restroom**[restruːm] 명 화장실
- **round-shaped** 형 둥근 모양의
- **shell**[ʃel] 명 (딱딱한) 껍데기, 껍질
- **sign**[sain] 명 몸짓, 신호, 표시
- **slowly**[slóuli] 부 천천히
- **snake**[sneik] 명 뱀
- **solve**[salv] 동 해결하다, 풀다
- **store**[stɔːr] 명 가게 동 저장하다
- **stripe**[straip] 명 줄무늬
- **succeed**[səksíːd] 동 성공하다
- **surprise**[sərpráiz] 동 놀라게 하다
- **tail**[teil] 명 꼬리
- **talent**[tǽlənt] 명 재능
- **temple**[témpl] 명 절, 사원
- **tool**[tuːl] 명 도구, 수단
- **unique**[juːníːk] 형 독특한
- **usually**[júːʒuəli] 부 대개, 보통
- **way**[wei] 명 방법, 방식
- **wear**[wɛər] 동 입다, 신다, 쓰다
- **whale**[hweil] 명 고래
- **while**[hwail] 접 ~하는 동안에
- **worm**[wəːrm] 명 벌레

Key Expressions

- **be good at** ~을 잘하다, ~에 능숙하다
- **dance to music** 음악에 맞춰 춤추다
- **find out** 알아보다
- **just as** 꼭 ~처럼
- **look for** ~을 찾다
- **look like** ~처럼 보이다, ~와 닮다
- **more than** ~ 이상(의)
- **not A but B** A가 아니고 B
- **on top of** ~의 위에
- **pull out** ~을 뽑다
- **take a rest** 휴식하다
- **talk with** ~와 이야기하다
- **watch out for** ~에 대해 조심하다, 경계하다
- **what else** 그 밖에, 그 외에

Word Power

※ 서로 반대되는 뜻을 가진 단어

- **female**(여성의) ↔ **male**(남성의)
- **slowly**(천천히) ↔ **fast**(빨리)
- **float**((액체 면에) 뜨다, 떠다니다) ↔ **sink**(가라앉다)
- **hide**(숨다, 감추다) ↔ **find**(찾다)

※ 서로 비슷한 뜻을 가진 단어

- **lucky**(운이 좋은) : **fortunate**(운이 좋은, 행운의)
- **pile**(쌓다, 포개다) : **stack**(쌓다, 포개다)
- **pattern**(무늬, 도안) : **design**(디자인, 무늬)
- **photograph**(사진) : **picture**(그림, 사진)
- **record**(기록하다, 등록하다; 기록) : **document**(기록하다; 기록(물))
- **solve**(해결하다, 풀다) : **deal with**(~을 해결하다)
- **surprise**(놀라게 하다) : **amaze**(몹시 놀라게 하다)
- **talent**(재능) : **gift**(타고난 재능), **capacity**(재능)
- **unique**(독특한) : **special**(특별한)
- **way**(방법) : **method**(방법, 방식)

English Dictionary

- **announcement** 발표, 소식
  → something important that someone tells people
  사람들에게 말하는 중요한 어떤 것

- **coconut** 코코넛 열매
  → a large brown nut with a hairy shell
  털이 있는 껍질을 가진 큰 갈색 견과

- **cotton** 면
  → a type of cloth made from soft fibres from a particular plant
  어떤 특별한 식물의 부드러운 섬유로 만들어지는 천의 일종

- **experiment** 실험, 시험
  → a scientific test you do to learn about something, or to show if an idea is true
  무엇인가 배우기 위해 또는 생각이 맞는지 보여주기 위해 하는 과학적 검사

- **fable** 우화
  → a story that teaches us something
  무엇인가를 우리에게 가르쳐 주는 이야기

- **floss** 치실질을 하다; 치실
  → to clean between your teeth with dental floss/special string that you use to clean between your teeth
  치실로 이 사이를 닦다 / 이 사이를 닦기 위해 사용하는 특별한 실

- **level** 정도, 수준
  → the amount or degree of something
  어떤 것의 양이나 정도

- **navy** 남색
  → a very dark blue color
  매우 진한 파란색

- **pattern** 무늬, 도안
  → a set of lines, shapes, or colours that are repeated regularly
  규칙적으로 반복되는 일련의 선, 모양, 색깔

- **photograph** 사진
  → a picture you take using a camera
  카메라를 사용하여 찍는 사진

- **pile** 쌓다, 포개다
  → to put a lot of things on top of each other
  차곡차곡 많은 것을 놓다

- **record** 기록하다, 등록하다
  → to write down information or store it on a computer
  컴퓨터에 정보를 적거나 저장하다

- **shell** (딱딱한) 껍데기, 껍질
  → the hard outside part of a nut or egg
  견과류나 알의 딱딱한 겉부분

- **surprise** 놀라게 하다
  → to make someone have a feeling of surprise
  누군가를 놀라움의 감정을 갖게 하다

- **talent** 재능
  → an ability to do something well
  어떤 것을 잘하는 능력

- **tool** 도구, 수단
  → a thing that you use for making or doing something
  어떤 것을 하거나 만들기 위해 사용하는 것

01 다음 문장의 빈칸에 들어갈 말로 알맞은 것은?

> Children have to wear helmets for _____ when they ride bikes.

① helper
② control
③ function
④ equipment
⑤ protection

02 다음 밑줄 친 부분과 의미가 가장 가까운 것을 고르시오.

> I need to <u>take a rest</u> a little.

① be tired
② take care of
③ make a mistake
④ sleep
⑤ relax

03 다음 문장의 빈칸에 알맞은 것은?

> Pull _____ the flag around the corner.

① up
② out
③ off
④ from
⑤ with

04 다음 중 밑줄 친 부분의 뜻풀이가 바르지 <u>않은</u> 것은?

① The scientists did a new <u>experiment</u> to learn more about monkeys. (실험)
② Do you need anything <u>else</u>? (또 다른)
③ She <u>piled</u> the boxes. (보관하다)
④ The <u>crow</u> flew up into a high tree. (까마귀)
⑤ We should use dental <u>floss</u> every day. (치실)

05 다음 빈칸에 공통으로 들어갈 말로 알맞은 것은?

> • I _____ my glasses and broke them.
> • He _____ his plate into the sink.

① dropped
② dried
③ carried
④ decreased
⑤ drank

서답형

06 다음 빈칸에 들어갈 알맞은 단어를 <보기>에서 찾아 쓰시오. (형태 변화 가능)

> ┤ 보기 ├
> unique   fable   carry

(1) I like reading Aesop's _____. They are fun.
(2) Karen was a woman of _____ talent.
(3) He always _____ a gun at that time.

07 다음 제시된 단어를 사용하여 자연스러운 문장을 만들 수 <u>없는</u> 것은? (형태 변화 가능)

> photograph   parrot   jar   floss

① To keep your teeth healthy, you have to _____ your teeth.
② There is water in the _____.
③ The man in this _____ is my grandfather.
④ The river is at its highest _____ for several years.
⑤ You can teach some _____ to say words.

08 다음 영영풀이에 해당하는 것은?

> a story that teaches us something

① fiction
② fable
③ myth
④ legend
⑤ language

01 다음 짝지어진 두 단어의 관계가 같도록 빈칸에 알맞은 말을 쓰시오. (주어진 철자가 있는 경우, 주어진 철자로 시작할 것)

(1) subtract : add = sink : f_____

(2) stupid : smart = male : _____

(3) good : nice = special : u_____

(4) soft : smooth = fortunate : _____

02 다음 빈칸에 알맞은 단어를 〈보기〉에서 골라 쓰시오. (형태 변화 가능)

┌─── 보기 ───┐
leave   floss   succeed   hide

(1) The little goats cry out and _____ around the house.

(2) People brush and _____ their teeth.

(3) They were happy that they _____ in finishing the project in time.

(4) I _____ my key in the car, so I can't open it.

03 다음 〈보기〉에서 빈칸에 공통으로 들어갈 단어를 골라 쓰시오.

┌─── 보기 ───┐
like   take   do   talk   look

(1) • We started to _____ for a house with a garden.
 • Koalas _____ like bears.

(2) • I just wanted to _____ to you.
 • He had a chance to _____ with a new student called Christina.

04 다음 우리말에 맞게 주어진 단어를 바르게 배열하시오.

(1) 그녀는 뱀을 보고 놀랐다.
(surprised, see, snake, she, a, was, to)
➡ _____

(2) 나는 남색 정장을 입었다.
(dressed, suit, a, was, in, I, navy)
➡ _____

(3) 사원은 소나무 사이에 위치하고 있다.
(is, trees, the, located, the, pine, temple, among)
➡ _____

05 다음 주어진 우리말에 맞게 빈칸을 채우시오.

(1) 우리는 이 실험을 위해 물 한 컵이 필요하다.
➡ We need _____ _____ _____ water for this _____.

(2) 수컷 새들은 그들의 짝을 찾기 위해 노래를 부른다.
➡ The _____ birds sing to _____ their mates.

[06~07] 다음 영영풀이에 해당하는 말을 주어진 철자로 시작하여 쓰시오.

06 ┌──────────────────────────┐
t_____ : an ability to do something well
└──────────────────────────┘

07 ┌──────────────────────────┐
n_____ : a very dark blue color
└──────────────────────────┘

Conversation

① 외모 묘사하기

> **A** What does your cat look like? 너의 고양이는 어떻게 생겼니?
> **B** It's small and it has grey hair. 작고 회색 털을 가지고 있어.

■ 'What does ~ look like?'는 '~는 어떻게 생겼니?'라는 의미로 주어의 외모나 생김새를 묻는 질문이다. 이 문장에서 like는 '~처럼'이라는 의미의 전치사이다.

■ 외모를 묘사할 때에는 'be동사 + 형용사' 혹은 'have + 형용사 + 명사'의 표현을 사용할 수 있다.

외모 묻기

- What does ~ look like? ~는 어떻게 생겼니?
- How does ~ look?
- How do you describe ~?
- Tell me what ~ looks like. ~는 어떻게 생겼는지 말해 줘.

like의 쓰임

- (동사) ~을 좋아하다 ex) She likes pizza.
- (전치사) ~와 비슷한 ex) She's wearing a dress like mine.
- (전치사) ~처럼   ex) Don't look at me like that.

핵심 Check

1. 다음 우리말과 일치하도록 빈칸에 알맞은 말을 쓰시오.

   A: _____ _____ it _____ like? (그것은 어떻게 생겼나요?)

   B: It's _____ _____ _____. (그것은 길고 검은색이에요.)

2. 다음 대화의 순서를 바르게 배열하시오.

   (A) Yes. I'm looking for my cap.   (B) It's red.

   (C) May I help you?   (D) What does it look like?

   _____ ➡ _____ ➡ _____ ➡ _____

2 정보 묻기

> **A** Can you tell me more about it? 그것에 대해 더 말해 줄래?
> **B** It has a long tail. 그것은 긴 꼬리를 가지고 있어.

■ 상대방에게 무엇인가에 대한 좀 더 많은 정보를 물어보기 위해서 'tell' 동사를 사용할 수 있다. 이때 tell 은 4형식 동사로 간접목적어와 직접목적어를 가질 수 있다. 'Can you tell me more about it?'에서 간접 목적어는 'me'이며, 직접목적어는 'more'이다. 'tell' 대신에 'explain', 'describe' 등의 동사로 바꾸어 쓸 수 있고, 이에 대해 모양, 무늬, 크기 등 여러 가지 특징의 정보로 대답할 수 있다.

정보를 묻는 표현

- Can[Could/Would] you tell me more about it? 그것에 대해 더 말해 줄래?
- Can[Could/Would] you explain more about it? 그것에 대해 더 설명해 줄래?
- Can[Could/Would] you describe it? 그것 좀 (자세히) 설명해 줄래?
- Can[Could/Would] you explain a little bit more? 좀 더 설명해 줄래?
- Can[Could/Would] you explain it more clearly? 그것을 더 분명하게 설명해 줄래?

■ 묘사나 정보를 묻는 대답에 사용할 수 있는 어휘

1. 무늬 종류
   - stripes, a striped pattern 줄무늬
   - check pattern 체크무늬
   - polka dots 물방울무늬
   - floral design[pattern] 꽃무늬
   - a star design 별무늬

2. 모양
   - round-shaped 둥근 모양의
   - ring-shaped 고리 모양의
   - heart-shaped 하트 모양의
   - be shaped like+명사 ~의 모양을 하고 있다
   - look like+명사 ~처럼 보이다. ~와 닮다

3. 색깔
   - violet 보라색
   - navy, Indian blue 남색
   - yellow 노란색
   - blue 파란색
   - red 빨간색
   - grey 회색
   - Olive green 올리브색

4. 크기
   - big, large 큰
   - small 작은
   - long 긴
   - short 짧은

핵심 Check

> **3.** 다음 우리말과 일치하도록 빈칸에 알맞은 말을 쓰시오.
>
> A: _____ _____ _____ more about it (그것에 대해 더 설명해 줄래?)
>
> B: It _____ _____ _____. (그것은 물방울무늬가 있어.)

A. Listen and Talk A 1

B: Excuse me. I'm ❶looking for my scarf.

W: ❷What does it look like?

B: ❸It's a long cotton scarf.

W: ❹Can you tell me more about it?

B: Well, it's grey.

W: OK. ❺I'll go and check.

B: 실례합니다. 저는 제 스카프 를 찾고 있어요.
W: 어떻게 생겼는데요?
B: 그것은 긴 면 스카프예요.
W: 그것에 대해 더 말해 줄래요?
B: 음, 회색이에요.
W: 알겠어요. 가서 확인해 볼게요.

❶ look for: ~을 찾다. look for 다음에는 명사나 동명사가 올 수 있다.
❷ 'What does ~ look like?'는 '~는 어떻게 생겼니?'라는 의미로 주어의 외모나 생김새를 묻는 질문이다. 이 문장에서 like는 '~처럼'이라는 의미의 전치사이다.
❸ It은 scarf를 대신 받아 주는 대명사로 쓰였다. long: 긴 cotton: 면
❹ Can you tell me more about it?은 추가 정보를 얻기 위해 묻는 표현이다.
❺ I'll = I will, go와 check는 등위접속사 and에 의해 병렬 구조로 연결되어 있다.

Check(√) True or False

(1) The boy's scarf is long and grey.　　　　　　T ☐ F ☐

(2) The boy's scarf is made of cotton.　　　　　　T ☐ F ☐

B. Listen and Talk C

M: May I help you?

G: Yes. I'm looking for my dog. His name is Prince.

M: ❶What does he look like?

G: ❷He's very small and has short white hair.

M: ❸Can you tell me more?

G: Well, he has a really long tail.

M: I see. And ❹one more thing. ❺Where did you lose him?

G: I lost him ❻near the main gate.

M: OK. I'll go and ❼make an announcement. Can you please wait here?

G: Sure. Thanks a lot.

M: 도와드릴까요?
G: 네. 제 개를 찾고 있어요. 이름 은 Prince예요.
M: 그가 어떻게 생겼나요?
G: 매우 작고 짧은 흰 털을 가지 고 있어요.
M: 더 얘기해 줄 수 있나요?
G: 음, 그는 무척 긴 꼬리를 가지 고 있어요.
M: 알겠습니다. 그리고 한 가지 더요. 어디서 잃어버렸나요?
G: 정문 근처에서 잃어버렸어요.
M: 좋아요. 가서 안내 방송을 하 겠습니다. 잠시 여기에서 기다 려 주시겠어요?
G: 네. 정말 감사합니다.

❶ What does he look like? = How does he look?: 그가 어떻게 생겼나요?
❷ is very small(매우 작다)와 has short white hair(짧은 흰 털을 가지고 있다)는 등위접속사 and에 의해 병렬 구조로 연결되어 있다.
❸ Can you tell me more (about your dog)?
❹ one more thing: 한 가지 더요.
❺ 의문사 where를 이용하여 장소를 묻는 표현이다.
❻ near는 '~ 근처에서'란 뜻으로 비슷한 어구로 'close to'가 있다.
❼ announcement: 발표, 소식. make an announcement: 발표하다, 방송을 하다

Check(√) True or False

(3) The girl lost her dog.　　　　　　T ☐ F ☐

(4) The man and the girl will make an announcement.　　　　　　T ☐ F ☐

Listen and Talk A-2

W: ❶May I help you?

B: Yes. I ❷lost my bag. ❸I think I left it in the restroom.

W: OK. What does it look like?

B: It's small and yellow.

W: ❹What else? ❺Tell me more about it.

B: Let me think. Oh, it has two pockets outside.

❶ May I help you? = Can I help you? = Do you need any help?: 도와드릴까요?

❷ lose − lost − lost: 잃어버리다, 분실하다

❸ I think (that) I left in the restroom. think 다음에 that절인 명사절을 목적어로 받을 수 있는데, 여기서 that은 생략이 가능하다.

❹ what else: 그 밖에, 그 외에

❺ Tell(4형식 동사) + me(간접목적어) + more about it(직접목적어). 여기서 more는 명사로 '더 많은 것'을 의미한다.

Listen and Talk A-3

W: Do you need help?

B: Yes. I lost my umbrella.

W: ❶What does it look like?

B: It's long and navy.

W: ❷Can you tell me more?

B: Yes. ❸It has a star pattern on it.

❶ What does it look like? = How does it look?: 그것은 어떻게 생겼나요?

❷ Can you tell me more (about your umbrella)?

❸ a star pattern: 별무늬

Listen and Talk A-4

W: ❶Do you need help?

B: Yes. ❷I'm looking for my cat.

W: What does it look like?

B: Well, ❸she's not very big and she has black hair.

W: Can you tell me more? Is there ❹anything special about her?

B: She has a short tail.

❶ Do you need (any) help? = Would you like any help? = Is there anything I can do to help you? = Can I do anything to help you?

❷ be + 동사-ing: ~하는 중이다(진행형) look for: ~을 찾다

❸ 여기서 she는 my cat을 가리킨다. hair: 털

❹ anything과 같이 -thing으로 끝나는 대명사는 형용사가 뒤에서 수식한다. ex) nothing special

Listen and Talk B-4

A: May I help you?

B: Yes. I'm looking for my ❶coin purse.

A: What does it look like?

B: It's red and has a ❷smiley face on it.

A: Can you tell me more about it?

B: It has a ❸key chain.

❶ coin purse: 동전 지갑

❷ smiley: 스마일 동그라미 속에 눈 두 개와 웃는 입 모양을 그려 넣은 단순한 얼굴 그림 ☺

❸ key chain: 열쇠 고리

Listen and Talk B

A: May I help you?

B: Yes. I'm looking for my hat.

A: What does it look like?

B: It's pink and ❶round-shaped.

A: Can you tell me more about ❷it?

B: It has a yellow ❸band.

❶ 모양을 나타내는 명사(heart, square 등)와 shaped가 합쳐져서 형용사가 된다. '명사-shaped'는 '~ 모양인'의 의미를 가진다.

❷ it = the hat

❸ band: 끈

Talk and Play

A: ❶What does Amy look like?

B: ❷She's tall and has long brown hair.

A: Can you tell me more?

B: ❸She's wearing short navy pants.

A: I ❹found her!

❶ 'What does ~ look like?'는 외모를 묻는 표현이다. 여기서 like는 '~처럼'이라는 의미의 전치사이다.

❷ 명사를 수식하는 형용사가 여러 개 나왔을 경우 '외형 (크기, 형상/길이) + 신구/색깔 + 재료'의 순서로 명사를 수식할 수 있다.

❸ 'She's wearing(= She is wearing)'은 현재진행형이다. navy: 남색

❹ find−found−found: 발견하다, 찾다

Review 1

G: Hi. ❶I think I lost my umbrella.

M: ❷What does it look like?

G: It's a big navy umbrella.

M: ❸Can you tell me more?

G: ❹It has a white flower pattern on it.

❶ I think (that) + 주어 + 동사 ~: 나는 ~라고 생각한다

❷ What does it look like? = How does it look?: 그것은 어떻게 생겼나요?

❸ Can you tell me more (about your umbrella)?

❹ a white flower pattern: 흰색 꽃무늬

다음 우리말과 일치하도록 빈칸에 알맞은 말을 쓰시오.

Listen and Talk A-1

B: Excuse me. I'm _____ _____ my scarf.

W: What does it look _____?

B: It's a long _____ scarf.

W: Can you _____ _____ _____ about it?

B: Well, it's _____.

W: OK. I'll _____ and _____.

Listen and Talk A-2

W: May _____ _____ _____?

B: Yes. I _____ my bag. I think I _____ it in the _____.

W: OK. _____ does it look _____?

B: _____ small and yellow.

W: _____ _____? Tell me _____ about it.

B: Let me think. Oh, it has _____ _____ _____.

Listen and Talk A-3

W: Do you need _____?

B: Yes. I _____ _____ _____.

W: What _____ _____ _____ like?

B: It's _____ _____ _____.

W: Can you _____ me more?

B: Yes. It has _____ _____ _____ _____ it.

Listen and Talk A-4

B: _____ _____ need help?

W: Yes. _____ _____ for my cat.

B: What does _____ _____ _____?

W: Well, she's _____ _____ _____ and she _____ black hair.

B: Can _____ _____ _____ more? Is there _____ _____ about her?

W: She has a _____ _____.

Listen and Talk B

A: May I help you?

B: Yes. _____ _____ _____ my cat.

A: What _____ _____ _____ _____?

B: _____ small and it _____ _____ hair.

A: _____ you tell me more _____ _____?

B: It _____ a long tail.

Listen and Talk B-2

A: _____ I help you?

B: Yes. _____ _____ _____ my _____.

A: _____ does it look _____?

B: It's small and red.

A: Can you _____ me more _____ it?

B: _____ _____ _____ _____ in it.

Listen and Talk C

M: May I help you?

G: Yes. I'm looking _____ my dog. _____ _____ is Prince.

M: _____ _____ _____ _____ _____?

G: He's very small and _____ _____ _____ hair.

M: _____ _____ tell me more?

G: Well, _____ has a _____ long tail.

M: I see. And _____ _____ _____. _____ did you lose him?

G: I _____ him near the _____ gate.

M: OK. _____ go and _____ _____ _____. Can you please _____ here?

G: Sure. Thanks a lot.

Talk and Play

A: What does Amy _____ _____?

B: She's _____ and has long _____ hair.

A: _____ _____ _____ _____ _____ _____?

B: She's _____ short navy _____.

A: I _____ her.

Review

G: Hi. I think I _____ my _____.

M: What _____ _____ look like?

G: It's a _____ _____ _____.

M: Can you _____ _____ _____ _____?

G: It _____ a white _____ _____ _____ it.

해석

A: 도와드릴까요?
B: 네. 저는 제 고양이를 찾고 있어요.
A: 그것은 어떻게 생겼나요?
B: 그것은 작고 회색 털을 가지고 있어요.
A: 그것에 대해 더 말해 주실 수 있나요?
B: 그것은 긴 꼬리를 가지고 있어요.

A: 도와드릴까요?
B: 네. 저는 제 지갑을 찾고 있어요.
A: 그것은 어떻게 생겼나요?
B: 그것은 작고 빨간색이에요.
A: 그것에 대해 더 말해 주실 수 있나요?
B: 그것 안에는 카드가 있어요.

M: 도와드릴까요?
G: 네. 제 개를 찾고 있어요. 이름은 Prince 예요.
M: 그가 어떻게 생겼나요?
G: 매우 작고 짧은 흰 털을 가지고 있어요.
M: 더 얘기해 줄 수 있나요?
G: 음, 그는 무척 긴 꼬리를 가지고 있어요.
M: 알겠습니다. 그리고 한 가지 더요. 어디서 잃어버렸나요?
G: 정문 근처에서 잃어버렸어요.
M: 좋아요. 가서 안내 방송을 하겠습니다. 잠시 여기에서 기다려 주시겠어요?
G: 네. 정말 감사합니다.

A: Amy는 어떻게 생겼니?
B: 그녀는 키가 크고 긴 갈색 머리야.
A: 더 말해 주겠니?
B: 그녀는 짧은 남색 바지를 입고 있어.
A: 그녀를 찾았어.

G: 안녕하세요. 제 우산을 잃어버린 것 같아요.
M: 그것은 어떻게 생겼나요?
G: 그것은 큰 남색 우산이에요.
M: 더 말해 주시겠어요?
G: 흰색 꽃무늬가 있어요.

[01~02] 다음 대화의 빈칸에 알맞은 것을 고르시오.

01

> B: _____ does Amy look like?
> G: She's tall and has long brown hair.

① What shape   ② How   ③ Where
④ What look   ⑤ What

02

> M: What does it look like?
> G: It's a big navy umbrella.
> M: _____
> G: It has a white flower pattern on it.

① Can you talk with me more?
② Do you need help?
③ Can you tell me more?
④ Can you talk to me?
⑤ Can you find my umbrella?

03 다음 대화의 빈칸에 들어갈 말로 적절하지 <u>않은</u> 것은?

> A: What does it look like?
> B: It's _____.

① long and navy   ② big and black
③ heart-shaped   ④ smart and kind
⑤ like a really big ball

04 주어진 문장의 앞에 나올 대화의 순서를 알맞게 쓰시오.

> (A) What does it look like?
> (B) Excuse me. I'm looking for my scarf.
> (C) Can you tell me more about it?
> (D) It's a long cotton scarf.

> Well, it's grey.

➡ _____

[01~04] 다음 대화를 읽고, 물음에 답하시오.

> W: May I help you?
> B: Yes. (①) I think I left it in the restroom. (②)
> W: OK. What does it look like?
> B: It's small and yellow. (③)
> W: What else?   (A)   me more about it.
> B: (④) Let me think. Oh, it has two pockets outside. (⑤)

01 위 대화의 ①~⑤ 중 주어진 문장이 들어갈 알맞은 곳은?

I lost my bag.

① ② ③ ④ ⑤

02 Where are they?

① the restroom ② the restaurant
③ the shop ④ the cafeteria
⑤ the Lost and Found

03 위 대화의 빈칸 (A)에 들어갈 말로 적절한 것은?

① Show ② Buy ③ Tell
④ Talk ⑤ Look

04 위 대화의 내용과 일치하지 않는 것을 고르시오.

① The woman helps the boy to find his bag.
② The boy's bag is small and has a pocket outside.
③ The woman wants to know more about the boy's bag.
④ The boy lost his bag.
⑤ The boy's bag is yellow.

[05~06] 다음 대화를 읽고, 물음에 답하시오.

> A: ___(A)___ I help you?
> B: Yes. ①I'm looking my scarf.
> A: ②What does it look like?
> B: ③It's blue.
> A: ④Can you tell me more about it?
> B: ⑤It has a star pattern on it.

05 위 대화의 빈칸 (A)에 들어갈 말로 적절하지 않은 것은?

① May ② Could ③ Can
④ Should ⑤ How may

서답형
06 위 대화의 ①~⑤ 중 어색한 곳을 고르고 고치시오.

_____ ➡ _____

[07~09] 다음 대화를 읽고, 물음에 답하시오.

> W: ①Do you need help?
> B: Yes. ②I'm looking for my cat.
> W: ③What does it look like?
> B: Well, she's not very big and she __(A)__ black hair.
> W: ④Can you tell me more? ⑤Is there special anything about her?
> B: She   (B)   a short tail.

07 위 대화의 빈칸 (A)와 (B)에 들어갈 말로 적절한 것은?

① is – has ② is – is
③ has – is ④ has – has
⑤ has – looks

08 위 대화의 ①~⑤ 중 어색한 곳을 고르고 고치시오.

_____ ➡ _____

09 위 대화의 내용과 일치하지 않는 것을 고르시오.

① The boy is looking for his cat.
② The cat is black.
③ The boy lost his cat.
④ The cat's tail is long.
⑤ The cat is female.

[10~13] 다음 대화를 읽고, 물음에 답하시오.

M: May I help you? (①)
G: Yes. <u>제 개를 찾고 있어요.</u> His name is Prince.
M: What does he look like?
G: He's very small and has short white hair. (②)
M: Can you tell me more? (③)
G: Well, he has a really long tail.
M: I see. And one more thing. (④)
G: I lost him near the main gate. (⑤)
M: OK. I'll go and ___(A)___ an announcement. Can you please wait here?
G: Sure. Thanks a lot.

10 위 대화의 ①~⑤ 중 주어진 문장이 들어갈 알맞은 곳은?

> Where did you lose him?

① ② ③ ④ ⑤

11 위 대화의 밑줄 친 우리말을 영작하시오.

➡ _____

12 위 대화의 빈칸 (A)에 들어갈 말로 적절한 것은?

① take ② make ③ do
④ let ⑤ hear

13 위 대화의 내용과 일치하지 않는 것을 고르시오.

① 개는 짧은 털을 가지고 있다.
② 개의 꼬리는 길다.
③ 여자아이는 개를 후문 근처에서 잃어버렸다.
④ 남자는 개를 찾는 방송을 할 것이다.
⑤ 개의 이름은 Prince이다.

[14~15] 다음 대화를 읽고, 물음에 답하시오.

A: What does Amy look like?
B: She's tall and ___(A)___ brown hair. (2단어)
A: Can you tell me more?
B: She's ___(B)___ navy pants. (2단어)
A: I ___(C)___ her!

14 다음 Amy의 사진을 보고 (A)와 (B)를 완성하시오.

(A) _____
(B) _____

15 위 대화의 빈칸 (C)에 들어갈 말로 적절한 것을 주어진 철자로 시작하여 쓰시오.

➡ f_____

[01~02] 다음 대화를 읽고, 물음에 답하시오.

> G: Hi. (A)(lost, my, think, I, I, umbrella)
> M: What does it look like?
> G: It's a big navy umbrella.
> M: Can you tell me more?
> G: (B)<u>흰색 꽃무늬가 있어요.</u>(a, pattern, on)

01 위 대화의 (A)에 주어진 단어를 알맞게 배열하시오.

➡ _____

02 위 대화의 (B)의 밑줄 친 우리말을 영어로 옮기시오.

➡ _____

[03~06] 다음 대화를 읽고, 물음에 답하시오.

> W: May I help you?
> B: Yes. I lost my bag. I think I left it ___(A)___ the restroom.
> W: OK. What does it look ___(B)___ ?
> B: It's small and ___(C)___ .
> W: What else? ⓐTell me more about it.
> B: Let me think. Oh, ___(D)___ .

03 위 대화의 빈칸 (A)와 (B)에 알맞은 전치사를 쓰시오.

(A) _____ (B) _____

04 위 그림을 참고하여 (C)에 알맞은 말을 쓰시오.

➡ _____

05 위 대화의 밑줄 친 ⓐ와 의미가 같게 주어진 단어를 이용해 문장을 쓰시오.

> (can)

➡ _____

06 그림을 참고하여, 주어진 단어를 이용해 (D)에 들어갈 문장을 완성하시오.

> (outside, pockets)

➡ _____

07 주어진 문장 앞에 나올 대화의 순서를 바르게 배열하시오.

> (A) Yes. I'm looking for my wallet.
> (B) It's small and red.
> (C) May I help you?
> (D) Can you tell me more about it?
> (E) What does it look like?

> There is a card in it.

➡ _____

08 다음 표를 보고 대화를 완성하시오.

Lost Pet Report	
type of animal	cat
color	black hair
size	not very big
anything special	short tail

> W: Do you need help?
> B: Yes. I'm looking for _____ _____.
> W: What does it look like?
> B: Well, she's _____ _____
>   and she has _____ _____.
> W: Can you tell me more? Is there anything special about her?
> B: She _____ _____

Grammar

교과서

1 주격 관계대명사

- Scientists **who** were studying crows did an experiment.
  까마귀를 연구하던 과학자들이 실험을 했다.

- We'll go to a restaurant **that** has a kids' menu. 우리는 아이들 식단이 있는 식당에 갈 것이다.

■ 관계대명사는 접속사와 대명사의 역할을 한다. 관계대명사절은 명사를 수식해 주는 절의 한 종류로 관계대명사절이 꾸며 주는 말을 선행사라고 하고 관계대명사는 앞의 선행사와 같은 대상을 가리킨다. 관계대명사절이 되기 전의 문장에서 주어로 쓰였으면 주격 관계대명사로, 소유격으로 쓰였으면 소유격 관계대명사로, 목적격으로 쓰였으면 목적격 관계대명사가 된다. 주격 관계대명사는 관계대명사절에서 주어 역할을 하므로 그 다음에는 동사가 온다.

- He is the man. He(=The man) met Mary yesterday.
  = He is the man **who** met Mary yesterday.

- He is the man. Mary met him(=the man) yesterday.
  = He is the man **whom** Mary met yesterday.

■ 관계대명사는 선행사에 따라 다음과 같이 사용되며, 목적격 관계대명사는 생략할 수 있다.

	주격	소유격	목적격
사람	who / that	whose	whom[who] / that
동물, 사물	which / that	whose / of which	which / that

- I'm looking for the man **who[that]** sent me the present. 나는 나에게 그 선물을 보낸 남자를 찾고 있다.

- I went to the concert **which** was free of charge. 나는 무료인 그 콘서트에 갔다.

■ 관계대명사 that은 who, whom과 which 대신 사용할 수 있으며 소유격은 없다. 또한 선행사가 '사람+동물[사물]'인 경우에는 반드시 that을 써야 한다.

- Look at the boy and his dog **that** are playing in the park. 공원에서 놀고 있는 소년과 그의 개를 보아라.

핵심 Check

1. 다음 우리말에 맞게 빈칸에 알맞은 말을 쓰시오.

(1) 그가 새 도서관을 디자인한 남자이다.

➡ He's the man _____ designed the new library.

(2) 나는 말을 할 수 있는 로봇을 가지고 싶다.

➡ I want to have a robot _____ can talk.

② 접속사 if

- **If** you think this bird is special, you are wrong.
  만약 당신이 이 새가 특별하다고 생각한다면, 당신이 틀렸다.

- Your English will improve **if** you study hard.
  네가 열심히 공부한다면, 너의 영어 실력이 향상될 것이다.

■ if는 '만약 ~한다면'이라는 뜻의 접속사로 문장 앞에 쓰여 그 문장을 다른 문장에 연결해 준다. if절은 조건을 나타내는 부사절이다. 접속사가 사용된 문장에서 접속사가 붙은 절을 종속절, 접속사가 붙지 않은 나머지 절을 주절이라고 하는데, 주절이 먼저 나올 수도 있고 종속절이 먼저 나올 수도 있다.

- You can come to the party **if** you want. 너는 네가 원하면 그 파티에 올 수 있어.

■ 접속사 unless는 '만약 ~하지 않는다면'의 뜻으로 'if ~ not'과 같은 의미이다.

- We won't go to the party **unless** we're invited.
  = We won't go to the party **if** we're **not** invited. 우리는 초대받지 않는다면 그 파티에 가지 않을 것이다.

■ 시간이나 조건의 접속사가 이끄는 부사절에서는 미래의 의미를 갖더라도 will을 쓰지 않고 현재시제를 쓴다.

- **If** it **rains** tomorrow, I won't go swimming. 내일 비가 오면 수영하러 안 갈 거야.

- I will go shopping **after** I **finish** doing my homework. 숙제를 끝낸 후에 나는 쇼핑하러 갈 거야.

■ if절이 명사 역할을 하는 경우도 있으며 (이때 if는 whether와 같은 의미이다.) 이때는 '~인지 아닌지'로 해석하며 미래를 나타낼 때에는 미래시제를 써야 한다.

- I wonder **if** she will be at home tomorrow. 나는 그녀가 내일 집에 있을지 궁금하다.

핵심 Check

2. 다음 우리말에 맞게 빈칸에 알맞은 말을 쓰시오.

(1) 만약 그들이 지금 떠난다면 기차를 탈 수 있다.

➡ They can catch the train _____ they leave now.

(2) 만약 학교가 일찍 끝난다면, 나는 해변에 갈 것이다.

➡ If school _____ early, I _____ _____ to the beach.

(3) 나는 그가 파티에 참석할 것인지 잘 모르겠다.

➡ I am not sure _____ he _____ take part in the party.

01 다음 빈칸에 들어갈 알맞은 것은?

> The girl _____ is standing next to him is my sister.

① which   ② what   ③ that   ④ whom   ⑤ whose

02 다음 문장에서 어법상 어색한 부분을 바르게 고쳐 쓰시오.

(1) I have a friend which lives in London.

_____ ➡ _____

(2) Read the magazine who is on the desk.

_____ ➡ _____

(3) You don't have to do so unless you don't want to.

_____, _____ ➡ _____

(4) If it will rain tomorrow, the picnic will be held inside.

_____ ➡ _____

03 다음 우리말에 맞게 괄호 안에 주어진 단어를 빈칸에 바르게 배열하시오.

(1) 만약 네가 내 여동생을 본다면, 이 책을 줘라.
   (see, you, my sister, if)

➡ _____ _____ _____ _____ _____, please give her
   this book.

(2) 우리는 재미있는 모자를 쓰고 있는 여자를 봤다.
   (was, a, hat, wearing, funny, who)

➡ We saw a woman _____ _____ _____ _____ _____
   _____.

04 다음 우리말을 영어로 옮길 때, 빈칸에 알맞은 것이 순서대로 짝지어진 것은?

> 그는 숙제를 끝내면 TV를 볼 것이다.
> ➡ He _____ TV if he _____ his homework.

① will watch – will finish   ② will watch – finishes
③ watches – will finish   ④ watches – finishes
⑤ watched – finished

01 다음 빈칸에 들어갈 수 있는 말이 다른 하나는?

① He wants to meet the woman _____ saved his son.
② I have a friend _____ is good at dancing.
③ There is a house _____ the roof is red.
④ The water _____ was flowing out of the bottle changed into ice.
⑤ Do you know the girl _____ wants to go abroad?

중요

02 다음 중 어법상 바르지 않은 것은?

① If school finishes early tomorrow, I will go to see a movie.
② I forget things unless I take notes.
③ I like the book that has many pictures.
④ Unless we take the subway, we will get there on time.
⑤ Your parents should visit the Louvre Museum if they go to Paris.

서답형

03 다음 괄호 안에서 알맞은 말을 고르시오.

(1) Degas loved painting dancers (which / who) were dancing on stage.
(2) Jane likes the *Starry Night* (who / which) Van Gogh painted.
(3) Do you know the girl (that / which) is wearing a red skirt?
(4) We will go on a picnic, (if / unless) it's fine.
(5) If you (will go / go) straight two blocks, you will find the building.

서답형

04 주어진 어휘를 이용하여 다음 우리말을 영어로 쓰시오.

> 당신은 휴식을 취하면 기분이 더 좋아질 거예요.
> (feel better, take a rest)

➡ _____

중요

05 다음 밑줄 친 that의 성격이 나머지 넷과 다른 것은?

① The dog that has a long tail belongs to Mr. Jones.
② This is the boy that showed me the way to the library.
③ There are lots of Korean dishes that taste delicious.
④ The book that Merriam bought for me is interesting.
⑤ I knew that you were going to ask this question.

06 다음 밑줄 친 부분의 의미가 다른 하나는?

① I would like a cup of coffee if you don't mind.
② I don't know if you can help me.
③ If you know the answer, please speak loudly.
④ If it's fine tomorrow, we'll go hiking.
⑤ If I sell the eggs, I can make money.

서답형

07 다음 문장에서 생략할 수 있는 것을 찾아 쓰시오.

(1) He never touched food which he didn't like.

➡ _____

(2) The man who is talking on the radio is famous.

➡ _____

08 다음 중 어법상 <u>어색한</u> 문장을 고르시오.

① If it will snow tomorrow, I'll go skiing.
② Unless you study hard, you can't pass the exam.
③ If I sell some milk, I can buy a chicken.
④ If you can't fall asleep easily, count numbers.
⑤ It is difficult to do unless you are a professional.

09 다음 중 어법상 옳은 문장을 고르시오.

① Leonardo da Vinch painted *the Mona Lisa* who is a very famous picture.
② I want to make a robot who can do the dishes.
③ This is the boy which she met the other day.
④ Emily likes to take pictures of flowers who are blooming.
⑤ Sam made two chairs that are comfortable to sit on.

10 다음 문장의 빈칸에 들어가기에 의미상 자연스러운 것은? (2개)

_____, you will get a good grade.

① Unless you listen to your teacher
② Unless you waste your time
③ If you use your cell phone during a class
④ If you pay attention to your teacher carefully
⑤ If you don't study hard

11 다음 두 문장을 한 문장으로 바르게 바꾸면?

• A koala is an animal.
• It has a big nose.

① A koala is that an animal has a big nose.
② A koala is an animal which it has a big nose.
③ A koala is an animal which has a big nose.
④ A koala is an animal which a big nose.
⑤ A koala is an animal who has a big nose.

12 다음 빈칸에 들어갈 알맞은 것은?

I bought a new camera _____.

① that I like a lot
② who works really well
③ which it looks very expensive
④ that I gave it to my son
⑤ that the shop sold it

서답형

13 다음 괄호 안에 주어진 단어들을 바르게 배열하여 문장을 완성하시오.

(class, there, no, today, if, is), I will go see a movie with my friend.

➡ _____

서답형

14 다음 그림을 보고 괄호 안에 주어진 어휘를 이용하여 빈칸을 알맞게 채우시오.

_____, you must go to the dentist. (have a toothache)

서답형

15 다음 우리말에 맞게 괄호 안의 어구를 바르게 배열하시오.

소년과 함께 잔디 위에 앉아 있는 개를 봐. (boy, the grass, sitting, that, is, on, a, with)
➡ Look at the dog _____.

➡ _____

16 다음 중 밑줄 친 부분의 쓰임이 잘못된 것은?

① What shall we do if it will begin snowing?
② If I travel to Europe, I will visit Oxford University in England.
③ If I have 100,000 won now, I'll buy a new backpack.
④ If you are hungry, you can eat the pizza on the table.
⑤ If I am hungry, I will eat ramyeon.

중요

17 다음 밑줄 친 부분의 쓰임이 어색한 것은?

① I want to buy a bag which has many pockets outside.
② Morris gave me a book which has many pictures.
③ Children who are under 120 cm cannot ride the roller coaster.
④ Mary likes the boy who came from Turkey.
⑤ Summer is the season who comes before fall.

중요

18 다음 빈칸에 들어갈 말을 순서대로 바르게 연결한 것은?

- _____ you go to bed early, you will be late for school tomorrow.
- _____ I get enough sleep, I will feel better.

① If – If
② If – Unless
③ Unless – If
④ Unless – Unless
⑤ When – However

19 다음 주어진 문장의 밑줄 친 부분과 동일한 역할을 하는 것을 두 개 고르시오.

Mike has a brother who plays the guitar very well.

① The lady who you met yesterday is my mom.
② Minsu met a girl who was very kind.
③ There are many girls who want to go swimming.
④ Who are you waiting for?
⑤ Find a friend who you can always depend on.

20 다음 주어진 문장과 의미가 같은 문장은?

You'll be late unless you hurry.

① You'll be late because you don't hurry.
② Hurry, so you will be late.
③ Hurry, and you will be late.
④ Hurry, or you will be late.
⑤ Hurry, but you will be late.

01 다음 두 문장을 관계대명사를 이용하여 한 문장으로 연결하시오.

(1) • This is a great book.
   • The book gave hope to many people.

   ➡ _____

   _____

(2) • Pilots are the persons.
   • They fly airplanes.

   ➡ _____

(3) • David has a brother.
   • He plays basketball well.

   ➡ _____

   _____

(4) • Kate bought some roses.
   • They smelled good.

   ➡ _____

   _____

(5) • Look at the man and his dog.
   • They are sleeping under the tree.

   ➡ _____

   _____

02 (중요) 다음 두 문장의 뜻이 같도록 빈칸에 알맞은 말을 쓰시오.

(1) Eat vegetables, and you can stay healthy.

   ➡ _____ you eat vegetables, you can stay healthy.

(2) Take the subway, or you'll be late.

   ➡ _____ you take the subway, you'll be late.

03 (중요) 다음 문장의 잘못된 부분을 바르게 고쳐 문장을 다시 쓰시오.

(1) This is a bird who can talk.

   ➡ _____

(2) Look at those musicians which are singing on the street.

   ➡ _____

(3) Alice lives in a house who has a beautiful garden.

   ➡ _____

   _____

(4) She is drawing two pictures that looks very similar.

   ➡ _____

(5) I like Cindy who she is very cool.

   ➡ _____

04 다음 문장을 어법에 맞게 고쳐 쓰시오.

(1) Kathy will go shopping in the afternoon if she will not be busy.

   ➡ _____

(2) If you will meet Morina tomorrow, can you tell her to call me?

   ➡ _____

   _____

(3) Unless you don't study hard, you won't pass the exam.

   ➡ _____

   _____

(4) Unless the weather is bad, I will not go hiking.

   ➡ _____

05 다음 〈보기〉의 (A)와 (B)에서 각각 서로 관계있는 문장을 선택한 후 관계대명사 who, whom, which 중 하나를 사용하여 한 문장으로 연결하시오.

> ─┤ 보기 ├─
>
> (A) • Don't take the umbrella.
> • Do you know the girl?
> • He is the tour guide.
> (B) • Jack met her in the park.
> • He will guide us in New York City.
> • I bought it last weekend.

(1) _____

(2) _____
_____

(3) _____
_____

06 다음 괄호 안에 주어진 어구를 이용하여 문장을 완성하시오.

(1) _____, I will swim in the sea. (go to Jeju-do)

(2) _____, I will let you play the computer games. (finish, your homework)

(3) _____, I will buy a T-shirt for Mom. (go shopping)

07 다음 빈칸을 어법에 맞게 채우시오.

> This is the house. Diana lives in the house.

(1) This is the house _____ .
(2) This is the house _____ .
(3) This is the house _____ .
(4) This is the house _____ .

08 다음 주어진 어구를 알맞게 배열하여 문장을 완성하시오.

(1) I, I, my, him, the street, pictures, actor, will, meet, take, favorite, if, with, on

➡ _____
_____

(2) you, it, the work, will, do, done, not, be, unless

➡ _____

09 두 문장을 관계대명사를 사용하여 한 문장으로 썼을 때, 빈칸에 해당하는 문장을 쓰시오.

(1) I want to get a robot.

_____

➡ I want to get a robot which can clean my room.

(2) _____
She is playing basketball.

➡ The girl who is playing basketball is my friend, Ann.

(3) This is a restaurant.

_____

➡ This is a restaurant that is famous for traditional Korean food.

(4) _____
The friend listens to me carefully.

➡ I want to have a friend that listens to me carefully.

10 다음 우리말을 if로 시작하여 10단어로 영작하시오.

> 오늘 학교가 일찍 끝나면, 나는 책을 읽을 거야.

➡ _____

Reading

Animals That Use Tools

People once thought that only humans can use tools. Now, scientists
are finding out that many animals can also use tools.

Macaque Monkeys

If you go to a Buddhist temple in Lop Buri, Thailand, watch out for
the Macaque monkeys. They may come to you and pull out your hair.
They use human hair to floss their teeth. If you are lucky, you may see
female monkeys that are teaching flossing to their babies. While the
babies are watching, the female monkeys floss their teeth very slowly.

This way, the baby monkeys learn to floss.
= By watching the female monkeys floss their teeth

tool 도구
once 한때, 예전에
only 오직, 단지
human 인간, 사람
Buddhist 불교의
temple 절, 사원
pull out ~을 뽑다
floss 치실질을 하다; 치실
female 여성의, 암컷의
while ~하는 동안에, ~과 동시에

📎 **확인문제**

● 다음 문장이 본문의 내용과 일치하면 T, 일치하지 않으면 F를 쓰시오.

1 Scientists are finding out that animals can't use tools. ☐

2 The Macaque monkeys may pull out your hair in the Buddhist temple in Lop Buri,
   Thailand. ☐

3 The Macaque monkeys use human hair to floss their teeth. ☐

4 While the babies are watching, the male monkeys floss their teeth very slowly. ☐

Octopuses

People don't usually think that octopuses are smart. However, octopuses are very smart, and they can also use tools. They use coconut shells for protection. When they can't find a good hiding place, they hide under coconut shells. Some octopuses even store coconut shells for later use. They pile the coconut shells and carry them to use later. How smart!

Crows

In Aesop's fable *The Thirsty Crow*, a crow drops stones into a jar to raise the level of water. You may think this is just a story, but it is not. Scientists who were studying crows did an experiment. They put a jar with water in front of a crow. A worm was floating on top of the water. However, the water level was low, so the crow could not eat the worm. The crow solved the problem just as in the fable. It dropped stones into the jar. If you think this bird is special, you are wrong. Scientists did the same experiment with other crows, and they all did the same, too.

octopus 문어
coconut 코코넛 열매
shell (딱딱한) 껍데기, 껍질
protection 보호
hide 숨다, 감추다
store 저장하다
pile 쌓다, 포개다
crow 까마귀
fable 우화, 동화
jar 병, 단지, 항아리
raise 올리다
level 높이, 정도, 수준
experiment 실험, 시험
float 뜨다, 떠오르다
solve 해결하다, 풀다

확인문제

● 다음 문장이 본문의 내용과 일치하면 T, 일치하지 않으면 F를 쓰시오.

1 Octopuses are very smart, and they can use tools. ☐

2 Octopuses use coconut shells to attack others. ☐

3 Octopuses always hide under coconut shells. ☐

4 Some octopuses carry coconut shells to use later. ☐

5 *The Thirsty Crow* is Aesop's fable. ☐

6 In an experiment, scientists put a jar filled with water in front of a crow. ☐

7 In the experiment, a worm was floating on top of the water. ☐

8 The crow in the experiment gave up eating the worm. ☐

• 우리말을 참고하여 빈칸에 알맞은 말을 쓰시오.

1 Animals _____ Use _____

2 People _____ _____ that only humans can use tools.

3 Now, scientists _____ _____ _____ that many animals can _____ use tools.

4 If you go to a Buddhist temple in Lop Buri, Thailand, _____ _____ _____ the Macaque monkeys.

5 They may come to you and _____ _____ your hair.

6 They use human hair _____ _____ _____ _____.

7 If you are lucky, you may see female monkeys _____ _____ _____ _____ to their babies.

8 _____ the babies are watching, the female monkeys _____ _____ _____ very slowly.

9 This way, the baby monkeys _____ _____ _____.

10 People _____ _____ _____ that octopuses are smart.

11 _____, octopuses are very smart, and they _____ _____ _____ tools.

12 They use coconut shells _____ _____.

---

1 도구를 사용하는 동물들

2 사람들은 한때 인간만이 도구를 사용할 수 있다고 생각했다.

3 이제 과학자들은 많은 동물들 역시 도구를 사용할 수 있다는 것을 밝혀내고 있다.

4 당신이 태국의 롭부리에 있는 절에 간다면, 마카크 원숭이들을 조심해야 한다.

5 그들이 당신에게 다가와 당신의 머리카락을 뽑을 수도 있다.

6 그들은 이빨을 치실질하기 위해서 사람의 머리카락을 사용한다.

7 만약 당신이 운이 좋으면, 당신은 새끼들에게 치실질하는 것을 가르치고 있는 암컷 원숭이들을 볼 수 있을 것이다.

8 새끼들이 지켜보고 있는 동안, 암컷 원숭이들은 아주 천천히 그들의 이빨을 치실질한다.

9 이런 방식으로, 새끼 원숭이들은 치실질을 배운다.

10 사람들은 대개 문어가 영리하다고 생각하지 않는다.

11 하지만, 문어는 매우 영리하고 또한 도구를 사용할 수 있다.

12 그들은 자신을 보호하기 위해 코코넛 껍데기를 사용한다.

13 When they can't find _____ _____ _____ _____, they _____ _____ coconut shells.

14 Some octopuses _____ _____ coconut shells _____ _____ _____.

15 They _____ the coconut shells and carry them _____ _____ _____.

16 _____ smart!

17 In Aesop's fable *The Thirsty Crow*, a crow _____ stones _____ a jar _____ _____ the level of water.

18 You may think _____ _____ _____ _____ _____, but it is not.

19 Scientists who were studying crows _____ _____ _____.

20 They put a jar _____ water _____ a crow.

21 A worm was floating _____ _____ _____ _____ water.

22 _____, the _____ _____ was _____, so the crow could not eat the worm.

23 The crow solved the problem _____ _____ in the fable.

24 It _____ stones _____ the jar.

25 If you think this bird is _____, you are _____.

26 Scientists did the same experiment _____ _____ _____, and they all _____ _____ _____, too.

---

13 그들이 숨을 만한 좋은 장소를 찾지 못했을 때, 그들은 코코넛 껍데기 아래로 숨는다.

14 어떤 문어들은 심지어 코코넛 껍데기를 나중에 쓰기 위해 모은다.

15 그들은 코코넛 껍데기를 쌓아두고 나중에 쓰기 위해서 가지고 다닌다.

16 얼마나 똑똑한가!

17 이솝 우화 '목마른 까마귀'에서 까마귀는 물 높이를 높이기 위해 항아리 안으로 돌을 떨어뜨린다.

18 당신은 이것이 그저 이야기라고 생각할 수 있지만, 그렇지 않다.

19 까마귀를 연구하던 과학자들이 실험을 했다.

20 그들은 까마귀 앞에 물이 든 항아리를 놓았다.

21 물 위에 벌레가 떠다니고 있었다.

22 하지만, 물 높이가 낮아서, 까마귀는 그 벌레를 먹을 수 없었다.

23 그 까마귀는 우화에서처럼 문제를 해결했다.

24 까마귀는 돌을 항아리 안으로 떨어뜨렸다.

25 만약 당신이 이 새가 특별하다고 생각한다면, 당신이 틀렸다.

26 과학자들은 다른 까마귀들에게도 똑같은 실험을 했고, 그들 모두가 똑같이 그렇게 했다.

● 우리말을 참고하여 본문을 영작하시오.

1 ▶ 도구를 사용하는 동물들

➡ _____

2 ▶ 사람들은 한때 인간만이 도구를 사용할 수 있다고 생각했다.

➡ _____

3 ▶ 이제 과학자들은 많은 동물들 역시 도구를 사용할 수 있다는 것을 밝혀내고 있다.

➡ _____

4 ▶ 당신이 태국의 롭부리에 있는 절에 간다면, 마카크 원숭이들을 조심해야 한다.

➡ _____

5 ▶ 그들이 당신에게 다가와 당신의 머리카락을 뽑을 수도 있다.

➡ _____

6 ▶ 그들은 이빨을 치실질하기 위해서 사람의 머리카락을 사용한다.

➡ _____

7 ▶ 만약 당신이 운이 좋으면, 당신은 새끼들에게 치실질하는 것을 가르치고 있는 암컷 원숭이들을 볼 수 있을 것이다.

➡ _____

8 ▶ 새끼들이 지켜보고 있는 동안, 암컷 원숭이들은 아주 천천히 그들의 이빨을 치실질한다.

➡ _____

9 ▶ 이런 방식으로, 새끼 원숭이들은 치실질을 배운다.

➡ _____

10 ▶ 사람들은 대개 문어가 영리하다고 생각하지 않는다.

➡ _____

11 ▶ 하지만, 문어는 매우 영리하고 또한 도구를 사용할 수 있다.

➡ _____

12 ▶ 그들은 자신을 보호하기 위해 코코넛 껍데기를 사용한다.

➡ _____

13 그들이 숨을 만한 좋은 장소를 찾지 못했을 때, 그들은 코코넛 껍데기 아래로 숨는다.

➡ _____

14 어떤 문어들은 심지어 코코넛 껍데기를 나중에 쓰기 위해 모은다.

➡ _____

15 그들은 코코넛 껍데기를 쌓아두고 나중에 쓰기 위해서 가지고 다닌다.

➡ _____

16 얼마나 똑똑한가!

➡ _____

17 이솝 우화 '목마른 까마귀'에서 까마귀는 물 높이를 높이기 위해 항아리 안으로 돌을 떨어뜨린다.

➡ _____

18 당신은 이것이 그저 이야기라고 생각할 수 있지만, 그렇지 않다.

➡ _____

19 까마귀를 연구하던 과학자들이 실험을 했다.

➡ _____

20 그들은 까마귀 앞에 물이 든 항아리를 놓았다.

➡ _____

21 물 위에 벌레가 떠다니고 있었다.

➡ _____

22 하지만, 물 높이가 낮아서, 까마귀는 그 벌레를 먹을 수 없었다.

➡ _____

23 그 까마귀는 우화에서처럼 문제를 해결했다.

➡ _____

24 까마귀는 돌을 항아리 안으로 떨어뜨렸다.

➡ _____

25 만약 당신이 이 새가 특별하다고 생각한다면, 당신이 틀렸다.

➡ _____

26 과학자들은 다른 까마귀들에게도 똑같은 실험을 했고, 그들 모두가 똑같이 그렇게 했다.

➡ _____

[01~03] 다음 글을 읽고, 물음에 답하시오.

Macaque Monkeys

If you go to a Buddhist temple in Lop Buri, Thailand, (A)[to watch / watch] out for the Macaque monkeys. They ⓐmay come to you and pull out your hair. They use human hair (B)[to floss / flossing] their teeth. If you are lucky, you may see female monkeys that (C)[is / are] teaching flossing to their babies. While the babies are watching, the female monkeys floss their teeth very slowly. This way, the baby monkeys learn to floss.

01 위 글의 괄호 (A)~(C)에서 어법상 알맞은 낱말을 골라 쓰시오.

(A)_____ (B)_____ (C)_____

02 위 글의 밑줄 친 ⓐmay와 의미가 다른 것을 고르시오.

① It may be true.
② You may go there at any moment.
③ It may rain at any moment.
④ He may be swimming in the pool.
⑤ He may have missed his train.

03 위 글의 내용과 일치하지 않는 것은?

① 태국의 롭부리에 있는 절에 간다면, 마카크 원숭이들을 조심해야 한다.
② 마카크 원숭이들이 당신에게 다가와 당신의 머리카락을 뽑을 수도 있다.
③ 마카크 원숭이들은 이빨을 치실질하기 위해서 사람의 머리카락을 사용한다.
④ 태국의 롭부리에 있는 절에서는 새끼들에게 치실질하는 것을 가르치고 있는 암컷 원숭이들을 항상 볼 수 있다.
⑤ 새끼들이 지켜보고 있는 동안, 암컷 원숭이들은 아주 천천히 그들의 이빨을 치실질한다.

[04~05] 다음 글을 읽고, 물음에 답하시오.

Octopuses

People don't usually think that octopuses are smart. However, octopuses are very smart, and ①they can also use tools. ②They use coconut shells for protection. When they can't find a good hiding place, ③they hide under coconut shells. Some octopuses even store coconut shells for later use. ④They pile the coconut shells and carry ⑤them to use later. How smart!

04 위 글의 밑줄 친 ①~⑤ 중에서 가리키는 대상이 나머지 넷과 다른 것은?

①　　　②　　　③　　　④　　　⑤

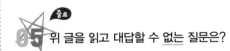

05 위 글을 읽고 대답할 수 없는 질문은?

① Do people usually think that octopuses are smart?
② Can octopuses use tools?
③ What do octopuses use as tools?
④ Where do octopuses hide when they can't find a good hiding place?
⑤ How many coconut shells do octopuses store?

[06~08] 다음 글을 읽고, 물음에 답하시오.

Crows

In Aesop's fable *The Thirsty Crow*, a crow drops stones into a jar ⓐto raise the level of water. You may think this is just a story, but it is not. Scientists who were studying crows did an experiment. They put a jar with water in front of a crow. A worm was floating on top of the water. However, the water level was (A)[low / high], so the crow could not eat the worm. The crow (B)[solved / gave up] the problem just as in the fable. It dropped stones into the jar. If you think this bird is special, you are (C)[right / wrong]. Scientists did the same experiment with other crows, and they all did the same, too.

중요

06 위 글의 괄호 (A)~(C)에서 문맥상 알맞은 낱말을 골라 쓰시오.

(A)＿＿＿＿ (B)＿＿＿＿ (C)＿＿＿＿

서답형

07 실험에서 까마귀가 도구를 사용했던 이유를 빈칸에 쓰시오. (6단어)

> The crow dropped stones into a jar ＿＿＿＿
> ＿＿＿＿＿＿＿＿＿＿＿＿＿ .

➡ ＿＿＿＿＿＿＿＿＿＿＿

08 위 글의 밑줄 친 ⓐto raise와 to부정사의 용법이 같은 것을 모두 고르시오.

① He grew up to be a brave soldier.
② My plan is to climb Mt. Everest.
③ I need a friend to talk with.
④ I have a lot of homework to do.
⑤ This river is dangerous to swim in.

[09~11] 다음 글을 읽고, 물음에 답하시오.

Macaque Monkeys

ⓐIf you will go to a Buddhist temple in Lop Buri, Thailand, watch out for the Macaque monkeys. (①) They may come to you and pull out your hair. (②) They use human hair ⓑto floss their teeth. (③) If you are lucky, you may see female monkeys that are teaching flossing to their babies. (④) This way, the baby monkeys learn to floss. (⑤)

중요

09 위 글의 흐름으로 보아, 주어진 문장이 들어가기에 가장 적절한 곳은?

> While the babies are watching, the female monkeys floss their teeth very slowly.

①   ②   ③   ④   ⑤

서답형

10 위 글의 밑줄 친 ⓐ에서 어법상 틀린 부분을 찾아 고치시오.

＿＿＿＿＿＿ ➡ ＿＿＿＿＿＿

11 위 글의 밑줄 친 ⓑto floss와 to부정사의 용법이 다른 것을 모두 고르시오.

① I have no time to waste.
② She visited my house to help me.
③ I went to the library to return the books.
④ My dream is to become a nurse.
⑤ She got up early to catch the train.

[12~14] 다음 글을 읽고, 물음에 답하시오.

Octopuses

People don't usually think that octopuses are smart. ____ⓐ____, octopuses are very smart, and they can also use tools. They use coconut shells ____ⓑ____ protection. When they can't find a good hiding place, they hide under coconut shells. Some octopuses even store coconut shells ____ⓒ____ later use. They pile the coconut shells and carry them to use later. How smart!

12 위 글의 빈칸 ⓐ에 들어갈 알맞은 말을 고르시오.

① Therefore   ② Besides
③ Instead   ④ However
⑤ For example

서답형

13 위 글의 빈칸 ⓑ와 ⓒ에 공통으로 들어갈 전치사를 쓰시오.

➡ _____

14 위 글의 내용과 일치하지 <u>않는</u> 것은?

① 사람들은 대개 문어가 영리하다고 생각하지 않는다.
② 문어들은 매우 영리하고 또한 도구를 사용할 수 있다.
③ 문어들은 숨을 만한 좋은 장소를 찾을 수 없을 때, 코코넛 껍데기 아래로 숨는다.
④ 몇몇 문어들은 나중에 사용하기 위해 코코넛 껍데기를 모은다.
⑤ 몇몇 문어들은 코코넛 껍데기를 쌓아 두고 바로 쓰기 위해 그것들을 가지고 다닌다.

[15~16] 다음 글을 읽고, 물음에 답하시오.

Crows

However, the water level was low, so the crow could not eat the worm. The crow solved the problem just as in the ____ⓐ____. It dropped stones into the jar. ⓑ<u>If you think this bird is ordinary, you are wrong.</u> Scientists did the same experiment with other crows, and they all did the same, too.

서답형

15 주어진 영영풀이를 참고하여 빈칸 ⓐ에 철자 f로 시작하는 단어를 쓰시오.

> a story which teaches a moral lesson and sometimes has animals as the main characters

➡ f_____

서답형

16 위 글의 밑줄 친 ⓑ에서 흐름상 어색한 부분을 찾아 고치시오.

_____ ➡ _____

[17~19] 다음 글을 읽고, 물음에 답하시오.

Animals ⓐ<u>That</u> Use Tools

People once thought ⓑ<u>that</u> only humans can use tools. Now, scientists are finding out that many animals can also use tools.

서답형

17 위 글의 밑줄 친 ⓐ, ⓑ와 문법적 쓰임이 같은 것을 각각 아래 〈보기〉에서 모두 골라 쓰시오.

┌─ 보기 ┐
① Look at the bird <u>that</u> is flying there.
② He said <u>that</u> the story was true.
③ I believe <u>that</u> you'll finish it in time.
④ This is the pen <u>that</u> I bought yesterday.
⑤ She told me <u>that</u> I was smart.
└──────────┘

ⓐ와 쓰임이 같은 것: _____
ⓑ와 쓰임이 같은 것: _____

18 위 글의 다음에 올 내용으로 가장 알맞은 것을 고르시오.

① 도구를 사용하는 많은 사람들
② 도구 사용에 관한 사람들의 생각
③ 동물의 지능에 관한 과학자들의 연구
④ 도구를 사용할 수 있는 많은 동물들
⑤ 도구를 사용한 과학자들의 연구

서답형

19 위 글의 내용과 일치하도록 다음 빈칸에 알맞은 말을 쓰시오.

> Now, scientists are finding out that not only humans but also many animals can _____ _____.

➡ _____

[20~22] 다음 글을 읽고, 물음에 답하시오.

Octopuses

People don't usually think that octopuses are smart. However, octopuses are very smart, and they can also use tools. ①They use coconut shells for protection. ②The coconut shell is a good place to sleep in. ③When they (A)[can / can't] find a good hiding place, they hide (B)[over / under] coconut shells. ④Some octopuses even store coconut shells for later use. ⑤They (C)[file / pile] the coconut shells and carry them to use later. How smart!

20 위 글의 ①~⑤ 중에서 전체 흐름과 관계 없는 문장은?

① ② ③ ④ ⑤

서답형

21 위 글의 괄호 (A)~(C)에서 문맥상 알맞은 낱말을 골라 쓰시오.

(A)_____ (B)_____ (C)_____

서답형

22 다음 질문에 대한 알맞은 대답을 빈칸에 쓰시오. (2단어)

> Q: What do the octopuses use as tools?
> A: They use _____ _____ as tools for protection.

[23~24] 다음 글을 읽고, 물음에 답하시오.

Giant Pandas

- Size: They grow 1.2m to 1.9m long and weigh up to 135kg.
- Food: They eat leaves, fish, and small animals.
- Home: They live in the wild, high up in the mountains of China.
- Amazing Facts: ⓐThey are very good at climbing trees. They take a rest on trees. They even walk from one tree to another.

23 위 글을 읽고 대답할 수 없는 질문은?

① How big are Giant Pandas?
② Where do Giant Pandas live?
③ How fast can Giant Pandas run?
④ What do Giant Pandas eat?
⑤ What is special about Giant Pandas?

서답형

24 위 글의 밑줄 친 ⓐ를 다음과 같이 바꿔 쓸 때 빈칸에 알맞은 말을 쓰시오.

> They climb trees _____ _____.

25 주어진 글 다음에 이어질 글의 순서로 가장 적절한 것은?

> People don't usually think that octopuses are smart.

> (A) When they can't find a good hiding place, they hide under coconut shells. Some octopuses even store coconut shells for later use.
> (B) They pile the coconut shells and carry them to use later. How smart!
> (C) However, octopuses are very smart, and they can also use tools. They use coconut shells for protection.

① (A) – (C) – (B)　　② (B) – (A) – (C)
③ (B) – (C) – (A)　　④ (C) – (A) – (B)
⑤ (C) – (B) – (A)

[26~28] 다음 글을 읽고, 물음에 답하시오.

Crows

(①) In Aesop's fable *The Thirsty Crow*, a crow drops stones into a jar to raise the level of water. (②) You may think this is just a story, but it is not. (③) Scientists who were studying crows did an experiment. (④) A worm was floating on top of the water. (⑤) However, the water level was low, so the crow could not eat the worm. ⓐ그 까마귀는 꼭 우화에서처럼 그 문제를 해결했다. It dropped stones into the jar. If you think this bird is special, you are wrong. Scientists did the same experiment with other crows, and they all did the same, too.

26 위 글의 흐름으로 보아, 주어진 문장이 들어가기에 가장 적절한 곳은?

> They put a jar with water in front of a crow.

①　　②　　③　　④　　⑤

27 위 글의 밑줄 친 ⓐ의 우리말에 맞게 주어진 어구를 이용하여 10 단어로 영작하시오.

> solved, just as

➡ _____

28 위 글의 요지로 알맞은 것을 고르시오.

① 이솝 우화 '목마른 까마귀'는 단지 이야기일 뿐이다.
② 까마귀는 영리한 동물이고 도구를 사용할 줄 안다.
③ 과학자들은 실험을 통해 까마귀를 연구했다.
④ 까마귀는 벌레를 먹는 것을 좋아한다.
⑤ 항아리의 수위가 낮으면 까마귀는 벌레를 먹을 수 없다.

29 다음 글의 제목으로 알맞은 것을 고르시오.

> People don't usually think that octopuses are smart. However, octopuses are very smart, and they can also use tools. They use coconut shells for protection. When they can't find a good hiding place, they hide under coconut shells. Some octopuses even store coconut shells for later use. They pile the coconut shells and carry them to use later. How smart!

① Animals with Special Talents
② The Amazing World of Nature
③ Octopuses Are Cleverer Than Humans!
④ Animals in the Fable
⑤ The Octopus, a Smart Animal!

[30~31] 다음 글을 읽고, 물음에 답하시오.

Crows

In Aesop's fable *The Thirsty Crow*, a crow drops stones into a jar to raise the level of water. You may think this is just a story, but it is not. Scientists who were studying crows did an experiment. ⓐThey put a jar with water in front of a crow. A worm was floating on top of the water. However, the water level was low, so the crow could not eat the worm. ⓑThe crow solved the problem just as in the fable. It dropped stones into the jar. If you think this bird is special, you are wrong. Scientists did the same experiment with other crows, and they all did the same, too.

서답형

30 위 글의 밑줄 친 ⓐ가 가리키는 것을 본문에서 찾아 쓰시오.

➡ _____

서답형

31 다음 빈칸 (A)와 (B)에 알맞은 단어를 넣어 위 글의 밑줄 친 ⓑ에 대한 설명을 완성하시오.

> When the crow could not eat the worm, it (A)_____ stones (B)_____ the jar to raise the level of water just as a crow does in Aesop's fable *The Thirsty Crow*.

[32~33] 주어진 글 다음에 이어질 글의 순서로 가장 적절한 것을 고르시오.

32

> If you go to a Buddhist temple in Lop Buri, Thailand, watch out for the Macaque monkeys.

> (A) While the babies are watching, the female monkeys floss their teeth very slowly. This way, the baby monkeys learn to floss.

> (B) They may come to you and pull out your hair. They use human hair to floss their teeth.

> (C) If you are lucky, you may see female monkeys that are teaching flossing to their babies.

① (A) – (C) – (B) ② (B) – (A) – (C)
③ (B) – (C) – (A) ④ (C) – (A) – (B)
⑤ (C) – (B) – (A)

33

> In Aesop's fable *The Thirsty Crow*, a crow drops stones into a jar to raise the level of water.

> (A) They put a jar with water in front of a crow. A worm was floating on top of the water. However, the water level was low, so the crow could not eat the worm. The crow solved the problem just as in the fable.

> (B) You may think this is just a story, but it is not. Scientists who were studying crows did an experiment.

> (C) It dropped stones into the jar. If you think this bird is special, you are wrong. Scientists did the same experiment with other crows, and they all did the same, too.

① (A) – (C) – (B) ② (B) – (A) – (C)
③ (B) – (C) – (A) ④ (C) – (A) – (B)
⑤ (C) – (B) – (A)

[01~03] 다음 글을 읽고, 물음에 답하시오.

ⓐAnimals That Uses Tools
People once thought that only humans can use tools. ⓑNow, scientists are finding out that many animals can also use tools.

중요
01 위 글의 밑줄 친 ⓐ에서 어법상 틀린 부분을 찾아 고치시오.

_____ ➡ _____

02 위 글의 밑줄 친 ⓑ에서 생략할 수 있는 단어를 찾아 쓰시오.

➡ _____

중요
03 위 글의 내용과 일치하도록 다음 빈칸 (A)와 (B)에 알맞은 말을 쓰시오.

There are many ____(A)____ that can use tools in addition to ____(B)____.

(A)_____ (B)_____

[04~06] 다음 글을 읽고, 물음에 답하시오.

Macaque Monkeys
If you go to a Buddhist temple in Lop Buri, Thailand, watch out for the Macaque monkeys. They may come to you and (A)[pull / push] out your hair. They use human hair to floss their teeth. If you are (B)[lucky / unlucky], you may see female monkeys that are teaching flossing to ⓐtheir babies. (C)[During / While] the babies are watching, the female monkeys floss their teeth very slowly. This way, the baby monkeys learn to floss.

중요
04 위 글의 괄호 (A)~(C)에서 문맥과 어법상 알맞은 낱말을 골라 쓰시오.

(A)_____ (B)_____ (C)_____

05 위 글의 밑줄 친 ⓐtheir가 가리키는 것을 본문에서 찾아 쓰시오.

➡ _____

06 다음 빈칸에 알맞은 단어를 넣어 Macaque 원숭이가 도구를 구하는 방법을 완성하시오. (본문의 단어를 변형할 것.)

They get the tools to floss their teeth by _____ _____ human hair.

[07~08] 다음 글을 읽고, 물음에 답하시오.

Octopuses
People don't usually think that octopuses are smart. However, octopuses are very smart, and they can also use tools. They use coconut shells for protection. When they can't find a good hiding place, they hide under coconut shells. Some octopuses even store coconut shells for later use. They __ⓐ__ the coconut shells and carry them to use later. How smart!

중요
07 다음 문장에서 위 글의 내용과 다른 부분을 찾아서 고치시오.

Octopuses are very smart, and they use coconut shells to prevent accidents.

_____ ➡ _____

08 주어진 영영풀이를 참고하여 빈칸 ⓐ에 철자 p로 시작하는 단어를 쓰시오.

> to lay objects on top of each other

➡ _____

[09~11] 다음 글을 읽고, 물음에 답하시오.

Crows

In Aesop's fable *The Thirsty Crow*, a crow drops stones into a jar to raise the level of water. You may think this is just a story, but it is not. Scientists who were studying crows did an experiment. They put a jar ___ⓐ___ water in front of a crow. A worm was floating on top of the water. However, the water level was low, so the crow could not eat the worm. The crow solved the problem just as in the fable. It dropped stones into the jar. ⓑIf you think this bird is special, you are wrong. Scientists did the same experiment ___ⓒ___ other crows, and they all did the same, too.

09 실험에서 까마귀가 사용한 도구가 무엇인지 본문에서 찾아 다음 빈칸에 쓰시오.

> When the crow could not eat the worm because of the low water level, it dropped _____ into the jar to raise the level of water.

10 위 글의 빈칸 ⓐ와 ⓒ에 공통으로 들어갈 전치사를 쓰시오.

➡ _____

11 위 글에서 밑줄 친 ⓑ처럼 말한 이유를 우리말로 쓰시오.

➡ _____

_____

[12~14] 다음 글을 읽고, 물음에 답하시오.

Octopuses

People don't usually think that octopuses are smart. However, octopuses are very smart, and they can also use tools. They use coconut shells for protection. When they can't find a good hiding place, they hide under coconut shells. ⓐ어떤 문어들은 심지어 코코넛 껍데기를 나중에 쓰기 위해 모은다. ⓑThey pile the coconut shells and to carry them to use later. How smart!

12 위 글을 읽고, 다음 질문에 대한 대답을 완성하시오. (8단어)

> Q: When do octopuses use coconut shells for protection?
> A: They use them _____
> _____ .

13 위 글의 밑줄 친 ⓐ의 우리말에 맞게 한 단어를 보충하여, 주어진 어휘를 알맞게 배열하시오.

> store / octopuses / some / use / coconut shells / even / for

➡ _____

_____

14 위 글의 밑줄 친 ⓑ에서 어법상 틀린 부분을 찾아 고치시오.

_____ ➡ _____

Words and Reading

Scientists are now finding out that many animals can use tools. Macaque
　　　　　　　　　　　　　　명사절을 이끄는 접속사
monkeys use human hair to floss their teeth. Octopuses hide under coconut
　　　　　　　　　부사적 용법(목적)　　　　　　　　　　전 ~ 아래
shells when they can't find a good hiding place. Crows can drop stones into
　　　　접 ~할 때　　　　　　　　명 숨기, 은신　　　　　　　　　　　~ 안으로
a jar to raise the level of water to eat the worm that is floating on top of the
　　　　　　　높이　　부사적 용법(목적)　벌레　= which(주격 관계대명사)　~ 위에
water.

구문해설 · find out: 알아내다 · tool: 도구, 수단 · hide: 숨다, 감추다 · drop: 떨어뜨리다

해석

과학자들은 이제 많은 동물들이 도구를 사용할 수 있다는 것을 알아내고 있다. 마카크 원숭이는 그들의 이빨을 치실질하기 위해 사람의 머리카락을 사용한다. 문어는 그들이 숨을 만한 좋은 장소를 찾지 못할 때 코코넛 껍질 아래 숨는다. 까마귀는 물의 높이를 올려 물 위에 떠 있는 벌레를 먹기 위해 항아리 안에 돌을 떨어뜨린다.

Think and Write

Animals with Special Talents

There are many animals that have special talents. An example is Einstein.
　　　　　~이 있다　　　　　　= which(주격 관계대명사)
He is an African Grey Parrot which can use 200 English words to talk with
　　　　　　　　　　　　　　= that(주격 관계대명사)　　　　　　　　부사적 용법(목적)
people. He can sing the "Happy Birthday" song.

There are many animals that have special talents. An example is Koko. She is
　　　　　~이 있다　　　선행사가 복수(animals)이므로 has (X)
a female gorilla which lives in America. She can talk with people in American
　　　　　　선행사가 단수(a female gorilla)이므로 live(X)　　　　　　　[도구·수단] ~으로
Sign Language. She knows more than 1,000 signs.
　　　　　　　　　　　more than: ~ 이상

구문해설 · special: 특별한 · talent: 재능 · female: 여성인, 암컷의 · Sign Language: 수화

특별한 재능을 가진 동물들
특별한 재능을 가진 많은 동물들이 있다. 한 예는 Einstein이다. 그는 사람들과 대화를 하기 위해 200개의 영어 단어를 사용할 수 있는 아프리카 회색앵무새이다. 그는 '생일 축하합니다' 노래를 부를 수 있다.
특별한 재능을 가진 많은 동물들이 있다. 한 예는 Koko이다. 그녀는 미국에 살고 있는 암컷 고릴라이다. 그녀는 수화로 사람들과 이야기할 수 있다. 그녀는 1,000개가 넘는 신호를 알고 있다.

Around the World

1. The longest snake ever is Medusa. She is 7.67 meters long.
　최상급 표현: 가장 ~한
2. Alley recorded the longest jump by a cat. Her record was 1.83 meters.

3. The oldest pig ever is Ernestine. He lived for 22 years and 359 days.

구문해설 · jump: 도약, 비약, 뜀, 뛰어오름

1. 지금까지 가장 긴 뱀은 Medusa이다. 그것은 길이가 7.67미터이다.
2. Alley는 가장 멀리 뛰는 고양이로 기록되었다. 그녀의 기록은 1.83 미터였다.
3. 지금까지 가장 오래 산 돼지는 Ernestine이다. 그는 22년 359일을 살았다.

Words & Expressions

01 다음 〈보기〉와 같은 관계가 되도록 빈칸에 알맞은 말을 쓰시오. (주어진 철자로 시작할 것)

> **보기**
> speak – talk

(1) stack ➡ p_____
(2) gift ➡ t_____
(3) deal with ➡ s_____
(4) amaze ➡ s_____

02 다음 우리말에 맞게 주어진 단어를 이용해 빈칸을 완성하시오.

> 너는 선생님의 발표를 들었니?
> ➡ Did you hear the teacher's _____?
> (announce)

03 다음 제시된 단어를 사용하여 자연스러운 문장을 만들 수 없는 것은? (형태 변화 가능)

> **보기**
> protection   pattern   whale   shell

① A _____ is the largest animal in the world.
② These are _____ of how to use tools.
③ Such a diet is believed to offer _____ against a number of cancers.
④ I like the shirt with a _____.
⑤ The kids were collecting _____ on the beach.

04 다음 빈칸에 공통으로 들어갈 단어를 쓰시오.

> • It was the lowest _____ of inflation for some years.
> • The water _____ of the Han River is averagely 10 meters.

05 다음 제시된 의미에 맞는 단어를 주어진 철자로 시작하여 빈칸에 쓰고, 알맞은 것을 골라 문장을 완성하시오.

> • c_____: a large brown nut with a hairy shell
> • t_____: a thing that you use for making or doing something
> • p_____: a picture you take using a camera

(1) Her _____ appeared on the front page of The New York Times.
(2) In my town, there are lots of _____ trees.
(3) In present day life, fire is a very useful _____.

06 다음 우리말과 일치하도록 괄호 안의 단어를 바르게 배열하시오.

(1) 문어의 몸은 가방처럼 생겼다.
   (like, a, the, bag, body, an, of, octopus, looks)
   ➡ _____

(2) 고릴라의 팔은 그것의 다리보다 길다.
   (of, than, the, a, longer, legs, arms, its, gorilla, are)
   ➡ _____

[07~08] 다음 대화는 그림에서 빨간 동그라미 물건을 찾는 내용이다. 그림과 일치하도록 (A)~(C)에서 알맞은 것을 고르시오.

07

G: Hi. I think I lost my umbrella.

M: What does it look like?

G: It's a (A)[small / big] (B)[pink / navy] umbrella.

M: Can you tell me more?

G: It has a white (C)[cloud / flower] pattern on it.

08

A: May I help you?

B: Yes. I'm looking for my (A)[scarf / bag].

A: What does it look like?

B: It's (B)[blue / grey].

A: Can you tell me more about it?

B: It has a (C)[star / heart] pattern on it.

09 다음 대화의 순서를 바르게 배열한 것은?

(A) It's a big silver bag.

(B) Excuse me. I'm looking for my bag. I left it in the restroom.

(C) OK. What does it look like?

(D) Alright. I'll go and check.

① (B) – (A) – (C) – (D)

② (B) – (A) – (D) – (C)

③ (B) – (C) – (A) – (D)

④ (C) – (A) – (B) – (D)

⑤ (C) – (B) – (A) – (D)

[10~11] 다음 대화를 읽고, 물음에 답하시오.

A: (A)_____

B: Yes. I'm looking for my bag.

A: (B)_____

B: It's big and orange.

A: (C)_____

B: ⓐIt has one big pocket outside.

10 위 대화의 빈칸 (A)~(C)에 들어갈 말을 〈보기〉에게 골라 기호를 쓰시오.

┤ 보기 ├

① How does it look like?

② Can you tell me more about it?

③ May I help you?

④ What does it look like?

⑤ Can you help me to find a pocket?

⑥ Can I tell you more about it?

⑦ What are you looking for?

(A) _____ (B) _____ (C) _____

11 위 대화의 밑줄 친 ⓐ이 가리키는 말을 주어진 단어를 이용해 찾아 쓰시오.

➡ _____ (be, which)

12 다음 중 짝지어진 대화가 <u>어색한</u> 것은?

① A: Do you need help?
　 B: I lost my wallet.
② A: What are you looking for?
　 B: I'm looking for my cat.
③ A: Can you tell me more?
　 B: It has a big blue star on it.
④ A: Where did you lose it?
　 B: I'll make an announcement.
⑤ A: Tell me more about it.
　 B: I lost it near the bus station.

Grammar

13 다음 밑줄 친 which와 용법이 <u>다른</u> 하나는?

I went to a shopping mall <u>which</u> was very far from my house.

① Tom is a student <u>who</u> studies art in a college.
② Look at the men <u>who</u> are dancing on the street.
③ I want to live in a house <u>that</u> has many rooms.
④ I don't know the girl <u>who</u> you met yesterday.
⑤ Julie is the girl <u>who</u> is wearing jeans and a white shirt.

14 관계대명사를 이용하여 만든 다음 문장을 원래의 두 문장으로 쓰시오.

Mr. Kim lives in a house which has many big windows.

➡ _____

15 다음 문장의 밑줄 친 부분과 쓰임이 같은 것은?

<u>If</u> it rains tomorrow, I will read a book at home.

① I think you should wait and see <u>if</u> the market improves.
② I wonder <u>if</u> I should go there or not.
③ <u>If</u> you take a taxi, you can get there in ten minutes.
④ I'd like to know <u>if</u> the bus has arrived.
⑤ <u>If</u> I were you, I would take part in the meeting.

16 다음 중 어법상 바르지 <u>않은</u> 것은?

Olivia ①will go ②shopping ③if she ④will have time ⑤in the afternoon.

①　　　②　　　③　　　④　　　⑤

17 다음 중 두 문장을 한 문장으로 만들 때 의미가 <u>다른</u> 하나는?

① I have to catch the train. It leaves at 8:45.
　→ I have to catch the train that leaves at 8:45.
② The boy sent me some flowers. I received them yesterday.
　→ The boy received some flowers yesterday that I sent.
③ I want to be a person. The person is loved by many people.
　→ I want to be a person who is loved by many people.
④ Mariana bought a book. She wanted to read it.
　→ Mariana bought a book that she wanted to read.
⑤ I called Jack yesterday. He lives in Seoul.
　→ I called Jack yesterday who lives in Seoul.

18 다음 우리말과 일치하도록 할 때, 빈칸에 알맞은 것은?

> 조용히 하지 않으면 너는 아이를 깨울 것이다.
> ➡ _____ you do not keep silent, you will wake up the baby.

① Because   ② When   ③ That
④ Unless   ⑤ If

19 다음 중 어법상 바르지 <u>않은</u> 것은?

① Diana has two puppies who are brown and white.
② Look at those birds that are sitting on the tree.
③ I met a girl who has the same name as me.
④ Jane saw a woman that was eating an apple.
⑤ This is an animal which has a long nose.

20 다음 중 어법상 <u>잘못된</u> 문장은?

① He won't pass the test unless he does his best.
② If I sell some milk, I can buy a chicken.
③ If my friend will look sad, I will invite her to dinner.
④ You should clean your room before your parents come tomorrow.
⑤ Is counting sheep helpful if I can't fall asleep?

21 다음 두 문장을 알맞은 관계대명사를 이용하여 하나의 문장으로 쓰시오.

> • This is the snack shop.
> • It is famous for corn dogs.

➡ _____
  _____

[22~23] 다음 글을 읽고, 물음에 답하시오.

Macaque Monkeys

  If you go to a Buddhist temple in Lop Buri, Thailand, watch out for the Macaque monkeys. They may come to you and pull out your hair. They use human hair to floss their teeth. If you are lucky, you may see female monkeys that are teaching flossing to their babies. While the babies are ⓐwatching, the female monkeys floss their teeth very slowly. This way, the baby monkeys learn to floss.

22 아래 〈보기〉에서 위 글의 밑줄 친 ⓐwatching과 문법적 쓰임이 같은 것의 개수를 고르시오.

> ┤ 보기 ├
> ① My hobby is making model cars.
> ② He stopped smoking.
> ③ Jane is helping her mom do the dishes.
> ④ Watching TV always makes me happy.
> ⑤ They are cleaning their house now.

① 1개   ② 2개   ③ 3개   ④ 4개   ⑤ 5개

23 다음 빈칸 (A)와 (B)에 알맞은 단어를 넣어 질문에 대한 알맞은 대답을 완성하시오.

> Q: How do the baby monkeys learn to floss?
> A: By (A)_____ the female monkeys (B)_____ their teeth very slowly.

[24~26] 다음 글을 읽고, 물음에 답하시오.

Octopuses

People don't usually think that octopuses are smart. (①) However, octopuses are very smart, and they can also use ___ⓐ___. (②) When they can't find a good hiding place, they hide under coconut shells. (③) Some octopuses even store coconut shells for later use. (④) They pile the coconut shells and carry them ___ⓑ___ later. (⑤) How smart!

24 위 글의 빈칸 ⓐ에 들어갈 알맞은 말을 고르시오.

① machines   ② engines   ③ systems
④ black ink   ⑤ tools

25 위 글의 흐름으로 보아, 주어진 문장이 들어가기에 가장 적절한 곳은?

> They use coconut shells for protection.

①   ②   ③   ④   ⑤

26 위 글의 빈칸 ⓑ에 use를 알맞은 형태로 쓰시오.

➡ _____

[27~28] 다음 글을 읽고, 물음에 답하시오.

Crows

In Aesop's fable *The Thirsty Crow*, ①a crow drops stones into a jar to raise the level of water. You may think this is just a story, but it is not. Scientists who were studying crows did an experiment. They put a jar with water in front of ②a crow. A worm was floating on top of the water. However, the water level was low, so ③the crow could not eat the worm.

The crow solved the problem just as in the fable. ④It dropped stones into the jar. If you think ⑤this bird is special, you are wrong. Scientists did the same experiment with other crows, and they all did the same, too.

27 위 글의 내용과 일치하지 <u>않는</u> 것은?

① 이솝 우화 '목마른 까마귀'에서 까마귀가 물 높이를 높이기 위해 항아리 안으로 돌을 떨어뜨린다.
② 실험에서 과학자들은 까마귀 앞에 물이 든 항아리를 놓았다.
③ 항아리 안의 물 위에 벌레 한 마리가 떠다니고 있었다.
④ 물높이가 낮아서 까마귀는 벌레를 먹을 수 없었다.
⑤ 실험 대상이었던 까마귀는 특별했다.

28 위 글의 밑줄 친 ①~⑤ 중에서 가리키는 대상이 나머지 넷과 <u>다른</u> 것은?

①   ②   ③   ④   ⑤

[29~30] 다음 글을 읽고, 물음에 답하시오.

Animals with Special Talents

There are many animals ___ⓐ___ have special talents. An example is Koko. She is a female gorilla ___ⓑ___ lives in America. She can talk with people in American Sign Language. She knows more than 1,000 signs.

29 위 글의 빈칸 ⓐ와 ⓑ에 공통으로 알맞은 말을 쓰시오.

➡ _____

30 다음 질문에 대한 알맞은 대답을 우리말로 쓰시오.

> Q: What is Koko's special talent?
>
> A: _____
>
> _____

단원별 예상문제

01 출제율 90%

다음 빈칸에 들어갈 알맞은 표현을 찾아 문장을 완성하시오.

to fix	to carry	suprised
carry	tool	floating
surprise	dropping	fix

(1) He's using a _____ _____ the door.

(2) It _____ me when he shouted in the dark.

(3) A tree branch was _____ down the river.

02 출제율 85%

다음 영영풀이에 해당하는 단어를 고르시오.

> something important that someone tells people

① management
② information
③ announcement
④ activity
⑤ lecture

03 출제율 100%

다음 주어진 우리말에 맞게 빈칸을 채우시오.

(1) Let us _____ that dogs can talk _____ us. (개가 우리처럼 말할 수 있다고 상상해 보자.)

(2) This is the best _____ _____ _____ the problem. (이것이 그 문제를 푸는 가장 좋은 방법이다.)

04 출제율 90%

다음 밑줄 친 부분과 의미가 가장 가까운 것은?

> The computer has become an important teaching tool.

① equipment
② type
③ object
④ way
⑤ sign

05 출제율 100%

다음 중 의미가 다른 하나를 고르시오.

① What does he look like?
② How does he look?
③ What's he like?
④ How do you describe him?
⑤ Tell me what he looks like.

[06~07] 다음 대화의 밑줄 친 부분에서 어색한 것의 개수를 고르시오.

06 출제율 90%

> B: Excuse me. ⓐI'm looking like my bag. I ⓑleft it in the restroom.
> W: OK. ⓒWhat does it look?
> B: ⓓIt's a big silver bag.
> W: Alright. ⓔIt'll go and check.

① 1개
② 2개
③ 3개
④ 4개
⑤ 5개

07 출제율 90%

> B: Excuse me. ⓐI'm looking for my cat.
> W: ⓑWhat does it look like?
> B: ⓒThey're small and white.
> W: ⓓCan you tell me more it?
> B: ⓔIt's wearing a T-shirt

① 1개
② 2개
③ 3개
④ 4개
⑤ 5개

07 다음 문장을 어법에 맞게 고쳐 쓰시오.

(1) I will see the doctor unless I don't feel better tomorrow.

➡ _____

(2) If I will get a ticket, I go to the concert.

➡ _____

(3) If it will snow tomorrow, we will go skiing.

➡ _____

[08~10] 다음 글을 읽고, 물음에 답하시오.

Macaque Monkeys

If you go to a Buddhist temple in Lop Buri, Thailand, watch out for the Macaque monkeys. They may come to you and pull out your hair. They use human hair to floss their teeth. If you are lucky, you may see female monkeys ⓐthat are teaching flossing to their babies. ⓑ새끼들이 지켜보고 있는 동안, 암컷 원숭이들은 아주 천천히 그들의 이빨을 치실질한다. This way, the baby monkeys learn to floss.

08 다음 질문에 대한 알맞은 대답을 본문에서 찾아 주어진 단어로 시작하여 쓰시오. (8단어)

Q: Why do the Macaque monkeys come to people and pull out their hair?
A: Because _____ .

09 위 글의 밑줄 친 ⓐthat과 바꿔 쓸 수 있는 단어를 쓰시오.

➡ _____

10 위 글의 밑줄 친 ⓑ의 우리말에 맞게 주어진 어휘를 이용하여 13 단어로 영작하시오.

While, watching, female, slowly

➡ _____

_____

[11~13] 다음 글을 읽고, 물음에 답하시오.

Crows

In Aesop's fable *The Thirsty Crow*, a crow drops stones into a jar to raise the level of water. You may think this is just a story, ⓐbut it is not. Scientists who were studying crows did an experiment. They put a jar with water in front of a crow. A worm was floating on top of the water. However, the water level was low, so the crow could not eat the worm. The crow solved the problem just as in the fable. It dropped stones into the jar. If you think this bird is special, you are wrong. Scientists did the same experiment with other crows, and they all ⓑdid the same, too.

11 위 글의 밑줄 친 ⓐ 문장 뒤에 생략된 말을 쓰시오.

➡ _____

12 다음 질문에 대한 알맞은 대답을 주어진 단어로 시작하여 쓰시오. (5단어)

Q: Why was it impossible for the crow to eat the worm which was floating on top of the water?
A: Because _____ .

13 위 글의 밑줄 친 ⓑ가 가리키는 것을 본문에서 찾아 쓰시오.

➡ _____

01 그림을 보고 표를 채우고, 내용과 일치하도록 대화를 완성하시오.

Lost Pet Report	
① type of animal	_____
② color	_____ hair
③ size	small
④ something special	_____ tail
⑤ lost place	near the library

A: May I help you?

B: Yes. _____

A: What does it look like?

B: _____ hair.

A: Can you tell me more about it?

B: It _____.

A: _____ did you lose it?

B: _____

02 관계대명사를 이용하여 직업을 설명하는 문장을 쓰시오.

(1) A pilot is a person _____.

(2) A painter is a person _____.

(3) A driver is a person _____.

(4) A baker is a person _____.

(5) A teacher is a person _____.

단원별 모의고사

01 다음 짝지어진 두 단어의 관계가 <u>다른</u> 하나를 고르시오.

① pattern – design
② way – method
③ photograph – picture
④ slowly – fast
⑤ record – document

02 다음 밑줄 친 부분과 바꾸어 쓸 수 있는 것을 고르시오.

> He is <u>trying to find</u> the book to read.

① looking at
② looking for
③ talking with
④ looking like
⑤ watching out

03 다음 〈보기〉의 어휘를 사용하여 문장을 완성하시오.

┌─ 보기 ─────────────────────────┐
  to   at   out   for   of   on
└───────────────────────────────┘

(1) I'm only interested in finding _____ what the fact are.
(2) He is good _____ solving difficult math problems.
(3) He added a lot of whipped cream _____ top _____ hot chocolate.
(4) They started to dance _____ music.

04 다음 우리말과 일치하도록 빈칸에 알맞은 말을 쓰시오.

(1) 너는 여행을 하는 동안 너의 모든 비용을 기록해야 한다.
➡ You should _____ all your expenses _____ your trip.
(2) 그는 컴퓨터를 사용하는 동안 먹는 중이다.
➡ He's eating _____ he is using a computer.

(3) Jane은 그녀의 학교에서 첫 여성 축구 팀 멤버이다.
➡ Jane is _____ _____ _____ soccer team member in her school.
(4) 우리 할머니는 항상 나에게 흥미로운 우화를 들려주셨다.
➡ My grandmother always _____ me some interesting _____.

[05~07] 다음 그림에서 빨간 동그라미로 표시된 것을 찾은 다음, 대화를 읽고 물음에 답하시오.

A: May I help you?
B: Yes. I'm looking for my (A)[hat / scarf / coin purse].
A: What does it look like?
B: It's red and has a (smile) face on it.
A: <u>그것에 대해 더 말해 주실 수 있나요?</u>
B: It has (B)[a lock / a key chain / a rock] on it.

05 위 대화의 괄호 (A)와 (B)에서 알맞은 것을 골라 쓰시오.

(A) _____   (B) _____

06 위 대화의 괄호 안의 smile을 알맞게 고치시오.

➡ _____

07 위 대화의 밑줄 친 우리말과 의미가 같도록 영작하시오. (7단어)

➡ _____

08 그림과 일치하지 <u>않는</u> 대화의 내용을 모두 고르고 알맞게 고치시오.

A: What does Steve look like?
B: He has long brown hair.
A: Can you tell me more?
B: He's wearing glasses and holding a racket.
A: I found her!

(1) _____ ➡ _____
(2) _____ ➡ _____
(3) _____ ➡ _____

[09~11] 다음 대화를 읽고, 물음에 답하시오.

M: May I ___ⓐ___ you?
G: Yes. I'm looking for my dog. His name ___ⓑ___ Prince.
M: What does he ___ⓒ___ like?
G: He's very small and ___ⓓ___ short white hair.
M: Can you tell me more?
G: Well, he ___ⓔ___ a really long tail.
M: I see. And one more thing. Where did you lose him?
G: <u>정문 근처에서 잃어버렸어요.</u>
M: OK. _____(A)_____ Can you please wait here?
G: Sure. Thanks a lot.

09 ⓐ~ⓔ의 빈칸을 주어진 동사를 이용해 채우시오. (형태 변화 가능)

| be look have help |

ⓐ _____ ⓑ _____ ⓒ _____ ⓓ _____ ⓔ _____

10 위 대화의 밑줄 친 우리말을 영작하시오.

➡ _____

11 위 대화의 빈칸 (A)에 알맞은 말을 고르시오.

① He's wearing a T-shirt.
② Tell me more about it.
③ I think I lost it.
④ I'll go and make an announcement.
⑤ It's a long cotton scarf.

12 다음 대화는 그림에서 빨간 동그라미 물건을 찾는 내용이다. 빈칸을 알맞게 채우시오.

G: Hi. I think I _____ my _____.
M: What does it look like?
G: It's a small _____ umbrella.
M: Can you tell me more?
G: It has _____ _____ _____ on it.

13 다음 괄호 안에 주어진 어휘를 이용하여 우리말을 영작하시오.

(1) 나는 11살인 개를 키운다. (have, a dog, old)
➡ _____

(2) 나는 경주에서 우승한 차가 마음에 든다.
(the car, like, win the race)
➡ _____

(3) 머리가 금발인 남자아이는 내 동생이다.
(boy, brother, has blond hair)
➡ _____

(4) 눈이 온다면 우리는 공원에 가지 않겠다.
(snows, won't, the park)
➡ _____

14 다음 두 문장을 한 문장으로 바르게 바꾼 것은?

> • Megan is talking with a girl.
> • The girl is wearing cute earrings.

① Megan is talking with a girl whom is wearing cute earrings.
② Megan is talking with a girl which is wearing cute earrings.
③ Megan is talking with a girl is wearing cute earrings.
④ Megan is talking with a girl who she is wearing cute earrings.
⑤ Megan is talking with a girl who is wearing cute earrings.

15 다음 빈칸에 공통으로 들어갈 단어는?

> • Is it OK _____ I smoke here?
> • I will watch TV _____ I finish my homework.

① if   ② unless   ③ how
④ that   ⑤ which

16 두 문장을 관계대명사를 사용하여 한 문장으로 썼을 때 빈칸에 다른 한 문장을 쓰시오.

(1) My mother bought me a new computer.

_____

➡ My mother bought me a new computer which worked really well.

(2) The man is my uncle.

_____

➡ The man who drove me to school is my uncle.

17 다음 문장의 밑줄 친 부분과 쓰임이 같은 것은?

> If I go to the beach, I'll swim in the sea.

① I'm not sure if I can do it.
② I'll tell her if she comes back.
③ I don't know if there is anything else I can do.
④ How can I tell if someone is my true friend or not?
⑤ I wonder if my child expresses himself well in English.

[18~20] 다음 글을 읽고, 물음에 답하시오.

Macaque Monkeys
If you go to a Buddhist temple in Lop Buri, Thailand, watch out for the Macaque monkeys. They may come to you and pull out your hair. They use human hair to floss their teeth. ⓐIf you are lucky, you may see female monkeys that are teaching flossing to their babies. While the babies are watching, the female monkeys floss their teeth very slowly. This way, the baby monkeys learn ⓑto floss.

18 위 글을 읽고 대답할 수 없는 질문은?

① Why do you have to watch out for the Macaque monkeys in the Buddhist temple in Lop Buri, Thailand?
② What do the Macaque monkeys use to floss their teeth?
③ Can you always see female monkeys teaching flossing to their babies?
④ What do the male monkeys teach to their babies?
⑤ How do the female monkeys teach flossing to their babies?

19 위 글의 밑줄 친 ⓐ에서 생략할 수 있는 것을 쓰시오.

➡ _____

20 위 글의 밑줄 친 ⓑto floss와 to부정사의 용법이 같은 것을 고르시오.

① Please tell me the way to go there.
② It is easy to solve the problem.
③ He must be foolish to believe her.
④ Give me a chair to sit on.
⑤ He practiced hard to win the game.

[21~22] 다음 글을 읽고, 물음에 답하시오.

Octopuses

People don't usually think that octopuses are smart. However, octopuses are very smart, and they can also use tools. They use coconut shells for protection. When they can't find a good hiding place, they hide under coconut shells. Some octopuses even ⓐstore coconut shells for later use. They pile the coconut shells and carry them to use later. How smart!

21 위 글의 내용과 일치하도록 다음 빈칸에 공통으로 들어갈 알맞은 단어를 쓰시오.

When octopuses can't find a good place to _____, they _____ under coconut shells for protection.

➡ _____

22 위 글의 밑줄 친 ⓐstore와 같은 의미로 쓰인 것을 고르시오.

① We can buy candies at a store.
② She has a vast store of knowledge.
③ He doesn't like store clothes.
④ We have a grain store.
⑤ Animals store food for the winter.

[23~24] 다음 글을 읽고, 물음에 답하시오.

Crows

In Aesop's fable *The Thirsty Crow*, a crow drops stones into a jar to raise the level of water. You may think this is just a story, but it is not. Scientists who were studying crows did an experiment. They put a jar with water in front of a crow. A worm was floating on top of the water. _____ⓐ_____, the water level was low, so the crow could not eat the worm. The crow solved ⓑthe problem just as in the fable. It dropped stones into the jar. If you think this bird is special, you are wrong. Scientists did the same experiment with other crows, and they all did the same, too.

23 위 글의 빈칸 ⓐ에 들어갈 알맞은 말을 고르시오.

① For instance   ② Moreover
③ In other words   ④ As a result
⑤ However

24 위 글의 밑줄 친 ⓑ가 가리키는 내용을 우리말로 쓰시오.

➡ _____
_____

Lesson 5

Living Healthily and Safely

 의사소통 기능

- 문제점이나 증상을 묻고 답하기
  A: What's wrong?
  B: I have a headache.

- 당부하기
  Make sure you take some medicine.

 언어 형식

- 목적격 관계대명사
  Another problem **(which/that)** you can have is neck pain.

- call A B
  We **call** such people smombies.

교과서

Words & Expressions

Key Words

- **accident** [ǽksidənt] 명 사고
- **addiction** [ədíkʃən] 명 중독
- **advice** [ædváis] 명 충고
- **another** [ənʌðər] 형 또 다른
- **around** [əráund] 부 주위에
- **author** [ɔ́:θər] 명 작가, 저자
- **back** [bæk] 명 등
- **blink** [bliŋk] 동 눈을 깜박이다
- **cause** [kɔːz] 동 야기하다
- **celebrity** [səlébrəti] 명 유명인사, 유명인
- **delicious** [dilíʃəs] 형 맛있는
- **dentist** [déntist] 명 치과의사
- **difficult** [dífikʌlt] 형 어려운
- **dry** [drai] 형 건조한, 마른
- **during** [djúəriŋ] 전 ~ 동안
- **example** [igzǽmpl] 명 예, 사례
- **exercise** [éksərsàiz] 명 운동
- **fever** [fí:vər] 명 열, 열병
- **headache** [hédeik] 명 두통
- **health** [helθ] 명 건강
- **hole** [houl] 명 구덩이, 구멍
- **hurt** [həːrt] 동 다치다
- **increase** [inkrí:s] 동 증가하다
- **intelligent** [intélədʒənt] 형 똑똑한, 지적인
- **meal** [mi:l] 명 식사
- **medicine** [médisn] 명 약
- **nervous** [nə́rvəs] 형 초조한, 불안한
- **pain** [pein] 명 아픔, 고통
- **prevent** [privént] 동 막다, 예방하다
- **promise** [prámis] 명 약속
- **regularly** [régjulərli] 부 규칙적으로
- **safety** [séifti] 명 안전
- **sign** [sain] 명 표지판
- **simple** [símpl] 형 단순한
- **skin** [skin] 명 피부
- **smart** [smɑːrt] 형 현명한, 말쑥한
- **sore** [sɔːr] 형 아픈, 쓰린
- **subject** [sʌ́bdʒikt] 명 과목
- **such** [sətʃ] 형 그러한
- **terrible** [térəbl] 형 끔찍한, 무서운
- **text** [tekst] 동 문자를 보내다
- **throat** [θrout] 명 목구멍
- **thumb** [θʌm] 명 엄지손가락
- **tip** [tip] 명 조언
- **toothache** [tú:θeik] 명 치통
- **unwise** [ənwáiz] 형 현명하지 않은
- **various** [véəriəs] 형 다양한
- **while** [hwail] 접 ~하는 동안
- **without** [wiðáut] 전 ~ 없이
- **zombie** [zámbi] 명 좀비, 반쯤 죽은 것 같은 사람

Key Expressions

- **a few** 몇몇의
- **a heating pad** 찜질 패드
- **all over the world** 전 세계적으로
- **be good at** ~ ~을 잘하다
- **eye level** 눈높이
- **fall asleep** 잠들다
- **for example** 예를 들어
- **from now on** 지금부터
- **get hurt** 다치다
- **get into** ~ (~한 상태에) 처하다
- **have a cold** 감기에 걸리다
- **have a fever** 열이 나다
- **have a runny nose** 콧물이 흐르다
- **have a sore throat** 목이 아프다
- **Here are**+복수 명사 여기에 ~가 있다
- **instead of** ~ ~ 대신에
- **look well** 건강해 보이다
- **take a rest** 휴식을 취하다, 쉬다
- **take medicine** 약을 먹다
- **talk to** ~ ~에게 말하다
- **text message** 문자 메시지
- **these days** 요즘
- **traffic light** 교통 신호등
- **try to**+동사원형 ~하려고 애쓰다[노력하다]
- **turn off** ~을 끄다
- **Why don't you**+동사원형 ~? ~하는 게 어때?

Word Power

※ 서로 반대되는 뜻을 가진 단어

- □ **wise** (현명한) ↔ **unwise** (현명하지 않은)
- □ **nervous** (초조한) ↔ **calm** (차분한)
- □ **dry** (건조한) ↔ **wet** (젖은)
- □ **without** (~ 없이) ↔ **with** (~을 가지고)
- □ **increase** (증가하다) ↔ **decrease** (감소하다)
- □ **careful** (조심하는) ↔ **careless** (부주의한)

- □ **well** (건강한) ↔ **ill** (아픈)
- □ **cheap** (싼) ↔ **expensive** (비싼)
- □ **interesting** (흥미로운) ↔ **uninteresting** (재미없는)
- □ **difficult** (어려운) ↔ **easy** (쉬운)
- □ **turn off** (끄다) ↔ **turn on** (켜다)
- □ **intelligent** (똑똑한) ↔ **stupid** (어리석은)

※ 서로 비슷한 뜻을 가진 단어

- □ **sore** : **painful** (아픈)
- □ **well** : **healthy** (건강한)
- □ **advice** : **tip** (조언, 충고)
- □ **prevent** : **inhibit** (막다)

- □ **terrible** : **awful** (끔찍한, 지독한)
- □ **nervous** : **anxious** (초조한, 불안한)
- □ **various** : **varied** (다양한)
- □ **pain** : **suffering** (고통)

English Dictionary

- □ **addiction** 중독
  → the problem when someone cannot stop doing something, or does something too much
  어떤 일을 하는 것을 멈출 수 없거나 너무 많이 할 때의 문제

- □ **blink** 눈을 깜박이다
  → to open and close your eyes very quickly
  매우 빨리 눈을 뜨고 감다

- □ **cause** 야기하다
  → to make something happen
  어떤 일이 발생하도록 하다

- □ **medicine** 약, 약물
  → a pill or a liquid that you take when you are sick to help you get better
  아플 때 나아지도록 하기 위해 복용하는 알약 또는 액체

- □ **pad** 패드
  → a thick piece of soft material
  부드러운 소재의 두꺼운 조각

- □ **pain** 고통
  → the feeling you have when a part of your body hurts
  신체의 일부가 아플 때 가지는 느낌

- □ **prevent** 막다, 예방하다
  → to stop something from happening, or stop someone from doing
  어떤 일이 일어나거나 누군가가 하는 것을 막다

- □ **regularly** 규칙적으로
  → at the same time every day, every week, etc.
  매일, 매주 등의 같은 시간에

- □ **rest** 휴식
  → a time when you relax or sleep
  쉬거나 잠을 자는 시간

- □ **safety** 안전
  → the state of being safe and protected from danger or harm
  위험이나 해로부터 안전하고 보호받는 상태

- □ **text** 문자를 보내다
  → to send someone a written message using a cell phone
  휴대전화를 이용하여 누군가에게 문자 메시지를 보내다

- □ **throat** 목구멍
  → the passage at the back of your mouth, where you swallow
  음식을 삼키는 입의 뒤쪽에 있는 통로

- □ **thumb** 엄지손가락
  → the short thick finger on your hand that helps you hold things
  물건을 집는 데 도움이 되는 손에 있는 짧고 두꺼운 손가락

서답형

01 다음 문장의 빈칸에 주어진 영어 설명에 해당하는 말을 쓰시오.

> used when one thing replaces another, or when you do a different thing

> • Turn off your smartphone during meals or meetings. You can talk to people _____ _____ texting them.

➡ _____

02 다음 빈칸에 공통으로 들어갈 말은? (대 · 소문자 무시)

> • I think you have a cold. _____ this medicine and make sure you _____ a good rest.

① take   ② get   ③ go
④ make   ⑤ look

서답형

03 다음 우리말에 맞게 빈칸에 알맞은 단어를 쓰시오.

> 너는 스마트폰을 볼 때 자주 눈을 깜박이지 않는다.

➡ When you look at your smartphone, you do not _____ often.

04 다음 글의 흐름상 빈칸에 들어갈 가장 적절한 단어는?

> Do you feel sad when you check your smartphone and there is no text message? If your answers are "yes," you may have smartphone _____.

① pain   ② author
③ addiction   ④ promise
⑤ celebrity

[05~06] 다음 영영풀이에 해당하는 단어를 고르시오.

05

> the feeling you have when a part of your body hurts

① sour   ② hurt
③ pain   ④ addiction
⑤ stress

중요

06

> at the same time every day, every week, etc.

① sometimes   ② always
③ carefully   ④ simply
⑤ regularly

서답형

07 다음 짝지어진 단어의 관계가 같도록 빈칸에 알맞은 말을 쓰시오.

> well : healthy = anxious : _____

08 다음 빈칸에 들어갈 말이 알맞게 짝지어진 것은?

> • Unwise or too much use of smartphones can _____ various problems.
> • When you look down at your smartphone, the stress on your neck _____s.

① prevent – decrease
② prevent – increase
③ hurt – prevent
④ cause – increase
⑤ cause – decrease

01 다음 빈칸에 들어갈 말을 〈보기〉에서 찾아 쓰시오. (필요하면 변형하여 쓰시오.)

┌── 보기 ──┐
nervous   well   have   smombie
└──────────┘

(1) I think he _____ a headache.

(2) You don't look _____. What's wrong?

(3) If you are a _____, you can have various safety problems.

(4) I get _____ when my smartphone is not around.

⭐중요
02 다음 영영풀이에 알맞은 단어를 〈보기〉에서 찾아 첫 번째 칸에 쓰고, 두 번째 칸에는 우리말 뜻을 쓰시오.

┌──── 보기 ────┐
pad   medicine   addiction   text
blink   fever   nervous   prevent
└──────────────┘

(1) _____: to stop something from happening, or stop someone from doing: _____

(2) _____: a pill or a liquid that you take when you are sick to help you get better: _____

(3) _____: the problem when someone cannot stop doing something, or does something too much: _____

03 다음 빈칸에 들어갈 알맞은 단어를 주어진 철자로 시작하여 쓰시오.

┌─────────────────────┐
• Many people like sending t_____ messages more than calling.

• Too much use of smartphones can c_____ dry eyes.
└─────────────────────┘

⭐중요
04 다음 우리말과 같은 표현이 되도록 문장의 빈칸을 채우시오.

(1) 스마트폰 없이 사는 것은 요즘 많은 사람들에게 어렵다.
  ➡ Living _____ smartphones is difficult for many of us these days.

(2) 우리는 그러한 사람들을 스몸비, 즉 스마트폰 좀비라고 부른다.
  ➡ We call _____ people smombies, smartphone zombies.

(3) 지금부터, 나는 매일 30분 동안 걸으려고 노력할 것이다.
  ➡ _____ _____ _____, I will try to walk for 30 minutes every day.

(4) 잠자리에서 스마트폰을 사용하면, 쉽게 잠들지 못할 거야.
  ➡ If you use your smartphone in bed, you may not _____ _____ easily.

05 다음 빈칸에 들어갈 말을 〈보기〉에서 골라 알맞은 형태로 고쳐 쓰시오.

┌──── 보기 ────┐
regular   nerve   addict   vary   text
└──────────────┘

(1) People may have smartphone _____ if they feel anxious when their smartphones are not around.

(2) Make sure you exercise _____.

(3) Unwise or too much use of smartphones can cause _____ problems.

(4) He did not notice the car because he was _____.

Conticonversation

1 문제점이나 증상을 묻고 답하기

> **A** What's wrong? 무슨 일이니?
> **B** I have a headache. 머리가 아파요.

- 상대방이 기분이 좋지 않거나 어딘가 아파 보일 때 What's wrong (with you)?라고 묻는다. What's the matter (with you)?라고 물을 수도 있다.

- **문제점이나 증상을 묻는 다양한 표현들**
"무슨 일 있니?"라는 의미로 What's wrong with you? / What's the matter? / Is there anything wrong? / What happened? / What's the problem? 등을 사용한다.

- **증상 답하기**
'나는 ~가 아프다.'는 'I have a/an+명사'로 나타내는데, 명사 자리에 아픈 증상이나 병명을 써서 어디가 아픈지를 표현한다. 아픈 증상을 나타내는 말은 주로 신체 부위 뒤에 '아픔, 통증'을 뜻하는 'ache'를 붙여 쓴다. 예를 들면 head(머리)에 ache를 붙이면 '두통'이라는 뜻의 'headache'가 된다. 이와 같은 형태로 요통 'backache', 귀앓이 'earache', 치통 'toothache' 등의 표현을 쓴다.

- A: You don't look well. 너 몸이 안 좋아 보여.
  What's wrong? 무슨 일 있니?
  B: I have a headache. 머리가 아파.

- A: What's the matter? 무슨 일 있니?
  B: My dog ate my homework. 내 개가 내 숙제를 먹어 버렸어.

- A: What's wrong, Peter? 무슨 일이니, Peter?
  B: I don't know, Ms. Kim, but my back hurts a lot. 모르겠어요, 김 선생님, 하지만 등이 매우 아파요.

핵심 Check

1. 다음 대화의 빈칸에 알맞은 말을 쓰시오.

   A: _____ _____ with your leg, Sam?

   B: I fell and hurt my foot while I was playing soccer.

2. 다음 주어진 문장과 같은 의미가 되도록 빈칸에 알맞은 말을 쓰시오.

   What's wrong?

   = Is there _____ _____?

② 당부하기

Make sure you take some medicine. 약을 꼭 먹도록 하렴.

- 상대방에게 당부하는 표현으로 '반드시 ~하도록 해라, ~을 확실히 해라'라는 의미의 'make sure ~'를 사용한다. make sure 다음에 접속사 that을 생략할 수 있고 당부하고자 하는 내용을 주어와 동사를 갖춘 문장으로 쓴다. 즉, sure 다음에는 '(that+)주어+동사'를 쓴다. 유사한 의미를 가진 표현으로 'You had better+동사원형 ~', 'Don't forget to+동사원형 ~', 'Remember to+동사원형 ~' 등이 있다.

당부하기 표현

- A: Well, make sure you take a warm bath. 음. 꼭 따뜻하게 목욕을 하도록 하렴.
  B: OK. Thanks a lot. 알았어요. 고마워요.
- A: I think I caught a cold. 나 감기에 걸린 것 같아.
  B: That's too bad. Make sure you take some medicine and relax. 안됐구나. 꼭 약을 먹고 쉬렴.
- Remember to call me when you leave. 떠날 때 나에게 전화하는 것을 기억해라.
- Don't forget to call me when you arrive. 도착하면 나에게 전화하는 것을 잊지 마.
- You had better call me when you arrive. 너는 도착하면 나에게 전화하는 것이 좋겠다.

- 상대방의 당부를 받아들일 때 make sure 다음에 긍정문이 오면 'OK. I will.'로 답하고, 부정문이 오면 'OK. I won't.'로 답한다.

- A: Make sure you give me a call when you get home. 집에 도착하면 내게 꼭 전화해.
  B: Okay, I will. 응. 그렇게 할게.
- A: Make sure you won't be late for the class again. 다시는 수업에 지각하지 마.
  B: Okay, I won't. 네. 안 할게요.

핵심 Check

3. 다음 대화의 빈칸에 들어갈 알맞은 것은?

　　A: Mom, can I play soccer with my friends after school?
　　B: Sure, but _____.

　　① you don't have to play soccer
　　② you can't
　　③ you had better not play soccer
　　④ don't forget to stay home after school
　　⑤ make sure you come home before dinner

A. Listen and Talk A-1

W: You ❶look sick. ❷What's wrong, Inho?

B: ❸I have a sore throat. I have a fever, too.

W: I think you have a cold. ❹Take this medicine and ❺make sure you take a good rest.

B: OK. Thank you.

W: 너 아파 보인다. 무슨 일이니, 인호야?
B: 목이 아파요. 열도 나요.
W: 감기에 걸린 것 같구나. 이 약을 먹고 좀 쉬도록 하렴.
B: 알겠어요. 감사합니다.

❶ 'look+형용사'는 '~처럼 보인다'는 의미이다.
❷ 문제점이나 증상을 묻는 표현으로 Is there anything wrong?, What happened?, What's the problem? 등으로 물을 수 있다.
❸ '나는 ~가 아프다.'는 표현으로 'I have a/an+명사'로 나타내는데, 명사 자리에 아픈 증상이나 병명을 써서 어디가 아픈지 표현한다.
❹ '약을 복용하다'라는 의미로 동사 take를 사용한다.
❺ 'make sure ~'는 상대방에게 당부하는 표현으로 '반드시 ~하도록 해라, ~을 확실히 해라'라는 의미다. '쉬다, 휴식을 취하다'는 표현에 동사 take를 사용한다.

Check(√) True or False

(1) Inho has a cold.　　　　　　　　　　　　　　　　　T ☐ F ☐

(2) The woman may be a school nurse.　　　　　　　　T ☐ F ☐

B. Listen and Talk C

W: ❶What's wrong, Andy?

B: Hello, Ms. Kim. My right thumb hurts.

W: Hmm. Do you use your smartphone a lot?

B: Yes, ❷I text a lot. Why?

W: I think you have texting thumb.

B: Texting thumb? What's texting thumb?

W: It's pain in your thumb. You can get it from ❸texting too much.

B: Oh, I didn't know that.

W: ❹Why don't you do some finger stretching exercises?

B: OK, I will.

W: And ❺make sure you don't text too much.

W: 무슨 일이니, Andy?
B: 안녕하세요, 김 선생님. 제 오른손 엄지손가락이 아파요.
W: 음. 너 스마트폰을 많이 사용하니?
B: 네, 저 문자를 많이 해요. 왜요?
W: 내 생각에 너는 texting thumb인 것 같아.
B: texting thumb이요? texting thumb이 뭐예요?
W: 엄지손가락에 통증이 있는 거야. 문자를 너무 많이 하면 생길 수 있어.
B: 오, 그건 몰랐네요.
W: 손가락 스트레칭 운동을 좀 하는 게 어떠니?
B: 네, 그럴게요.
W: 그리고 문자를 너무 많이 하지 않도록 하렴.

❶ 문제점이나 증상을 물어볼 때 사용하는 표현으로 'What's the matter?'로 바꾸어 쓸 수 있다.
❷ text는 동사로 '문자를 보내다'는 의미다.
❸ 전치사 from 뒤의 texting은 전치사의 목적어로 사용된 동명사이다.
❹ 'Why don't you+동사원형 ~?'은 '~하는 게 어때?'라는 뜻으로 제안이나 권유를 할 때 사용하는 표현이다.
❺ 상대방에게 당부하는 표현으로 '반드시 ~하도록 해라, ~을 확실히 해라'라는 의미이다.

Check(√) True or False

(3) Andy's right thumb hurts.　　　　　　　　　　　　T ☐ F ☐

(4) Andy won't do any finger stretching exercises.　　T ☐ F ☐

Listen and Talk A-2

W: ❶What's wrong, Peter?

B: I don't know, Ms. Kim, but ❷my back hurts a lot.

W: ❸Put a heating pad on it.

B: OK, I will.

W: And ❹make sure you do some stretching exercises.

❶ Is there anything wrong?, What happened?, What's the problem? 등과 같은 표현으로 문제점이나 증상을 물어볼 때 사용한다.

❷ 여기서 back은 명사로 '등'을 의미한다. a lot은 동사 hurts를 수식하는 부사구로 '많이'의 의미다.

❸ put A on B 형태로 'A를 B에 놓다'는 의미다.

❹ 상대방에게 당부하는 표현으로 '반드시 ~하도록 해라, ~을 확실히 해라'라는 의미다.

Listen and Talk A-3

W: ❶What's the matter, Chris?

B: I have a terrible toothache.

W: ❷Here is some medicine. Take this.

B: Thank you.

W: And make sure you ❸go to the dentist.

B: OK, I will.

❶ 문제점이나 증상을 물어볼 때 사용하는 표현이다.

❷ 'Here is+단수 명사'로 '여기에 ~가 있다'는 의미다

❸ go to the dentist는 '치과에 가다'는 의미다.

Listen and Talk A-4

W: What's wrong with your leg, Sam?

B: I fell and hurt my foot ❶while I was playing soccer.

W: Can you walk?

B: Yes, but it hurts a lot.

W: ❷Why don't you put some ice on it? And make sure you don't play soccer until next week.

❶ while은 접속사로 '~하는 동안'의 의미다.

❷ 'Why don't you+동사원형 ~?'은 '~하는 게 어때?'라는 의미이다.

Listen and Talk B-1

A: You don't ❶look well. What's wrong?

B: I have a headache.

A: ❷That's too bad. Make sure you ❸take some medicine.

B: OK, I will.

❶ 'look+형용사'로 여기서 well은 형용사로 '건강한'의 의미다.

❷ 상대방의 안 좋은 일이나 소식에 대해 '안 됐다'라는 의미다.

❸ take는 '복용하다, 먹다'의 의미다.

Listen and Talk B-2

A: You don't look well. What's wrong?

B: I have a cold.

A: That's too bad. Make sure you ❶go see a doctor.

B: OK, I will.

❶ 'go see a doctor'는 '병원에 가다'는 의미로 해석한다.

Review 1

G: ❶What's wrong, Mike?

B: ❷I have a terrible headache.

G: I think you ❸should take some medicine.

B: OK, I will.

❶ Is there anything wrong?, What happened?, What's the problem? 등과 같은 표현으로 문제점이나 증상을 물어볼 때 사용한다.

❷ '나는 ~가 아프다.'는 표현으로 'I have a/an+명사'로 나타내는데, 명사 자리에 아픈 증상이나 병명을 써서 어디가 아픈지 표현한다.

❸ 상대방에게 조언을 할 때 조동사 should를 사용한다.

Review 2

M: What's the matter, Mina?

G: I ❶have a sore throat. I also ❷have a runny nose.

M: I think you have a cold. Make sure you get some rest.

G: OK, I will.

❶ 'have a sore throat'는 '목이 아프다'는 의미다.

❷ 'have a runny nose'는 '콧물이 난다'는 의미다.

● 다음 우리말과 일치하도록 빈칸에 알맞은 말을 쓰시오.

Listen and Talk A-1

W: You look sick. _____ _____, Inho?

B: I _____ _____ _____ _____ . I _____ _____ _____, too.

W: I think you _____ _____ _____. _____ this medicine and _____ _____ you _____ a good rest.

B: OK. Thank you.

해석

W: 너 아파 보인다. 무슨 일이니, 인호야?
B: 목이 아파요. 열도 나요.
W: 감기에 걸린 것 같구나. 이 약을 먹고 좀 쉬도록 하렴.
B: 알겠어요. 감사합니다.

Listen and Talk A-2

W: What's _____, Peter?

B: I don't know, Ms. Kim, but my back _____ a lot.

W: _____ a heating pad _____ it.

B: OK, I will.

W: And _____ _____ you do some stretching exercises.

W: 무슨 일이니, Peter?
B: 모르겠어요, 김 선생님, 등이 아파요.
W: 그곳에 찜질 패드를 올려놓으렴.
B: 네, 그럴게요.
W: 그리고 스트레칭 운동을 하렴.

Listen and Talk A-3

W: What's the _____, Chris?

B: I _____ _____ terrible toothache.

W: _____ _____ some medicine. _____ this.

B: Thank you.

W: And _____ _____ you go to the dentist.

B: OK, I will.

W: 무슨 일이니, Chris?
B: 저는 심한 치통이 있어요.
W: 여기 약이 있단다. 이것을 먹으렴.
B: 감사합니다.
W: 그리고 치과에 가도록 하렴.
B: 네, 알겠어요.

Listen and Talk A-4

W: What's _____ _____ your leg, Sam?

B: I fell and hurt my foot _____ I was playing soccer.

W: Can you walk?

B: Yes, but it _____ a lot.

W: _____ _____ _____ put some ice on it? And _____ _____ you don't play soccer _____ next week.

W: 다리에 무슨 문제가 있니, Sam?
B: 축구를 하다가 넘어져서 발을 다쳤어요.
W: 걸을 수는 있겠니?
B: 네, 하지만 많이 아파요.
W: 얼음을 그 위에 올려놓는 게 어떠니? 그리고 다음 주까지는 축구를 하지 않도록 하렴.

Listen and Talk B

1. **A:** You don't _____ _____. What's wrong?
   B: I _____ a headache.
   A: _____ _____ _____. Make sure you _____ some medicine.
   B: OK, I _____.

2. **A:** You _____ _____ _____. What's _____?
   B: I have a _____.
   A: That's too bad. _____ _____ you go see a doctor.
   B: OK, I will.

Listen and Talk C

W: What's _____, Andy?
B: Hello, Ms. Kim. My right _____ hurts.
W: Hmm. Do you use your smartphone _____ _____?
B: Yes, I _____ a lot. Why?
W: I think you _____ texting thumb.
B: Texting thumb? What's texting thumb?
W: It's _____ in your thumb. You can _____ it from _____ too much.
B: Oh, I didn't know that.
W: _____ _____ _____ do some finger stretching exercises?
B: OK, I will.
W: And _____ _____ you don't text too much.

Review 1

G: What's wrong, Mike?
B: I _____ _____ _____ headache.
G: I think you _____ _____ some medicine.
B: OK, I will.

Review 2

M: What's _____ _____, Mina?
G: I _____ _____ _____ _____ _____. I also have a _____ nose.
M: I think you have a cold. _____ _____ you get some rest.
G: OK, I will.

1. A: 너 몸이 안 좋아 보여. 무슨 일 있니?
   B: 머리가 아파.
   A: 안됐다. 약을 먹으렴.
   B: 응, 그렇게.

2. A: 너 몸이 안 좋아 보여. 무슨 일 있니?
   B: 감기에 걸렸어.
   A: 안됐다. 병원에 가도록 하렴.
   B: 응, 그렇게.

W: 무슨 일이니, Andy?
B: 안녕하세요, 김 선생님. 제 오른손 엄지손가락이 아파요.
W: 음. 너 스마트폰을 많이 사용하니?
B: 네, 저 문자를 많이 해요. 왜요?
W: 내 생각에 너는 texting thumb인 것 같아.
B: texting thumb이요? texting thumb이 뭐예요?
W: 엄지손가락에 통증이 있는 거야. 문자를 너무 많이 하면 생길 수 있어.
B: 오, 그건 몰랐네요.
W: 손가락 스트레칭 운동을 좀 하는 게 어떠니?
B: 네, 그럴게요.
W: 그리고 문자를 너무 많이 하지 않도록 하렴.

G: 무슨 일 있니, Mike?
B: 머리가 너무 아파.
G: 너는 약을 먹는 것이 좋겠다.
B: 알겠어, 그렇게.

M: 무슨 일 있니, 미나야?
G: 목이 아파요. 그리고 콧물도 나요.
M: 내 생각에 네가 감기에 걸린 것 같구나. 좀 쉬도록 하렴.
G: 네, 그럴게요.

01 다음 우리말에 맞도록 빈칸에 들어갈 알맞은 말을 쓰시오.

> 좀 쉬도록 하렴.

➡ _____ _____ you get some rest.

02 다음 대화의 빈칸에 들어갈 말로 어색한 것은?

> W: _____, Sam?
> B: I fell and hurt my foot while I was playing soccer.

① What's wrong with you
② What's the matter with you
③ What happened
④ What do you mean
⑤ What's wrong with your leg

03 다음 대화의 빈칸에 들어갈 말로 어색한 것은?

> W: You look sick. What's wrong, Inho?
> B: I have a sore throat. I have a fever, too.
> W: I think you have a cold. _____
> B: OK. Thank you.

① Don't forget to go see a doctor.
② Make sure you take a good rest.
③ Remember to go to the dentist.
④ You should drink a lot of water.
⑤ Take this medicine.

04 다음 대화의 밑줄 친 우리말에 맞게 문장의 빈칸을 채우시오.

> A: You don't look well. What's wrong?
> B: 머리가 아파요.

➡ I _____ _____ headache.

[01~02] 다음 대화를 읽고 물음에 답하시오.

> W: _____(A)_____, Chris?
> B: I have a terrible toothache.
> W: Here is some medicine. __(B)__ this.
> B: Thank you.
> W: And make sure you go to the dentist.
> B: OK, I will.

01 위 대화의 빈칸 (A)에 들어갈 말로 <u>어색한</u> 것은?

① What's wrong
② What's the problem
③ What's the matter
④ How's it going
⑤ Is there anything wrong

02 위 대화의 빈칸 (B)에 들어갈 말로 알맞은 것은?

① Want　　　　② Bring
③ Leave　　　　④ Make
⑤ Take

03 다음 대화의 순서를 바르게 배열한 것은?

> (A) I have a sore throat. I also have a runny nose.
> (B) I think you have a cold. Make sure you get some rest.
> (C) OK, I will.
> (D) What's the matter, Mina?

① (A) – (B) – (C) – (D)
② (B) – (A) – (C) – (D)
③ (B) – (C) – (A) – (D)
④ (D) – (A) – (B) – (C)
⑤ (D) – (B) – (A) – (C)

[04~06] 다음 대화를 읽고 물음에 답하시오.

> G: (A)What's wrong, Mike?
> B: I ___ⓐ___ a terrible headache.
> G: (B)You should take some medicine.
> B: OK, I will.

04 위 대화의 빈칸 ⓐ에 들어갈 말로 알맞은 것은?

① take　　　　② make
③ catch　　　　④ explain
⑤ have

서답형

05 위 대화의 밑줄 친 (A)와 같은 뜻이 되도록 다음 문장의 빈칸을 채우시오.

> = What's _____ _____ with you
> = What _____

06 위 대화의 밑줄 친 (B)와 바꾸어 쓸 수 <u>없는</u> 것은?

① You had better take some medicine.
② Make sure you take some medicine.
③ Don't forget to take some medicine.
④ Remember to take some medicine.
⑤ Don't remember to take some medicine.

07 다음 대화의 밑줄 친 부분의 의도로 알맞은 것은?

> A: You don't look well. What's wrong?
> B: I have a headache.
> A: That's too bad. <u>Make sure you take some medicine.</u>
> B: OK, I will.

① 안부 묻기　　　　② 의무 표현하기
③ 요청하기　　　　④ 당부하기
⑤ 의견 묻기

[08~10] 다음 대화를 읽고 물음에 답하시오.

W: What's the matter, Chris?
B: I have a terrible (A)toothache.
W: (B)여기 약이 있단다. Take this.
B: Thank you.
W: And _____ (C) _____ .
B: OK, I will.

서답형

08 다음 문장은 밑줄 친 (A)에 대한 영어 설명이다. 빈칸에 알맞은 단어를 쓰시오.

> a _____ in a tooth

➡ _____

서답형

09 위 대화의 밑줄 친 (B)의 우리말에 맞게 다음 문장의 빈칸을 완성하시오.

➡ _____ _____ some medicine.

10 위 대화의 빈칸 (C)에 들어갈 말로 가장 적절한 것은?

① make sure you do some exercises
② don't play soccer
③ make sure you go to the dentist
④ make sure you don't text too much
⑤ you need to eat well

[11~13] 다음 대화를 읽고 물음에 답하시오.

W: (A)무슨 일이니, Andy?
B: Hello, Ms. Kim. My right thumb hurts.
W: Hmm. (①) Do you use your smartphone a lot?
B: Yes, I text a lot. Why?
W: (②) I think you have texting thumb.
B: Texting thumb? (③) What's texting thumb?
W: (④) You can get it from texting too much.
B: Oh, I didn't know that. (⑤)

W: Why don't you do some finger stretching exercises?
B: OK, I will.
W: And make sure you don't text too much.

서답형

11 위 대화의 밑줄 친 (A)의 우리말에 맞게 주어진 단어를 이용하여 영어로 쓰시오.

> what, matter, with

➡ _____

서답형

12 다음 주어진 문장이 들어갈 위치로 알맞은 것은?

> It's pain in your thumb.

①   ②   ③   ④   ⑤

13 위 대화의 내용과 일치하지 않는 것은?

① Andy uses his smartphone a lot.
② Andy texts a lot.
③ Andy feels pain in his right thumb.
④ Ms. Kim advises Andy to do some finger stretching exercises.
⑤ Ms. Kim doesn't text too much.

14 다음 중 짝지어진 대화가 어색한 것은?

① A: What's wrong?
   B: I have a headache.
② A: What's the matter, Chris?
   B: I have a terrible toothache.
③ A: Here is some medicine. Take this.
   B: Thank you.
④ A: You don't look well. Is there anything wrong?
   B: No problem. I have a headache.
⑤ A: I have a sore throat. I have a fever, too.
   B: I think you have a cold.

[01~02] 다음 대화를 읽고 물음에 답하시오.

W: You look sick. What's _____ⓐ_____, Inho?
B: I _____ⓑ_____ a sore throat. I have a fever, too.
W: I think you _____ⓒ_____ a cold. (A)이 약을 먹고 꼭 충분히 쉬도록 하렴.
B: OK. Thank you.

01 위 대화의 흐름상 빈칸 ⓐ~ⓒ에 알맞은 말을 쓰시오.

➡ ⓐ _____ ⓑ _____ ⓒ _____

02 위 대화의 밑줄 친 (A)의 우리말에 맞게 주어진 어구를 이용하여 영어로 쓰시오.

> medicine, and, make, take you, a, good rest

➡ _____

03 다음 대화의 밑줄 친 우리말에 맞게 주어진 단어를 이용하여 빈칸을 채우시오.

> W: (A)다리에 무슨 문제가 있니, Sam?
> B: I fell and hurt my foot (B)축구를 하다가.
> W: Can you walk?
> B: Yes, but it hurts a lot.
> W: Why don't you put some ice on it? And (C)축구를 하지 않도록 하렴 until next week.

➡ (A) _____
    (wrong, with, leg)
  (B) _____
    (while, was, soccer)
  (C) _____
    (make, sure, play)

[04~05] 다음 대화를 읽고 물음에 답하시오.

W: What's wrong, Andy?
B: Hello, Ms. Kim. My right thumb hurts.
W: Hmm. Do you use your smartphone a lot?
B: Yes, I text a lot. Why?
W: I think you have texting thumb.
B: Texting thumb? What's texting thumb?
W: _____(A)_____ You can get it from texting too much.
B: Oh, I didn't know that.
W: Why don't you do some finger stretching exercises?
B: OK, I will.
W: And _____(B)_____.

04 위 대화의 내용으로 보아 Andy의 질문에 대한 답으로 (A)에 들어갈 알맞은 말을 완성하시오.

➡ It's _____ in your _____.

05 위 대화의 빈칸 (B)에 들어갈 Ms. Kim의 충고를 완성하시오.

➡ _____ _____ you _____ _____ too much

06 다음 대화의 충고를 읽고, 빈칸에 들어갈 말을 주어진 단어를 이용하여 완성하시오.

> A: What's wrong, Peter?
> B: _____
> A: I think you need to eat well. Try to eat lots of fresh fruit and vegetables. And make sure you exercise regularly.
> B: OK, I will.

➡ _____ (get, tire, easily)

Grammar

교과서

1 목적격 관계대명사

> • Another problem **(which/that)** you can have is neck pain.
> 네가 가질 수 있는 또 다른 문제는 목 통증이다.

- 관계대명사절에서 관계대명사의 역할이 목적어일 때 이것을 목적격 관계대명사라고 하며, 관계대명사절의 첫머리에 위치해야 한다.

- 목적격 관계대명사는 수식하는 선행사가 사람이면 who나 whom, that을, 사람이 아니면 which나 that을 쓴다. 목적격 관계대명사는 생략될 수 있다.
  - I know the man **(who/whom/that)** you met yesterday. 나는 네가 어제 만난 그 남자를 알아.
  - This is the book **(which/that)** I have chosen. 이것이 내가 고른 책이다.

- 목적격 관계대명사절을 만들 때 특히 주의할 것은 동사 뒤에 목적어가 없다는 것인데, 이것은 앞에 있는 관계대명사가 동사의 목적어 역할을 하기 때문이다.
  - The person is my father. I respect **him(=the person)** the most.
    = The person **(who/whom/that)** I respect the most is my father.
  - John is reading the book. He bought **it(=the book)** last Saturday.
    = John is reading the book **(which/that)** he bought last Saturday.

- 목적격 관계대명사가 전치사의 목적어인 경우 전치사는 관계대명사절의 끝에 오거나 관계대명사 앞에 올 수 있다. 전치사가 관계대명사절의 끝에 올 경우에는 관계대명사를 생략할 수 있다. 전치사가 관계대명사 앞에 올 경우에는 관계대명사 that을 쓸 수 없으며, 관계대명사를 생략하지 않는다.
  - This is the pen **(which/that)** he wrote the novel with. 이것은 그가 그 소설을 쓰는 데 썼던 펜이다.
    = This is the pen with **which** he wrote the novel.
    = This is the pen with that he wrote the novel. (×)

핵심 Check

1. 다음 우리말에 맞게 빈칸에 알맞은 말을 쓰시오.
   (1) 나는 John이 말한 그 사람을 알고 있어요.
      ➡ I know the man _____ John mentioned.
   (2) 그는 엄마가 만들어 주는 피자를 먹는 것을 좋아한다.
      ➡ He likes to eat the pizza _____ his mom makes.

② call A B

> • We **call** such people smombies. 우리는 그런 사람들을 스몸비라고 부른다.
>
> • We **elected** her chairman. 우리는 그녀를 의장으로 선출했다.

■ 'call A B'는 'A를 B라고 부르다'라는 의미로, 문법적으로는 call 다음의 명사[대명사] A를 목적어, 그리고 B에 해당하는 명사를 목적격 보어로 볼 수 있는 5형식 구문이다.

• They will **call** their daughter Sophie. 그들은 그들의 딸을 Sophie라고 부를 것이다.

■ call A B와 유사하게 목적격 보어 자리에 명사가 올 수 있는 동사로는 make, name, elect, consider 등이 있다.

call A B	A를 B라고 부르다
name A B	A를 B라고 이름 짓다
make A B	A를 B로 만들다
elect A B	A를 B로 선출하다
consider A B	A를 B로 여기다[생각하다]

• I **consider** him a friend. 나는 그를 친구로 생각한다.

■ 동사 다음에 두 개의 명사가 목적어, 목적격 보어로 쓰인다는 점에서는 consider, believe 등의 동사와 유사해 보이지만, call은 목적격 보어로 형용사나 to부정사를 취하지 않는다는 점에 유의한다.

• Can we **call** it a success? 우리가 그것을 성공이라고 부를 수 있느냐?

• We **named** her Mina. 우리는 그녀를 Mina라고 이름 지었다.

• She **made** her son a teacher. 그녀는 그녀의 아들을 선생님으로 만들었다.

• I **believe** him honest. 나는 그가 정직하다고 생각한다.

핵심 Check

2. 다음 우리말에 맞게 빈칸에 알맞은 말을 쓰시오.

(1) 우리는 이것을 text neck이라고 부른다.

➡ We _____ this _____ _____.

(2) 그의 발명은 그를 부자로 만들었다.

➡ His invention _____ him a _____ _____.

01 다음 빈칸에 들어갈 말로 알맞지 <u>않은</u> 것을 <u>모두</u> 고르시오.

> The friend _____ I met yesterday is Sue.

① who   ② whose   ③ whom
④ that   ⑤ which

02 다음 문장에서 어법상 <u>어색한</u> 부분을 바르게 고쳐 쓰시오.

(1) He showed me the photos who he had taken in Spain.

＿＿＿＿＿＿＿＿＿ ➡ ＿＿＿＿＿＿＿＿＿

(2) The children which Ms. Collins is teaching are smart.

＿＿＿＿＿＿＿＿＿ ➡ ＿＿＿＿＿＿＿＿＿

(3) We call the lion to be the king of beasts.

＿＿＿＿＿＿＿＿＿ ➡ ＿＿＿＿＿＿＿＿＿

beast: 짐승 the king of beasts: 백수 (百獸)의 왕

03 다음 우리말에 맞게 괄호 안에 주어진 단어를 바르게 배열하시오.

(1) 이것이 어제 내가 산 신발들이다. (I, the shoes, yesterday, are, bought, these, which)

➡ ＿＿＿＿＿＿＿＿＿＿＿＿＿＿＿＿＿＿＿

(2) 우리는 우리 물고기를 Ernie라고 불렀다. (we, Ernie, our, fish, called)

➡ ＿＿＿＿＿＿＿＿＿＿＿＿＿＿＿＿＿＿＿

04 다음 우리말을 영어로 옮길 때, 빈칸에 알맞은 말이 순서대로 짝지어진 것은?

> 우리는 화면의 화살표를 커서라고 부른다.
> ➡ We call ＿＿＿＿＿＿ ＿＿＿＿＿＿.

① the arrow on the screen – a cursor
② a cursor – the arrow on the screen
③ the arrow – a cursor on the screen
④ a cursor on the screen – the arrow
⑤ on the screen a cursor – the arrow

01 다음 〈보기〉의 밑줄 친 부분과 다르게 쓰인 것은?

> ┌─ 보기 ─
> There are various things <u>that</u> you can do to prevent this.

① Tom bought the book <u>that</u> he wanted to read.

② Wayne met the girl <u>who</u> looked very intelligent at the party.

③ Susan is the girl <u>who</u> I gave some flowers yesterday.

④ The skirt <u>which</u> she is wearing is pretty.

⑤ I want to marry a woman <u>that</u> I love.

02 다음 빈칸에 들어갈 수 있는 말이 다른 하나는?

① Mr. Lee was my teacher _____ taught me math.

② A computer is a thing _____ people do many things with.

③ This is the pen _____ was on the table.

④ Are there any students _____ name hasn't been called?

⑤ Christina Rossetti is the poet _____ I like most.

03 다음 빈칸에 알맞지 <u>않은</u> 것은?

> We _____ him our class president.

① elected   ② made
③ appointed   ④ considered
⑤ took

04 다음 괄호 안에서 알맞은 말을 고르시오.

(1) I know the boy (which / that) everyone likes.

(2) Monica wants to see *the Mona Lisa* (who / which) Leonardo da Vinci painted.

(3) There was a program in (that / which) I really wanted to take part.

(4) Sharon wore the earrings (whom / which) I gave to her.

(5) We (call / consider) her to be a genius.

➡ (1) _____ (2) _____ (3) _____
   (4) _____ (5) _____

05 다음 우리말을 주어진 어휘를 이용하여 영어로 쓰시오.

> 나는 할아버지께서 내게 해 주신 이야기들을 아직 기억한다. (the stories, still, my grandfather, tell)

➡ _____

  _____

06 다음 중 어법상 바르지 <u>않은</u> 것은?

① The movie made her a star.

② Which do you consider to be the most important?

③ They elected Obama President of the USA.

④ They named their baby James.

⑤ We call such music as hip hop.

07 다음 중 어법상 옳은 문장은?

① This is the book who my sister bought last night.
② We sometimes have to eat side dishes whom we don't like.
③ This is the house which she lives.
④ This is something that you should bear in mind.
⑤ James is the only friend which he can trust.

08 다음 밑줄 친 that의 용법이 나머지 넷과 다른 것은?

① My opinion is that he really doesn't understand you.
② This is an animal that has a long nose.
③ The movie that Mike and I watched yesterday was interesting.
④ The cookies that she made were very delicious.
⑤ Jerry never touched the food that he didn't like.

09 다음 중 〈보기〉와 문장의 형식이 다르게 쓰인 것은?

┌─ 보기 ├─
They called their dog Lucky.
└──────────

① As it is very cold outside, please keep yourself warm.
② We elected him President.
③ Jeff made his son a desk.
④ We found the boy asleep in the sofa.
⑤ Ms. Han named her cat Willow.

서답형
10 다음 문장에서 생략할 수 있는 것을 찾아 쓰시오.

(1) The sport that Frank can play well is basketball.
(2) The girl whom you met last night is my sister.
(3) *Annie* is the story of an 11-year-old girl who is named Annie.

➡ (1) _____ (2) _____ (3) _____

11 다음 두 문장을 한 문장으로 바르게 바꾼 것은?

• BJ is a rap singer.
• I like BJ the most.

① BJ is whom a rap singer I like the most.
② BJ is a rap singer which I like the most.
③ BJ is a rap singer who like the most.
④ BJ is a rap singer who I like him the most.
⑤ BJ is a rap singer whom I like the most.

12 다음 중 밑줄 친 부분의 쓰임이 잘못된 것은?

① His success abroad has made <u>him a national hero</u> in Korea.
② They <u>call it strange</u>.
③ I <u>consider it to be</u> the best novel I have written in my life.
④ The students <u>elected her as president</u> of their class.
⑤ The town <u>chose Mr. White as mayor</u>.

13 다음 두 문장을 관계대명사를 사용하여 한 문장으로 바꾸시오.

(1) • New York is a big city.
　　• Many people visit New York every year.

　➡ _____

　_____

(2) • My favorite subject is math.
　　• I'm good at math.

　➡ _____

　_____

(3) • The man was my math teacher.
　　• I saw the man at the mall.

　➡ _____

　_____

(4) • She is a famous movie star.
　　• Many people like her.

　➡ _____

　_____

(5) • I was surprised at the speed.
　　• He learned to speak with the speed.

　➡ _____

　_____

　_____

(6) • Do you know the girl?
　　• Anne is talking to the girl.

　➡ _____

　_____

　_____

14 다음 빈칸에 자연스러운 의미가 되도록 들어갈 알맞은 것은?

> We _____ Chicago the Windy City.

① call　　　　　② want
③ give　　　　　④ regard
⑤ have

15 다음 밑줄 친 부분의 쓰임이 어색한 것은?

① This is the road which leads to the library.
② Fall is the season which comes after summer.
③ Philip loves the girl who I love.
④ The young boy to that Jane is talking is Alex.
⑤ The famous man lives in the town which Tom visited last year.

16 우리말에 맞게 괄호 안의 어휘를 바르게 배열하시오.

(1) 우리는 셰익스피어를 영국의 국민 시인이라고 부른다. (we, Shakespeare, poet, England's, call, national)

　➡ _____

(2) 나는 그를 겁쟁이라고 생각한다. (I, him, coward, be, consider, a, to)

　➡ _____

17 주어진 문장의 밑줄 친 부분과 용법이 같은 것을 두 개 고르시오.

> The spaghetti that Suji made for me yesterday was delicious.

① There was no hope that she would recover her health.
② The actor who I like the most is Robert.
③ I didn't know who you were talking about.
④ The movie which I want to watch is *Alita*.
⑤ They must be swallows that have come back from the south.

Grammar 서술형 시험대비

01 다음 두 문장을 관계대명사를 이용하여 한 문장으로 연결하여 쓰시오.

(1) • I bought the snack.
 • Everyone likes the snack.

 ➡ _____

 _____

(2) • *Romeo and Juliet* is the movie.
 • Helen saw *Romeo and Juliet*.

 ➡ _____

 _____

(3) • The person is my sister.
 • I love the person the most.

 ➡ _____

 _____

(4) • The author is C. S. Lewis.
 • I like the author the most.

 ➡ _____

 _____

(5) • Look at the boy.
 • Mary is talking to the boy.

 ➡ _____

 _____

(6) • Look at Chris and his dog.
 • Bella is playing with them.

 ➡ _____

 _____

02 다음 괄호 안에 주어진 말을 바르게 배열하여 문장을 완성하시오.

(1) (people / New York City / the Big Apple / call)

 ➡ _____

(2) (people / hero / him / consider / may / some / a / as / not)

 ➡ _____

(3) (they / her / the Boxer of the Year / named)

 ➡ _____

(4) (ability / him / his / person / made / famous / a)

 ➡ _____

(5) (leader / him / we / be / elected / to / a)

 ➡ _____

(6) (followers / a genius / him / his / be / believed / to)

 ➡ _____

(7) (they / Mike / fool / regard / as / a)

 ➡ _____

03 다음 그림을 보고 괄호 안에 주어진 어휘를 이용하여 문장을 완성하시오.

(the park in the sky / the rooftop garden / call)
➡ We _____.

04 다음 문장에서 <u>잘못된 부분</u>을 바르게 고쳐 문장을 다시 쓰시오.

(1) Andy is the boy which Hajun met in Canada.

➡ _____

(2) The table who my dad made for me is sturdy.

➡ _____

(3) Hemingway is the author whom I like him the most.

➡ _____

(4) The book which he wrote it is fun.

➡ _____

(5) Can I borrow the book about that you told me?

➡ _____

05 두 문장을 관계대명사를 사용하여 한 문장으로 썼을 때, 빈칸에 해당하는 문장을 쓰시오.

(1) • I ate the chocolate cake.
+ • _____
➡ I ate the chocolate cake which my grandmother made.

(2) • Do you remember the people?
+ • _____
➡ Do you remember the people whom we met on the plane?

(3) • _____
+ • He will drive the car while he stays in New York.
➡ He wants to rent a car that he will drive while he stays in New York.

(4) • _____
+ • You can depend on the friend.
➡ Do you have a friend whom you can depend on?

06 다음 문장을 어법에 맞게 고쳐 쓰시오.

(1) They called him to be Mr. Long.
➡ _____

(2) They regarded him their leader.
➡ _____

07 괄호 안에 주어진 어휘를 이용하여 우리말에 맞게 영작하시오.

(1) 우리는 그곳에 매우 바람이 많이 불기 때문에 Chicago를 the Windy City라고 부른다. (it, there, call, windy, because, very) (we로 시작할 것)

➡ _____

(2) 나는 나의 엄마가 내게 만들어 주신 과자를 좋아한다. (like, the cookies, for, make)

➡ _____

(3) 내가 가장 방문하고 싶은 나라는 프랑스이다. (the country, visit, the most)

➡ _____

(4) Harry는 작년에 나와 함께 일했던 파트너였다. (the partner, that, worked)

➡ _____

Be Smart with Your Smartphones!

without: '~ 없이' (전치사)
Living without smartphones is difficult for many of us these days.
동명사(주어): 단수로 취급 → 단수 동사 is를 쓴다.   요즈음

However, unwise or too much use of smartphones can cause various
    unwise와 too much가 or로 연결, 뒤에 나온 use를 수식

problems.

Are you a smombie?

All over the world, people are walking around like zombies. Their
    전 세계에 걸쳐   좀비처럼

heads are down, and their eyes are on their smartphones. We call such
                        그들의 눈은 스마트폰을 향하고 있다   call A B: A를 B라고 부르다

people smombies, smartphone zombies. If you are a smombie, you
    smombies와 smartphone zombies는 동격

can have various safety problems. You may not see a hole in the street,
                                        추측(~일지도 모른다)

so you may fall and get hurt. You may get into a car accident, too. So
그래서   다치다

what can you do to prevent these problems? It's simple. Do not look at
                to부정사의 부사적 용법(목적)   앞에 나온 다양한 안전 관련 문제들

your smartphone while you are walking!
                ~하는 동안

Do you have dry eyes or text neck?

Smartphones can cause various health problems. One example is dry
                                    스마트폰이 야기할 수 있는 건강 문제의 한 예

eyes. When you look at your smartphone, you do not blink often. Then
when 이하는 시간의 부사절로 '~할 때'라는 의미

your eyes will feel dry.
            feel은 감각동사로 형용사가 보어로 쓰였다.

without ~ 없이
cause 일으키다, 야기하다
various 다양한, 여러 가지의
such 그런, 그러한
zombie 좀비 (반쯤 죽은 것 같은 사람)
hole 구덩이
prevent 방지하다, 막다
simple 간단한
text neck 거북목 증후군
dry eye 안구 건조증
text 문자 메시지; (휴대 전화로) 문자를 보내다

확인문제

● 다음 문장이 본문의 내용과 일치하면 T, 일치하지 <u>않으면</u> F를 쓰시오.

1 Living without smartphones is difficult for many of us these days. ☐

2 Smombies are smart zombies. ☐

3 Smombies can have various social problems. ☐

4 Smombies may not see a hole in the street, so they may fall and get hurt. ☐

Another problem you can have is neck pain. When you look down at
problem과 you 사이에 목적격 관계대명사 which/that이 생략되어 있다.　　　　　　　　　　　　～을 내려다보다

your smartphone, the stress on your neck increases. Too much use of
　　　　　　　　　　　　　　　형용사구

your smartphone, for example, too much texting, can cause neck pain.
　　　　　　　　　　Too much use of your smartphone의 한 예

We call this text neck.
　　call A B: A를 B라고 부르다

Here are some tips for these problems. For dry eyes, try to blink
여기 ～이 있다　　　　　　　　　　　　　　　try to+동사원형: ～하려고 노력하다. cf. try+-ing: 한번 ～해 보다

often. For text neck, move your smartphone up to your eye level. You
　　　　　　　　　　　　　　　　　　～까지

can also do some neck stretching exercises.

How do you feel when you don't have your smartphone with you?

Do you feel nervous when your smartphone is not around? Do
　　　　　　　　　　when 이하는 시간의 부사절로 '～할 때'라는 의미　　　　　주위에(부사)

you feel sad when you check your smartphone and there is no text
feel은 감각동사로 형용사가 보어로 쓰였다.　　　　　　　　　　　　　　　～이 없다

message? If your answers are "yes," you may have smartphone
　　　　　　　　　　　　　　　　　　　추측(～일지도 모른다)　　= smartphone addiction

addiction. There are various things you can do to prevent this. For
things와 you 사이에는 목적격 관계대명사 that 또는 which 생략
～이 있다　　　　　　　　　　　　　　　to부정사의 부사적 용법(목적)

example, turn off your smartphone during meals or meetings. You can
　　　　　～을 끄다　　　　　　　～ 중에

talk to people instead of texting them.
　　　　～ 하는 대신에. 뒤에 동명사가 온다.　= people

blink (눈을) 깜박거리다

pain 통증. 고통

look down at ～을 내려다보다

increase 증가하다

eye level 눈높이

stretch 늘이다. 뻗다

nervous 초조한

around 주위에

addiction 중독

meal 식사

instead of ～ 대신에

확인문제

● 다음 문장이 본문의 내용과 일치하면 T, 일치하지 않으면 F를 쓰시오.

1 When you look at your smartphone, your eyes will feel dry,

   so you should not blink often. ☐

2 When you look down at your smartphone, the stress on your back increases. ☐

3 Too much texting can cause neck pain called text neck. ☐

4 If you feel nervous when your smartphone is not around, you may have smartphone

   addiction. ☐

5 There are few things you can do to prevent smartphone addiction. ☐

6 You can talk to people instead of texting them to prevent smartphone addiction. ☐

● 우리말을 참고하여 빈칸에 알맞은 말을 쓰시오.

1 _____ _____ _____ Your Smartphones!

2 _____ _____ _____ is difficult for many of us these days.

3 However, _____ _____ _____ _____ _____ of smartphones can cause various problems.

4 Are you _____ _____?

5 All over the world, people are walking around _____ _____.

6 Their heads are down, and their eyes are _____ _____ _____.

7 We call _____ _____ smombies, smartphone zombies.

8 If you are a smombie, you can have _____ _____ _____.

9 You _____ _____ _____ a hole in the street, _____ you may fall and get hurt.

10 You may _____ _____ a car accident, too.

11 So what can you do _____ _____ these problems?

12 It's _____.

13 Do not look at your smartphone _____ you are _____!

14 Do you have _____ _____ or _____ _____?

15 Smartphones can cause various _____ _____.

16 One example is _____ _____.

---

1 스마트폰을 현명하게 사용하라!

2 스마트폰 없이 사는 것은 요즘 많은 사람들에게 어렵다.

3 하지만 스마트폰을 현명하지 않게 사용하거나 너무 과도하게 사용하는 것은 다양한 문제를 야기할 수 있다.

4 당신은 스몸비인가요?

5 전 세계적으로 사람들이 좀비처럼 걸어다니고 있다.

6 그들의 머리는 아래를 향하고, 그들의 눈은 스마트폰을 향하고 있다.

7 우리는 그런 사람들을 스몸비, 즉 스마트폰 좀비라고 부른다.

8 만약 당신이 스몸비라면, 당신은 다양한 안전 관련 문제들을 겪을 수 있다.

9 당신은 거리에 있는 구덩이를 보지 못할 수도 있고, 그래서 넘어져서 다칠지도 모른다.

10 당신은 또한 교통사고를 당할지도 모른다.

11 그렇다면 이런 문제들을 방지하기 위해 무엇을 할 수 있을까?

12 간단하다.

13 걷고 있는 동안에는 스마트폰을 보지 마라!

14 당신은 안구 건조증이나 거북목 증후군이 있나요?

15 스마트폰은 다양한 건강상의 문제를 일으킬 수 있다.

16 한 가지 예가 안구 건조증이다.

서답형

05 위 글의 밑줄 친 ⓐ에서 어법상 **틀린** 부분을 찾아 고쳐 쓰시오.

_____ ➡ _____

06 아래 〈보기〉에서 위 글의 밑줄 친 ⓑto blink와 to부정사의 용법이 같은 것의 개수를 고르시오.

┌─ 보기 ┬─
① I found it useless to teach you math.
② She came here to have a talk with you.
③ It is dangerous to play with matches.
④ Your fault is to talk too much.
⑤ I decided to help those young children.
└─────┘

① 1개 ② 2개 ③ 3개 ④ 4개 ⑤ 5개

중요

07 위 글의 주제로 알맞은 것은?

① the cause of dry eyes and the tips to prevent them
② health problems from smartphones and tips for them
③ some tips for avoiding text neck caused by smartphones
④ the increase of the stress due to smartphones
⑤ the importance of neck stretching for a healthy life

[08~10] 다음 글을 읽고 물음에 답하시오.

How do you feel when you don't have your smartphone with you?

Do you feel (A)[nervous / nervously] when your smartphone is not around? Do you feel (B)[sad / sadly] when you check your smartphone and there is no text message?

If your answers are "yes," you may have smartphone ___ⓐ___. There are various things you can do (C)[preventing / to prevent] this. For example, turn off your smartphone during meals or meetings. You can talk to people instead of texting ⓑthem.

서답형

08 위 글의 괄호 (A)~(C)에서 어법상 알맞은 것을 골라 쓰시오.

➡ (A) _____ (B) _____ (C) _____

서답형

09 주어진 영영풀이를 참고하여 빈칸 ⓐ에 철자 a로 시작하는 단어를 쓰시오.

┌──────────────────────┐
1. the condition of taking harmful drugs and being unable to stop taking them
2. a very strong desire or need for something
└──────────────────────┘

➡ _____

서답형

10 위 글의 밑줄 친 ⓑthem이 가리키는 것을 본문에서 찾아 쓰시오.

➡ _____

[11~14] 다음 글을 읽고 물음에 답하시오.

ⓐLiving without smartphones is difficult for many of us these days. However, unwise or too much use of smartphones can cause various problems.

ⓑ_____

All over the world, people are walking around like zombies. Their heads are down, and their eyes are on their smartphones. We call such people smombies, smartphone zombies. If you are a smombie, you can have various safety problems. You may not see a hole in the street, so you may fall and get hurt. You may get into a car accident, too. So what can you do to prevent these problems? It's simple. Do not look at your smartphone while you are walking!

11 위 글의 밑줄 친 ⓐLiving과 문법적 쓰임이 같은 것을 모두 고르시오.

① The boy reading a book is my son.
② I saw you running on the ground.
③ My brother is good at dancing.
④ My hobby is watching movies.
⑤ Look at the flying bird.

12 위 글의 빈칸 ⓑ에 들어갈 문장으로 알맞은 것은?

① Living without smartphones is difficult.
② Are you a smombie?
③ See a hole in the street!
④ You should prevent a car accident.
⑤ A smombie isn't a troublemaker!

서답형

13 위 글의 내용과 일치하도록 다음 빈칸 (A)와 (B)에 알맞은 단어를 본문에서 찾아 쓰시오.

> You must not look at your (A)_____ while you are walking to prevent various (B)_____ problems.

14 위 글을 읽고 대답할 수 없는 질문은?

① Is it easy for many of us to live without smartphones these days?
② Can too much use of smartphones cause problems?
③ What does a smombie mean?
④ What problems do smombies have?
⑤ What is the most dangerous problem that smombies may have?

[15~17] 다음 글을 읽고 물음에 답하시오.

Do you have dry eyes or text neck?

Smartphones can cause various health problems. One example is dry eyes. When you look ___ⓐ___ your smartphone, you do not blink often. Then your eyes will feel dry.

ⓑAnother problem you can have is neck pain. When you look down ___ⓐ___ your smartphone, the stress on your neck increases. Too much use of your smartphone, for example, too much texting, can cause neck pain. We call this text neck.

Here are some tips for these problems. ___ⓒ___ dry eyes, try to blink often. ___ⓒ___ text neck, move your smartphone ⓓup to your eye level. You can also do some neck stretching exercises.

15 위 글의 빈칸 @와 ⓒ에 각각 공통으로 들어갈 전치사가 바르게 짝지어진 것은?

① for – From ② at – For
③ at – From ④ for – To
⑤ on – For

서답형

16 위 글의 밑줄 친 문장 ⓑ에 생략된 단어를 넣어 문장을 다시 쓰시오.

➡ _____

17 위 글의 밑줄 친 @up to와 같은 의미로 쓰인 것은?

① He's not up to the job.
② It's up to you.
③ The temperature went up to 35°C.
④ What's she up to?
⑤ She is looking up to you.

[18~21] 다음 글을 읽고 물음에 답하시오.

How do you feel when you don't have your smartphone with you?

ⓐDo you feel nervous when your smartphone is around? Do you feel sad when you check your smartphone and there is no text message?

If your answers are "yes," you may have smartphone addiction. There are various things you can do to prevent ⓑthis. For example, turn off your smartphone during meals or meetings. You can talk to people instead of texting them.

서답형

18 위 글의 밑줄 친 @에서 흐름상 어색한 부분을 찾아 고치시오.

➡ _____

서답형

19 위 글의 밑줄 친 ⓑthis가 가리키는 것을 본문에서 찾아 영어로 쓰시오.

➡ _____

서답형

20 다음 질문에 대한 알맞은 대답을 영어로 쓰시오. (두 가지)

Q: What can you do to prevent smartphone addiction?

➡ (1) _____
(2) _____

21 위 글의 주제로 알맞은 것을 고르시오.

① living without your smartphone
② feeling sad when using a smartphone
③ how to get many text messages
④ smartphone addiction and its prevention
⑤ the danger of smartphone addiction

[22~24] 다음 글을 읽고 물음에 답하시오.

Minho: Yesterday, I fell on the street and got hurt. I was texting and I didn't see a hole.
 ↳ Reply: Do not use your smartphone while you are walking.

Emma: My eyes feel dry when I use my smartphone.
 ↳ Reply: Try to blink often.

Suji: I have neck pain ⓐwhen I text a lot.
 ↳ Reply: Move your smartphone up to your eye level and do some neck stretching exercises.

Eric: I think I have smartphone addiction.
 ↳ Reply: Turn off your smartphone during meals or meetings and talk to people instead of texting them.

서답형

22 다음 질문에 대한 알맞은 대답을 주어진 단어로 시작하여 쓰시오. (8~9 단어)

> **Q:** Why did Minho fall on the street and get hurt yesterday?

A: Because ＿＿＿＿＿＿＿＿＿＿＿＿＿＿ .

23 위 글의 밑줄 친 ⓐwhen과 같은 의미로 쓰인 것을 **모두** 고르시오.

① When I was a boy, I was very smart.
② I don't know when I should go.
③ Time goes very fast when I'm busy.
④ When did she promise to meet him?
⑤ When can you come?

24 위 글의 내용과 일치하지 <u>않는</u> 것은?

① 민호는 걷는 동안에는 스마트폰을 사용하지 말아야 한다.
② Emma는 스마트폰을 사용할 때 눈이 건조하다고 느낀다.
③ 수지는 문자를 많이 보낼 때 목 통증이 있다.
④ Eric은 스마트폰을 눈높이까지 들고, 목 스트레칭 운동을 해야 한다.
⑤ Eric은 식사나 회의 중에는 스마트폰을 끄고 문자를 보내는 대신에 사람들과 이야기해야 한다.

[25~27] 다음 글을 읽고 물음에 답하시오.

How do you feel when you don't have your smartphone with you?

 Do you feel nervous when your smartphone is not around? (①) Do you feel sad when you check your smartphone and there is no text message?
 (②) If your answers are "yes," you may have smartphone (A)[addition / addiction]. (③)
 ⓐ＿＿＿ , turn (B)[on / off] your smartphone during meals or meetings. (④) You can talk to people (C)[instead of / because of] texting them. (⑤)

25 위 글의 ①~⑤ 중 다음 주어진 문장이 들어갈 알맞은 곳은?

> There are various things you can do to prevent this.

①   ②   ③   ④   ⑤

26 위 글의 빈칸 ⓐ에 들어갈 알맞은 것은?

① For example   ② Thus
③ Moreover   ④ However
⑤ On the other hand

27 위 글의 괄호 (A)~(C)에서 문맥상 알맞은 낱말을 골라 쓰시오.

➡ (A) _____ (B) _____ (C) _____

[28~30] 다음 글을 읽고 물음에 답하시오.

Living without smartphones is difficult for many of us these days. However, unwise or too much use of smartphones can cause various problems.

Are you a smombie?

All over the world, people are ⓐwalking around like zombies. Their heads are down, and their eyes are on their smartphones. We call such people smombies, smartphone zombies. If you are a smombie, you can have various ___(A)___ problems. You may not see a hole in the street, so you may fall and get hurt. You may get into a car accident, too. So what can you do to prevent these problems? It's simple. Do not look at your smartphone while you are walking!

28 위 글의 빈칸 (A)에 들어갈 알맞은 것은?

① health   ② mental
③ economical   ④ safety
⑤ physical

29 아래 〈보기〉에서 위 글의 밑줄 친 ⓐwalking과 문법적 쓰임이 다른 것의 개수를 고르시오.

┌─── 보기 ───┐
① Look at the boy underline{singing} on the street.
② Thank you for underline{helping} me solve it.
③ My hobby is underline{taking} pictures.
④ She is underline{making} an apple pie.
⑤ underline{Keeping} a diary every day is difficult.
└──────────┘

① 1개   ② 2개   ③ 3개   ④ 4개   ⑤ 5개

30 위 글의 주제로 알맞은 것은?

① the comfortable living by using smartphones
② the difficulty of living without using smartphones
③ the increase of people like zombies all over the world
④ a car accident which is caused by smombies
⑤ various safety problems due to unwise use of smartphones

[01~03] 다음 글을 읽고 물음에 답하시오.

Living without smartphones (A)[is / are] difficult for many of us these days. However, unwise or too much use of smartphones can cause various problems.

Are you a smombie?

All over the world, people are walking around (B)[like / alike] zombies. Their heads are down, and their eyes are on their smartphones. We call such people smombies, smartphone zombies. If you are a smombie, you can have various ⓐsafety problems. You may not see a hole in the street, so you may fall and get hurt. You may get into a car accident, too. So what can you do to prevent these problems? (C)[Its / It's] simple. Do not look at your smartphone while you are walking!

01 위 글의 괄호 (A)~(C)에서 어법상 알맞은 낱말을 골라 쓰시오.

➡ (A) _____ (B) _____ (C) _____

02 다음 빈칸 (A)~(C)에 알맞은 단어를 넣어 smombies에 대한 설명을 완성하시오.

> They are people who are walking around like (A)_____ with their (B)_____ hanging down, and their (C)_____ on their smartphones.

03 위 글의 밑줄 친 ⓐ의 예 두 가지를 본문에서 찾아 우리말로 쓰시오.

➡ (1) _____
   (2) _____

[04~06] 다음 글을 읽고 물음에 답하시오.

Do you have dry eyes or text neck?

Smartphones can cause various health problems. One example is dry eyes. When you look at your smartphone, you do not ___ⓐ___ often. Then your eyes will feel dry.

Another problem you can have is neck pain. ⓑ스마트폰을 내려다볼 때, 목에 가해지는 압박이 증가한다. Too much use of your smartphone, for example, too much texting, can cause neck pain. We call this ⓒtext neck.

Here are some tips for these problems. For dry eyes, try to ___ⓓ___ often. For text neck, move your smartphone up to your eye level. You can also do some neck stretching exercises.

04 주어진 영영풀이를 참고하여 빈칸 ⓐ와 ⓓ에 공통으로 들어갈 단어를 철자 b로 시작하여 쓰시오.

> to shut your eyes and very quickly open them again

➡ _____

05 위 글의 밑줄 친 ⓑ의 우리말에 맞게 한 단어를 보충하여, 주어진 어휘를 알맞게 배열하시오. (when으로 시작할 것)

> your neck / down / the stress / when / look / your smartphone / at / you / increases / ,

➡ _____
   _____

06 What does the underlined ©text neck mean? Fill in the blanks with the suitable words.

> It means the neck pain which is caused by (A)_____ _____ _____ of your smartphone like too much (B)_____ .

[07~09] 다음 글을 읽고 물음에 답하시오.

> Living without smartphones is difficult for many of us these days. However, ⓐunwise or too much use of smartphones can cause various problems.
>
> **Are you a smombie?**
> All over the world, people are walking around like zombies. Their heads are down, and their eyes are on their smartphones. ⓑ 우리는 그런 사람들을 스몸비, 즉 스마트폰 좀비라고 부른다. If you are a smombie, you can have various safety problems. ©You may not see a hole in the street, so you may fall and get hurt. You may get into a car accident, too. So what can you do to prevent these problems? It's simple. Do not look at your smartphone while you are walking!

07 위 글의 밑줄 친 ⓐ의 예를 본문에서 찾아 우리말로 쓰시오. (30~35자)

➡ _____

_____

08 위 글의 밑줄 친 ⓑ의 우리말에 맞게 주어진 어휘를 이용하여 7 단어로 영작하시오.

> such, smombies

➡ _____

09 위 글의 밑줄 친 ©를 다음과 같이 바꿔 쓸 때 빈칸에 들어갈 알맞은 말을 쓰시오.

➡ _____ you may not see a hole in the street, you may fall and get hurt.

[10~11] 다음 글을 읽고 물음에 답하시오.

> **Do you have dry eyes or text neck?**
> Smartphones can cause various health problems. One example is ⓐdry eyes. When you look at your smartphone, you do not blink often. Then your eyes will feel dry.
>
> Another problem you can have is neck pain. When you look down at your smartphone, the stress on your neck increases. Too much use of your smartphone, ⓑfor example, too much texting, can cause neck pain. We call this text neck.
>
> Here are some tips for these problems. For dry eyes, try to blink often. For text neck, move your smartphone up to your eye level. You can also do some neck stretching exercises.

10 위 글의 밑줄 친 ⓐdry eyes의 원인과 이 문제를 위한 조언을 우리말로 쓰시오.

➡ 원인: _____

조언: _____

11 위 글의 밑줄 친 ⓑfor example과 바꿔 쓸 수 있는 단어를 두 단어로 쓰시오.

➡ _____

Talk and Play

A: What's wrong?
상대방이 기분이 좋지 않거나 어딘가 아파 보일 때 사용함.(= What's the matter?)
B: I have a fever.
'나는 ~가 아프다'는 표현으로 'have+a/an+병명/증상' 형태를 사용.
A: That's too bad. Make sure you get some rest.
상대방이 안 좋은 일을 당했을 때 사용하는 표현.(= I'm sorry to hear that.)
B: OK, I will.　　상대방에게 당부하는 표현.(반드시 ~하도록 하다, ~을 확실히 하다)

구문해설 ・**fever**: 열　・**make sure**: 확실히 ~하다　・**rest**: 휴식

After You Read B

Be Smart with Your Smartphones!

Minho: Yesterday, I fell on the street and got hurt. I was texting and I didn't
　　　　　　　　　　　　　　　　　　　　　　　　　　　　　　　　　현재분사
see a hole.
┗, Reply: Do not use your smartphone while you are walking.

Emma: My eyes feel dry when I use my smartphone.
　　　　　　feel은 감각동사로 형용사가 보어로 쓰였다.
┗, Reply: Try to blink often.
　　　　　　명사적 용법(목적어)

Suji: I have neck pain when I text a lot.
　　　　　　　　　　　　때(접속사)
┗, Reply: Move your smartphone up to your eye level and do some
　　　　　　　　　　　　　　　　　　　~까지
neck stretching exercises.

Eric: I think I have smartphone addiction.
　　　　　　　　　　　　스마트폰 중독
┗, Reply: Turn off your smartphone during meals or meetings and
　　　　　~을 끄다 ↔ turn on
talk to people instead of texting them.
　~ 대신에 (뒤에 명사 또는 동명사가 온다.)　= people

구문해설 ・**hole**: 구덩이　・**blink**: (눈을) 깜박거리다　・**text**: 문자 메시지; (휴대 전화로) 문자를 보내다
・**stretch**: 늘이다, 뻗다　・**addiction**: 중독　・**meal**: 식사　・**instead of**: ~ 대신에

Around the World

This sign says, "Be careful of using your smartphone while you are walking."
　　　　　　　　　　　　　전치사 of의 목적어로 동명사　　　　　접속사(~하는 동안)
There are traffic lights on the ground, so people can see them while they are
　　　　　　　　　　　　　　　　　　　그래서　　　　　= traffic lights
using their smartphones.
현재분사
This sign on the ground means, "This side of the street is for people who are
　　　　　형용사구　　　　　　　　　　　　　　　　　　　　　주격 관계대명사
texting."

구문해설 ・**say**: (신문・게시・편지・책 따위가) ~라고 씌어져 있다　・**mean**: 의미하다

해석

A: 무슨 일이니?
B: 나는 열이 나.
A: 안됐다. 좀 쉬도록 하렴.
B: 응, 알겠어.

스마트폰을 현명하게 사용하라!
민호: 어제, 나는 길에서 넘어져서 다쳤다. 나는 문자를 보내고 있었고 구덩이를 보지 못했다.
→ 대답: 걷는 동안에는 스마트폰을 사용하지 마라.
Emma: 나는 스마트폰을 사용할 때 눈이 건조하다고 느낀다.
→ 대답: 눈을 자주 깜박이도록 노력해라.
수지: 나는 문자를 많이 보낼 때 목 통증이 있다.
→ 대답: 스마트폰을 눈높이까지 들고, 목 스트레칭 운동을 해라.
Eric: 나는 스마트폰 중독인 것 같다.
→ 대답: 식사나 회의 중에는 스마트폰을 끄고 문자를 보내는 대신에 사람들과 이야기해라.

이 표지판은 "걷는 동안 스마트폰 사용을 주의하세요."라는 의미이다.
땅바닥에 신호등이 있어서, 사람들이 스마트폰을 사용하는 동안에도 신호등을 볼 수 있다.
땅바닥에 있는 이 표지판은 "길의 이쪽은 문자를 보내고 있는 사람들을 위한 곳입니다."라는 의미이다.

01 다음 주어진 두 단어의 관계가 같도록 빈칸에 알맞은 단어를 쓰시오. (주어진 철자로 시작할 것)

> expensive : cheap = stupid : i_____

02 다음 글의 빈칸 ⓐ와 ⓑ에 들어갈 단어가 바르게 짝지어진 것은?

> Living ___ⓐ___ smartphones is difficult for many of us these days. However, unwise or too much use of smartphones can ___ⓑ___ various problems.

① with – prevent
② with – cause
③ without – prevent
④ without – cause
⑤ without – decrease

[03~04] 다음 영영풀이에 해당하는 것을 고르시오.

03

> to spread out your arms, legs, or body as far as possible

① text   ② blink
③ stretch   ④ cause
⑤ prevent

04

> in the state of sleep; sleeping

① asleep   ② sour
③ intelligent   ④ various
⑤ simple

05 빈칸에 공통으로 들어갈 말을 주어진 철자로 시작하여 쓰시오.

> • The c_____ of the accident is not clear. The police are still looking into it.
> • Too much use of smartphones can c_____ dry eyes.

➡ _____

06 다음 밑줄 친 부분의 뜻이 잘못된 것은?

① Make sure you get some rest. (확실히 ~하라)
② I think you have computer game addiction! (중독)
③ My eyes are so dry. I try to blink often. (눈을 감다)
④ Don't look at your smartphone while you are walking! (~ 하는 동안)
⑤ When you look down at your smartphone, the stress on your neck increases. (압박)

07 다음 대화의 빈칸에 들어갈 말로 알맞지 않은 것은?

> W: _____, Chris?
> B: I have a terrible toothache.
> W: Here is some medicine. Take this.
> B: Thank you.

① What's the matter
② What's the problem
③ Is there anything wrong
④ What do you mean
⑤ What's wrong with you

[08~10] 다음 대화를 읽고 물음에 답하시오.

W: ⓐWhat's wrong, Andy?

B: Hello, Ms. Kim. My right thumb hurts.

W: Hmm. (①) Do you use your smartphone a lot?

B: Yes, I ⓑtext a lot. Why? (②)

W: I think you have texting thumb.

B: Texting thumb? (③)

W: It's ⓒpain in your thumb. You can get it from texting too much. (④)

B: Oh, I didn't know (A)that.

W: Why don't you ⓓdo some finger stretching exercises?

B: OK, I will. (⑤)

W: And make sure ⓔyou text too much.

08 주어진 문장이 들어갈 위치로 알맞은 것은?

> What's texting thumb?

① ② ③ ④ ⑤

09 밑줄 친 (A)that이 가리키는 것을 우리말로 쓰시오.

➡ _____

10 위 대화의 밑줄 친 ⓐ~ⓔ 중, 흐름상 어색한 것은?

① ⓐ ② ⓑ ③ ⓒ ④ ⓓ ⑤ ⓔ

11 다음 대화의 밑줄 친 부분 중 어법상 어색한 것은?

> W: What's ⓐwrong with your leg, Sam?
>
> B: I fell and hurt my foot ⓑwhile I was playing soccer.
>
> W: Can you walk?
>
> B: Yes, but it ⓒhurts a lot.
>
> W: ⓓWhy don't you put some ice on it? And ⓔmake sure don't play soccer until next week.

① ⓐ ② ⓑ ③ ⓒ ④ ⓓ ⑤ ⓔ

12 다음 중 짝지어진 대화가 어색한 것은?

① A: I have a headache.
  B: That's too bad.

② A: Make sure you take some medicine.
  B: OK, I will.

③ A: What's the matter, Chris?
  B: I have a terrible toothache.

④ A: I fell and hurt my foot while I was playing soccer.
  B: That sounds good.

⑤ A: Here is some medicine. Take this. And make sure you go to the dentist.
  B: OK, I will.

13 다음 대화의 밑줄 친 부분에 대한 설명으로 적절하지 <u>않은</u> 것은?

> W: ⓐWhat's the matter, Chris?
>
> B: I ⓑhave a terrible toothache.
>
> W: Here is some medicine. ⓒTake this.
>
> B: Thank you.
>
> W: And ⓓmake sure you go to the dentist.
>
> B: ⓔOK, I will.

① ⓐ: 문제점에 대해 물어볼 때 사용하는 표현이다.

② ⓑ: 이가 매우 아프다는 뜻이다.

③ ⓒ: '가져가다'라는 의미로 사용되었다.

④ ⓓ: 상대방에게 당부할 때 사용하는 표현이다.

⑤ ⓔ: 상대방의 조언에 '그렇게 하겠다'는 긍정의 표현이다.

Grammar

14 다음 밑줄 친 부분 중 어법상 어색한 것은?

> He was very ①intelligent, ②so we ③all called ④him ⑤to be Einstein.

① ② ③ ④ ⑤

15 다음 중 두 문장을 한 문장으로 만들 때 의미가 <u>다른</u> 하나는?

① This is the book.
 + John read the book last week.
 ➡ This is the book which John read last week.

② Grace sent an email to the boy.
 + Grace loved him.
 ➡ Grace sent an email to the boy whom she loved.

③ The card was sent to Sue.
 + I bought the card yesterday.
 ➡ Sue sent the card that I bought yesterday.

④ Remember to include all the expenses.
 + You spent the expenses.
 ➡ Remember to include all the expenses that you spent.

⑤ Those are the flowers.
 + Rachel planted them this spring.
 ➡ Those are the flowers Rachel planted this spring.

16 〈보기〉의 밑줄 친 which와 용법이 <u>다른</u> 하나는?

┌─── 보기 ───
│ Yesterday I watched the movie <u>which</u> he recommended.
└

① Herold is the only person <u>that</u> I want to meet now.

② I like the dog <u>which</u> my friend gave to me.

③ I employed a young man <u>who</u> Jenny liked a lot.

④ He is wearing a jacket <u>which</u> has two pockets.

⑤ The teacher <u>whom</u> I like most teaches math.

17 다음 문장의 빈칸에 알맞지 <u>않은</u> 것은?

| They _____ him to be their leader. |

① called   ② chose
③ considered   ④ wanted
⑤ elected

18 다음 밑줄 친 부분 중 생략할 수 있는 것은?

① Nick Larson is the man <u>that</u> lives in this town.

② Where did you buy <u>that</u> watch?

③ It is certain <u>that</u> he will come.

④ I like the robot <u>that</u> Kirk bought for me.

⑤ His dress is <u>that</u> of a gentleman.

19 괄호 안에 주어진 어휘를 사용해 다음을 영작하시오. (that 사용 금지)

(1) *Jane Eyre*는 Yumi가 어제 읽은 책이다. (the book, read)
 ➡ _____

(2) 내가 입고 있는 재킷은 나의 할머니로부터의 선물이다. (jacket, wear, a present)
 ➡ _____

(3) 사람들은 그러한 음식을 fajitas라고 부른다. (call, such, fajitas)
 ➡ _____

(4) 그 축제는 그 도시를 방문하기에 인기 있는 장소로 만들었다. (a, popular, visit)
 ➡ _____

Reading

[20~22] 다음 글을 읽고 물음에 답하시오.

Are you a smombie?

All over the world, people are walking around like zombies. Their heads are down, and their eyes are ⓐ their smartphones. We call such people smombies, smartphone zombies. (①) You may not see a hole in the street, so you may fall and get hurt. (②) You may get ⓑ a car accident, too. (③) So what can you do ©to prevent these problems? (④) It's simple. (⑤) Do not look at your smartphone while you are walking!

20 위 글의 흐름으로 보아, 주어진 문장이 들어가기에 가장 적절한 곳은?

> If you are a smombie, you can have various safety problems.

①   ②   ③   ④   ⑤

21 위 글의 빈칸 ⓐ와 ⓑ에 들어갈 전치사가 바르게 짝지어진 것은?

① from – into   ② in – at
③ on – into   ④ from – to
⑤ on – for

22 위 글의 밑줄 친 ©to prevent와 to부정사의 용법이 다른 것을 고르시오. (2개)

① She was pleased to see her son.
② He was the first man to land on the moon.
③ You are too young to understand it.
④ He is studying English to get a good job.
⑤ He promised me to come back soon.

[23~25] 다음 글을 읽고 물음에 답하시오.

ⓐ

Smartphones can cause various health problems. One example is dry eyes. When you look at your smartphone, you do not blink often. Then your eyes will feel dry.

(A)[Another / The other] problem you can have is neck pain. When you look down at your smartphone, the stress on your neck (B)[decreases / increases]. Too much use of your smartphone, ⓑ, too much texting, can cause neck pain. We call this text neck.

Here are some (C)[advices / tips] for these problems. For dry eyes, try to blink often. For text neck, move your smartphone up to your eye level. You can also do some neck stretching exercises.

23 위 글의 빈칸 ⓐ에 들어갈 문장으로 알맞은 것은?

① Blink often when using a smartphone!
② Does the stress on the neck increase?
③ What is the main reason of text neck?
④ Do you have dry eyes or text neck?
⑤ Do some neck stretching exercises!

24 위 글의 빈칸 ⓑ에 들어갈 알맞은 것은?

① in addition   ② for example
③ however   ④ in fact
⑤ as a result

25 위 글의 괄호 (A)~(C)에서 문맥이나 어법상 알맞은 낱말을 골라 쓰시오.

➡ (A) _____ (B) _____ (C) _____

[26~27] 다음 글을 읽고 물음에 답하시오.

How do you feel when you don't have your smartphone with you?

ⓐ스마트폰이 주위에 없을 때 당신은 초조한 기분이 드는가? Do you feel sad when you check your smartphone and there is no text message?

If your answers are "yes," you may have smartphone addiction. There are various things you can do to prevent this. ⓑFor example, turn off your smartphone while meals or meetings. You can talk to people instead of texting them.

26 위 글의 밑줄 친 ⓐ의 우리말에 맞게 주어진 어휘를 이용하여 10 단어로 영작하시오. (Do로 시작할 것)

nervous, around

➡ _____

_____

27 위 글의 밑줄 친 ⓑ에서 어법상 틀린 부분을 찾아 고치시오.

_____ ➡ _____

[28~29] 다음 글을 읽고 물음에 답하시오.

Minho: Yesterday, I fell on the street and got hurt. I was texting and I didn't see a hole.
↳ Reply: Do not use your smartphone while you are walking.

Emma: My eyes feel dry when I use my smartphone.
↳ Reply: Try to blink often.

Suji: I have neck pain when I text a lot.
↳ Reply: Move your smartphone up to your eye level and do some neck stretching exercises.

Eric: I think I have smartphone addiction.
↳ Reply: Turn off your smartphone during meals or meetings and talk to people __ⓐ__ .

28 위 글의 빈칸 ⓐ에 들어갈 알맞은 말은?

① instead of looking at them
② besides texting them
③ through SNS
④ instead of texting them
⑤ besides emailing them

29 Fill in the blanks with the suitable words.

Q1: Who should try to blink often? Q2: Why should he[she] try to blink often?

➡ Q1: _____ should try to blink often.

Q2: Because the eyes _____ _____ when he[she] uses the smartphone.

[30~31] 다음 글을 읽고 물음에 답하시오.

How do you feel when you don't have your smartphone with you?

Do you feel nervous when your smartphone is not around? Do you feel sad when you check your smartphone and there is no text message?

If your answers are "yes," you may have smartphone addiction. There are various things you can do to prevent this. For example, turn off your smartphone during meals or meetings. You can talk to people instead of __ⓐ__ them.

30 위 글을 읽고 스마트폰 중독이라고 생각할 수 있는 경우 두 가지를 우리말로 쓰시오.

➡ (1) _____

(2) _____

_____

31 위 글의 빈칸 ⓐ에 text를 알맞은 형태로 쓰시오.

➡ _____

출제율 90%

01 다음 짝지어진 단어의 관계가 같도록 빈칸에 알맞은 말을 쓰시오.

sore : painful = varied : _____

출제율 95%

02 다음 영영풀이에 해당하는 단어는?

a famous person

① author　　　② promise
③ celebrity　　④ zombie
⑤ hole

출제율 85%

03 다음 빈칸에 우리말에 맞게 알맞은 단어를 쓰시오. (주어진 철자로 시작하시오.)

• 여기에 이런 문제에 대한 몇 가지 조언이 있다.
(A) _____ _____ some tips for these problems.
• 스마트폰이 주위에 없을 때 당신은 초조한 기분이 드는가?
(B) Do you feel n_____ when your smartphone is not around?

[04~05] 다음 대화를 읽고 물음에 답하시오.

A: (A)너 몸이 안 좋아 보여. What's wrong?
B: I have a headache.
A: _____ (B) _____ Make sure you take some medicine.
B: OK, I will.

출제율 95%

04 위 대화의 밑줄 친 (A)의 우리말에 맞게 주어진 문장을 채우시오.

➡ You don't _____ _____.

출제율 95%

05 위 대화의 (B)에 들어갈 말로 알맞은 것을 모두 고르시오.

① That sounds good.
② I'm sorry to hear that.
③ I'm pleased to hear that.
④ That's too bad.
⑤ How are you doing?

출제율 95%

06 다음 (A)~(C)에 알맞은 말이 바르게 짝지어진 것은?

Smartphones can cause (A)[simple / various] health problems. One example is dry eyes. When you look at your smartphone, you do not blink often. Then your eyes will feel (B)[dry / wet]. Another problem you can have is neck pain. When you look down at your smartphone, the stress on your neck [decreases / increases].

	(A)	(B)	(C)
①	simple	wet	increases
②	simple	dry	decreases
③	various	wet	decreases
④	various	dry	increases
⑤	various	dry	decreases

출제율 95%

07 다음 대화의 밑줄 친 부분 중 어법상 어색한 것은?

W: You ⓐlook sick. What's wrong, Inho?
B: I ⓑhave a sore throat. I ⓒhave a fever, too.
W: I think you ⓓhave cold. Take this medicine and ⓔmake sure you take a good rest.
B: OK. Thank you.

① ⓐ　② ⓑ　③ ⓒ　④ ⓓ　⑤ ⓔ

W: _____(A)_____, Andy?

B: Hello, Ms. Kim. My right thumb hurts.

W: Hmm. Do you use your smartphone a lot?

B: Yes, I text a lot. Why?

W: I think you have texting thumb.

B: Texting thumb? What's texting thumb?

W: _____(B)_____. You can get it from texting too much.

B: Oh, I didn't know that.

W: ⓐ손가락 스트레칭 운동을 좀 하는 게 어떠니?

B: OK, I will.

W: And _____(C)_____.

08 위 대화의 빈칸 (A)~(C)에 들어갈 말로 알맞은 것을 〈보기〉에서 찾아 쓰시오.

┌─ 보기 ─┐
- What can I do for you
- What's wrong
- It's pain in your thumb
- don't forget to text message to me
- make sure you don't text too much
└────────┘

➡ (A) _____
(B) _____
(C) _____

09 위 대화의 밑줄 친 ⓐ의 우리말에 맞게 주어진 단어를 이용하여 영어로 쓰시오.

why, you, do, some, stretching exercises

➡ _____

10 다음 대화의 빈칸에 들어갈 말로 알맞은 것은?

W: What's wrong, Peter?

B: I don't know, Ms. Kim, but my back hurts a lot.

W: Put a heating pad on it.

B: OK, I will.

W: And _____.

① you should not forget to lock the door
② you had better text a lot
③ make sure you do some stretching exercises
④ make sure you give me a call when you get home
⑤ make sure you get enough sleep tonight

11 다음 문장에서 어법상 어색한 것을 바르게 고쳐 문장을 다시 쓰시오.

(1) The pizza who my dad made was really delicious.

➡ _____
_____

(2) I know the girl which you are talking about.

➡ _____
_____

(3) We elected class president Chris.

➡ _____

(4) The game that we saw it was very boring.

➡ _____

(5) He called me as Queen.

➡ _____

12 다음 빈칸에 들어갈 말을 <u>모두</u> 고르시오.

> Jane is the girl _____ Peter met in the park.

① who

② whose

③ whom

④ which

⑤ that

13 다음 중 어법상 바르지 <u>않은</u> 것은?

① Do you like the hat you bought yesterday?

② Arnold calls his daughter *My Little Princess*.

③ I met the lady with whom you had dinner last Saturday.

④ They called the ship to be Titanic.

⑤ *Yesterday* is the song that I can sing in English.

14 다음 우리말을 괄호 안에 주어진 어휘를 이용하여 영작하시오. (that 사용 금지)

(1) 우리는 그러한 춤을 Salsa라고 부른다. (such, call, a dance, 6 단어)

➡ _____

(2) 아무도 Nicole이 만든 스파게티를 좋아하지 않았다. (spaghetti, make, 7 단어)

➡ _____

(3) 우리는 Alex를 우리 동아리의 회장으로 선출했다. (elect, president, club, 7 단어)

➡ _____

(4) 그녀는 내가 가장 좋아하는 가수이다. (the singer, most, 8 단어)

➡ _____

[15~17] 다음 글을 읽고 물음에 답하시오.

Are you a smombie?

All over the world, people are walking around ⓐlike zombies. Their heads are down, and their eyes are on their smartphones. We call such people smombies, smartphone zombies. If you are a smombie, you can have various safety problems. You may not see a hole in the street, so you may fall and get hurt. You may get into a car accident, too. So what can you do to prevent ⓑthese problems? It's simple. Do not look at your smartphone while you are __(A)__!

15 위 글의 빈칸 (A)에 들어갈 가장 알맞은 것은?

① talking

② walking

③ studying

④ eating

⑤ playing

16 위 글의 밑줄 친 ⓐlike와 의미가 다른 것은?

① He ran like the wind.

② You do it like this.

③ I had a chance to meet people of like mind.

④ Don't look at me like that.

⑤ Students were angry at being treated like children.

17 위 글의 밑줄 친 ⓑthese problems와 바꿔 쓸 수 있는 말을 본문에서 찾아 쓰시오.

➡ _____

[18~19] 다음 글을 읽고 물음에 답하시오.

Do you have dry eyes or text neck?

Smartphones can cause various ___ⓐ___ problems. One example is dry eyes. When you look at your smartphone, you do not blink often. Then your eyes will feel dry.

Another problem you can have is neck pain. When you look down at your smartphone, the stress on your neck increases. Too much use of your smartphone, for example, too much texting, can cause neck pain. We call this text neck.

Here are some tips for these problems. For dry eyes, try to blink often. For text neck, move your smartphone up to your eye level. You can also do some neck stretching exercises.

✏ 출제율 95%
18 위 글의 빈칸 ⓐ에 들어갈 알맞은 것은?

① safety　　　　　② social
③ environment　　④ mental
⑤ health

✏ 출제율 90%
19 위 글의 내용과 일치하지 <u>않는</u> 것은?

① 스마트폰 사용은 안구 건조증을 일으킬 수 있다.
② 스마트폰 사용은 목 통증을 일으킬 수 있다.
③ 스마트폰을 내려다볼 때, 목에 가해지는 압박이 감소한다.
④ 안구 건조증에는, 눈을 자주 깜박이려고 노력해야 한다.
⑤ 거북목 증후군에는 당신의 눈높이까지 스마트폰을 위로 올려야 한다.

[20~22] 다음 글을 읽고 물음에 답하시오.

There are a few things I need to change to have a ___ⓐ___ life.

First, I don't exercise much. From now on, I will try to walk for 30 minutes every day.

Second, I think I eat too much fast food. I will eat fast food only once a week.

Third, I often eat at night. I will not eat after 10 o'clock.

I will try my best ⓑto keep these promises.

✏ 출제율 95%
20 위 글의 빈칸 ⓐ에 healthy의 비교급을 쓰시오.

➡ _____

✏ 출제율 100%
21 위 글을 읽고 더 건강한 생활을 하기 위해 필자가 바꾸어야 할 세 가지를 우리말로 쓰시오.

(1) _____
　　➡ _____
(2) _____
　　➡ _____
(3) _____
　　➡ _____

✏ 출제율 90%
22 아래 〈보기〉에서 위 글의 밑줄 친 ⓑto keep과 to부정사의 용법이 다른 것의 개수를 고르시오.

┌─ 보기 ─┐
① This chair seems comfortable <u>to sit</u> on.
② I have no friends <u>to help</u> me.
③ I found it difficult <u>to persuade</u> them.
④ I was shocked <u>to hear</u> the tragic news.
⑤ What a fool he is <u>to say</u> such a foolish thing!

① 1개　② 2개　③ 3개　④ 4개　⑤ 5개

서술형 실전문제

01 다음 그림을 보고 아래 대화의 빈칸에 알맞은 단어를 쓰시오.

> G: What's _____, Mike?
> B: I _____ _____ terrible _____.
> G: I think you _____ _____ some medicine.
> B: OK, I _____.

02 다음 대화를 읽고 아래의 표를 완성하시오.

> W: What's wrong, Andy?
> B: Hello, Ms. Kim. My right thumb hurts.
> W: Hmm. Do you use your smartphone a lot?
> B: Yes, I text a lot. Why?
> W: I think you have texting thumb.
> B: Texting thumb? What's texting thumb?
> W: It's pain in your thumb. You can get it from texting too much.
> B: Oh, I didn't know that.
> W: Why don't you do some finger stretching exercises?
> B: OK, I will.
> W: And make sure you don't text too much.

- Problem: _____ _____ (_____ in your thumb)
- Advice: (1) do some _____ _____
  _____ (2) don't _____ too much

03 괄호 안에 주어진 단어를 이용하여 다음 대화를 완성하시오.

> M: _____(A)_____, Mina?
> G: I _____(B)_____. I also have a runny nose.
> M: I think you have a cold. _____(C)_____
> G: OK, I will.

➡ (A) _____ (what, matter)

  (B) _____ (a sore throat)

  (C) _____ (make, you, some rest)

04 다음 두 문장을 관계대명사를 사용하여 한 문장으로 바꾸시오.

(1) • The book is about nature.
  • I'm reading the book.
  ➡ _____

(2) • Kenya is the country.
  • John wants to visit the country.
  ➡ _____

(3) • J. K. Rowling is a famous novelist.
  • Many people like her.
  ➡ _____

(4) • I want to know the name of the girl.
  • I met her at the party.
  ➡ _____

(5) • Start by identifying the people.
  • You want to work with the people.
  ➡ _____

(6) • The rate can be very slow.
  • Hair grows at the rate.
  ➡ _____

Living (A)[with / without] smartphones is difficult for many of us these days. However, unwise or too much use of smartphones can cause various problems.

Are you a smombie?

All over the world, people are walking around like zombies. ⓐ그들의 머리는 아래를 향하고, 그들의 눈은 스마트폰을 향하고 있다. We call such people smombies, smartphone zombies. If you are a smombie, you can have various safety problems. You may not see a (B)[hole / whole] in the street, so you may fall and get hurt. You may get into a car accident, too. So what can you do to (C)[prevent / protect] these problems? It's simple. Do not look at your smartphone while you are walking!

Do you have dry eyes or text neck?

Smartphones can cause various health problems. One example is dry eyes. When you look at your smartphone, you do not blink often. Then your eyes will feel dry.

Another problem you can have is neck pain. ⓐUnderlined{When you look up at your smartphone, the stress on your neck increases.} Too much use of your smartphone, for example, too much texting, can cause ⓑneck pain. We call this text neck.

Here are some tips for these problems. For dry eyes, try to blink often. For text neck, move your smartphone up to your eye level. You can also do some neck stretching exercises.

05 위 글의 괄호 (A)~(C)에서 문맥상 알맞은 낱말을 골라 쓰시오.

➡ (A) _____ (B) _____ (C) _____

06 위 글의 밑줄 친 ⓐ의 우리말에 맞게 한 단어를 보충하여, 주어진 어휘를 알맞게 배열하시오.

their smartphones / are / on / are / their eyes / and / their heads / ,

➡ _____

_____

07 다음 빈칸 (A)와 (B)에 알맞은 단어를 넣어 질문에 답하시오.

Q: Why may smombies fall and get hurt in the street?
A: Because they look at their (A)_____ while they are walking and may not see a (B)_____ in the street.

08 위 글의 내용과 일치하도록 다음 빈칸 (A)와 (B)에 알맞은 단어를 쓰시오.

One of the health problems smartphones can cause is (A)_____ _____ and another problem is (B)_____ _____.

09 위 글의 밑줄 친 ⓐ에서 흐름상 어색한 부분을 찾아 고치시오.

_____ ➡ _____

10 위 글의 밑줄 친 ⓑneck pain의 원인과 이 문제를 위한 조언을 우리말로 쓰시오.

➡ 원인: _____

_____

조언: (1) _____

(2) _____

01 다음 주어진 문제점과 그에 맞는 충고를 찾아서 〈보기〉와 같이 적절한 대화를 완성하시오.

Problem		Advice	
• headache	• toothache	• take some medicine	• get some rest
• cold	• sore throat	• go see a doctor	• drink a lot of water
• fever	• runny nose	• go to the dentist	• take a warm bath

┤ 보기 ├

A: You don't look well. What's wrong?

B: I have a headache.

A: That's too bad. Make sure you take some medicine.

B: OK, I will.

(1) _____

_____

(2) _____

_____

02 다음은 Big Ben의 사진이다. 그림을 참고하고 괄호 안에 주어진 어휘를 이용하여 문장을 완성하시오.

(the clock tower / call)

➡ People _____.

03 다음 내용을 바탕으로 건강한 생활을 위한 다짐을 하는 글을 쓰시오.

My problems are that	**I'll try to ....**
e.g. I don't exercise much	e.g. walk for 30 minutes every day

There are a few things I need (A)_____ to have a healthier life.

First, I don't exercise much. (B)_____, I will try to walk for 30 minutes every day.

Second, I think I eat too much fast food. I will eat fast food only (C)_____.

Third, I often eat at night. I will not eat (D)_____ 10 o'clock.

I will try (E)_____ to keep these promises.

단원별 모의고사

01 다음 단어에 대한 영어 설명이 <u>어색한</u> 것은?

① zombie: in stories and movies, a dead body that moves by magic

② blink: to open and close your eyes very quickly

③ prevent: to try to allow something to happen

④ simple: not difficult or complicated

⑤ traffic light: a set of colored lights at the side of the road that show when cars are allowed to move

02 다음 짝지어진 단어의 관계가 같도록 빈칸에 알맞은 말을 쓰시오.

> well : healthy = suffering: _____

03 다음 영영풀이에 해당하는 단어는?

> able to learn and understand things quickly

① intelligent   ② various

③ careful   ④ dry

⑤ stupid

04 다음 대화의 빈칸에 공통으로 들어갈 말은?

> W: You look sick. What's wrong, Inho?
>
> B: I _____ sore throat. I _____ fever, too.
>
> W: I think you _____ cold. Take this medicine and make sure you take a good rest.
>
> B: OK. Thank you.

① catch   ② take a   ③ make

④ turn a   ⑤ have a

05 다음 대화의 순서가 바르게 배열된 것은?

> (A) I fell and hurt my foot while I was playing soccer.
>
> (B) Yes, but it hurts a lot.
>
> (C) Can you walk?
>
> (D) What's wrong with your leg, Sam?

① (A) – (C) – (B) – (D)

② (B) – (C) – (D) – (A)

③ (C) – (D) – (A) – (B)

④ (D) – (A) – (C) – (B)

⑤ (D) – (B) – (A) – (C)

06 다음 중 짝지어진 대화가 <u>어색한</u> 것은?

① A: What's wrong, Peter?

    B: I don't know, Ms. Kim, but my back hurts a lot.

② A: What's the matter with you, Jenny? You don't look well.

    B: I won first prize in the singing contest.

③ A: What's wrong with your legs, Andy?

    B: I fell and hurt them while I was playing soccer.

④ A: I have a runny nose. I have a fever, too.

    B: Take this medicine and make sure you take a good rest.

⑤ A: You don't look well. What's wrong?

    B: I couldn't sleep well last night. I'm so tired.

07 다음 대화의 빈칸에 들어갈 말로 어색한 것은?

> A: What's the matter, Inho?
> B: _____

① I have a headache.
② I have a fever.
③ I have a stomachache.
④ I hurt my back.
⑤ Make sure you take some medicine.

[08~09] 다음 대화를 읽고 물음에 답하시오.

> W: What's wrong, Peter?
> B: I don't know, Ms. Kim, but my back hurts a lot.
> W: Put a heating pad on ⓐit.
> B: OK, I will.
> W: And _____(A)_____ .

08 밑줄 친 ⓐit이 가리키는 것을 Ms. Kim의 입장에서 영어로 쓰시오.

➡ _____

09 위 대화의 빈칸 (A)에 들어갈 말로 어색한 것은?

① don't remember to do some stretching exercises
② make sure you do some stretching exercises
③ remember to do some stretching exercises
④ don't forget to do some stretching exercises
⑤ you had better do some stretching exercises

10 다음 대화의 빈칸 (A)에 들어갈 당부의 표현으로 가장 어색한 것은?

> A: You don't look well. What's wrong?
> B: I have a runny nose.
> A: That's too bad. Make sure ____(A)____ .
> B: OK, I will.

① you go see a doctor
② you take some medicine
③ you get some rest
④ you go to the dentist
⑤ you take a warm bath

[11~12] 다음 대화를 읽고 물음에 답하시오.

> W: What's wrong, Andy?
> B: Hello, Ms. Kim. My right thumb hurts.
> W: Hmm. Do you use your smartphone a lot?
> B: Yes, I text a lot. Why?
> W: I think you have texting thumb.
> B: Texting thumb? What's texting thumb?
> W: It's pain in your thumb. You can get (A)it from texting too much.
> B: Oh, I didn't know that.
> W: Why don't you do some finger stretching exercises?
> B: OK, I will.
> W: And make sure you don't text too much.

11 Andy가 Ms. Kim을 만난 이유로 알맞은 것은?

① Because he texted a lot.
② Because his right thumb hurt.
③ Because he lost his smartphone.
④ To ask her what exercises to do.
⑤ To make sure he would not text too much.

12 위 대화의 밑줄 친 (A)it이 가리키는 것을 영어로 쓰시오.

➡ _____

13 괄호 안에 주어진 어휘를 이용하여 우리말을 영작하시오.

(1) Cameron은 Gillian이 가장 좋아하는 감독이다. (the director, best)

➡ _____

(2) 우리는 Jason이 우리에게 해준 이야기를 좋아했다. (the story, tell, 7단어)

➡ _____

(3) 그의 사업은 그를 백만장자로 만들었다. (business, a millionaire)

➡ _____

(4) 우리는 Bali를 신들의 섬이라고 부른다. (the island of gods)

➡ _____

14 다음 빈칸에 공통으로 들어갈 단어는?

| • Let's _____ the world a better place. |
| • I will _____ him do his homework. |

① call   ② make

③ elect   ④ consider

⑤ name

15 두 문장을 관계대명사를 사용하여 한 문장으로 썼을 때 빈칸의 문장을 쓰시오.

(1) • Mr. Lee is the teacher.

• _____

➡ Mr. Lee is the teacher whom every student respects.

(2) • There are various things.

• _____

➡ There are various things that you can do to prevent this.

16 다음 중 어법상 바르지 않은 것은?

① His music has made him a citizen of the world.

② They elected Jane club leader.

③ They considered their son to be a genius.

④ She named him after Harry Porter.

⑤ We want to call this cup as Cookie Eater.

17 어법상 어색한 것을 바르게 고쳐 문장을 다시 쓰시오.

(1) He is a gentleman which I built a good trust on.

➡ _____

_____

(2) These are the pants who I bought yesterday.

➡ _____

(3) She doesn't consider an artist him.

➡ _____

(4) This is the issue about that we need to express our opinion.

➡ _____

_____

(5) Ella received some flowers that her boy friend had sent them to her.

➡ _____

_____

(6) They call it as 'Non La'.

➡ _____

[18~20] 다음 글을 읽고 물음에 답하시오.

Do you have dry eyes or text neck?

Smartphones can cause various health problems. One example is dry eyes. When you look at your smartphone, you do not blink often. Then your eyes will feel (A)[dry / drily].

Another problem you can have (B)[is / are] neck pain. When you look down at your smartphone, the stress on your neck increases. Too much use of your smartphone, for example, too much texting, can cause neck pain. ⓐWe call this text neck.

Here are some tips for ⓑthese problems. For dry eyes, try to blink often. For text neck, move your smartphone up to your eye level. You can also do some neck (C)[stretching / stretched] exercises.

18 위 글의 괄호 (A)~(C)에서 어법상 알맞은 낱말을 골라 쓰시오.

➡ (A) _____ (B) _____ (C) _____

19 위 글의 밑줄 친 ⓐ와 문장의 형식이 다른 것을 모두 고르시오.

① I painted the door green.
② She sent me a long letter.
③ He found this book easily.
④ Each girl kept her love a secret.
⑤ I gave her the book.

20 위 글의 밑줄 친 ⓑthese problems에 해당하지 않는 것을 고르시오.

① Your eyes will feel dry.
② You often blink.
③ You can have neck pain.
④ The stress on your neck increases.
⑤ Too much texting can cause text neck.

[21~22] 다음 글을 읽고 물음에 답하시오.

How do you feel when you don't have your smartphone with you?

Do you feel nervous when your smartphone is not around? Do you feel sad when you check your smartphone and there is no text message?

If your answers are "yes," you may have smartphone addiction. ⓐThere are various things you can do to prevent this. For example, turn off your smartphone during meals or meetings. You can talk to people instead of texting them.

21 위 글의 밑줄 친 ⓐ에서 things와 you 사이에 생략된 단어를 모두 고르시오.

① which   ② who
③ what   ④ that
⑤ whom

22 위 글의 내용과 일치하지 않는 것은?

① 스마트폰이 주위에 없을 때 초조한 기분이 들면 스마트폰 중독일지도 모른다.
② 스마트폰을 확인했을 때 아무런 문자 메시지가 없을 경우 슬픈 기분이 들면 스마트폰 중독일지도 모른다.
③ 스마트폰 중독을 예방하기 위해 할 수 있는 일은 별로 없다.
④ 스마트폰 중독을 예방하기 위해 식사나 회의 중에는 스마트폰을 꺼야 한다.
⑤ 스마트폰 중독을 예방하기 위해 문자를 보내는 대신에 사람들과 이야기를 할 수 있다.

INSIGHT
on the textbook

교과서 파헤치기

※ 다음 영어를 우리말로 쓰시오.

01 round	_____	22 anyone	_____
02 discount	_____	23 explain	_____
03 afraid	_____	24 combination	_____
04 purple	_____	25 upgrade	_____
05 expensive	_____	26 recycling	_____
06 condition	_____	27 upcycle	_____
07 used	_____	28 hold	_____
08 almost	_____	29 trash	_____
09 large	_____	30 clothes	_____
10 price	_____	31 through	_____
11 throw	_____	32 creative	_____
12 bucket	_____	33 sewing	_____
13 strap	_____	34 decorate	_____
14 instrument	_____	35 get a discount	_____
15 rubber band	_____	36 take ~(돈) off	_____
16 upcycling	_____	37 throw away	_____
17 knife	_____	38 let me think	_____
18 environment	_____	39 be good for	_____
19 each	_____	40 be about	_____
20 understand	_____	41 hear from	_____
21 meaning	_____	42 for example	_____
		43 cut off	_____

단어 Test

※ 다음 우리말을 영어로 쓰시오.

01 안경

02 가방

03 흥미로운

04 음악의

05 청바지

06 행사

07 ~처럼, ~와 같이

08 물건

09 양로원

10 (도구장비) 세트

11 바느질하다

12 아래 부분, 바닥

13 어깨

14 마지막으로

15 ~를 통해

16 조합, 결합

17 가죽 끈

18 이해하다

19 양동이

20 쓰레기

21 할인

22 비싼

23 던지다

24 환경

25 장식하다

26 재활용

27 악기

28 의미

29 칼

30 거의

31 중고의

32 가격

33 설명하다

34 개최하다, 열다

35 ~에 의해 만들어지다

36 ~을 찾다

37 ~처럼 들리다

38 ~을 자르다

39 ~에 좋다

40 예를 들어

41 버리다

42 할인을 받다

43 ~에 관해 말하다

※ 다음 영영풀이에 알맞은 단어를 <보기>에서 골라 쓴 후, 우리말 뜻을 쓰시오.

1 _____ : a reduction in the usual price of something: _____

2 _____ : the things that people wear, such as shirts, coats, trousers, and dresses: _____

3 _____ : particular idea that a word, expression, or sign represents: _____

4 _____ : the air, water, and land on Earth, which is affected by man's activities: _____

5 _____ : two or more different things that exist together or put together: _____

6 _____ : giving a lot of attention to something because you want to find out more about it: _____

7 _____ : an object used for producing music: _____

8 _____ : to tell someone about something in a way that is clear or easy to understand: _____

9 _____ : involving the use of imagination to produce new ideas or things: _____

10 _____ : to make something look more attractive by putting something pretty on it: _____

11 _____ : a bag for carrying things that has two shoulder straps and is carried on the back: _____

12 _____ : things that you throw away because you no longer want or need them: _____

13 _____ : shaped like a circle or a ball: _____

14 _____ : an open container with a handle that is used especially to hold and carry water and other liquids: _____

15 _____ : having the color of blue and red mixed together: _____

16 _____ : the process of treating things that have already been used so that they can be used again: _____

보기			
bucket	combination	trash	creative
discount	recycling	environment	meaning
backpack	clothes	round	decorate
explain	instrument	purple	interested

※ 다음 우리말과 일치하도록 빈칸에 알맞은 것을 골라 쓰시오.

1 _____ Talk _____ Upcycling
　　A. about　　　　　B. let's

2 Hi, _____ _____ .
　　A. members　　　　B. club

3 _____ you know, this _____ Environment Day is _____ upcycling.
　　A. about　　　B. year's　　　C. as

4 Before we talk about _____ group's event idea for that day, I want you _____ _____ the _____ of "upcycling."
　　A. to　　B. meaning　　C. each　　D. understand

5 _____ anyone _____ upcycling?
　　A. explain　　　B. can

6 Yes. The word "_____" is a _____ of "upgrade" and "_____."
　　A. combination　　B. recycling　　C. upcycling

7 _____ recycling, upcycling is _____ for the _____ .
　　A. good　　　B. environment　　C. like

8 _____ you upcycle, you make new and _____ things _____ _____ things.
　　A. old　　B. when　　C. from　　D. better

9 Good. Now, _____ _____ about _____ group's idea for the event.
　　A. talk　　B. each　　C. let's

10 _____ start _____ Pei's group.
　　A. with　　　B. let's

11 _____ group wants _____ _____ a trashion show.
　　A. hold　　B. to　　C. my

12 "Trashion" is a _____ of "_____" and "_____."
　　A. fashion　　B. combination　　C. trash

13 We'll use _____ to make _____ .
　　A. clothes　　B. trash

14 We want _____ students to become _____ in upcycling _____ the show.
　　A. interested　　B. through　　C. other

15 A trashion show _____ _____ fun!
　　A. like　　　B. sounds

16 What _____ your _____ , Eric?
　　A. group　　　B. about

17 My group is _____ to _____ musical _____ from old things.
　　A. make　　B. going　　C. instruments

1 업사이클링에 대해 이야기해 봅시다.

2 동아리 회원 여러분, 안녕하세요.

3 여러분도 알다시피 올해의 환경의 날은 업사이클링에 관한 것입니다.

4 각 그룹이 그날에 할 행사 아이디어를 이야기하기 전에 여러분이 '업사이클링'의 의미를 이해하기를 바랍니다.

5 누가 업사이클링의 뜻을 설명해 줄 수 있나요?

6 네. '업사이클링'이란 단어는 "upgrade"와 "recycling"이 결합한 것입니다.

7 재활용과 마찬가지로 업사이클링도 환경에 좋아요.

8 업사이클링을 하면, 여러분은 오래된 것들로 새롭고 더 좋은 것을 만들어요.

9 좋아요. 이제 각 그룹의 행사 아이디어에 대해 이야기해 봅시다.

10 Pei의 그룹부터 시작하죠.

11 저희 그룹은 트래션 쇼를 하고 싶습니다.

12 "트래션(Trashion)"은 "trash"와 "fashion"이 결합한 말입니다.

13 저희는 옷을 만들기 위해 쓰레기를 이용할 것입니다.

14 저희는 이 쇼를 통해서 다른 학생들이 업사이클링에 관심을 갖게 되기를 바랍니다.

15 트래션 쇼라니 멋지겠구나!

16 너희 그룹은 어떠니, Eric?

17 저희 그룹은 낡은 물건으로 악기를 만들려고 합니다.

18 We'll _____ drums _____ old plastic _____ .
A. buckets   B. from   C. make

19 We'll _____ make a guitar _____ old boxes and _____ bands.
A. from   B. also   C. rubber

20 We _____ to play _____ instruments _____ a mini-concert.
A. the   B. plan   C. in

21 Thank you, Eric. Now, _____ _____ _____ Sumi's group.
A. hear   B. let's   C. from

22 My group _____ make bags _____ old _____ .
A. clothes   B. from   C. will

23 _____ _____ , we'll _____ blue jeans.
A. use   B. example   C. for

24 _____ _____ this bag.
A. at   B. look

25 This was _____ _____ Hajun, one _____ our group members.
A. of   B. made   C. by

26 _____ _____ nice?
A. it   B. isn't

27 We'll make _____ bags and _____ them _____ Environment Day.
A. sell   B. on   C. more

28 We're _____ to give all the money _____ a _____ home.
A. nursing   B. going   C. to

29 _____ a _____ idea.
A. great   B. that's

30 _____ ideas are _____ so _____ .
A. creative   B. your   C. all

31 I _____ everyone _____ _____ hard for Environment Day.
A. work   B. to   C. want

32 _____ _____ the legs _____ the blue jeans.
A. of   B. off   C. cut

33 _____ the bottom _____ .
A. together   B. sew

34 _____ shoulder _____ from one _____ the legs.
A. of   B. straps   C. make

35 _____ the _____ to the _____ of the jeans.
A. top   B. sew   C. straps

36 _____ the bag _____ pins _____ buttons.
A. and   B. decorate   C. with

18 낡은 플라스틱 양동이로 드럼을 만들 겁니다.

19 또한 저희는 낡은 상자와 고무 줄로 기타를 만들 겁니다.

20 저희는 소규모 음악회를 열어 그 악기들로 연주할 계획입니다.

21 고맙다, Eric. 그럼 이제 수미의 그룹 의견을 들어 보자.

22 저희 그룹은 낡은 옷으로 가방을 만들 거예요.

23 예를 들어 청바지를 이용할 거예요.

24 이 가방을 보세요.

25 이것은 저희 모둠원 중 한 명인 하준이가 만들었어요.

26 멋지지 않나요?

27 우리는 가방을 더 많이 만들어서 환경의 날에 팔 거예요.

28 번 돈을 모두 양로원에 줄 예정이에요.

29 훌륭한 생각이구나.

30 너희들의 발상은 모두 아주 창의적이구나.

31 너희들 모두 환경의 날을 위해 열심히 노력하길 바란다.

32 청바지의 다리 부분을 잘라낸다.

33 아래쪽을 붙여서 바느질한다.

34 다리 한 짝으로 어깨끈을 만든다.

35 청바지의 윗부분에 어깨끈을 바느질한다.

36 핀이나 단추로 가방을 장식한다.

※ 다음 우리말과 일치하도록 빈칸에 알맞은 말을 쓰시오.

1 _____ Talk _____ Upcycling

2 Hello, _____ _____.

3 _____ _____ _____, this year's Environment Day is _____ _____.

4 _____ we _____ _____ each group's event idea for that day, I want you _____ _____ the meaning of "_____."

5 Can anyone _____ _____?

6 Yes. The word "_____" is a _____ of "upgrade" and "recycling."

7 _____ recycling, upcycling _____ _____ _____ the environment.

8 _____ you _____, you make new and better things _____ _____ _____.

9 Good. Now, _____ _____ _____ each group's idea for the event.

10 _____ _____ _____ with Pei's group.

11 My group wants to _____ _____ trashion _____.

12 "Trashion" is _____ _____ _____ "trash" and "fashion."

13 We'll use trash _____ _____ _____.

14 We want other students to _____ _____ _____ upcycling _____ the show.

15 A trashion show _____ _____ _____!

16 _____ _____ your group, Eric?

17 My group _____ _____ _____ make musical _____ from old things.

1 업사이클링에 대해 이야기해 봅시다

2 동아리 회원 여러분, 안녕하세요.

3 여러분도 알다시피 올해의 환경의 날은 업사이클링에 관한 것입니다.

4 각 그룹이 그날에 할 행사 아이디어를 이야기하기 전에 여러분이 '업사이클링'의 의미를 이해하기를 바랍니다.

5 누가 업사이클링의 뜻을 설명해 줄 수 있나요?

6 네. '업사이클링'이란 단어는 "upgrade"와 "recycling"이 결합한 것입니다.

7 재활용과 마찬가지로 업사이클링도 환경에 좋아요.

8 업사이클링을 하면, 여러분은 오래된 것들로 새롭고 더 좋은 것을 만들어요.

9 좋아요. 이제 각 그룹의 행사 아이디어에 대해 이야기해 봅시다.

10 Pei의 그룹부터 시작하죠.

11 저희 그룹은 트래션 쇼를 하고 싶습니다.

12 "트래션(Trashion)"은 "trash"와 "fashion"이 결합한 말입니다.

13 저희는 옷을 만들기 위해 쓰레기를 이용할 것입니다.

14 저희는 이 쇼를 통해서 다른 학생들이 업사이클링에 관심을 갖게 되기를 바랍니다.

15 트래션 쇼라니 멋지겠구나!

16 너희 그룹은 어떠니, Eric?

17 저희 그룹은 낡은 물건으로 악기를 만들려고 합니다.

18 We'll make drums _____ old plastic _____.

19 We'll _____ make a guitar _____ old boxes and _____ _____.

20 We _____ _____ _____ the _____ in a mini-concert.

21 Thank you, Eric. Now, _____ _____ _____ Sumi's group.

22 My group will _____ bags _____ _____ _____.

23 _____ _____, we'll use blue _____.

24 _____ _____ this bag.

25 This _____ _____ _____ Hajun, _____ _____ our group members.

26 _____ _____ nice?

27 We'll make _____ bags and sell them _____ _____ _____.

28 We're going to give _____ _____ _____ to a _____ _____.

29 That's a _____ _____.

30 _____ ideas are all so _____.

31 I _____ everyone _____ _____ _____ for Environment Day.

32 _____ _____ the legs of the _____ _____.

33 _____ the bottom _____.

34 Make _____ _____ from _____ of the legs.

35 _____ the straps _____ the top of the jeans.

36 _____ the bag _____ pins and buttons.

---

18 낡은 플라스틱 양동이로 드럼을 만들 겁니다.

19 또한 저희는 낡은 상자와 고무 줄로 기타를 만들 겁니다.

20 저희는 소규모 음악회를 열어 그 악기들로 연주할 계획입니다.

21 고맙다, Eric. 그럼 이제 수미의 그룹 의견을 들어 보자.

22 저희 그룹은 낡은 옷으로 가방을 만들 거예요.

23 예를 들어 청바지를 이용할 거 예요.

24 이 가방을 보세요.

25 이것은 저희 모둠원 중 한 명인 하준이가 만들었어요.

26 멋지지 않나요?

27 우리는 가방을 더 많이 만들어 서 환경의 날에 팔 거예요.

28 번 돈을 모두 양로원에 줄 예정 이에요.

29 훌륭한 생각이구나.

30 너희들의 발상은 모두 아주 창 의적이구나.

31 너희들 모두 환경의 날을 위해 열심히 노력하길 바란다.

32 청바지의 다리 부분을 잘라낸다.

33 아래쪽을 붙여서 바느질한다.

34 다리 한 짝으로 어깨끈을 만든다.

35 청바지의 윗부분에 어깨끈을 바 느질한다.

36 핀이나 단추로 가방을 장식한다.

※ 다음 문장을 우리말로 쓰시오.

1 ▶ Let's Talk about Upcycling

➡ _____

2 ▶ Hello, club members.

➡ _____

3 ▶ As you know, this year's Environment Day is about upcycling.

➡ _____

4 ▶ Before we talk about each group's event idea for that day, I want you to understand the meaning of "upcycling."

➡ _____

5 ▶ Can anyone explain upcycling?

➡ _____

6 ▶ Yes. The word "upcycling" is a combination of "upgrade" and "recycling."

➡ _____

7 ▶ Like recycling, upcycling is good for the environment.

➡ _____

8 ▶ When you upcycle, you make new and better things from old things.

➡ _____

9 ▶ Good. Now, let's talk about each group's idea for the event.

➡ _____

10 ▶ Let's start with Pei's group.

➡ _____

11 ▶ My group wants to hold a trashion show.

➡ _____

12 ▶ "Trashion" is a combination of "trash" and "fashion."

➡ _____

13 ▶ We'll use trash to make clothes.

➡ _____

14 ▶ We want other students to become interested in upcycling through the show.

➡ _____

15 ▶ A trashion show sounds like fun!

➡ _____

16 ▶ What about your group, Eric?

➡ _____

17 ▶ My group is going to make musical instruments from old things.

➡ _____

18 We'll make drums from old plastic buckets.
➡ _____

19 We'll also make a guitar from old boxes and rubber bands.
➡ _____

20 We plan to play the instruments in a mini-concert.
➡ _____

21 Thank you, Eric. Now, let's hear from Sumi's group.
➡ _____

22 My group will make bags from old clothes.
➡ _____

23 For example, we'll use blue jeans.
➡ _____

24 Look at this bag.
➡ _____

25 This was made by Hajun, one of our group members.
➡ _____

26 Isn't it nice?
➡ _____

27 We'll make more bags and sell them on Environment Day.
➡ _____

28 We're going to give all the money to a nursing home.
➡ _____

29 That's a great idea.
➡ _____

30 Your ideas are all so creative.
➡ _____

31 I want everyone to work hard for Environment Day.
➡ _____

32 Cut off the legs of the blue jeans.
➡ _____

33 Sew the bottom together.
➡ _____

34 Make shoulder straps from one of the legs.
➡ _____

35 Sew the straps to the top of the jeans.
➡ _____

36 Decorate the bag with pins and buttons.
➡ _____

※ 다음 괄호 안의 단어들을 우리말에 맞도록 바르게 배열하시오.

1 (about / Talk / Upcycling / Let's)
➡ _____

2 (members. / hello, / club)
➡ _____

3 (know, / you / as / Environment / is / this / Day / year's / upcycling. / about)
➡ _____

4 (talk / before / about / we / idea / each / event / group's / day, / that / for / I / to / you / want / "upcycling."/ the / understand / of / meaning)
➡ _____

5 (upcycling? / explain / anyone / can)
➡ _____

6 (yes. / the / "upcycling" / is / word / a / "recycling."/ and / combination / of / and / "upgrade")
➡ _____

7 (recycling, / is / like / upcycling / the / good / environment. / for)
➡ _____

8 (you / upcycle, / when / you / new / make / things / and / old / better / from / things.)
➡ _____

9 (good. / let's / talk / now, / about / each / idea / the / group's / event. / for)
➡ _____

10 (start / group. / let's / Pei's / with)
➡ _____

11 (wants / my / hold / trashion / a / group / show. / to)
➡ _____

12 (is / "trash" / a / "fashion." / combination / and / "trashion" / of)
➡ _____

13 (use / make / we'll / clothes. / to / trash)
➡ _____

14 (other / we / to / want / students / in / become / through / show. / the / interested / upcycling)
➡ _____

15 (show / like / a / trashion / fun! / sounds)
➡ _____

16 (about / Eric? / what / group / your)
➡ _____

17 (group / to / my / is / musical / going / instruments / from / things. / make / old)
➡ _____

1 업사이클링에 대해 이야기해 봅시다

2 동아리 회원 여러분, 안녕하세요.

3 여러분도 알다시피 올해의 환경의 날은 업사이클링에 관한 것입니다.

4 각 그룹이 그날에 할 행사 아이디어를 이야기하기 전에 여러분이 '업사이클링'의 의미를 이해하기를 바랍니다.

5 누가 업사이클링의 뜻을 설명해 줄 수 있나요?

6 네. '업사이클링'이란 단어는 "upgrade"와 "recycling"이 결합한 것입니다.

7 재활용과 마찬가지로 업사이클링도 환경에 좋아요.

8 업사이클링을 하면, 여러분은 오래된 것들로 새롭고 더 좋은 것을 만들어요.

9 좋아요. 이제 각 그룹의 행사 아이디어에 대해 이야기해 봅시다.

10 Pei의 그룹부터 시작하죠.

11 저희 그룹은 트래션 쇼를 하고 싶습니다.

12 "트래션(Trashion)"은 "trash"와 "fashion"이 결합한 말입니다.

13 저희는 옷을 만들기 위해 쓰레기를 이용할 것입니다.

14 저희는 이 쇼를 통해서 다른 학생들이 업사이클링에 관심을 갖게 되기를 바랍니다.

15 트래션 쇼라니 멋지겠구나!

16 너희 그룹은 어떠니, Eric?

17 저희 그룹은 낡은 물건으로 악기를 만들려고 합니다.

18 (drums / we'll / from / plastic / make / buckets. / old)

➡ _____

19 (also / a / we'll / make / boxes / guitar / from / rubber / old / bands. / and)

➡ _____

20 (instruments / plan / the / we / to / play / mini-concert. / in / a)

➡ _____

21 (you, / Eric. / thank // now, / group. / from / let's / hear / Sumi's)

➡ _____

22 (will / my / group / bags / clothes. / make / from / old)

➡ _____

23 (example, / for / use / jeans. / we'll / blue)

➡ _____

24 (this / at / bag. / look)

➡ _____

25 (was / Hajun, / this / made / by / one / our / of / members. / group)

➡ _____

26 (nice? / it / isn't)

➡ _____

27 (we'll / bags / more / make / and / them / Day. / sell / Environment / on)

➡ _____

28 (going / we're / give / to / money / all / to / the / home. / a / nursing)

➡ _____

29 (a / idea. / that's / great)

➡ _____

30 (ideas / all / creative. / so / your / are)

➡ _____

31 (everyone / work / I / to / want / hard / Day. / for / Environment)

➡ _____

32 (the / cut / off / legs / jeans. / the / blue / of)

➡ _____

33 (the / bottom / together. / sew)

➡ _____

34 (shoulder / from / make / straps / the / of / one / legs.)

➡ _____

35 (the / sew / to / straps / the / jeans. / the / top / of)

➡ _____

36 (the / decorate / bag / and / bottons. / pins / with)

➡ _____

18 낡은 플라스틱 양동이로 드럼을 만들 겁니다.

19 또한 저희는 낡은 상자와 고무 줄로 기타를 만들 겁니다.

20 저희는 소규모 음악회를 열어 그 악기들로 연주할 계획입니다.

21 고맙다. Eric. 그럼 이제 수미의 그룹 의견을 들어 보자.

22 저희 그룹은 낡은 옷으로 가방을 만들 거예요.

23 예를 들어 청바지를 이용할 거예요.

24 이 가방을 보세요.

25 이것은 저희 모둠원 중 한 명인 하준이가 만들었어요.

26 멋지지 않나요?

27 우리는 가방을 더 많이 만들어서 환경의 날에 팔 거예요.

28 번 돈을 모두 양로원에 줄 예정이에요.

29 훌륭한 생각이구나.

30 너희들의 발상은 모두 아주 창의적이구나.

31 너희들 모두 환경의 날을 위해 열심히 노력하길 바란다.

32 청바지의 다리 부분을 잘라낸다.

33 아래쪽을 붙여서 바느질한다.

34 다리 한 짝으로 어깨끈을 만든다.

35 청바지의 윗부분에 어깨끈을 바느질한다.

36 핀이나 단추로 가방을 장식한다.

※ 다음 우리말을 영어로 쓰시오.

1 업사이클링에 대해 이야기해 봅시다

➡ _____

2 동아리 회원 여러분, 안녕하세요.

➡ _____

3 여러분도 알다시피 올해의 환경의 날은 업사이클링에 관한 것입니다.

➡ _____

4 각 그룹이 그날에 할 행사 아이디어를 이야기하기 전에 여러분이 '업사이클링'의 의미를 이해하기를 바랍니다.

➡ _____

➡ _____

5 누가 업사이클링의 뜻을 설명해 줄 수 있나요?

➡ _____

6 네. '업사이클링'이란 단어는 "upgrade"와 "recycling"이 결합한 것입니다.

➡ _____

7 재활용과 마찬가지로 업사이클링도 환경에 좋아요.

➡ _____

8 업사이클링을 하면, 여러분은 오래된 것들로 새롭고 더 좋은 것을 만들어요.

➡ _____

9 좋아요. 이제 각 그룹의 행사 아이디어에 대해 이야기해 봅시다.

➡ _____

10 Pei의 그룹부터 시작하죠.

➡ _____

11 저희 그룹은 트래션 쇼를 하고 싶습니다.

➡ _____

12 "트래션(Trashion)"은 "trash"와 "fashion"이 결합한 말입니다.

➡ _____

13 저희는 옷을 만들기 위해 쓰레기를 이용할 것입니다.

➡ _____

14 저희는 이 쇼를 통해서 다른 학생들이 업사이클링에 관심을 갖게 되기를 바랍니다.

➡ _____

15 트래션 쇼라니 멋지겠구나!

➡ _____

16 너희 그룹은 어떠니, Eric?

➡ _____

17 저희 그룹은 낡은 물건으로 악기를 만들려고 합니다.

➡ _____

18 낡은 플라스틱 양동이로 드럼을 만들 겁니다.
➡ _____

19 또한 저희는 낡은 상자와 고무줄로 기타를 만들 겁니다.
➡ _____

20 저희는 소규모 음악회를 열어 그 악기들로 연주할 계획입니다.
➡ _____

21 고맙다, Eric. 그럼 이제 수미의 그룹 의견을 들어 보자.
➡ _____

22 저희 그룹은 낡은 옷으로 가방을 만들 거예요.
➡ _____

23 예를 들어 청바지를 이용할 거예요.
➡ _____

24 이 가방을 보세요.
➡ _____

25 이것은 저희 모둠원 중 한 명인 하준이가 만들었어요.
➡ _____

26 멋지지 않나요?
➡ _____

27 우리는 가방을 더 많이 만들어서 환경의 날에 팔 거예요.
➡ _____

28 번 돈을 모두 양로원에 줄 예정이에요.
➡ _____

29 훌륭한 생각이구나.
➡ _____

30 너희들의 발상은 모두 아주 창의적이구나.
➡ _____

31 너희들 모두 환경의 날을 위해 열심히 노력하길 바란다.
➡ _____

32 청바지의 다리 부분을 잘라낸다.
➡ _____

33 아래쪽을 붙여서 바느질한다.
➡ _____

34 다리 한 짝으로 어깨끈을 만든다.
➡ _____

35 청바지의 윗부분에 어깨끈을 바느질한다.
➡ _____

36 핀이나 단추로 가방을 장식한다.
➡ _____

※ 다음 우리말과 일치하도록 빈칸에 알맞은 말을 쓰시오.

Around the World

1. Kids, I want _____ _____ music _____ _____ you.

2. But we _____ have _____ musical instruments.

3. I _____ _____ you.

4. I _____ a good idea.

5. Oh, _____ you!

6. I _____ _____ musical instruments _____ trash.

7. The world _____ _____ _____.

8. We _____ _____ music.

9. This is the power of _____.

1. 얘들아, 너희에게 음악 수업을 해주고 싶구나.
2. 하지만 우리는 악기가 하나도 없어.
3. 내가 도와줄 수 있어.
4. 나에게 좋은 생각이 있어.
5. 오, 고맙습니다!
6. 나는 쓰레기로 악기를 만들 수 있어.
7. 세상은 우리에게 쓰레기를 보내줬어.
8. 우리는 음악으로 되돌려 준다.
9. 이것이 업사이클링의 힘이란다.

Think and Write

1. _____ _____ Idea: Blue Jeans Basket

2. You _____ : old blue _____, _____ kit, scissors, buttons and pins

3. Step: 1 _____ _____ a leg of the old blue jeans.

4. 2 Cut out a piece _____ make the _____ _____ the basket.

5. 3 _____ the bottom _____ the leg.

6. 4 _____ _____ buttons and pins.

1. 창의적인 업사이클링 아이디어: 청바지 바구니
2. 준비물: 낡은 청바지, 바느질 도구 세트, 가위, 단추와 장식 핀
3. 단계: 1 낡은 청바지의 다리를 자른다.
4. 2 바구니의 바닥을 만들기 위해 한 조각을 자른다.
5. 3 바닥을 다리 부분과 꿰맨다.
6. 4 단추와 핀으로 장식한다.

구석구석 지문 Test

※ 다음 우리말을 영어로 쓰시오.

Around the World

1. 얘들아, 너희에게 음악 수업을 해주고 싶구나.
➡ _____

2. 하지만 우리는 악기가 하나도 없어.
➡ _____

3. 내가 도와줄 수 있어.
➡ _____

4. 나에게 좋은 생각이 있어.
➡ _____

5. 오, 고맙습니다!
➡ _____

6. 나는 쓰레기로 악기를 만들 수 있어.
➡ _____

7. 세상은 우리에게 쓰레기를 보내줬어.
➡ _____

8. 우리는 음악으로 되돌려 준다.
➡ _____

9. 이것이 업사이클링의 힘이란다.
➡ _____

Think and Write

1. 창의적인 업사이클링 아이디어: 청바지 바구니
➡ _____

2. 준비물: 낡은 청바지, 바느질 도구 세트, 가위, 단추와 장식 핀
➡ _____

3. 단계: 1. 낡은 청바지의 다리를 자른다.
➡ _____

4. 2. 바구니의 바닥을 만들기 위해 한 조각을 자른다.
➡ _____

5. 3. 바닥을 다리 부분과 꿰맨다.
➡ _____

6. 4. 단추와 핀으로 장식한다.
➡ _____

※ 다음 영어를 우리말로 쓰시오.

01	snake	
02	navy	
03	photograph	
04	restroom	
05	gorilla	
06	lucky	
07	succeed	
08	announcement	
09	temple	
10	while	
11	usually	
12	worm	
13	solve	
14	protection	
15	level	
16	parrot	
17	cotton	
18	talent	
19	slowly	
20	record	
21	octopus	

22	shell	
23	male	
24	imagine	
25	crow	
26	pattern	
27	surprise	
28	once	
29	experiment	
30	tail	
31	also	
32	wear	
33	store	
34	not A but B	
35	be good at	
36	pull out	
37	look like	
38	dance to music	
39	watch out for	
40	take a rest	
41	what else	
42	find out	
43	just as	

※ 다음 우리말을 영어로 쓰시오.

01 숨다, 감추다 _____

02 방법, 방식 _____

03 쌓다, 포개다 _____

04 우화, 동화 _____

05 치실질을 하다; 치실 _____

06 ~을 두고 가다, 떠나다 _____

07 휴대하다 _____

08 둥근 모양의 _____

09 몸짓, 신호, 표시 _____

10 도구, 수단 _____

11 병, 단지 _____

12 [물체가] (액체 면에) 뜨다 _____

13 줄무늬 _____

14 예, 예제 _____

15 또한 _____

16 코코넛 열매 _____

17 떨어뜨리다 _____

18 독특한 _____

19 실험, 시험 _____

20 보호 _____

21 성공하다 _____

22 무늬, 도안 _____

23 절, 사원 _____

24 천천히 _____

25 사진 _____

26 상상하다 _____

27 면 _____

28 대개, 보통 _____

29 남자의, 수컷의 _____

30 문어 _____

31 앵무새 _____

32 고릴라 _____

33 벌레 _____

34 발표, 소식 _____

35 ~ 이상(의) _____

36 알아내다 _____

37 ~의 위에 _____

38 휴식하다 _____

39 A가 아니고 B _____

40 ~을 찾다 _____

41 ~을 잘하다 _____

42 ~을 뽑다 _____

43 ~처럼 보이다, ~와 닮다 _____

※ 다음 영영풀이에 알맞은 단어를 <보기>에서 골라 쓴 후, 우리말 뜻을 쓰시오.

1 _____ : a story that teaches us something: _____

2 _____ : a large brown nut with a hairy shell: _____

3 _____ : to make someone have a feeling of surprise: _____

4 _____ : the hard outside part of a nut or egg: _____

5 _____ : the amount or degree of something: _____

6 _____ : a very dark blue color: _____

7 _____ : an ability to do something well: _____

8 _____ : a picture you take using a camera: _____

9 _____ : a type of cloth made from soft fibres from a particular plant: _____

10 _____ : a scientific test you do to learn about something, or to show if an idea is true: _____

11 _____ : to clean between your teeth with dental floss/special string that you use to clean between your teeth: _____

12 _____ : something important that someone tells people: _____

13 _____ : to put a lot of things on top of each other: _____

14 _____ : to write down information or store it on a computer: _____

15 _____ : a thing that you use for making or doing something: _____

16 _____ : a set of lines, shapes, or colours that are repeated regularly: _____

보기			
pattern	record	cotton	announcement
photograph	navy	surprise	level
tool	experiment	floss	coconut
fable	shell	pile	talent

※ 다음 우리말과 일치하도록 빈칸에 알맞은 말을 쓰시오.

해석

Listen and Talk A-1

B: Excuse me. I'm _____ _____ my scarf.

W: What does it _____ _____?

B: It's _____ _____ _____ scarf.

W: Can you _____ _____ _____ about it?

B: Well, it's _____.

W: OK. I'll _____ and _____.

B: 실례합니다. 저는 제 스카프를 찾고 있어요.
W: 어떻게 생겼는데요?
B: 그것은 긴 면 스카프예요.
W: 그것에 대해 더 말해 줄래요?
B: 음, 회색이에요.
W: 알겠어요. 가서 확인해 볼게요.

Listen and Talk A-2

W: _____ I _____ you?

B: Yes. I _____ my bag. I _____ I _____ it in the restroom.

W: OK. What _____ it _____ _____?

B: _____ small and _____.

W: _____ _____? _____ me _____ about it.

B: _____ me _____. Oh, it _____ two pockets _____.

W: 도와드릴까요?
B: 네. 저는 제 가방을 잃어버렸어요. 제 생각엔 화장실에 두고 온 것 같아요.
W: 알겠어요. 그것은 어떻게 생겼나요?
B: 작고 노란색이에요.
W: 또 다른 건요? 그것에 대해 더 말해 주세요.
B: 어디 보자. 오, 바깥쪽에 두 개의 주머니가 있어요.

Listen and Talk A-3

W: Do you _____ _____?

B: Yes. I _____ _____ _____.

W: What does it _____ _____?

B: _____ long and _____.

W: Can you _____ _____ _____?

B: Yes. It _____ _____ _____ _____ on it.

W: 도움이 필요하신가요?
B: 네. 저는 제 우산을 잃어버렸어요.
W: 그것은 어떻게 생겼나요?
B: 길고 남색이에요.
W: 더 말해 주시겠어요?
B: 네. 별무늬가 있어요.

Listen and Talk A-4

B: _____ _____ _____ help?

W: Yes. _____ _____ _____ my cat.

B: _____ does it _____ _____?

W: Well, she's not very big and she _____ _____ _____.

B: _____ _____ _____ me more? Is there _____ _____ about her?

W: She has a _____ _____.

B: 도움이 필요하신가요?
W: 네. 저는 고양이를 찾고 있어요.
B: 그것은 어떻게 생겼나요?
W: 음, 그렇게 크지는 않고 털이 검은색이에요.
B: 더 말해 주시겠어요? 특별한 점이 있나요?
W: 그것은 짧은 꼬리를 가지고 있어요.

Listen and Talk B

A: _____ _____ _____ you?

B: Yes. _____ _____ _____ my cat.

A: _____ does it look _____?

B: It's small and it _____ _____ _____.

A: _____ _____ _____ _____ more about it?

B: It has a _____ _____.

Listen and Talk B-2

A: _____ I _____ you?

B: Yes. I'm _____ _____ my _____.

A: _____ does it _____ _____?

B: _____ _____ and red.

A: Can you tell me _____ _____ it?

B: There _____ a card _____ it.

Listen and Talk C

M: May _____ _____ _____?

G: Yes. _____ _____ _____ my dog. _____ name is Prince.

M: _____ does he _____ like?

G: He's very small and has _____ _____ _____.

M: Can you _____ _____ _____?

G: Well, he has a _____ _____ _____.

M: I see. And _____ _____ thing. Where _____ you _____ him?

G: I _____ him _____ the main gate.

M: OK. I'll go and _____ _____ _____. Can you please _____ here?

G: Sure. Thanks _____ _____.

Talk and Play

A: What _____ Amy _____ _____?

B: She's tall and has _____ _____ _____.

A: _____ _____ _____ me more?

B: She's _____ short _____ pants.

A: I _____ her.

Review

G: Hi. I _____ I _____ my umbrella.

M: _____ _____ _____ _____ _____ _____?

G: It's a big _____ umbrella.

M: Can you _____ me _____?

G: It _____ a white flower _____ _____ it.

A: 도와드릴까요?
B: 네. 저는 제 고양이를 찾고 있어요.
A: 그것은 어떻게 생겼나요?
B: 그것은 작고 회색 털을 가지고 있어요.
A: 그것에 대해 더 말해 주실 수 있나요?
B: 그것은 긴 꼬리를 가지고 있어요.

A: 도와드릴까요?
B: 네. 저는 제 지갑을 찾고 있어요.
A: 그것은 어떻게 생겼나요?
B: 그것은 작고 빨간색이에요.
A: 그것에 대해 더 말해 주실 수 있나요?
B: 그것 안에는 카드가 있어요.

M: 도와드릴까요?
G: 네. 제 개를 찾고 있어요. 이름은 Prince 예요.
M: 그가 어떻게 생겼나요?
G: 매우 작고 짧은 흰 털을 가지고 있어요.
M: 더 얘기해 줄 수 있나요?
G: 음, 그는 무척 긴 꼬리를 가지고 있어요.
M: 알겠습니다. 그리고 한 가지 더요. 어디서 잃어버렸나요?
G: 정문 근처에서 잃어버렸어요.
M: 좋아요. 가서 안내 방송을 하겠습니다. 잠시 여기에서 기다려 주시겠어요?
G: 네. 정말 감사합니다.

A: Amy는 어떻게 생겼니?
B: 그녀는 키가 크고 긴 갈색 머리야.
A: 더 말해 주겠니?
B: 그녀는 짧은 남색 바지를 입고 있어.
A: 그녀를 찾았어.

G: 안녕하세요. 제 우산을 잃어버린 것 같아요.
M: 그것은 어떻게 생겼나요?
G: 그것은 큰 남색 우산이에요.
M: 더 말해 주시겠어요?
G: 흰색 꽃무늬가 있어요.

※ 다음 우리말에 맞도록 대화를 영어로 쓰시오.

Listen and Talk A-1

B: _____

W: _____

B: _____

W: _____

B: _____

W: _____

B: 실례합니다. 저는 제 스카프를 찾고 있어요.
W: 어떻게 생겼는데요?
B: 그것은 긴 면 스카프예요.
W: 그것에 대해 더 말해 줄래요?
B: 음, 회색이에요.
W: 알겠어요. 가서 확인해 볼게요.

Listen and Talk A-2

W: _____

B: _____

W: _____

B: _____

W: _____

B: _____

W: 도와드릴까요?
B: 네. 저는 제 가방을 잃어버렸어요. 제 생각엔 화장실에 두고 온 것 같아요.
W: 알겠어요. 그것은 어떻게 생겼나요?
B: 작고 노란색이에요.
W: 또 다른 건요? 그것에 대해 더 말해 주세요.
B: 어디 보자. 오, 바깥쪽에 두 개의 주머니가 있어요.

Listen and Talk A-3

W: _____

B: _____

W: _____

B: _____

W: _____

B: _____

W: 도움이 필요하신가요?
B: 네. 저는 제 우산을 잃어버렸어요.
W: 그것은 어떻게 생겼나요?
B: 길고 남색이에요.
W: 더 말해 주시겠어요?
B: 네. 별무늬가 있어요.

Listen and Talk A-4

B: _____

W: _____

B: _____

W: _____

B: _____

W: _____

B: 도움이 필요하신가요?
W: 네. 저는 고양이를 찾고 있어요.
B: 그것은 어떻게 생겼나요?
W: 음, 그렇게 크지는 않고 털이 검은색이에요.
B: 더 말해 주시겠어요? 특별한 점이 있나요?
W: 그것은 짧은 꼬리를 가지고 있어요.

Listen and Talk B

A: _____

B: _____

A: _____

B: _____

A: _____

B: _____

A: 도와드릴까요?
B: 네. 저는 제 고양이를 찾고 있어요.
A: 그것은 어떻게 생겼나요?
B: 그것은 작고 회색 털을 가지고 있어요.
A: 그것에 대해 더 말해 주실 수 있나요?
B: 그것은 긴 꼬리를 가지고 있어요.

Listen and Talk B-2

A: _____

B: _____

A: _____

B: _____

A: _____

B: _____

A: 도와드릴까요?
B: 네. 저는 제 지갑을 찾고 있어요.
A: 그것은 어떻게 생겼나요?
B: 그것은 작고 빨간색이에요.
A: 그것에 대해 더 말해 주실 수 있나요?
B: 그것 안에는 카드가 있어요.

Listen and Talk C

M: _____

G: _____

M: _____

G: _____

M: _____

G: _____

M: _____

G: _____

M: _____

G: _____

M: 도와드릴까요?
G: 네. 제 개를 찾고 있어요. 이름은 Prince 예요.
M: 그가 어떻게 생겼나요?
G: 매우 작고 짧은 흰 털을 가지고 있어요.
M: 더 얘기해 줄 수 있나요?
G: 음, 그는 무척 긴 꼬리를 가지고 있어요.
M: 알겠습니다. 그리고 한 가지 더요. 어디서 잃어버렸나요?
G: 정문 근처에서 잃어버렸어요.
M: 좋아요. 가서 안내 방송을 하겠습니다. 잠시 여기에서 기다려 주시겠어요?
G: 네. 정말 감사합니다.

Talk and Play

A: _____

B: _____

A: _____

B: _____

A: _____

A: Amy는 어떻게 생겼니?
B: 그녀는 키가 크고 긴 갈색 머리야.
A: 더 말해 주겠니?
B: 그녀는 짧은 남색 바지를 입고 있어.
A: 그녀를 찾았어.

Review

G: _____

M: _____

G: _____

M: _____

G: _____

G: 안녕하세요. 제 우산을 잃어버린 것 같아요.
M: 그것은 어떻게 생겼나요?
G: 그것은 큰 남색 우산이에요.
M: 더 말해 주시겠어요?
G: 흰색 꽃무늬가 있어요.

※ 다음 우리말과 일치하도록 빈칸에 알맞은 것을 골라 쓰시오.

1 Animals _____ Use _____

    A. Tools   B. That

2 People _____ _____ that _____ humans can use tools.

    A. thought   B. only   C. once

3 Now, scientists are _____ _____ that many animals can _____ use tools.

    A. out   B. also   C. finding

4 If you go to a Buddhist temple _____ Lop Buri, Thailand, _____ _____ _____ the Macaque monkeys.

    A. out   B. in   C. for   D. watch

5 They _____ come to you and _____ _____ your hair.

    A. out   B. may   C. pull

6 They use human hair _____ _____ their _____ .

    A. teeth   B. floss   C. to

7 If you are lucky, you may see _____ monkeys _____ _____ teaching _____ to their babies.

    A. flossing   B. are   C. female   D. that

8 _____ the babies are _____ , the female monkeys _____ their _____ very slowly.

    A. floss   B. teeth   C. watching   D. while

9 This _____ , the baby monkeys learn _____ _____ .

    A. floss   B. way   C. to

10 People _____ _____ _____ that octopuses are smart.

    A. think   B. don't   C. usually

11 _____ , octopuses are very smart, and they _____ also _____ tools.

    A. use   B. however   C. can

12 They _____ coconut _____ for _____ .

    A. protection   B. shells   C. use

---

1 도구를 사용하는 동물들

2 사람들은 한때 인간만이 도구를 사용할 수 있다고 생각했다.

3 이제 과학자들은 많은 동물들 역시 도구를 사용할 수 있다는 것을 밝혀내고 있다.

4 당신이 태국의 롭부리에 있는 절에 간다면, 마카크 원숭이들을 조심해야 한다.

5 그들이 당신에게 다가와 당신의 머리카락을 뽑을 수도 있다.

6 그들은 이빨을 치실질하기 위해서 사람의 머리카락을 사용한다.

7 만약 당신이 운이 좋으면, 당신은 새끼들에게 치실질하는 것을 가르치고 있는 암컷 원숭이들을 볼 수 있을 것이다.

8 새끼들이 지켜보고 있는 동안, 암컷 원숭이들은 아주 천천히 그들의 이빨을 치실질한다.

9 이런 방식으로, 새끼 원숭이들은 치실질을 배운다.

10 사람들은 대개 문어가 영리하다고 생각하지 않는다.

11 하지만, 문어는 매우 영리하고 또한 도구를 사용할 수 있다.

12 그들은 자신을 보호하기 위해 코코넛 껍데기를 사용한다.

13 When they _____ _____ a good _____ place, they _____ under coconut shells.

    A. hide   B. find   C. hiding   D. can't

14 Some octopuses even _____ coconut shells later _____.

    A. use   B. store   C. for

15 They _____ the coconut shells and _____ them to use _____.

    A. later   B. carry   C. pile

16 _____ _____!

    A. smart   B. how

17 In Aesop's fable *The Thirsty Crow*, a crow _____ stones _____ a jar _____ the level of water.

    A. to   B. drops   C. into   D. raise

18 You _____ _____ this is _____ a story, but it is not.

    A. just   B. think   C. may

19 Scientists who _____ _____ crows did an _____.

    A. experiment   B. studying   C. were

20 They _____ a jar _____ water in _____ of a crow.

    A. front   B. with   C. put

21 A _____ was _____ on _____ of the water.

    A. top   B. floating   C. worm

22 However, the _____ _____ was _____, so the crow _____ not eat the worm.

    A. low   B. level   C. could   D. water

23 The crow _____ the problem _____ in the fable.

    A. as   B. solved   C. just

24 It _____ stones _____ the jar.

    A. into   B. dropped

25 If you think this bird is _____, you are _____.

    A. wrong   B. special

26 Scientists did the same _____ other crows, and they all _____ the _____, too.

    A. same   B. with   C. experiment   D. did

---

13 그들이 숨을 만한 좋은 장소를 찾지 못했을 때, 그들은 코코넛 껍데기 아래로 숨는다.

14 어떤 문어들은 심지어 코코넛 껍데기를 나중에 쓰기 위해 모은다.

15 그들은 코코넛 껍데기를 쌓아두고 나중에 쓰기 위해서 가지고 다닌다.

16 얼마나 똑똑한가!

17 이솝 우화 '목마른 까마귀'에서 까마귀는 물 높이를 높이기 위해 항아리 안으로 돌을 떨어뜨린다.

18 당신은 이것이 그저 이야기라고 생각할 수 있지만, 그렇지 않다.

19 까마귀를 연구하던 과학자들이 실험을 했다.

20 그들은 까마귀 앞에 물이 든 항아리를 놓았다.

21 물 위에 벌레가 떠다니고 있었다.

22 하지만, 물 높이가 낮아서, 까마귀는 그 벌레를 먹을 수 없었다.

23 그 까마귀는 우화에서처럼 문제를 해결했다.

24 까마귀는 돌을 항아리 안으로 떨어뜨렸다.

25 만약 당신이 이 새가 특별하다고 생각한다면, 당신이 틀렸다.

26 과학자들은 다른 까마귀들에게도 똑같은 실험을 했고, 그들 모두가 똑같이 그렇게 했다.

※ 다음 우리말을 참고하여 빈칸에 알맞은 것을 고르시오.

1 Animals _____ Use _____

2 People _____ _____ that only humans _____ _____ tools.

3 Now, scientists are _____ _____ that many animals _____ _____ use tools.

4 If you _____ _____ a Buddhist _____ in Lop Buri, Thailand, _____ _____ _____ the Macaque monkeys.

5 They _____ _____ to you and _____ _____ your hair.

6 They use human hair _____ _____ _____ _____ .

7 If you are lucky, you may see _____ monkeys that _____ _____ _____ to their babies.

8 _____ the babies _____ _____ , the female monkeys _____ _____ _____ very slowly.

9 _____ _____ , the baby monkeys _____ _____ _____ .

10 People don't _____ _____ that _____ are smart.

11 _____ , octopuses are very smart, and they _____ _____ _____ tools.

12 They use coconut _____ _____ _____ .

1 도구를 사용하는 동물들

2 사람들은 한때 인간만이 도구를 사용할 수 있다고 생각했다.

3 이제 과학자들은 많은 동물들 역시 도구를 사용할 수 있다는 것을 밝혀내고 있다.

4 당신이 태국의 롭부리에 있는 절에 간다면, 마카크 원숭이들을 조심해야 한다.

5 그들이 당신에게 다가와 당신의 머리카락을 뽑을 수도 있다.

6 그들은 이빨을 치실질하기 위해서 사람의 머리카락을 사용한다.

7 만약 당신이 운이 좋으면, 당신은 새끼들에게 치실질하는 것을 가르치고 있는 암컷 원숭이들을 볼 수 있을 것이다.

8 새끼들이 지켜보고 있는 동안, 암컷 원숭이들은 아주 천천히 그들의 이빨을 치실질한다.

9 이런 방식으로, 새끼 원숭이들은 치실질을 배운다.

10 사람들은 대개 문어가 영리하다고 생각하지 않는다.

11 하지만, 문어는 매우 영리하고 또한 도구를 사용할 수 있다.

12 그들은 자신을 보호하기 위해 코코넛 껍데기를 사용한다.

13 When they _____ find a good _____ _____, they _____ _____ coconut shells.

14 Some octopuses _____ _____ coconut shells _____ _____ _____.

15 They _____ the coconut shells and _____ them _____ _____ _____.

16 _____ smart!

17 In Aesop's _____ *The Thirsty Crow*, a crow _____ stones into a _____ _____ _____ the level of water.

18 You _____ _____ this is _____ a story, _____ it is not.

19 Scientists _____ _____ _____ crows did an _____.

20 They _____ a jar with water _____ _____ _____ a crow.

21 A _____ was floating _____ _____ _____ the water.

22 _____, the water _____ was _____, so the crow _____ _____ eat the worm.

23 The crow _____ the problem _____ _____ in the fable.

24 It _____ stones _____ the jar.

25 _____ you think this bird is _____, you are _____.

26 Scientists did the _____ _____ with _____ crows, and they all did the same, _____.

---

13 그들이 숨을 만한 좋은 장소를 찾지 못했을 때, 그들은 코코넛 껍데기 아래로 숨는다.

14 어떤 문어들은 심지어 코코넛 껍데기를 나중에 쓰기 위해 모은다.

15 그들은 코코넛 껍데기를 쌓아두고 나중에 쓰기 위해서 가지고 다닌다.

16 얼마나 똑똑한가!

17 이솝 우화 '목마른 까마귀'에서 까마귀는 물 높이를 높이기 위해 항아리 안으로 돌을 떨어뜨린다.

18 당신은 이것이 그저 이야기라고 생각할 수 있지만, 그렇지 않다.

19 까마귀를 연구하던 과학자들이 실험을 했다.

20 그들은 까마귀 앞에 물이 든 항아리를 놓았다.

21 물 위에 벌레가 떠다니고 있었다.

22 하지만, 물 높이가 낮아서, 까마귀는 그 벌레를 먹을 수 없었다.

23 그 까마귀는 우화에서처럼 문제를 해결했다.

24 까마귀는 돌을 항아리 안으로 떨어뜨렸다.

25 만약 당신이 이 새가 특별하다고 생각한다면, 당신이 틀렸다.

26 과학자들은 다른 까마귀들에게도 똑같은 실험을 했고, 그들 모두가 똑같이 그렇게 했다.

※ 다음 문장을 우리말로 쓰시오.

1 Animals That Use Tools

➡ _____

2 People once thought that only humans can use tools.

➡ _____

3 Now, scientists are finding out that many animals can also use tools.

➡ _____

4 If you go to a Buddhist temple in Lop Buri, Thailand, watch out for the Macaque monkeys.

➡ _____

5 They may come to you and pull out your hair.

➡ _____

6 They use human hair to floss their teeth.

➡ _____

7 If you are lucky, you may see female monkeys that are teaching flossing to their babies.

➡ _____

8 While the babies are watching, the female monkeys floss their teeth very slowly.

➡ _____

9 This way, the baby monkeys learn to floss.

➡ _____

10 People don't usually think that octopuses are smart.

➡ _____

11 However, octopuses are very smart, and they can also use tools.

➡ _____

12 They use coconut shells for protection.

➡ _____

13 (they / find / when / hiding / can't / place, / good / a / they / shells. / hide / under / coconut)

➡ _____

14 (even / some / store / octopuses / for / use. / coconut / later / shells)

➡ _____

15 (the / shells / they / coconut / pile / them / and / later. / to / carry / use)

➡ _____

16 (smart! / how)

➡ _____

17 (The / fable / Crow, / Aesop's / Thirsty / in / stones / a / drops / crow / to / jar / into / raise / a / water. / the / of / level)

➡ _____

➡ _____

18 (think / you / just / may / a / this / story, / is / not. / is / but / it)

➡ _____

19 (were / crows / did / experiment. / who / scientists / an / studying)

➡ _____

20 (put / water / they / with / jar / a / front / a / in / crow. / of)

➡ _____

21 (top / was / worm / water. / a / floating / the / of / on)

➡ _____

22 (the / level / low, / however, / water / was / crow / so / eat / the / not / worm. / could / the)

➡ _____

23 (solved / crow / the / problem / as / the / just / in / fable. / the)

➡ _____

24 (stones / the / dropped / it / jar. / into)

➡ _____

25 (this / you / if / special, / think / bird / is / wrong. / are / you)

➡ _____

26 (did / same / scientists / the / experiment / crows, / with / other / and / did / same, / too. / all / they / the)

➡ _____

➡ _____

13 그들이 숨을 만한 좋은 장소┊ 찾지 못했을 때, 그들은 코코┊ 껍데기 아래로 숨는다.

14 어떤 문어들은 심지어 코코┊ 껍데기를 나중에 쓰기 위해 ┊은다.

15 그들은 코코넛 껍데기를 쌓아┊고 나중에 쓰기 위해서 가지┊다닌다.

16 얼마나 똑똑한가!

17 이솝 우화 '목마른 까마귀'에서┊까마귀는 물 높이를 높이기 위┊해 항아리 안으로 돌을 떨어┊린다.

18 당신은 이것이 그저 이야기라고┊생각할 수 있지만, 그렇지 않다┊

19 까마귀를 연구하던 과학자들이┊실험을 했다.

20 그들은 까마귀 앞에 물이 든 항┊아리를 놓았다.

21 물 위에 벌레가 떠다니고 있었┊다.

22 하지만, 물 높이가 낮아서, 까마┊귀는 그 벌레를 먹을 수 없었다┊

23 그 까마귀는 우화에서처럼 문제┊를 해결했다.

24 까마귀는 돌을 항아리 안으로┊떨어뜨렸다.

25 만약 당신이 이 새가 특별하다┊고 생각한다면, 당신이 틀렸다.

26 과학자들은 다른 까마귀들에게┊도 똑같은 실험을 했고, 그들 모┊두가 똑같이 그렇게 했다.

※ 다음 우리말을 영어로 쓰시오.

1 도구를 사용하는 동물들

➡ _____

2 사람들은 한때 인간만이 도구를 사용할 수 있다고 생각했다.

➡ _____

3 이제 과학자들은 많은 동물들 역시 도구를 사용할 수 있다는 것을 밝혀내고 있다.

➡ _____

4 당신이 태국의 롭부리에 있는 절에 간다면, 마카크 원숭이들을 조심해야 한다.

➡ _____

5 그들이 당신에게 다가와 당신의 머리카락을 뽑을 수도 있다.

➡ _____

6 그들은 이빨을 치실질하기 위해서 사람의 머리카락을 사용한다.

➡ _____

7 만약 당신이 운이 좋으면, 당신은 새끼들에게 치실질하는 것을 가르치고 있는 암컷 원숭이들을 볼 수 있을 것이다.

➡ _____

8 새끼들이 지켜보고 있는 동안, 암컷 원숭이들은 아주 천천히 그들의 이빨을 치실질한다.

➡ _____

9 이런 방식으로, 새끼 원숭이들은 치실질을 배운다.

➡ _____

10 사람들은 대개 문어가 영리하다고 생각하지 않는다.

➡ _____

11 하지만, 문어는 매우 영리하고 또한 도구를 사용할 수 있다.

➡ _____

12 그들은 자신을 보호하기 위해 코코넛 껍데기를 사용한다.

➡ _____

13 그들이 숨을 만한 좋은 장소를 찾지 못했을 때, 그들은 코코넛 껍데기 아래로 숨는다.

➡ _____

14 어떤 문어들은 심지어 코코넛 껍데기를 나중에 쓰기 위해 모은다.

➡ _____

15 그들은 코코넛 껍데기를 쌓아두고 나중에 쓰기 위해서 가지고 다닌다.

➡ _____

16 얼마나 똑똑한가!

➡ _____

17 이솝 우화 '목마른 까마귀'에서 까마귀는 물 높이를 높이기 위해 항아리 안으로 돌을 떨어뜨린다.

➡ _____

18 당신은 이것이 그저 이야기라고 생각할 수 있지만, 그렇지 않다.

➡ _____

19 까마귀를 연구하던 과학자들이 실험을 했다.

➡ _____

20 그들은 까마귀 앞에 물이 든 항아리를 놓았다.

➡ _____

21 물 위에 벌레가 떠다니고 있었다.

➡ _____

22 하지만, 물 높이가 낮아서, 까마귀는 그 벌레를 먹을 수 없었다.

➡ _____

23 그 까마귀는 우화에서처럼 문제를 해결했다.

➡ _____

24 까마귀는 돌을 항아리 안으로 떨어뜨렸다.

➡ _____

25 만약 당신이 이 새가 특별하다고 생각한다면, 당신이 틀렸다.

➡ _____

26 과학자들은 다른 까마귀들에게도 똑같은 실험을 했고, 그들 모두가 똑같이 그렇게 했다.

➡ _____

※ 다음 우리말과 일치하도록 빈칸에 알맞은 말을 쓰시오.

Around the World

1. The _____ snake _____ is Medusa.

2. She is 7.67 meters _____.

3. Alley _____ the longest jump by a cat.

4. Her _____ was 1.83 meters.

5. _____ _____ pig ever is Ernestine.

6. He _____ _____ 22 years and 359 days.

1. 지금까지 가장 긴 뱀은 Medusa이다.
2. 그것은 길이가 7.67미터이다.
3. Alley는 가장 멀리 뛰는 고양이로 기록되었다.
4. 그녀의 기록은 1.83 미터였다.
3. 지금까지 가장 오래 산 돼지는 Ernestine이다.
5. 그는 22년 359일을 살았다.

Think and Write

1. Animals _____ Special Talents

2. _____ _____ many animals that _____ special talents.

3. An _____ is Einstein.

4. He is an African Grey Parrot _____ can use 200 English words _____ _____ with people.

5. He _____ _____ the "Happy Birthday" song.

6. There _____ many animals _____ have special _____.

7. _____ _____ is Koko.

8. She is a _____ gorilla which _____ in America.

9. She can _____ _____ people _____ American Sign Language.

10. She knows _____ _____ 1,000 signs.

1. 특별한 재능을 가진 동물들
2. 특별한 재능을 가진 많은 동물들이 있다.
3. 한 예는 Einstein이다.
4. 그는 사람들과 대화를 하기 위해 200개의 영어 단어를 사용할 수 있는 아프리카 회색앵무새이다.
5. 그는 '생일 축하합니다' 노래를 부를 수 있다.
6. 특별한 재능을 가진 많은 동물들이 있다.
7. 한 예는 Koko이다.
8. 그녀는 미국에 살고 있는 암컷 고릴라이다.
9. 그녀는 수화로 사람들과 이야기할 수 있다.
10. 그녀는 1,000개가 넘는 신호를 알고 있다.

※ 다음 우리말을 영어로 쓰시오.

Around the World

1. 지금까지 가장 긴 뱀은 Medusa이다.
   ➡ _____

2. 그것은 길이가 7.67미터이다.
   ➡ _____

3. Alley는 가장 멀리 뛰는 고양이로 기록되었다.
   ➡ _____

4. 그녀의 기록은 1.83 미터였다.
   ➡ _____

5. 지금까지 가장 오래 산 돼지는 Ernestine이다.
   ➡ _____

6. 그는 22년 359일을 살았다.
   ➡ _____

Think and Write

1. 특별한 재능을 가진 동물들
   ➡ _____

2. 특별한 재능을 가진 많은 동물들이 있다.
   ➡ _____

3. 한 예는 Einstein이다.
   ➡ _____

4. 그는 사람들과 대화를 하기 위해 200개의 영어 단어를 사용할 수 있는 아프리카 회색앵무새이다.
   ➡ _____

5. 그는 '생일 축하합니다' 노래를 부를 수 있다.
   ➡ _____

6. 특별한 재능을 가진 많은 동물들이 있다.
   ➡ _____

7. 한 예는 Koko이다.
   ➡ _____

8. 그녀는 미국에 살고 있는 암컷 고릴라이다.
   ➡ _____

9. 그녀는 수화로 사람들과 이야기할 수 있다.
   ➡ _____

10. 그녀는 1,000개가 넘는 신호를 알고 있다.
    ➡ _____

※ 다음 영어를 우리말로 쓰시오.

01	advice
02	celebrity
03	during
04	unwise
05	sore
06	fever
07	simple
08	blink
09	thumb
10	prevent
11	throat
12	health
13	skin
14	nervous
15	various
16	hole
17	subject
18	dry
19	meal
20	medicine
21	regularly

22	intelligent
23	difficult
24	hurt
25	promise
26	accident
27	safety
28	example
29	increase
30	author
31	terrible
32	addiction
33	cause
34	pain
35	from now on
36	all over the world
37	fall asleep
38	instead of ~
39	get into ~
40	take a rest
41	have a sore throat
42	for example
43	look well

※ 다음 우리말을 영어로 쓰시오.

01 엄지손가락

02 구덩이, 구멍

03 건강

04 어려운

05 약속

06 규칙적으로

07 단순한

08 초조한, 불안한

09 충고

10 막다, 예방하다

11 다치다

12 ~ 동안

13 피부

14 눈을 깜박이다

15 다양한

16 유명인사, 유명인

17 아픈, 쓰린

18 현명하지 않은

19 과목

20 약

21 열, 열병

22 건조한, 마른

23 똑똑한, 지적인

24 목구멍

25 식사

26 증가하다

27 치과의사

28 현명한, 말쑥한

29 운동

30 중독

31 ~ 없이

32 치통

33 안전

34 작가, 저자

35 ~ 대신에

36 몇몇의

37 요즈음

38 콧물이 흐르다

39 예를 들어

40 휴식을 취하다, 쉬다

41 ~하려고 애쓰다[노력하다]

42 잠들다

43 지금부터

※ 다음 영영풀이에 알맞은 단어를 <보기>에서 골라 쓴 후, 우리말 뜻을 쓰시오.

1 _____ : a time when you relax or sleep: _____

2 _____ : a thick piece of soft material: _____

3 _____ : to make something happen: _____

4 _____ : a hollow place in something solid or in the surface of something:
   _____

5 _____ : to open and close your eyes very quickly: _____

6 _____ : at the same time every day, every week, etc.: _____

7 _____ : the feeling you have when a part of your body hurts: _____

8 _____ : to send someone a written message using a cell phone: _____

9 _____ : the passage at the back of your mouth, where you swallow: _____

10 _____ : to become larger or greater in size, amount, number, etc.: _____

11 _____ : a pill or a liquid that you take when you are sick to help you get better:
   _____

12 _____ : to stop something from happening, or stop someone from doing:
   _____

13 _____ : the state of being safe and protected from danger or harm: _____

14 _____ : the short thick finger on your hand that helps you hold things: _____

15 _____ : physical activity that is done in order to become stronger and healthier:
   _____

16 _____ : the problem when someone cannot stop doing something, or does something
   too much: _____

보기			
throat	medicine	exercise	cause
prevent	addiction	rest	text
hole	thumb	blink	increase
pad	pain	regularly	safety

※ 다음 우리말과 일치하도록 빈칸에 알맞은 말을 쓰시오.

 해석

Listen and Talk A-1

W: You _____ _____. _____ _____, Inho?

B: I _____ _____ _____ _____ . I _____ _____ _____, too.

W: I think you _____ _____ _____. _____ this _____ and _____ you _____ a good _____.

B: OK. _____ _____.

Listen and Talk A-2

W: What's _____, Peter?

B: I don't know, Ms. Kim, but my _____ _____ _____ _____.

W: _____ a heating pad _____ it.

B: OK, _____ _____.

W: And _____ _____ you do some _____ _____.

Listen and Talk A-3

W: What's the _____, Chris?

B: I _____ _____ terrible _____.

W: _____ _____ some _____. _____ this.

B: Thank you.

W: And _____ _____ you go to the _____.

B: OK, _____ _____.

Listen and Talk A-4

W: What's _____ _____ your leg, Sam?

B: I _____ and _____ my foot _____ I was playing soccer.

W: _____ you _____?

B: Yes, but it _____ a lot.

W: _____ _____ _____ put some ice on it? And _____ _____ you _____ soccer _____ next week.

Listen and Talk B

1. **A:** You _____ _____ _____. What's _____?
   B: I _____ _____ _____.
   A: _____ _____ _____. _____ you _____ some medicine.
   B: OK, I _____.

2. **A:** You _____ _____ _____. What's _____?
   B: I _____ _____ _____.
   A: That's too bad. _____ _____ you go see a _____.
   B: OK, _____ _____.

Listen and Talk C

W: What's _____, Andy?
B: Hello, Ms. Kim. My right _____ _____.
W: Hmm. Do you _____ your smartphone _____ _____?
B: Yes, I _____ _____ _____. Why?
W: I think you _____ _____ _____.
B: Texting thumb? What's texting thumb?
W: It's _____ in _____ _____. You can _____ it _____ _____ too much.
B: Oh, I _____ _____ that.
W: _____ _____ _____ do some finger stretching exercises?
B: OK, I will.
W: And _____ _____ _____ _____ _____ too much.

Review 1

G: What's _____, Mike?
B: I _____ _____ _____ _____.
G: I think you _____ _____ _____ _____.
B: OK, _____ _____.

Review 2

M: What's _____ _____, Mina?
G: I _____ _____ _____ _____. I also _____ _____ _____.
M: I think you have a _____. _____ _____ you _____ _____ _____.
G: OK, _____ _____.

1. A: 너 몸이 안 좋아 보여. 무슨 일 있니?
   B: 머리가 아파.
   A: 안됐다. 약을 먹으렴.
   B: 응, 그럴게.

2. A: 너 몸이 안 좋아 보여. 무슨 일 있니?
   B: 감기에 걸렸어.
   A: 안됐다. 병원에 가도록 하렴.
   B: 응, 그럴게.

W: 무슨 일이니, Andy?
B: 안녕하세요, 김 선생님. 제 오른손 엄지손가락이 아파요.
W: 음. 너 스마트폰을 많이 사용하니?
B: 네, 저 문자를 많이 해요. 왜요?
W: 내 생각에 너는 texting thumb인 것 같아.
B: texting thumb이요? texting thumb이 뭐예요?
W: 엄지손가락에 통증이 있는 거야. 문자를 너무 많이 하면 생길 수 있어.
B: 오, 그건 몰랐네요.
W: 손가락 스트레칭 운동을 좀 하는 게 어떠니?
B: 네, 그럴게요.
W: 그리고 문자를 너무 많이 하지 않도록 하렴.

G: 무슨 일 있니, Mike?
B: 머리가 너무 아파.
G: 너는 약을 먹는 것이 좋겠다.
B: 알겠어, 그럴게.

M: 무슨 일 있니, 미나야?
G: 목이 아파요. 그리고 콧물도 나요.
M: 내 생각에 네가 감기에 걸린 것 같구나. 좀 쉬도록 하렴.
G: 네, 그럴게요.

※ 다음 우리말과 일치하도록 빈칸에 알맞은 말을 쓰시오.

1 _____ _____ _____ Your Smartphones!

2 _____ _____ _____ is difficult for many of us _____ _____.

3 However, _____ _____ _____ _____ _____ of smartphones _____ _____ various problems.

4 _____ you _____ _____?

5 _____ _____ _____ _____, people are _____ _____ _____ _____.

6 Their heads are _____, and their eyes are _____ _____ _____.

7 We _____ _____ _____ _____ _____, smartphone zombies.

8 If you are a smombie, you can have _____ _____.

9 You _____ _____ _____ a hole in the street, _____ you _____ _____ and _____.

10 You _____ _____ _____ a car accident, _____.

11 So what can you do _____ _____ _____ _____?

12 It's _____.

13 _____ _____ _____ your smartphone _____ you are _____!

14 Do you have _____ _____ or _____?

15 Smartphones can cause _____ _____ _____.

16 _____ _____ is _____ _____.

한글 해석

1 스마트폰을 현명하게 사용하라!
2 스마트폰 없이 사는 것은 요즘 많은 사람들에게 어렵다.
3 하지만 스마트폰을 현명하지 않게 사용하거나 너무 과도하게 사용하는 것은 다양한 문제를 야기할 수 있다.
4 당신은 스몸비인가요?
5 전 세계적으로 사람들이 좀비처럼 걸어다니고 있다.
6 그들의 머리는 아래를 향하고, 그들의 눈은 스마트폰을 향하고 있다.
7 우리는 그런 사람들을 스몸비, 즉 스마트폰 좀비라고 부른다.
8 만약 당신이 스몸비라면, 당신은 다양한 안전 관련 문제들을 겪을 수 있다.
9 당신은 거리에 있는 구덩이를 보지 못할 수도 있고, 그래서 넘어져서 다칠지도 모른다.
10 당신은 또한 교통사고를 당할지도 모른다.
11 그렇다면 이런 문제들을 방지하기 위해 무엇을 할 수 있을까?
12 간단하다.
13 걷고 있는 동안에는 스마트폰을 보지 마라!
14 당신은 안구 건조증이나 거북목 증후군이 있나요?
15 스마트폰은 다양한 건강상의 문제를 일으킬 수 있다.
16 한 가지 예가 안구 건조증이다.

17 When you _____ _____ your smartphone, you do not _____ _____.

18 Then your eyes _____ _____ _____.

19 _____ _____ you can have _____ _____ _____.

20 When you _____ _____ _____ your smartphone, the _____ _____ your neck _____.

21 _____ _____ _____ of your smartphone, for example, _____ _____ _____, can cause _____ _____.

22 We _____ this _____ _____.

23 _____ _____ _____ _____ for these problems.

24 For _____ _____, _____ _____ _____ often.

25 For text neck, _____ your smartphone _____ _____ _____ _____ _____.

26 You _____ _____ do some _____ _____ _____.

27 _____ _____ _____ _____ when you don't have your smartphone with you?

28 Do you _____ _____ when your smartphone is not _____?

29 Do you _____ _____ when you check your smartphone and there is _____ _____ _____?

30 If your _____ are "yes," you may have _____ _____.

31 There are various things you can do _____ _____ _____.

32 _____ _____, _____ _____ _____ your smartphone _____ meals or meetings.

33 You _____ talk to people _____ _____ _____ them.

17	스마트폰을 볼 때, 당신은 눈을 자주 깜박거리지 않는다.
18	그러면 눈이 건조하다고 느낄 것이다.
19	일어날 수 있는 또 다른 문제는 목 통증이다.
20	스마트폰을 내려다볼 때, 목에 가해지는 압박이 증가한다.
21	스마트폰을 너무 많이 사용하는 것은, 예를 들어, 너무 많이 문자를 하는 것은 목 통증을 일으킬 수 있다.
22	이런 증상을 거북목 증후군이라고 부른다.
23	여기에 이런 문제들을 위한 몇 가지 조언이 있다.
24	안구 건조증에는, 눈을 자주 깜박이려고 노력해라.
25	거북목 증후군에는 당신의 눈높이까지 스마트폰을 위로 올려라.
26	목 스트레칭 운동 또한 할 수 있다.
27	스마트폰이 없을 때 어떤 기분이 드나요?
28	스마트폰이 주위에 없을 때 당신은 초조한 기분이 드는가?
29	스마트폰을 확인했을 때 아무런 문자 메시지가 없으면 슬픈 기분이 드는가?
30	만약 당신의 대답이 '그렇다'이면, 당신은 스마트폰 중독일지도 모른다.
31	이것을 방지하기 위해 할 수 있는 일은 여러 가지가 있다.
32	예를 들어, 식사나 회의 중에는 스마트폰을 꺼라.
33	문자를 보내는 대신에 사람들과 이야기를 할 수 있다.

※ 다음 문장을 우리말로 쓰시오.

1 ▶ Be Smart with Your Smartphones!

➡ _____

2 ▶ Living without smartphones is difficult for many of us these days.

➡ _____

3 ▶ However, unwise or too much use of smartphones can cause various problems.

➡ _____

4 ▶ Are you a smombie?

➡ _____

5 ▶ All over the world, people are walking around like zombies.

➡ _____

6 ▶ Their heads are down, and their eyes are on their smartphones.

➡ _____

7 ▶ We call such people smombies, smartphone zombies.

➡ _____

8 ▶ If you are a smombie, you can have various safety problems.

➡ _____

9 ▶ You may not see a hole in the street, so you may fall and get hurt.

➡ _____

10 ▶ You may get into a car accident, too.

➡ _____

11 ▶ So what can you do to prevent these problems?

➡ _____

12 ▶ It's simple.

➡ _____

13 ▶ Do not look at your smartphone while you are walking!

➡ _____

14 ▶ Do you have dry eyes or text neck?

➡ _____

15 ▶ Smartphones can cause various health problems.

➡ _____

16 ▶ One example is dry eyes.

➡ _____

17 When you look at your smartphone, you do not blink often.

➡ _____

18 Then your eyes will feel dry.

➡ _____

19 Another problem you can have is neck pain.

➡ _____

20 When you look down at your smartphone, the stress on your neck increases.

➡ _____

21 Too much use of your smartphone, for example, too much texting, can cause neck pain.

➡ _____

22 We call this text neck.

➡ _____

23 Here are some tips for these problems.

➡ _____

24 For dry eyes, try to blink often.

➡ _____

25 For text neck, move your smartphone up to your eye level.

➡ _____

26 You can also do some neck stretching exercises.

➡ _____

27 How do you feel when you don't have your smartphone with you?

➡ _____

28 Do you feel nervous when your smartphone is not around?

➡ _____

29 Do you feel sad when you check your smartphone and there is no text message?

➡ _____

30 If your answers are "yes," you may have smartphone addiction.

➡ _____

31 There are various things you can do to prevent this.

➡ _____

32 For example, turn off your smartphone during meals or meetings.

➡ _____

33 You can talk to people instead of texting them.

➡ _____

※ 다음 괄호 안의 단어들을 우리말에 맞도록 바르게 배열하시오.

1 (Smart / Be / with / Smartphones! / Your)
➡ _____

2 (without / living / is / smartphones / for / difficult / of / many / us / days. / these)
➡ _____

3 (unwise / however, / or / much / too / of / use / can / smartphones / problems. / various / cause)
➡ _____

4 (you / are / smombie? / a)
➡ _____

5 (over / all / world, / the / are / people / around / walking / zombies. / like)
➡ _____

6 (heads / their / down, / are / and / eyes / their / are / smartphones. / their / on)
➡ _____

7 (call / we / people / such / smombies, / zombies. / smartphone)
➡ _____

8 (you / if / a / are / smombie, / can / you / various / have / problems. / safety)
➡ _____

9 (may / you / see / not / hole / a / the / in / street, / you / so / fall / may / hurt. / get / and)
➡ _____

10 (may / you / into / get / car / a / too. / accident,)
➡ _____

11 (what / so / you / can / to / do / problems? / these / prevent)
➡ _____

12 (simple. / it's)
➡ _____

13 (not / do / at / look / smartphone / your / you / while / walking! / are)
➡ _____

14 (you / do / dry / have / or / eyes / neck? / text)
➡ _____

15 (can / smartphones / cause / problems. / health / various)
➡ _____

16 (example / one / eyes. / dry / is)
➡ _____

1 스마트폰을 현명하게 사용하라!

2 스마트폰 없이 사는 것은 요즘 많은 사람들에게 어렵다.

3 하지만 스마트폰을 현명하지 않게 사용하거나 너무 과도하게 사용하는 것은 다양한 문제를 야기할 수 있다.

4 당신은 스몸비인가요?

5 전 세계적으로 사람들이 좀비처럼 걸어다니고 있다.

6 그들의 머리는 아래를 향하고, 그들의 눈은 스마트폰을 향하고 있다.

7 우리는 그런 사람들을 스몸비, 즉 스마트폰 좀비라고 부른다.

8 만약 당신이 스몸비라면, 당신은 다양한 안전 관련 문제들을 겪을 수 있다.

9 당신은 거리에 있는 구덩이를 보지 못할 수도 있고, 그래서 넘어져서 다칠지도 모른다.

10 당신은 또한 교통사고를 당할지도 모른다.

11 그렇다면 이런 문제들을 방지하기 위해 무엇을 할 수 있을까?

12 간단하다.

13 걷고 있는 동안에는 스마트폰을 보지 마라!

14 당신은 안구 건조증이나 거북목 증후군이 있나요?

15 스마트폰은 다양한 건강상의 문제를 일으킬 수 있다.

16 한 가지 예가 안구 건조증이다.

17 (you / when / at / look / smartphone, / your / do / you / not / often. / blink)
➡ _____

18 (your / then / will / eyes / dry. / feel)
➡ _____

19 (problem / another / can / you / is / have / pain. / neck)
➡ _____

20 (you / when / down / look / your / at / smartphone, / stress / the / on / increases. / neck / your)
➡ _____

21 (much / too / of / use / smartphone, / your / example, / for / much / too / texting, / cause / can / pain. / neck)
➡ _____
_____

22 (call / we / neck. / text / this)
➡ _____

23 (are / here / tips / some / for / problems. / these)
➡ _____

24 (dry / for / eyes, / to / try / often. / blink)
➡ _____

25 (text / for / neck, / your / move / smartphone / to / up / level. / eye / your)
➡ _____

26 (can / you / do / also / neck / some / exercises. / stretching)
➡ _____

27 (do / how / feel / you / you / when / have / don't / smartphone / you? / with / your)
➡ _____

28 (you / do / nervous / feel / when / smartphone / your / around? / not / is)
➡ _____

29 (you / do / sad / feel / you / when / check / smartphone / your / and / is / there / text / message? / no)
➡ _____
_____

30 (your / if / answers / "yes," / are / may / you / addiction. / smartphone / have)
➡ _____

31 (are / there / things / various / can / you / to / do / this. / prevent)
➡ _____

32 (example, / for / off / turn / smartphone / your / meals / meetings. / during / or)
➡ _____

33 (can / you / talk / people / to / of / instead / them. / texting)
➡ _____

17 스마트폰을 볼 때, 당신은 눈을 자주 깜박거리지 않는다.
18 그러면 눈이 건조하다고 느낄 것이다.
19 일어날 수 있는 또 다른 문제는 목 통증이다.
20 스마트폰을 내려다볼 때, 목에 가해지는 압박이 증가한다.
21 스마트폰을 너무 많이 사용하는 것은, 예를 들어, 너무 많이 문자를 하는 것은 목 통증을 일으킬 수 있다.
22 이런 증상을 거북목 증후군이라고 부른다.
23 여기에 이런 문제들을 위한 몇 가지 조언이 있다.
24 안구 건조증에는, 눈을 자주 깜박이려고 노력해라.
25 거북목 증후군에는 당신의 눈높이까지 스마트폰을 위로 올려라.
26 목 스트레칭 운동 또한 할 수 있다.
27 스마트폰이 없을 때 어떤 기분이 드나요?
28 스마트폰이 주위에 없을 때 당신은 초조한 기분이 드는가?
29 스마트폰을 확인했을 때 아무런 문자 메시지가 없으면 슬픈 기분이 드는가?
30 만약 당신의 대답이 '그렇다'이면, 당신은 스마트폰 중독일지도 모른다.
31 이것을 방지하기 위해 할 수 있는 일은 여러 가지가 있다.
32 예를 들어, 식사나 회의 중에는 스마트폰을 꺼라.
33 문자를 보내는 대신에 사람들과 이야기를 할 수 있다.

※ 다음 우리말을 영어로 쓰시오.

1 스마트폰을 현명하게 사용하라!

➡ _____

2 스마트폰 없이 사는 것은 요즘 많은 사람들에게 어렵다.

➡ _____

3 하지만 스마트폰을 현명하지 않게 사용하거나 너무 과도하게 사용하는 것은 다양한 문제를 야기할 수 있다.

➡ _____

4 당신은 스몸비인가요?

➡ _____

5 전 세계적으로 사람들이 좀비처럼 걸어다니고 있다.

➡ _____

6 그들의 머리는 아래를 향하고, 그들의 눈은 스마트폰을 향하고 있다.

➡ _____

7 우리는 그런 사람들을 스몸비, 즉 스마트폰 좀비라고 부른다.

➡ _____

8 만약 당신이 스몸비라면, 당신은 다양한 안전 관련 문제들을 겪을 수 있다.

➡ _____

9 당신은 거리에 있는 구덩이를 보지 못할 수도 있고, 그래서 넘어져서 다칠지도 모른다.

➡ _____

10 당신은 또한 교통사고를 당할지도 모른다.

➡ _____

11 그렇다면 이런 문제들을 방지하기 위해 무엇을 할 수 있을까?

➡ _____

12 간단하다.

➡ _____

13 걷고 있는 동안에는 스마트폰을 보지 마라!

➡ _____

14 당신은 안구 건조증이나 거북목 증후군이 있나요?

➡ _____

15 스마트폰은 다양한 건강상의 문제를 일으킬 수 있다.

➡ _____

16 한 가지 예가 안구 건조증이다.

➡ _____

17 스마트폰을 볼 때, 당신은 눈을 자주 깜박거리지 않는다.

➡ _____

18 그러면 눈이 건조하다고 느낄 것이다.

➡ _____

19 일어날 수 있는 또 다른 문제는 목 통증이다.

➡ _____

20 스마트폰을 내려다볼 때, 목에 가해지는 압박이 증가한다.

➡ _____

21 스마트폰을 너무 많이 사용하는 것은, 예를 들어, 너무 많이 문자를 하는 것은 목 통증을 일으킬 수 있다.

➡ _____

22 이런 증상을 거북목 증후군이라고 부른다.

➡ _____

23 여기에 이런 문제들을 위한 몇 가지 조언이 있다.

➡ _____

24 안구 건조증에는, 눈을 자주 깜박이려고 노력해라.

➡ _____

25 거북목 증후군에는 당신의 눈높이까지 스마트폰을 위로 올려라.

➡ _____

26 목 스트레칭 운동 또한 할 수 있다.

➡ _____

27 스마트폰이 없을 때 어떤 기분이 드나요?

➡ _____

28 스마트폰이 주위에 없을 때 당신은 초조한 기분이 드는가?

➡ _____

29 스마트폰을 확인했을 때 아무런 문자 메시지가 없으면 슬픈 기분이 드는가?

➡ _____

30 만약 당신의 대답이 '그렇다'이면, 당신은 스마트폰 중독일지도 모른다.

➡ _____

31 이것을 방지하기 위해 할 수 있는 일은 여러 가지가 있다.

➡ _____

32 예를 들어, 식사나 회의 중에는 스마트폰을 꺼라.

➡ _____

33 문자를 보내는 대신에 사람들과 이야기를 할 수 있다.

➡ _____

※ 다음 우리말과 일치하도록 빈칸에 알맞은 말을 쓰시오.

Talk and Play

1. A: What's _____?

2. B: I _____ _____ _____.

3. A: That's too bad. _____ _____ you get _____ _____.

4. B: OK, _____ _____.

1. A: 무슨 일이니?
2. B: 나는 열이 나.
3. A: 안됐다. 좀 쉬도록 하렴.
4. B: 응, 알겠어.

After You Read B

1. _____ _____ _____ Your Smartphones!

2. Minho: Yesterday, I _____ on the street and _____ _____.

3. I _____ _____ and I _____ _____ a hole.

4. Reply: _____ _____ use your smartphone _____ you _____ _____.

5. Emma: My eyes _____ _____ when I use my smartphone.

6. Reply: _____ _____ _____ often.

7. Suji: I have neck pain _____ I _____ _____ _____ _____.

8. Reply: Move your smartphone _____ _____ your _____ _____ and do some neck _____ _____.

9. Eric: I think I _____ _____ _____.

10. Reply: _____ _____ your smartphone _____ meals or meetings and talk to people _____ _____ _____ them.

1. 스마트폰을 현명하게 사용하라!
2. 민호: 어제, 나는 길에서 넘어져서 다쳤다.
3. 나는 문자를 보내고 있었고 구덩이를 보지 못했다.
4. 대답: 걷는 동안에는 스마트폰을 사용하지 마라.
5. Emma: 나는 스마트폰을 사용할 때 눈이 건조하다고 느낀다.
6. 대답: 눈을 자주 깜박이도록 노력해라.
7. 수지: 나는 문자를 많이 보낼 때 목 통증이 있다.
8. 대답: 스마트폰을 눈높이까지 들고, 목 스트레칭 운동을 해라.
9. Eric: 나는 스마트폰 중독인 것 같다.
10. 대답: 식사나 회의 중에는 스마트폰을 끄고 문자를 보내는 대신에 사람들과 이야기해라.

Around the World

1. This sign says, "_____ _____ of _____ your smartphone _____ you are walking."

2. _____ _____ traffic lights on the ground, _____ people can see them _____ they _____ _____ their smartphones.

3. This sign on the ground _____, "This _____ of the street is for people _____ _____ _____ _____."

1. 이 표지판은 "걷는 동안 스마트폰 사용을 주의하세요."라는 의미이다.
2. 바닥에 신호등이 있어서, 사람들이 스마트폰을 사용하는 동안에도 신호등을 볼 수 있다.
3. 바닥에 있는 이 표지판은 "길의 이쪽 편은 문자를 보내고 있는 사람들을 위한 곳입니다."라는 의미이다.

※ 다음 우리말을 영어로 쓰시오.

Talk and Play

1. A: 무슨 일이니?
➡ _____

2. B: 나는 열이 나.
➡ _____

3. A: 안됐다. 좀 쉬도록 하렴.
➡ _____

4. B: 응, 알겠어.
➡ _____

After You Read B

1. 스마트폰을 현명하게 사용하라!
➡ _____

2. 민호: 어제, 나는 길에서 넘어져서 다쳤다.
➡ _____

3. 나는 문자를 보내고 있었고 구덩이를 보지 못했다.
➡ _____

4. 대답: 걷는 동안에는 스마트폰을 사용하지 마라.
➡ _____

5. Emma: 나는 스마트폰을 사용할 때 눈이 건조하다고 느낀다.
➡ _____

6. 대답: 눈을 자주 깜박이도록 노력해라.
➡ _____

7. 수지: 나는 문자를 많이 보낼 때 목 통증이 있다.
➡ _____

8. 대답: 스마트폰을 눈높이까지 들고, 목 스트레칭 운동을 해라.
➡ _____

9. Eric: 나는 스마트폰 중독인 것 같다.
➡ _____

10. 대답: 식사나 회의 중에는 스마트폰을 끄고 문자를 보내는 대신에 사람들과 이야기해라.
➡ _____

Around the World

1. 이 표지판은 "걷는 동안 스마트폰 사용을 주의하세요."라는 의미이다.
➡ _____

2. 바닥에 신호등이 있어서, 사람들이 스마트폰을 사용하는 동안에도 신호등을 볼 수 있다.
➡ _____

3. 바닥에 있는 이 표지판은 "길의 이쪽 편은 문자를 보내고 있는 사람들을 위한 곳입니다."라는 의미이다.
➡ _____

영어 기출 문제집

적중100

1학기

정답 및 해설

동아 | 윤정미

중 2

영어 기출 문제집

1학기

정답 및 해설

동아 | 윤정미

중 2

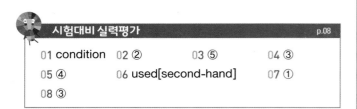
Ideas for Saving the Earth

시험대비 실력평가
p.08

01 condition 02 ② 03 ⑤ 04 ③
05 ④ 06 used[second-hand] 07 ①
08 ③

01 둘은 동의어 관계이다. 할인 – 상태
02 get to+장소: ~에 도착하다 / have to+동사원형: ~ 해야 한다
03 nursing home은 '양로원'이다.
04 음악을 만들어 내기 위해 사용되는 물건
05 어떤 예쁜 것을 위에 놓음으로써 물건을 더 매력적으로 보이게 만들다
06 used = second-hand '중고의'
07 동명사 recycling이 뒤에 있고, 글의 의미상 '~와 같은'의 의미를 가지는 전치사 like가 와야 한다. 야구 글러브를 찾고 있다는 의미로 for가 적절하다.
08 trash와 fashion이 결합한 말이다.

서술형 시험대비
p.09

01 (1) interested (2) kit (3) instruments (4) discount
02 (1) hold, 열다, 개최하다 (2) much, 많은
   (3) explain, 설명하다 (4) creative, 창의적인
03 (1) Cut off (2) sounds like
   (3) throw, away (4) take
04 (1) musical (2) meaning
   (3) combination (4) take, off
05 (t)rash, (c)ombination
06 (1) different (2) environment (3) creative (4) once
   (5) rubber (6) almost (7) through (8) expensive
   decorate, 장식하다, 꾸미다

01 (1) become 뒤에 형용사가 필요하다. '관심 있는'은 interested 가 적절하다. (2) sewing kit 바느질 세트(반짇고리) (3) 콘서트 에서 악기를 연주할 계획이다. (4) 할인을 받을 수 있나요?
02 (1) 저희 그룹은 트래션 쇼를 하고 싶습니다. (2) 저 동그란 안 경은 얼마인가요? (3) 누가 업사이클링의 의미를 설명할 수 있

나요? (4) 너희들의 발상은 정말 창의적이구나.
03 (1) cut off: ~을 자르다 (2) sound like+명사: ~처럼 들리다 (3) throw away: ~을 버리다 (4) 여기서 take는 '선택하다, 사다'는 의미이다.
04 (1) 명사 instruments(악기)와 어울리는 music의 형용사 형 태가 적절하다. (2) 나는 여러분들이 업사이클링의 의미를 이해 하길 원합니다. mean의 명사형인 meaning이 적절하다. (3) 동사 combine의 명사형 combination이 적절하다. (4) '할인 을 받을 수 있나요?'라는 물음에 '1달러 할인해 줄게요.'라는 의 미가 적절하므로 '할인하다'라는 take off가 적절하다.
05 (1) trash: 쓰레기 (2) combination: 조합

교과서
Conversation

핵심 Check
p.10~11

1 How much 2 price 3 ① 4 ⑤

교과서 대화문 익히기

Check(√) True or False
p.12

1 F 2 T 3 F 4 T

교과서 확인학습
p.14~15

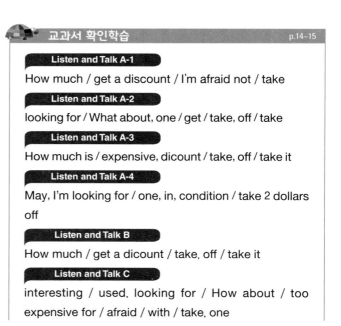

Listen and Talk A-1
How much / get a discount / I'm afraid not / take

Listen and Talk A-2
looking for / What about, one / get / take, off / take

Listen and Talk A-3
How much is / expensive, dicount / take, off / take it

Listen and Talk A-4
May, I'm looking for / one, in, condition / take 2 dollars off

Listen and Talk B
How much / get a dicount / take, off / take it

Listen and Talk C
interesting / used, looking for / How about / too expensive for / afraid / with / take, one

시험대비 기본평가 p.16

01 looking for 02 ⑤ 03 ② 04 get

01 'I'm looking for ~.'는 '나는 ~을 찾고 있다.'라는 뜻으로, 찾고 있는 물건이 무엇인지 말할 때 사용하는 표현이다.

02 밑줄 친 문장은 신발의 가격을 묻는 표현으로 ⑤번 '이 신발의 가격은 얼마인가요?'가 적절하다.

03 B의 마지막 말은 '좋아요'라고 했기 때문에 파란 티셔츠를 구입한다는 말이 오는 것이 가장 적절하다. ①은 '또 다른 셔츠를 보여주세요.'라는 표현으로 처음 본 물건이 마음에 들지 않거나 다른 옷을 보고 싶을 때 사용하는 표현이다. ④의 Here you are.는 물건을 건네줄 때 사용하는 표현으로 '여기 있습니다.'라는 뜻이다.

04 get a discount가 '할인을 받다'라는 뜻이며 '내가 할인을 받을 수 있나요?'라는 표현으로 Can I get a discount?를 사용한다.

시험대비 실력평가 p.17~18

01 ③	02 ⑤	03 ④	04 ②
05 ⑤	06 ④		07 That's expensive for me.
08 backpack	09 ⑤		10 used[second-hand]
11 ②	12 ④		

01 B의 대답으로 보아 빈칸에는 둥근 안경의 가격을 묻는 표현이 적절하다. round glasses가 복수명사이므로 복수동사 are가 적절하다.

02 할인해 줄 수 있나요?라는 물음에 대한 답으로 No라고 했기 때문에 '유감스럽지만 안 돼'라는 말이 적절하다.

03 제시된 문장은 가격을 말하는 표현이므로 가격이 얼마인지 묻는 표현이 적절하다. ④번은 '이 책은 할인 중인가요?'라는 뜻이다. on sale은 '할인 중'이라는 의미다.

04 ②번은 '어디서 가방을 살 수 있나요?'라는 표현이고, 나머지는 모두 매장에서 가방을 살 수 있는지 묻는 표현이다.

05 얼마를 할인한다는 의미로 'take+돈+off'를 사용한다.

06 '어서 오세요'라는 인사말에 (D) 네라고 답하고 신발 가격을 묻는 말이 오고 (A) 신발 가격을 말해주고 (B) 할인 여부를 물어

보는 말이 온다. 마지막으로 (C) 할인을 해주겠다는 말이 오면 된다.

07 주어는 대명사 that이 오고, expensive가 형용사이므로 be동사가 와야 한다.

08 one은 앞에 나온 명사를 대신하는 부정대명사다.

09 ⑤번의 What are you looking for? 는 사고자 하는 물건이 무엇인지 물어보는 말이다. look at은 '~ 을 보다'는 의미로 '시계를 보고 있는 중입니다.'는 어색하다.

10 사용된 결과로 더럽거나 더 이상 좋은 상태에 있지 않은

11 깎아줄 수 있는지 묻는 말에 '일 년 밖에 되지 않아 거의 새 것이다'라고 했으므로 할인을 해주지 않는다는 표현이 와야 한다.

12 가게 주인은 15달러하는 빨간색 시계를 깎아주지 않아 B는 10달러하는 파란색 시계를 대신 구입한 것이다.

서술형 시험대비 p.19

01 Can I get a discount?

02 She will pay ten dollars.

03 (A) How much is this yellow backpack?
(B) How[What] about this red one?
(C) I'll take it.

04 used / How much is it / get a dicount / afraid / lage numbers

05 I'll take 3 dollars off.

01 할인을 받는 의미로 get a discount를 사용한다.

02 정상 가격은 12달러인데 남자가 2달러를 할인해 주겠다고 했기 때문에 여자가 지불할 금액은 10달러이다.

03 (A) 가격을 물어볼 때 'How much+동사+주어?' 를 이용한다.
(B) '~은 어때요?'라는 표현은 'How[What] about ~?'을 이용하고 '빨간색 가방은 어떤가요?'라는 의미이므로 앞에 나온 a backpack을 대신하는 부정 대명사 one을 이용한다. (C) 물건을 선택할 때 동사 take를 사용한다.

05 '할인을 하다, 깎아주다'는 표현으로 'take 금액 off'를 사용한다.

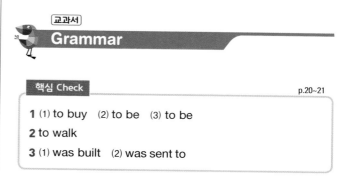

교과서 Grammar

핵심 Check p.20~21

1 (1) to buy (2) to be (3) to be

2 to walk

3 (1) was built (2) was sent to

시험대비 기본평가
p.22

01 (1) cleans → is cleaned (2) is → was
　 (3) sit → to sit (4) to not play → not to play

02 ⑤

03 were injured / was broken / to be / to exercise

04 (1) to know (2) was cleaned

01 (1) 바닥이 청소되는 것이므로 수동태가 적절하다. (2) 과거이므로 was가 적절하다. (3) ask의 목적격보어로 to부정사가 적절하다. (4) to부정사의 부정형은 'not to+동사원형'으로 쓴다.

02 책이 쓰여지는 것이므로 수동태가 적절하다.

03 (1) 그들이 부상을 입은 것이므로 수동태가 적절하다. (2) 꽃병이 깨진 것이므로 수동태가 적절하다. (3) want의 목적격보어로 to부정사가 적절하다. (4) advise의 목적격보어로 to부정사가 적절하다.

04 (1) want의 목적격보어로 to부정사가 적절하다. (2) 방이 청소되는 것이므로 수동태가 적절하다.

시험대비 실력평가
p.23~25

01 ③　　02 ④　　03 (1) to (2) for (3) of
04 ⑤　　05 ④　　06 ①
07 ②　　08 ①　　09 ⑤　　10 ④

11 (1) *The Mona Lisa* was painted by Leonardo da Vinci.
　 (2) The famous player was surprised at her movements.
　 (3) The house was not broken by the tornado.
　 (4) Ms. Jackson told Tom to clean the windows.
　 (5) The teacher expected his students to do their best.

12 ⑤　　　13 to join / to do　　　14 ③
15 ①　　　16 ③　　　17 ②

18 (1) Sujin painted the picture.
　 (2) Casa Mila was built by Antonio Gaudi.
　 (3) A model plane was made for me by my father.
　 (4) Her homework will be finished by Kate by the end of this week.
　 (5) By whom was the house built?

01 ③ 수동태는 'be+과거분사'의 형태이므로 was built가 되어야 한다.

02 ask의 목적격보어로 to부정사가 적절하다.

03 직접목적어를 주어로 한 수동태에서 간접목적어 앞에 (1) teach는 전치사 to를, (2) buy는 전치사 for를, (3) ask는 전치사 of를 쓴다.

04 tell의 목적격보어로 to부정사가 적절하다.

05 Her pictures taken at the party were shown to me by Mary.

06 make는 목적격보어로 to부정사가 아니라 원형부정사를 쓴다.

07 ① A difficult question was asked of her by them. ③ These books will be sent to you tomorrow morning. ④ The window was broken by Mike yesterday. ⑤ The telephone was invented by Alexander Bell in 1876.

08 ask, tell, advise, want, expect는 모두 목적격보어로 to부정사가 와야 한다

09 cautious: 주의 깊은, 신중한 ⑤ The doctor wanted Harry to get well soon.

10 dust: 먼지 / be covered with: ~로 덮여 있다 / be pleased with: ~에 기뻐하다

11 (1), (3) Mona Lisa가 그려지고, 집이 부서지지 않은 것이므로 수동태가 적절하다. (2) be surprised at: ~에 놀라다 (4), (5) tell과 expect는 목적격보어로 to부정사를 쓴다.

12 turn on은 구동사로 하나의 동사처럼 취급하여 be turned on으로 나타낸다. on을 빠뜨리지 않도록 주의한다.

13 want와 allow는 목적격보어로 to부정사를 쓴다.

14 make는 직접목적어를 주어로 한 수동태에서 간접목적어 앞에 for를 쓴다.

15 시제가 saw로 과거형이므로 was seen으로 쓰고, 목적격 보어 flying은 그대로 써준다. 원형부정사일 경우에는 to부정사로 써야 한다.

16 want는 목적격보어로 to부정사를 쓴다.

17 ② make는 사역동사이므로 목적격보어로 동사원형이 와야 하며, 나머지는 모두 to부정사가 와야 한다.

18 (3) make는 직접목적어를 주어로 하는 수동태만 가능하다. (4) 미래 시제의 수동태는 'will be+과거분사'이다. (5) 의문사 who가 whom으로 바뀌는 것에 주의한다.

서술형 시험대비
p.26~27

01 (1) Angelina was taught English by Williams last year.
　 (2) English was taught (to) Angelina by Williams last year.

02 (1) to draw (2) to read (3) to solve
　 (4) not to drive (5) to clean

03 (1) The floor was covered with a beautiful carpet.
　 (2) The book was not written in Korean.
　 (3) Animals there were taken care of by people.
　 (4) The watch was given (to) me two years ago by my father.
　 (5) A book was bought for me by her.

04 (1) I made a basket.
　 (2) *I and the village* was painted by Marc Chagall in 1911.

4　정답 및 해설

(3) A rotten tooth was pulled out by the dentist.

(4) Matthew kindly showed me the way to the National Museum.

(5) Dust covered him while he was walking along the road.

05 (1) She wants Steve to come home early.

(2) He believed his students to be diligent.

(3) He asked me to drive a car very carefully.

(4) My boss forced me to sign the agreement.

(5) The doctor told me not to do exercise too much.

06 (1) The airplane was invented by the Wright brothers.

(2) The house was built by him in 1963.

(3) Handerson is not interested in playing the guitar.

(4) He will be told of the news by his sister tomorrow.

(5) Soup was cooked for Christina by John.

07 (1) The woman asked the man to carry her bag.

(2) Emma advised me to wait till tomorrow.

(3) Peter told Sylvia to dance with him.

(4) They expected him to participate in the festival.

(5) Good health enabled him to finish the plan.

08 (1) study   (2) to call

01 teach는 직접목적어를 주어로 한 수동태에서 간접목적어 앞에 전치사 to를 쓴다.

02 (1) encourage (2) tell (3) order (4) warn (5) ask는 모두 목적격보어로 to부정사를 쓴다

03 (1) be covered with: ~로 덮여 있다 (2) 수동태의 부정은 'be+not+과거분사'이다. (3) take good care of를 하나의 동사처럼 생각해서 'be taken good care of'로 써야 한다. (4) give는 직접목적어를 주어로 한 수동태에서는 간접목적어 앞에 전치사 to를 써야 한다. (5) buy 는 직접목적어를 주어로 하는 수동태만 가능하다.

04 (3) pulled out은 하나의 동사로 취급해서 was pulled out으로 써야 한다. (4) show는 직접목적어를 주어로 한 수동태에서 간접목적어 앞에 전치사 to를 쓴다. (5) be covered는 by가 아니라 with를 쓴다.

05 (1) want (2) believe (3) ask (4) force 등의 동사는 목적격보어로 to부정사가 와야 한다. (5) to부정사의 부정형은 'not to+동사원형'으로 쓴다.

06 (1) 비행기가 발명되는 것이므로 수동태 (2) 수동태는 'be+ 과거분사' (3) be interested in: ~에 흥미가 있다 (4) tomorrow가 있는 수동태이므로 미래형 'will be+과거분사'로 써야 한다. (5) cook은 직접목적어를 주어로 한 수동태에서는 간접목적어 앞에 for를 쓴다.

07 ask, advise, tell, expect, enable 등은 모두 목적격보어로 to부정사가 와야 한다.

08 (1) 사역동사 have는 목적격보어로 원형부정사를 쓴다. (2) would like는 목적격보어로 to부정사를 쓴다.

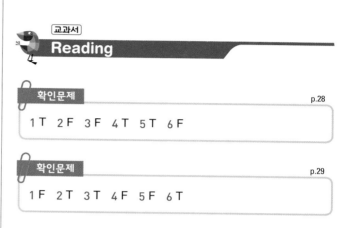

교과서 Reading

확인문제　　　　　　　　　p.28

1 T　2 F　3 F　4 T　5 T　6 F

확인문제　　　　　　　　　p.29

1 F　2 T　3 T　4 F　5 F　6 T

교과서 확인학습 A　　　　　p.30~31

01 about Upcycling
02 club members
03 As you know
04 each group's event idea, you to understand
05 explain upcycling
06 a combination of
07 Like recycling, is good for
08 from old things
09 for the event
10 Let's start with
11 to hold a trashion show
12 a combination of
13 We'll use trash
14 become interested in
15 sounds like fun
16 What about
17 make musical instruments
18 make, from
19 from old boxes, rubber bands
20 plan to play the instruments
21 let's hear from
22 make bags from
23 For example
24 Look at
25 was made by
26 Isn't it
27 sell them on Environment Day
28 to a nursing home
29 a great idea
30 all so creative
31 to work hard
32 Cut off
33 Sew, together
34 Make shoulder straps
35 to the top of
36 Decorate, with

1 Let's Talk about Upcycling

2 Hello, club members.

3 As you know, this year's Environment Day is about upcycling.

4 Before we talk about each group's event idea for that day, I want you to understand the meaning of "upcycling."

5 Can anyone explain upcycling?

6 Yes. The word "upcycling" is a combination of "upgrade" and "recycling."

7 Like recycling, upcycling is good for the environment.

8 When you upcycle, you make new and better things from old things.

9 Good. Now, let's talk about each group's idea for the event.

10 Let's start with Pei's group.

11 My group wants to hold a trashion show.

12 "Trashion" is a combination of "trash" and "fashion."

13 We'll use trash to make clothes.

14 We want other students to become interested in upcycling through the show.

15 A trashion show sounds like fun!

16 What about your group, Eric?

17 My group is going to make musical instruments from old things.

18 We'll make drums from old plastic buckets.

19 We'll also make a guitar from old boxes and rubber bands.

20 We plan to play the instruments in a mini-concert.

21 Thank you, Eric. Now, let's hear from Sumi's group.

22 My group will make bags from old clothes.

23 For example, we'll use blue jeans.

24 Look at this bag.

25 This was made by Hajun, one of our group members.

26 Isn't it nice?

27 We'll make more bags and sell them on Environment Day.

28 We're going to give all the money to a nursing home.

29 That's a great idea.

30 Your ideas are all so creative.

31 I want everyone to work hard for Environment Day.

32 Cut off the legs of the blue jeans.

33 Sew the bottom together.

34 Make shoulder straps from one of the legs.

35 Sew the straps to the top of the jeans.

36 Decorate the bag with pins and buttons.

시험대비 실력평가

01 ③   02 ⑤   03 ②

04 (A) other (B) through (C) like   05 ⑤

06 ③   07 ②   08 more bags

09 the bags → all the money

10 4 → 1 → 3 → 5 → 2   11 ⓐ with ⓑ to

12 one of the legs   13 ④   14 ③

15 at → for   16 ④   17 ①, in

18 ②   19 like   20 ②

21 I want everyone to work hard for Environment Day.

22 (A) old clothes   (B) Environment Day (C) all the money

23 one   24 directions

25 ① cut off a leg of the old blue jeans
  ② cut out a piece to make the bottom of the basket
  ③ sew the bottom to the leg
  ④ decorate with pins and buttons

26 ①   27 For instance   28 ④

29 Hajun, one of our group members, made this.

30 for → to   31 Lastly   32 decorate

33 To the top of the jeans.   34 ①, ③   35 ③

36 to become

37 They will make drums and a guitar.

01 recycling과 '마찬가지로' upcycling도 환경에 좋다.

02 ⓐ와 ⑤ 명사적 용법(목적격보어), ①과 ③ 부사적 용법(목적), ②와 ④ 형용사적 용법

03 '오래된 것들로' 새롭고 더 좋은 것들을 만든다고 해야 하므로 from이 적절하다.

04 (A) '다른' 학생들이라고 해야 하므로 other가 적절하다. another + 단수 명사, (B) 이 쇼를 '통해서'라고 해야 하므로 through가 적절하다. though: 비록 ~이지만, (C) '멋지겠구나'라고 해야 하므로 like가 적절하다. sound like fun: 재미있을 것 같다, sound like: ~처럼 들리다, alike: (아주) 비슷한 (명사 앞에는 안 씀)

05 ⑤ 소규모 음악회를 여는 장소는 알 수 없다. ① "trash"와 "fashion"이 결합한 말, ② 쓰레기, ③ 다른 학생들이 업사이클

링에 대해 관심을 가지게 되는 것, ④ 낡은 물건

06 위 글은 '두 그룹의 행사 아이디어'에 관한 글이다.

07 ② 앞의 내용의 예가 나오고 있으므로 For example(예를 들면)이 가장 적절하다. ① 그러나, ③ 그러므로, ④ 게다가, ⑤ 그 결과

08 가방을 더 많이 만들어서 환경의 날에 팔 것이라고 했기 때문에, them은 '더 많은 가방'을 가리킨다.

09 수미의 그룹은 낡은 옷으로 가방을 만들어 팔아서, 번 '돈'을 모두 양로원에 줄 예정이다.

10 4 청바지의 다리 부분을 잘라내기 → 1 아래쪽을 붙여서 바느질 하기 → 3 다리 한 짝으로 어깨 끈을 만들기 → 5 청바지의 윗 부분에 어깨끈을 바느질하기 → 2 핀과 단추로 가 방을 장식 하기

11 ⓐ 'with' pins and buttons: 핀과 단추들로, 핀과 단추들을 가지고, ⓑ 'to' the top of the jeans: 청바지의 윗 부분에

12 어깨 끈을 만들기 위해 청바지의 '다리 한 짝'이 필요하다.

13 ③번의 '업사이클링'의 의미를 이해하기를 바란다는 말과 ⑤번의 누가 업사이클링의 뜻을 설명해 줄 수 있느냐는 말 사이의 '업사이클링'은 새로운 물건을 만들기 위해 폐기물을 사용하는 것이라는 ④번 문장은 전체 글의 흐름에서 벗어난다.

14 upcycling은 upgrade의 'up'과 recycling의 'cycling'을 합 친 말이다.

15 재활용과 마찬가지로 upcycling도 '환경에 좋다'고 해야 하므 로 at을 for로 고쳐야 한다. be good at: ~을 잘하다, be good for: ~에 좋다

16 ④ 부사적 용법(결과), ⓐ와 나머지는 다 명사적 용법

17 ① be interested in: ~에 관심이 있다. 나머지는 다 from

18 ② 만족한, ① 지루한, ③ 우울한, ④ 부끄러운, ⑤ 실망한

19 sound like: ~처럼 들리다

20 ②번 다음 문장의 This에 주목한다. 주어진 문장의 this bag을 받고 있으므로 ②번이 적절하다.

21 'want+목적어+to부정사' 구문을 사용하면 된다.

22 (A) '낡은 옷'으로 가방을 만들기, (B) '환경의 날'에 가방을 팔 아서 (C) '번 돈'을 모두 양로원에 드리기

23 ⓐ 한 가지, ⓑ a basket을 가리키는 부정대명사

24 directions: 지시, 무엇을 할지, 어떻게 할지 혹은 어떤 장소에 어떻게 도착할지를 말해주는 지시, these 뒤이므로 복수 형태로 쓰는 것이 적절하다.

25 ① 낡은 청바지의 다리 부분을 자르기, ② 바구니의 바닥을 만들 기 위해 한 조각을 자르기, ③ 바닥을 다리 부분과 꿰매기 ④ 단추 와 핀으로 장식하기

26 ① (A)의 drums가 주어진 글의 musical instruments에 해 당하므로 제일 먼저 오고 (C)에서 also 로 악기의 예를 계속 설 명하므로 (A) 다음에 (C)가 이어지고 (B)의 the instruments 가 앞에서 말한 악기들을 가리키므로 (C) 다음에 (B)가 와야 한

다. 그러므로 (A)-(C)-(B)의 순서가 적절하다.

27 for example = for instance: 예를 들면

28 ⓑ look at: ~을 보다 ⓓ on+특정한 날

29 by 다음의 행위자를 능동태의 주어로 바꾸고 동격에 해당하는 부분 앞뒤로 콤마를 찍는 것이 적절하다.

30 수여동사 give는 간접목적어 앞에 전치사 to를 쓴다.

31 lastly: 마지막으로, 끝으로(무엇을 열거하면서 마지막 요소 앞 에 붙이는 말)

32 뭔가를 덧붙여 어떤 것을 더 매력적으로 만들다: decorate(장 식하다)

33 끈을 '청바지의 꼭대기'에 바느질해야 한다.

34 hold[have] a trashion show: 트래션 쇼를 열다

35 문맥상 upcycling이 되어야 한다. / upgrading: 등급상승

36 want+목적어+to부정사를 써야 한다.

서술형 시험대비 p.40~41

01 to understand
02 The word "upcycling" is a combination of "upgrade" and "recycling."
03 old → new,　new → old
04 trash
05 How about your group
06 드럼: 낡은 플라스틱 양동이　기타: 낡은 상자와 고무줄
07 We're going to give a nursing home all the money.
08 hardly → hard
09 wants to understand → wants club members to understand
10 each groups' → each group's
11 (A) make clothes　(B) trashion show
12 (A) drums　(B) a guitar

01 'want+목적어+to부정사'로 써야 한다.

02 The word와 "upcycling"은 동격이므로 같이 붙여 쓰면 된다.

03 업사이클을 할 때 '오래된' 것들로부터 '새롭고' 더 좋은 것들을 만들게 된다고 하는 것이 적절하다.

04 사용한 종이, 빈 병, 그리고 쓰레기 음식과 같은 원치 않는 물건 들 혹은 폐기물, trash: 쓰레기

05 What about ~? = How about ~?: ~은 어때?

06 드럼은 '낡은 플라스틱 양동이'로, 기타는 '낡은 상자와 고무줄' 로 만들 것이다.

07 전치사 to를 없애고 간접목적어(a nursing home), 직접 목적 어(all the money) 순서로 쓰면 된다.

08 너희들 모두 환경의 날을 위해 열심히 노력하길 바란다고 해야 하 기 때문에, hard로 고쳐야 한다. hardly: 거의 ~ 아니다[없다]

09 Mr. Brown은 '동아리 회원들'이 "upcycling"의 의미를 이해 하기를 원한다.

7

10 each는 뒤에 단수 명사를 써야 한다.

11 '옷을 만들기' 위해 쓰레기를 사용하고 '트래션 쇼'를 열 것이다.

12 낡은 플라스틱 양동이로 '드럼'을, 낡은 상자와 고무줄로 '기타'를 만들 것이다.

영역별 핵심문제

01 better   **02** ④   **03** ③   **04** ①

05 ②   **06** ⑤   **07** ④   **08** ④

09 clock   **10** ④   **11** ⑤   **12** ②

13 ①, ③, ④   **14** ⑤

15 (1) was made for me by my mom

  (2) were given to Emily by Jonathan, was given some flowers by Jonathan

  (3) made me wash his car

  (4) painted *Girl in the Woods*

  (5) was put off on account of the rain (by them)

16 (1) These chocolate cookies were baked by me.

  (2) We want to wash our clothes.

  (3) Her sister was taken care of by Judy.

  (4) The thief will be caught by the police.

  (5) She told me to wash my hands before dinner.

17 ⑤   **18** ②   **19** ④

20 (1) A doll was made for her by her mother.

  (2) Most of the doors in this building are made of wood.

  (3) I was brought up by my grandparents.

  (4) The teacher warned his students to hand in their homework by Friday.

  (5) I believe Ella to be very smart.

21 ④   **22** As you know   **23** ①

24 ③   **25** ⑤   **26** in a mini-concert

27 ③번, of → by   **28** ②

01 반의어 관계다. 비싼 : 싼 = 더 나은 : 더 나쁜

02 ⓐ는 '~은 어때요?'라는 의미로 How about ~?이 적절하고, ⓑ는 물건을 샀다는 의미로 take를 사용한다.

03 음악을 만들어 내기 위해 사용되는 물건

04 더 많이 알고 싶기 때문에 어떤 것에 더 많은 관심을 가지는

05 Nancy는 비치백의 끈을 잡았다. / 그녀는 잠옷 끈을 어깨 위로 끌어올렸다.

06 like는 전치사로 '~처럼, ~와 같이'라는 뜻이다.

07 M의 대답으로 보아 할인을 해준다는 말이 온다.

08 '그건 제게 너무 비쌉니다.'라는 말 다음에 '할인을 받을 수 있나요?'라는 말이 오는 것이 자연스럽다.

09 one은 앞에 나온 같은 종류의 명사를 대신하는 부정대명사로 clock을 가리킨다.

10 그것은 단지 일 년 밖에 되지 않았다고 했기 때문에 '거의 새 것이

다'라는 의미가 적절하므로 used를 new로 바꾼다.

11 ②는 '너는 무엇을 할 거니?' '음. 생각해 볼게.'라는 말로 자연스럽다. ⑤는 축구공의 가격을 물어보는 말에 '1달러 할인해 줄게요'라고 하는 말은 어색하다.

12 Andy는 축구공을 1달러 할인받은 가격인 5달러에 구입한다.

13 A의 대답으로 보아 빈칸에는 가격을 물어보는 표현이 자연스럽다.

14 ① We want you to join our club. ② The cookies were cooked by Eric. ③ Mr. Gilbert would like his students to do their best. ④ The airplane was invented by the Wright brothers.

15 (1), (2) 직접목적어를 주어로 한 수동태에서 make는 간접목적어 앞에 전치사 for를, give는 to를 쓴다. (3) make는 사역동사로 목적격보어로 원형부정사를 쓰지만 수동태에서 는 to부정사로 바뀐다. (4) 수동태는 'be+과거분사'의 형태이다. (5) 구동사는 하나의 어휘처럼 취급한다.

16 수동태는 'be+과거분사+by 행위자'의 형태이며, want와 tell은 목적격보어로 to부정사가 온다.

17 'want+목적어+to부정사: (목적어)가 ~하기를 원하다' ②번의 have는 사역동사로 목적격보어로 원형부정사가 온다.

18 The light는 동사 turned off의 행위의 대상이므로 수동태로 써야 적절하다.

19 have는 사역동사이므로 목적격보어로 원형부정사가 온다.

20 (1) make는 간접목적어를 주어로 수동태를 만들 수 없다. (동사의 의미 때문에 만들 수 없는 것임) (2) be made of: ~로 만들어지다(물리적 변 화), be made from: ~로 만들어지다(화학적 변화) (3) 구동사는 하나의 동 사처럼 취급한다. 동사와 함께 이어지는 어휘나 전치사 by를 빠뜨리기 쉬우므로 주의한다. (4), (5) warn, believe의 목적격보어로 to부정사가 적절하다.

21 ④ recycling과 upcycling의 차이점은 알 수 없다. ① upcycling, ② '업사이클링'이란 단어는 "upgrade"와 "recycling"이 결합한 것이다. ③ upcycling은 오래된 것들을 이용하여 새롭고 더 좋은 것들을 만들므로 환경에 좋다. ⑤ Pei의 그룹

22 as는 접속사로 '~하다시피[~하듯이]'의 뜻으로 쓰였다.

23 ⓑ와 ①은 '~와 (똑)같이[마찬가지로], ~처럼(전치사)', ②와 ④ ~을 좋아하다(동사), ③ 비슷한 것(명사), ⑤ (예를 들어) ~와 같은

24 ③ 낡은 '플라스틱' 양동이로 드럼을 만들 것이다.

25 Eric의 그룹은 낡은 물건들로 '악기'를 만들 것이다. ① 실험 도구, ② 자동차, ③ 의사소통 기구, ④ 건설장비

26 '소규모 음악회'에서 악기를 연주할 것이다.

27 수동태의 행위자 앞에 'by'를 쓰는 것이 적절하다.

28 ② 창의적인, 앞에서 훌륭한 생각이라고 했기 때문에, 발상이 모두 '창의적'이라고 하는 것이 적절하다. ① 따분한, 재미없는, ③ 흔한, ④ 지루한, ⑤ 구식의

8 정답 및 해설

01 creative   02 ③   03 (A) Sew   (B) Decorate

04 ④   05 ②   06 I'll take it.

07 (A) How about this red clock?

    (B) Can I get a discount?

08 how much is this blue clock with the large numbers?

09 ②   10 ③   11 ③   12 ④

13 (1) Were the students taught English by Emma?

     Was English taught to the students by Emma?

   (2) A lot of data can be sent through the Internet (by us).

   (3) *The Dance Class* was painted by Edgar Degas.

14 (1) give → to give

   (2) to wait → wait

15 (1) was painted by

   (2) was invented by

   (3) was pleased with

16 ②   17 ⑤   18 environment

19 ②   20 ⑤

21 (A) clothes   (B) trashion show   (C) upcycling

22 ③   23 this bag   24 ②

25 (1) Cut off   (2) Sew   (3) from

   (4) Sew   (5) Decorate

26 ④

---

01 유의어 관계다. 쓰레기 = 창의적인

02 단어나 표현 또는 표시가 나타내는 특정한 생각

03 upcycling은 upgrade와 recycling을 결합한 것이다. 재활용과 마찬가지로 업사이클링도 환경에 좋다. 업사이클링을 하면 여러분은 오래된 것들로 새롭고 더 나은 것을 만든다.

05 ①은 '이 시계는 할인 중인가요?'라는 뜻으로 yes/no로 대답을 하는 것이 자연스럽다. ③ '돈을 얼마나 가지고 있니?' ④ '이 신발 가격은 얼마인가요?'라는 뜻으로 적절해 보이지만 these shoes는 복수형이므로 They are ~로 답해야 한다.

07 (A)는 시계를 찾고 있다는 말에 대해 빨간색 시계가 어떠냐고 제안하는 말이 적절하고, (B)의 앞에 저에게는 너무 비싸다는 말이 있으므로 '할인을 받을 수 있을까요?'라는 말이 자연스럽다.

08 가격을 물어볼 때 'how much is[are] ~?'를 사용하고, 이 파란색 시계(this blue clock)가 주어이므로 단수동사 is를 사용한다.

09 ⓑ everything은 '모든 것'이라는 의미지만 단수 취급한다. are를 is로 바꾸어야 한다.

10 B의 대답이 사지 않겠다고 했기 때문에 할인을 하지 않는다는 표현이 적절하다.

11 ① The key was stolen by Bill. ② Presents were given to all the children. ④ Was her homework finished by her? ⑤ The spaghetti was made by my dad.

12 Tell them to come to my birthday party.

13 (1) 직접목적어를 주어로 하는 수동태에서 teach는 전치사 to를 간접목적어 앞에 붙여야 한다.(2) 조동사의 수동태는 '조동사+be+과거분사'의 형태로 쓴다. (3) 수동태는 'be+ 과거분사'의 형태로 쓴다.

14 (1) ask의 목적격보어로 to부정사가 와야 한다. (2) make는 사역동사이므로 목적격보어로 동사원형이 와야 한다.

15 (1), (2) 목적어가 주어로 나와 있으므로 수동태로 답을 작성한다. (3) be pleased는 전치사 with를 쓴다.

16 ⓐ와 ② ~하다시피[~하듯이] (접속사), ① (자격, 기능 등이) ~로(서) (전치사), ③ [보통 as ~ as ⋯로 형용사·부사 앞에서] ~와 같을 정도로(지시부사), ④ ~ 때문에(접속사), ⑤ (비례) ~함에 따라(접속사)

17 ⓑ talk about: ~에 대해 말하다, ⓒ event idea for that day: '그날(환경의 날)에 할' 행사 아이디어

18 upcycling은 '환경'에 좋다.

19 hold a show: 쇼를 열다

20 ⑤ 명사적 용법, ⓑ와 나머지는 다 부사적 용법 ① 형용사 수식, ② 원인, ③ 목적, ④ 이유

21 Pei의 그룹은 쓰레기를 사용하여 '옷'을 만들고 '트래션 쇼'를 준비할 것이다. 그들은 그 쇼를 통해 다른 학생들이 '업사이클링'에 관심을 가지게 되기를 바란다.

22 ③ 수미의 그룹이 얼마나 많은 돈을 벌기를 기대하는지는 대답할 수 없다. ① Bags from old clothes. ② On Environment Day. ④ They are going to give all the money to a nursing home. ⑤ He wants everyone to work hard for Environment Day.

23 하준이가 만든 '가방'을 가리킨다.

24 ① 저축하다, ② 기부하다, ③ 간직하다, ④ 저장[보관]하다, ⑤ 재활용하다

25 ① 청바지의 다리 부분을 '자르기', ② 아래쪽을 붙여서 '바느질하기', ③ 다리 '한 짝으로' 어깨 끈을 만들기, ④ 청바지의 윗부분에 어깨끈을 '바느질하기', ⑤ 핀이나 단추로 가방을 '장식하기'

26 '지퍼'는 필요한 재료가 아니다.

---

01 15 dollars / one year / 10 dallars / the large numbers, He will[is going to] buy the blue clock.

02 (A) How much is this black bag?

   (B) I'll take 2 dollars off.

03 round glasses / 18 dollars / I'm afraid not

04 (1) Ms. Brown asked the students to clean the classroom.

(2) His parents expected him to win the contest.

(3) The boss warned the driver to drive very carefully.

05 The book was not written in Korean.

06 (1) not to be late   (2) not to give up

07 interesting → interested

08 A trashion show sounds like fun!

09 (A) musical instruments   (B) old plastic buckets
(C) from   (D) the instruments

10 (A) clothes   (B) Isn't   (C) to

11 낡은 옷으로 가방을 만들어 환경의 날에 가방을 판 다음, 번 돈을 양로원에 줄 예정이라는 것

12 wants to work → wants everyone to work

01 소년은 무엇을 살 것인가?

02 (A)는 B의 대답으로 볼 때 검정색 가방의 가격을 묻고 있다는 것을 알 수 있다. (B) 그림에서 15달러를 13달러로 할인해 주고 있다는 것을 알 수 있다. 그래서 2달러 깎아 준다는 표현이 적절하다.

03 Jenny가 사려고 하는 물건은 둥근 안경(round glasses)이고, 가격은 18달러다. 할인을 받을 수 있느냐는 질문에 남자가 No 라고 말했으므로 '안 될 것 같아요(I'm afraid not.)'라는 말이 오는 것이 적절하다.

04 ask, expect, warn 등은 목적격보어로 to부정사를 쓴다.

05 그 책이 주어이므로 수동태로 쓴다.

06 ask와 encourage는 목적격보어로 to부정사를 쓰고 부정사의 부정은 not을 앞에 붙인다.

07 '흥미를 가지게 되는 것'이므로 interested가 적절하다.

08 sound like: ~하게 들리다

09 (A) 오래된 물건들로 '악기'를 만들기, (B) '낡은 플라스틱 양동이'로 드럼을 만들기, (C) 낡은 상자와 고무줄'로' 기타를 만들기, (D) 소규모 음악회를 열어 '그 악기들'로 연주하기

10 (A) '낡은 옷'으로 가방을 만들 것이라고 해야 하므로 clothes가 적절하다. cloths: cloth(옷감, 천)의 복수, (B) 그것은 멋지지 '않나요?'라고 해야 하므로 Isn't가 적절하다. (C) give는 to를 사용하여 3형식으로 고친다.

11 ① '낡은 옷으로 가방을 만들 것이다.', ② '환경의 날에 가방을 팔 것이다.', ③ '번 돈을 모두 양로원에 줄 것이다.' 라는 내용을 포함해서 쓰면 정답.

12 Mr. Brown은 '모든 사람들'이 환경의 날을 위해 열심히 노력하길 바란다.

창의사고력 서술형 문제   p.54

|모범답안|

01 (1) A: May I help you?
B: Yes. How much is this scarf?

A: It's 6 dollars.
B: Can I get a discount?
A: OK. I'll take 2 dollars off.
B: I'll take it.

(2) A: May I help you?
B: Yes. How much is this T-shirt?
A: It's 10 dollars.
B: Can I get a discount?
A: No, I'm afraid not. Sorry.
B: Then, I don't think I'll take it.

02 (1) Mom wants Minsu to clean his room.

(2) Mom wants Mina to do the dishes.

(3) Mom wants me to walk the dog.

03 (A) directions(또는 steps)   (B) cut
(C) Second   (D) decorate

단원별 모의고사   p.55~58

01 ③   02 upgrade   03 ①   04 ⑤

05 (A) How much   (B) It's 20 dallars
(C) take 2 dallars off

06 am looking for / get a discount / take, off / 12

07 (1) How much is this pink skirt?

(2) I'll take 1 dollar off.

08 ④   09 ⑤   10 ⑤   11 ③

12 I'll take the blue one.

13 (1) We made this flower pot from an ice cream bowl.

(2) The song, *Yesterday*, was written by the Beatles.

(3) Some cookies were cooked for us by her.

(4) Picasso was laughed at at first (by people).

14 ②   15 was heard to open the window by me

16 close → to close   17 I believe her to be kind.

18 (this year's) Environment Day   19 ①

20 (A) Pei's group   (B) Environment Day   21 ②

22 ③   23 ⑤   24 member → members

25 Your ideas are all so creative. 혹은 All your ideas are so creative.

01 ③: 물건을 사기 위해 지불해야 하는 금액 = price(가격)

02 반의어 관계다. 비싼 : 값싼 = 격하시키다 : 개선시키다

03 이해하기 쉽고 분명한 방식으로 어떤 것을 말해주다

04 첫 번째 빈칸은 할인을 하다는 의미로 take off를 사용하고, 두 번째 빈칸은 물건을 사다는 의미로 take를 쓴다.

05 (A)는 티셔츠의 가격을 물어보는 표현(How much)이 오고

(B)는 셔츠의 가격이 20달러(It's 20 dollars)라는 말이 오고 (C)는 2달러 깎아 준다(take 금액 off)는 표현이 오는 것이 자연스럽다.

07 (1)은 B의 대답으로 보아 분홍 스커트의 가격을 묻는 말이 오는 것이 자연스럽고 (2)는 '깎아 주실 수 있어요?'라는 물음에 대한 답으로, 그림에서 10달러에서 9달러로 1달러 할인을 해준다는 걸 알 수 있다.

08 ⓐ의 one은 앞에 나온 backpack을 가리키는 부정대명사고, ⓑ의 it은 15달러 하는 the red backpack을 가리킨다.

09 ⑤ 도와 드릴까요?라는 물음에 '좋군요. 그걸 살게요.'라는 답은 적절하지 않다.

10 ① 한정사로 '하나의' ② 강조의 의미로 '단 하나의' ③ 강조의 의미로 '단 하나의' ④ 1을 의미한다. ⑤ 명사를 대신하는 부정대명사

11 ③ 파란색 시계가 얼마나 오래 되었는지는 대화에서 언급되어 있지 않다.

12 take는 물건을 '사다, 선택하다'라는 뜻이다.

13 (1) 보통 We나 They가 주어일 경우 by us나 by them을 생략한다. (3) cook은 직접목적어를 주어로 하는 수동태만 가능하며 간접목적어 앞에 전치사 for를 쓴다. (4) laugh at은 하나의 동사처럼 취급되므로 수동태로 바뀌어도 at을 빠뜨리면 안 된다. by people은 생략할 수 있다.

14 ② ask의 목적격보어로 to부정사가 적절하다.

15 hear는 목적격보어로 원형부정사를 쓰지만, 수동태에서는 원형부정사를 to부정사로 바꿔 주어야 한다.

16 ask의 목적격보어로 to부정사가 적절하다.

17 believe는 목적격보어로 to부정사를 쓴다.

18 '(올해의) 환경의 날'을 가리킨다.

19 start with: ~와 함께 출발하다

20 'Pei의 그룹'이 '환경의 날'을 위한 행사 아이디어에 대해 말할 것이다.

21 ② 몇 명의 학생들이 upcycling에 관심이 있는지는 대답할 수 없다. ① Pei's group. ③ He thinks a trashion show sounds like fun. ④ From old things. ⑤ Sumi.

22 ③ 좋아하다(동사) ⓐ와 나머지는 모두 전치사로 '~와 같은, ~처럼'의 뜻이다.

23 Mr. Brown은 '모든 사람들이' 환경의 날을 위해 열심히 일하기를 원한다.

24 ~ 중의 하나: one of 복수명사

25 all을 소유격 앞에 써도 된다.

Lesson 4

The Amazing World of Animals

시험대비 실력평가
p.62

01 ⑤　　02 ⑤　　03 ②　　04 ③
05 ①　　06 (1) fables　(2) unique　(3) carried
07 ④　　08 ②

01 have to: ~해야 한다 / wear: 입다 / protection: 보호
02 take a rest: 휴식하다
03 pull out: ~을 뽑다
04 ③ pile: 쌓다, 포개다
05 drop: 떨어뜨리다
06 (1) fable: 우화, 동화 (2) unique: 독특한 (3) carry: 휴대하다
07 ① floss: 치실질을 하다 ② jar: 병, 단지 ③ photograph: 사진 ④ level: 높이, 정도, 수준 ⑤ parrots, parrot: 앵무새
08 fable: 우화

서술형 시험대비
p.63

01 (1) (f)loat　(2) female　(3) (u)nique　(4) lucky
02 (1) hide　(2) floss　(3) succeeded　(4) left
03 (1) look　(2) talk
04 (1) She was surprised to see a snake.
　(2) I was dressed in a navy suit.
　(3) The temple is located among the pine trees.
05 (1) a cup[glass] of, experiment　(2) male, find
06 (t)alent
07 (n)avy

01 (1) 반의어 관계, subtract: 빼다 add: 더하다 sink: 가라앉다 float: ([물체가] [액체 면에]) 뜨다, 떠다니다 (2) 반의어 관계, stupid: 멍청한 smart: 똑똑한 male: 남자의, 수컷의 female: 여성의, 암컷의 (3) 동의어 관계, good: 좋은 nice: 좋은 special: 특별한 unique: 독특한 (4) soft: 부드러운 smooth: 매끄러운 fortunate: 운이 좋은, 행운의 lucky: 운이 좋은
02 (1) hide: 숨다, 감추다 (2) floss: 치실질을 하다 (3) succeed: 성공하다 (4) leave: ~을 두고 가다
03 (1) look for: ~을 찾다 / look like: ~처럼 보이다, ~와 닮다 (2) talk to: ~에게 말하다 / talk with: ~와 이야기하다

04 (1) surprise: 놀라게 하다 (2) navy: 남색 (3) temple: 절, 사원

05 (1) a cup[glass] of ~: 한 컵의 / experiment: 실험, 시험 (2) male: 남자의 / 수컷의 find: 찾다

06 talent: 재능

07 navy: 남색

Conversation 〔교과서〕

핵심 Check   p.64~65

1 What does, look, long and black
2 (C) → (A) → (D) → (B)
3 Can you explain / has polka dots

교과서 대화문 익히기

Check(√) True or False   p.66

1 T 2 T 3 T 4 F

교과서 확인학습   p.68~69

Listen and Talk A-1

looking for / like / cotton / tell me more / grey / go, check

Listen and Talk A-2

I help you / lost, left, restroom / What, like / It's / What else, more / two pockets outside

Listen and Talk A-3

help / lost my umbrella / does it look / long and navy / tell / a star pattern on

Listen and Talk A-4

Do you / I'm looking / it look like / not very big, has / you tell me, anything special / short tail

Listen and Talk B

I'm looking for / does it look like / It's, has grey / Can, about it / has

Listen and Talk B-2

May / I'm looking for, wallet / What, like / tell, about /

There is a card

Listen and Talk C

for, His name / What does he look like / has short white / Can you / he, really / one more thing, Where / lost, main / I'll, make an announcement / wait

Talk and Play

look like / tall, brown / Can you tell me more / wearing, pants / found

Review

lost, umbrella / does it / big navy umbrella / tell me more / has, flower pattern on

시험대비 기본평가   p.70

01 ⑤   02 ③   03 ④
04 (B) - (A) - (D) - (C)

01 'What does ~ look like?'는 '~는 어떻게 생겼니?'라는 의미로 외모나 생김새를 묻는 질문이다.

02 어떻게 생겼는지 질문하고 또 다른 정보를 묻는 상황이므로 ③이 어울린다.

03 외모나 형태를 물어보고 있으므로 성격을 나타내고 있는 ④는 어울리지 않는다.

04 look for: ~을 찾다 / scarf: 스카프, 목도리 / cotton: 면 / long: 긴

시험대비 실력평가   p.71~72

01 ①   02 ⑤   03 ③   04 ②
05 ④   06 ① looking → looking for   07 ④
08 ⑤ special anything → anything special   09 ④
10 ④   11 I'm looking for my dog.   12 ②
13 ③   14 (A) has long   (B) wearing short
13 (f)ound

01 ① 다음에 나오는 인칭대명사 it을 사용하기 위해서는 지칭되는 명사가 나와야 한다.

02 잃어버린 물건을 찾기 위해서 간 장소이므로 분실물 보관소이다.

03 Tell me more about it.: 그것에 대해 더 말해 주세요. ④는 Talk to me more가 되어야 한다.

04 ② 가방 바깥쪽에 2개의 주머니가 있다.

05 should: ~해야 한다

06 look for: ~을 찾다

07 have: 가지고 있다, she는 3인칭 단수형이므로 has가 적절하다.

08 anything과 같이 -thing으로 끝나는 대명사는 형용사가 뒤에서 수식한다.

12 정답 및 해설

09 남자아이의 고양이는 꼬리가 짧다.

10 잃어버린 장소를 말하는 문장 앞에 와야 한다.

11 look for: ~을 찾다

12 make an announcement: 방송을 하다

13 ③ main gate: 정문 / near: 근처

14 (1) 명사를 수식하는 형용사가 여러 개 나왔을 경우 '외형(크기, 형상/길이) + 신구/색깔 + 재료'의 순서로 명사를 수식할 수 있다. (2) wear: 입다 / navy: 남색

15 find–found–found: 찾다

서술형 시험대비
p.73

01 I think I lost my umbrella.

02 It has a white flower pattern on it.

03 (A) in 또는 at   (B) like

04 yellow

05 Can you tell me more about it?

06 it has two pockets outside

07 (C) – (A) – (E) – (B) – (D)

08 my cat, no very big, black hair, has a short tail

02 pattern: 무늬, 도안

03 in[at]: ~에서 / look like: ~처럼 보이다, ~와 닮다

04 yellow: 노란색

05 Can you tell me more?는 '더 말해 주시겠어요?'라는 의미로 추가적인 정보를 물을 때 사용한다.

06 have: 가지다 / pocket: 주머니 / outside: 바깥에, 밖에

07 May I help you?: 도와드릴까요? / look for: ~을 찾다 / look like: ~처럼 보이다, ~와 닮다 / small: 작은

08 look for: ~을 찾다 / cat: 고양이 / lost: 잃어버린 / hair: 털 / short: 짧은 / tail: 꼬리

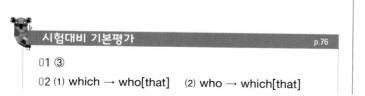

교과서
Grammar

핵심 Check
p.74~75

1 (1) who[that]   (2) which[that]

2 (1) if   (2) ends, will go   (3) if, will

시험대비 기본평가
p.76

01 ③

02 (1) which → who[that]   (2) who → which[that]

(3) 뒤에 나오는 don't 삭제 또는 unless → if

(4) will rain → rains

03 (1) If you see my sister

(2) who was wearing a funny hat

04 ②

01 선행사가 The girl로 사람이며 is standing의 주어 역할을 하므로 주격 관계대명사 who나 that이 적절하다.

02 (1) 선행사가 사람이므로 which를 who나 that으로 고쳐야 한다. (2) 선행사가 사물이므로 who를 which나 that으로 고쳐야 한다. (3) unless는 'if ~ not'의 의미이므로 뒤에 나오는 don't를 삭제하거나 unless를 if로 고쳐야 한다. (4) 조건의 접속사가 이끄는 부사절에서는 미래의 의미를 갖더라도 will을 쓰지 않고 현재시제를 쓰므로 will rain을 rains로 고쳐야 한다.

03 (1) if는 '만약 ~한다면'이라는 뜻의 접속사이다. (2) 선행사가 사람이므로 who를 쓴다.

04 조건의 접속사가 이끄는 부사절에서는 미래의 의미를 갖더라도 will을 쓰지 않고 현재시제를 쓴다.

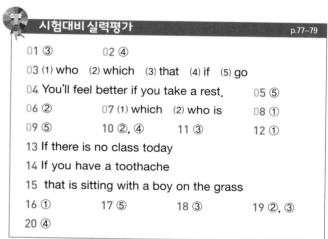

시험대비 실력평가
p.77~79

01 ③   02 ④

03 (1) who   (2) which   (3) that   (4) if   (5) go

04 You'll feel better if you take a rest.   05 ⑤

06 ②   07 (1) which   (2) who is   08 ①

09 ⑤   10 ②, ④   11 ③   12 ①

13 If there is no class today

14 If you have a toothache

15 that is sitting with a boy on the grass

16 ①   17 ⑤   18 ③   19 ②, ③

20 ④

01 모두 주격으로 사용된 관계대명사 that이 들어갈 수 있지만 ③번은 소유격 관계대명사 of which가 들어가야 한다.

02 ④ unless = if ~ not이므로 Unless가 아니라 If가 되어야 한다.

03   (1) 선행사가 사람이므로 who, (2) 선행사가 사물이므로 which, (3) 선행사가 사람이므로 that (4) 의미상 if (5) 조건의 부사절에서는 미래시제 대신에 현재시제를 쓴다.

04 조건의 부사절에서는 미래시제 대신에 현재시제를 쓰므로 if 절은 현재시제로 쓰고, 주절은 미래시제로 쓴다.

05 ⑤번은 접속사이지만 나머지는 모두 관계대명사이다.

06 ②번만 know의 목적절을 이끄는 '~인지 아닌지'로 쓰였다.

07 목적격 관계대명사와 '주격 관계대명사+be동사'는 생략할 수 있다.

08 ① 조건절이 미래의 일을 나타낼 때에도 조건절의 시제는 현재형을 쓴다.

09 관계대명사의 선행사가 사람이면 who, whom이나 that을 쓰

고 사물이면 which나 that을 쓴다. bloom: 꽃이 피(게 하)다, 개화하다

10 의미상 ②, ④가 적절하다. unless = if ~ not

11 선행사가 동물이므로 which나 that을 이용하고 주격이므로 주어로 쓰인 it은 쓰지 말아야 한다.

12 ②번에서는 who를 which나 that으로 바꿔야 하고, ③~ ⑤에서는 관계대명사는 접속사와 대명사 역할을 하므로 it이 없어야 한다.

13 if절은 'if+주어+동사 ~'의 어순으로 쓴다.

14 '이가 아프면 치과 의사에게 가야 한다.'는 말로 조건을 나타내는 if를 이용한다.

15 주격 관계대명사 다음에 동사를 써야 한다.

16 ① What shall we do if it begins snowing?

17 선행사가 사물이므로 which나 that을 써야 한다.

18 unless = if ~ not

19 주어진 문장과 ②, ③번의 who는 주격 관계대명사이다. ①, ⑤번은 목적격 관계대명사, ④번은 의문대명사이다.

20 unless는 'if ~ not'의 의미로 '명령문, or ~(~해라, 그렇지 않으면)'로 바꿔 쓸 수 있다.

서술형 시험대비
p.80~81

01 (1) This is a great book which[that] gave hope to many people.
  (2) Pilots are the persons who[that] fly airplanes.
  (3) David has a brother who[that] plays basketball well.
  (4) Kate bought some roses which[that] smelled good.
  (5) Look at the man and his dog that are sleeping under the tree.

02 (1) If (2) Unless

03 (1) This is a bird which[that] can talk.
  (2) Look at those musicians who[that] are singing on the street.
  (3) Alice lives in a house which[that] has a beautiful garden.
  (4) She is drawing two pictures that look very similar.
  (5) I like Cindy who is very cool.

04 (1) Kathy will go shopping in the afternoon if she is not busy.
  (2) If you meet Morina tomorrow, can you tell her to call me?
  (3) Unless you study hard, you won't pass the exam. 또는 If you don't study hard, you won't

pass the exam.
  (4) If the weather is bad, I will not go hiking.

05 (1) Don't take the umbrella which I bought last weekend.
  (2) Do you know the girl whom Jack met in the park?
  (3) He is the tour guide who will guide us in New York City.

06 (1) If I go to Jeju-do
  (2) If you finish your homework
  (3) If I go shopping

07 (1) which Diana lives in
  (2) that Diana lives in
  (3) in which Diana lives
  (4) Diana lives in

08 (1) If I meet my favorite actor on the street, I will take pictures with him.
  (2) The work will not be done unless you do it.

09 (1) It can clean my room.
  (2) The girl is my friend, Ann.
  (3) It is famous for traditional Korean food.
  (4) I want to have a friend.

10 If school finishes early today, I will read a book.

01 (1), (4) 선행사가 사물이므로 관계대명사 which나 that을 써야 한다. (2), (3) 선행사가 사람이므로 관계대명사 who나 that을 써야 한다. (5) 선행사가 '사람+동물'이므로 관계대명사 that을 써야 한다.

02 명령문 + and ~: '~해라, 그러면'(= If ~) / 명령문 + or ~: '~해라, 그렇지 않으면'(Unless = If ~ not)

03 (1), (3) 선행사가 사물이므로 관계대명사 which나 that을 써야 한다. (2) 선행사가 사람이므로 관계대명사 who나 that을 써야 한다. (4) two pictures가 선행사이므로 look이 되어야 한다. (5) 관계대명사가 접속사와 대명사의 역할을 하므로 she를 삭제해야 한다.

04 (1), (2) 조건절에서는 현재시제로 미래시제를 대신한다. (3), (4) unless = if ~ not

05 (1) 선행사가 사물이므로 which를 쓴다. (2) 선행사가 사람이고 목적격이므로 whom을 쓴다. (3) 선행사가 사람이고 주격이므로 who를 쓴다.

06 조건절에서는 현재시제로 미래시제를 대신한다.

07 선행사가 사물이므로 which나 that을 쓴다. 전치사를 관계대명사 앞으로 옮길 수 있으나 관계대명사 that은 전치사 다음에 쓸 수 없다. 목적격 관계대명사는 생략 가능하다

08 조건절에서는 현재시제로 미래시제를 대신하며, unless는 'if ~ not'의 의미이다.

09 주격 관계대명사는 선행사가 사람이면 who나 that, 사물이나 동물이면 which나 that을 쓰고, 관계대명사절에서 주어 역할을 하며 다음에 동사가 나온다.

10 조건절에서는 현재시제로 미래시제를 대신한다.

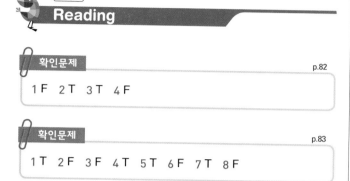

교과서
Reading

확인문제
p.82

1 F   2 T   3 T   4 F

확인문제
p.83

1 T   2 F   3 F   4 T   5 T   6 F   7 T   8 F

교과서 확인학습 A
p.84~85

01 That, Tools   02 once, thought
03 are finding out, also   04 watch out for
05 pull out   06 to floss their teeth
07 that are teaching flossing
08 While, floss their teeth   09 learn to floss
10 don't usually think
11 However, can also use   12 for protection
13 a good hiding place, hide under
14 even store, for later use
15 pile, to use later   16 How
17 drops, into, to raise
18 this is just a story
19 did an experiment   20 with, in front of
21 on top of the   22 However, water level, low
23 just as   24 dropped, into   25 special, wrong
26 with other crows, did the same

교과서 확인학습 B
p.86~87

1 Animals That Use Tools
2 People once thought that only humans can use tools.
3 Now, scientists are finding out that many animals can also use tools.
4 If you go to a Buddhist temple in Lop Buri, Thailand, watch out for the Macaque monkeys.

5 They may come to you and pull out your hair.
6 They use human hair to floss their teeth.
7 If you are lucky, you may see female monkeys that are teaching flossing to their babies.
8 While the babies are watching, the female monkeys floss their teeth very slowly.
9 This way, the baby monkeys learn to floss.
10 People don't usually think that octopuses are smart.
11 However, octopuses are very smart, and they can also use tools.
12 They use coconut shells for protection.
13 When they can't find a good hiding place, they hide under coconut shells.
14 Some octopuses even store coconut shells for later use.
15 They pile the coconut shells and carry them to use later.
16 How smart!
17 In Aesop's fable *The Thirsty Crow*, a crow drops stones into a jar to raise the level of water.
18 You may think this is just a story, but it is not.
19 Scientists who were studying crows did an experiment.
20 They put a jar with water in front of a crow.
21 A worm was floating on top of the water.
22 However, the water level was low, so the crow could not eat the worm.
23 The crow solved the problem just as in the fable.
24 It dropped stones into the jar.
25 If you think this bird is special, you are wrong.
26 Scientists did the same experiment with other crows, and they all did the same, too.

시험대비 실력평가
p.88~93

01 (A) watch (B) to floss (C) are   02 ②
03 ④   04 ⑤   05 ⑤
06 (A) low (B) solved (C) wrong
07 to raise the level of water   08 ①, ⑤
09 ④   10 will go → go   11 ①, ④
12 ④   13 for   14 ⑤   15 (f)able
16 ordinary → special   17 ①, ④ / ②, ③, ⑤
18 ④   19 use tools   20 ②
21 (A) can't (B) under (C) pile
22 coconut shells   23 ③
24 very well   25 ④   26 ④

15

02 ②번은 허가를 나타내어 '~해도 좋다'라는 뜻이고, ⓐ와 나머지는 다 추측을 나타내어 '~일지도 모른다'라는 뜻이다.

03 ④ 항상 볼 수 있는 것이 아니라, '만약 당신이 운이 좋으면 볼 수 있다.'

04 ⑤ them은 '문어'가 아니라 '코코넛 껍데기'를 지칭한다.

05 ⑤ 문어들이 몇 개의 코코넛 껍데기를 저장하는 지는 대답할 수 없다. ① No. ② Yes. ③ Coconut shells. ④ They hide under coconut shells.

06 (A) 물 높이가 '낮아서' 까마귀는 그 벌레를 먹을 수 없었다고 해야 하므로 low가 적절하다. (B) 그 까마귀는 우화에서처럼 문제를 '해결했다'고 해야 하므로 solved가 적절하다. give up: 포기하다, (C) 이 새가 특별하다고 생각한다면, 당신이 '틀렸다'고 해야 하므로 wrong이 적절하다.

07 까마귀는 '물 높이를 높이기 위해' 항아리 안으로 돌을 떨어 뜨렸다.

08 ⓐ와 ①, ⑤는 부사적 용법,
② 명사적 용법(보어),
③과 ④ 형용사적 용법

09 ④번 다음 문장의 This way에 주목한다. 주어진 문장의 내용을 받고 있으므로 ④번이 적절하다.

10 조건의 부사절에서는 현재시제가 미래시제를 대신한다.

11 ⓑ와 ②, ③, ⑤는 부사적 용법(목적), ① 형용사적 용법, ④ 명사적 용법

12 앞에 나오는 내용과 상반되는 내용이 뒤에 이어지므로 However가 가장 적절하다. ① 그러므로, ② 게다가, ③ 대신에, ⑤ 예를 들면

13 ⓑ for protection: 보호하기 위해,
ⓒ for later use: 나중에 쓰기 위해서

14 ⑤ 몇몇 문어들은 코코넛 껍데기를 '나중에' 쓰기 위해 가지고 다닌다.

15 fable: 우화, 도덕적 교훈을 가르치고, 가끔 동물을 주인공으로 다루는 이야기

16 이 새가 '특별하다'고 생각한다면 당신이 틀렸다고 해야 하므로, ordinary를 special로 고치는 것이 적절하다. ordinary: 보통의, 평범한

17 ⓐ: 관계대명사, ⓑ: 접속사

18 본문의 끝에서 이제 과학자들은 많은 동물들 역시 도구를 사용할 수 있다는 것을 밝혀내고 있다고 했기 때문에, 다음에 올 내용으로는 ④번이 적절하다.

19 이제 과학자들은 인간들뿐만 아니라 많은 동물들도 '도구를 사용할 수 있다'는 것을 밝혀내고 있다. not only A but also B: A뿐만 아니라 B도

20 ①에서 언급한 protection에 대한 설명이 ③에서 계속되고 있는데, 그 사이의 '코코넛 껍데기는 잠자기에 좋은 장소'라는 ② 번 문장은 전체 글의 흐름에서 벗어난다.

21 (A)와 (B) 숨을 만한 좋은 장소를 찾을 수 '없을' 때, 코코넛 껍데기 '아래로' 숨는다고 해야 하므로 각각 can't와 under가 적절하다. (C) 코코넛 껍데기를 '쌓아두고' 나중에 쓰기 위해서 그것들을 가지고 다닌다고 해야 하므로 pile이 적절하다. pile: (물건을 차곡차곡) 쌓다[포개다], file: 서류철

22 그들은 보호를 위한 도구로 '코코넛 껍데기'를 사용한다.

23 ③ 자이언트 판다가 얼마나 빨리 달릴 수 있는지는 대답할 수 없다. ① They grow 1.2m to 1.9m long and weigh up to 135kg. ② They live in the wild, high up in the mountains of China. ④ They eat leaves, fish, and small animals. ⑤ They are very good at climbing trees. They take a rest on trees. They even walk from one tree to another.

24 be good at ~ing: ~을 잘하다

25 (C)의 However가 주어진 글과 반대되는 내용을 이끄는 것이므로 제일 먼저 오고 (C)에서 언급한 protection에 대한 설명이 (A)에서 계속되므로 (C) 다음에 (A)가 이어지고 (B)의 the coconut shells가 (A)의 마지막에 나오는 coconut shells를 가리키므로 (A) 다음에 (B)가 와야 한다. 그러므로 (C)-(A)-(B)의 순서가 적절하다.

26 주어진 문장의 They에 주목한다. ④번 앞 문장의 Scientists를 가리키므로 ④번이 적절하다.

27 just as: 꼭 ~처럼

28 까마귀는 영리한 동물이고 도구를 사용할 줄 안다는 내용의 글이다.

29 위 글은 문어들이 매우 영리하다는 것을 설명하는 글이므로, '문어, 영리한 동물!'이 제목으로 적절하다.

30 '과학자들'을 가리킨다.

31 까마귀가 벌레를 먹을 수 없었을 때, 그것은 이솝 우화 '목마른 까마귀'의 까마귀가 그러는 것처럼 수위를 높이기 위해 항아리 '안으로' '돌을 떨어뜨렸다.'

32 (B)의 They가 주어진 글의 the Macaque monkeys를 가리키므로 제일 먼저 오고 (A)의 the female monkeys가 (C)의 female monkeys를 가리키므로 (C) 다음에 (A)가 와야 한다. 그러므로 (B)-(C)-(A)의 순서가 적절하다.

33 (B)의 this가 주어진 글의 내용을 가리키므로 제일 먼저 오고 (A)의 They가 (B)의 Scientists를 가리키므로 (B) 다음에 (A)가 이어지고 (C)의 It이 (A)의 마지막에 나오는 The crow를 가리키므로 (A) 다음에 (C)가 와야 한다. 그러므로 (B)-(A)-(C)의 순서가 적절하다.

01 Uses → Use   02 that

03 (A) animals   (B) humans

04 (A) pull   (B) lucky   (C) While

05 female monkeys   06 pulling out

07 to prevent accidents → for protection

08 pile   09 stones   10 with

11 과학자들이 다른 까마귀들에게도 똑같은 실험을 했고, 그들 모두가 똑같이 그렇게 했기 때문이다.

12 when they can't find a good hiding place

13 Some octopuses even store coconut shells for later use.

14 to carry → carry

01 선행사인 Animals가 복수이므로 Use가 적절하다.

02 목적어에 해당하는 명사절을 이끄는 접속사 that을 생략할 수 있다.

03 '인간들' 외에도 도구를 사용할 수 있는 많은 '동물들'이 있다. in addition to: ~에 더하여, ~뿐 아니라

04 (A) 당신의 머리카락을 '뽑을 수도' 있다고 해야 하므로 pull이 적절하다. push: 밀다, (B) 만약 네가 '운이 좋으면'이라고 해야 하므로 lucky가 적절하다. unlucky: 불행한, (C) 뒤에 '주어+동사'가 이어지므로 While이 적절하다. during 다음에는 기간을 나타내는 명사가 나온다.

05 새끼들에게 치실질하는 것을 가르치고 있는 '암컷 원숭이들'을 가리킨다.

06 전치사 by 다음에 동명사로 쓰는 것이 적절하다.

07 문어들은 매우 영리하고, 사고를 예방하기 위해서가 아니라 '보호를 위해' 코코넛 껍데기를 사용한다.

08 물건들을 서로 겹쳐 놓다, pile: (물건을 차곡차곡) 쌓다[포개다]

09 까마귀가 낮은 물 높이 때문에 벌레를 먹을 수 없었을 때, 그것은 물 높이를 높이기 위해 항아리 안으로 돌을 떨어뜨렸다.

10 ⓐ a jar with water: 물이 든 항아리, ⓒ with other crows: 다른 까마귀들에게도

11 다른 까마귀들도 똑같이 했기 때문에, 이 새가 특별하다고 생각한다면 당신이 틀렸다.

12 그들을 '숨을 만한 좋은 장소를 찾지 못할 때' 보호를 위해 그들은 코코넛 껍데기 아래로 숨는다.

13 'later'를 보충하면 된다.

14 'pile'과 병렬구문을 이루도록 하는 것이 적절하다.

01 (1) (p)ile   (2) (t)alent   (3) (s)olve   (4) (s)urprise

02 announcement   03 ②   04 level

05 (c)oconut   (t)ool   (p)hotograph

    (1) photograph   (2) coconut   (3) tool

06 (1) The body of an octopus looks like a bag.

    (2) The arms of a gorilla are longer than its legs.

07 (A) big (B) navy (C) flower

08 (A) scarf (B) blue (C) star

09 ③   10 (A) ③ (B) ④ (C) ②

11 the bag which is big and orange

12 ④   13 ④

14 Mr. Kim lives in a house. It has many big windows.

15 ③   16 ④   17 ②   18 ⑤

19 ①   20 ③

21 This is the snack shop which[that] is famous for corn dogs.

22 ②   23 (A) watching (B) floss[flossing]

24 ⑤   25 ②   26 to use   27 ⑤

28 ①   29 that 또는 which

30 그녀는 사람들과 수화로 말할 수 있다. 그녀는 1,000개가 넘는 신호를 안다.

01 주어진 보기는 유의어의 관계이다. (1) stack: 쌓다, 포개다 / pile 쌓다, 포개다 (2) gift: 타고난 재능 / talent: 재능 (3) deal with: ~을 해결하다 / solve: 해결하다, 풀다 (4) amaze: 몹시 놀라게 하다 / surprise: 놀라게 하다

02 announce: 발표하다 / announcement: 발표, 소식

03 ① whale, whale: 고래 ② examples, example: 예, 예제 ③ protection, protection: 보호 ④ pattern, pattern: 무늬, 도안 ⑤ shells, shell: (딱딱한) 껍데기, 껍질

04 level: 높이, 정도, 수준

05 (1) photograph: 사진 (2) coconut: 코코넛 열매 (3) tool: 도구

06 (1) body: 몸 / look like: ~처럼 보이다, ~와 닮다 / bag: 가방 (2) arm: 팔 / loner than ~: ~보다 긴 / gorilla: 고릴라

07 small: 작은 / big: 큰 / pink: 분홍색 / navy: 남색 / cloud pattern: 구름무늬 / flower pattern: 꽃무늬

08 (A) scarf: 스카프, 목도리

    (B) blue: 파란색 / grey: 회색

    (C) star pattern: 별무늬

09 (B) 화장실에 가방을 두고 와서, 가방을 찾고 있다고 말한다. (C) 이에 가방의 생김새를 물어본다. (A) 큰 은색 가방이라고 대답한다. (D) (직원이) 가서 확인해 본다고 말한다.

10 (A) May I help you?: 도와드릴까요?

    (B) 크기와 색깔이 대답으로 나왔으므로, 생김새를 묻는 질문이 어울린다.

    (C) 가방의 다른 특징을 설명하는 대답을 하므로, 또 다른 특징을 묻는 질문이 어울린다.

11 명사+관계대명사 which+동사 ~: ~인 명사

12 어디서 잃어버렸는지 물어보는 질문에, 방송을 하겠다는 대답은

13 ④번은 목적격 관계대명사이고 나머지는 모두 주격 관계대명사이다.

14 선행사가 사물이므로 which로 연결한 문장이다.

15 주어진 문장과 ③번은 조건을 나타내는 부사절을 이끌고 있다. ①, ②, ④번은 '~인지 아닌지'의 뜻으로 명사절을 이끌고 있다. ⑤ 가정법에 쓰인 if이다.

16 조건의 부사절에서는 현재시제로 미래시제를 대신하므로 has가 적절하다.

17 ② I received some flowers yesterday that the boy sent me.

18 조건을 나타내는 부사절을 이끄는 if가 적절하다.

19 선행사가 동물이므로 which나 that이 알맞다.

20 ③ 시간이나 조건을 나타내는 부사절에서는 현재시제가 미래시제를 대신한다.

21 선행사가 사물이므로 which나 that을 이용한다.

22 ⓐ와 ③번 ⑤번은 현재분사, ① 동명사(보어), ② 동명사(목적어), ④ 동명사(주어)

23 새끼 원숭이들은 암컷 원숭이들이 아주 천천히 그들의 이빨을 치실질하는 것을 보면서 치실질을 배운다. (A) 전치사 by 다음에 동명사로 쓰는 것이 적절하다. (B) 지각동사 watch+목적어+동사원형 또는 현재분사

24 문어가 보호를 위해 코코넛 껍데기를 사용하는 것은 '도구'를 사용하는 것에 해당하므로 tools가 적절하다.

25 주어진 문장의 'protection'에 주목한다. ②번 다음 문장의 내용이 'protection'에 대한 설명에 해당하므로 ②번이 적절하다.

26 '나중에 쓰기 위해'라고 해야 하므로, 부사적 용법(목적)의 to부정사로 쓰는 것이 적절하다.

27 ⑤ '이 새가 특별하다고 생각한다면, 당신이 틀렸다'고 했다.

28 ①은 이솝 우화 '목마른 까마귀'에 나오는 까마귀를 가리키고, 나머지는 다 과학자들이 행한 실험 대상인 까마귀를 가리킨다.

29 선행사가 동물이고 주어 자리이므로, 주격 관계대명사 that이나 which를 쓰는 것이 적절하다.

30 Sign Language: 수화

단원별 예상문제
p.102~105

01 (1) tool to fix　(2) surprised　(3) floating　**02** ③

03 (1) imagine, like　(2) way to solve　**04** ①

05 ③　　**06** ③　　**07** ②　　**08** ⑤

09 ④　　**10** ③

11 She's not big but her legs are very strong.

12 Coco can stand on two legs and dance to music.

13 ②, ⑤

14 (1) If school finishes early today

　　(2) If the weather is nice tomorrow

　　(3) Unless you exercise hard

　　(4) Unless you try hard

15 ③　　　　**16** unless　　**17** ③　　　**18** ④

19 (1) The students who exercise every day are healthy.

　　(2) The girl who is eating an ice cream is kind.

　　(3) She has a machine which makes cotton candy.

　　(4) If the weather is good tomorrow, we'll go to the park and fly kites.

20 ②　　　　**21** ④

22 새끼들이 지켜보고 있는 동안, 암컷 원숭이들이 아주 천천히 그들의 이빨을 치실질 함으로써

23 ③　　　**24** (A) hiding (B) carry (C) How

25 weight → weigh　　　　**26** ④

01 (1) tool: 도구, 수단 / to fix: 고치기 위해서(to부정사의 부사적 용법) (2) surprise: 놀라게 하다 (3) float: [물체가] (액체 면에) 뜨다, 떠다니다

02 announcement: 발표, 소식 / 사람들에게 말하는 중요한 어떤 것

03 (1) imagine: 상상하다 / like: ~와 같이 (2) way: 방법, 방식 / way to 동사: ~하는 방식 / solve: 해결하다, 풀다

04 tool: 도구, 수단 / equipment: 장치, 설비

05 ③ 'What's ~ like?'는 '~는 어때?'라는 뜻으로 성격, 성품 또는 상태를 묻는 질문이다.

06 ⓐ I'm looking like → I'm looking for, look for: ~을 찾다 ⓒ What does it look like?: 그것은 어떻게 생겼나요? ⓔ It'll → I'll, 사람이 가서 확인하는 것이니, 사물 주어 It이 아니라 사람 주어 I가 나와야 한다.

07 ⓒ They're → It's ⓓ Can you tell me more about it? about이 들어가야 한다.

08 안내 방송을 하는 동안 기다려 달라는 말이 적절하다.

09 ① help ② is ③ look ④ has ⑤ lost

10 잃어버린 개의 크기가 매우 작다고 했다. not very small → very small

11 but: 하지만 / leg: 다리 / very: 매우

12 can: ~할 수 있다 / dance to music: 음악에 맞춰 춤추다

13 선행사가 사람이고 주격이므로 who나 that을 써야 한다.

14 unless = if ~ not

15 ③ 선행사가 사람과 사물이므로 관계대명사는 that을 써야 한다.

16 unless = if ~ not

17 선행사가 사람일 때와 사물일 때 모두 쓰일 수 있는 것은 that이다.

18 조건절이 미래의 일을 나타낼 때에도 조건절의 시제는 현재형을 쓴다.

19 (1)~(3) 선행사가 사람이면 who를, 사물이나 동물이면 which를 쓴다. (4) 조건절에서는 현재시제로 미래시제를 대신한다.

20 ①번에서 마카크 원숭이들이 당신에게 다가와 당신의 머리카락을 뽑을 수도 있다고 한 다음 ③번에서 그 이유를 설명하고 있는데, 그 사이의 '그들은 사람들과 노는 것을 좋아한다.'는 ②번 문장은 전체 글의 흐름에서 벗어난다.

21 ⓐ watch out for: ~을 경계하다[조심하다], ⓑ teach는 to를 사용하여 3형식으로 고친다.

22 암컷 원숭이들은 새끼들이 지켜보고 있는 동안 아주 천천히 그들의 이빨을 치실질함으로써 새끼들에게 치실질을 가르친다.

23 숨을 만한 좋은 장소를 찾지 못할 때, 그들은 코코넛 껍데기 아래로 숨는다는 말이 이어지므로, ③번 '보호'를 위해 코코넛 껍데기를 사용한다고 하는 것이 적절하다. ① 공격, ② 예방, ④ 수리, ⑤ 절약, 저축

24 (A) '숨기에 좋은 장소'라고 해야 하므로 동명사형 hiding이 적절하다. hiding place: 은신처; 은폐 장소, hide를 쓰려면 a good place to hide라고 하는 것이 적절하다. (B) pile과 병렬구문을 이뤄야 하므로 carry가 적절하다. (C) 뒤에 형용사가 나오므로 How가 적절하다. How 형용사 또는 부사 (주어+동사)!, What a[an] 형용사 명사 (주어+동사)!

25 동사를 써야 하므로 weight를 weigh로 고치는 것이 적절하다. weight: (명사) 무게

26 ④ 얼룩말의 수명은 알 수 없다.

🦉 서술형 실전문제   p.106~107

01 (1) What does it look like?
(2) How does it look?

02 pattern

03 (1) I teach sign language to gorillas.
(2) They have a black and white stripe on their wings.

04 (1) hurry, will, miss   (2) rains, will not go
(3) won't be, see

05 (1) Ann lives in the house which[that] has a beautiful garden.
(2) These are the pictures which[that] were painted by Picasso.
(3) I want to play with the boy who[that] has a new board game.

06 (1) The old lady who is 80 years old still looks healthy.
(2) She has a bird that can repeat after people's words.
(3) If you help me, I will be happy. 또는 I will be happy if you help me.

07 (1) I will see the doctor if I don't feel better tomorrow.

(2) If I get a ticket, I'll go to the concert.
(3) If it snows tomorrow, we will go skiing.

08 they use human hair to floss their teeth

09 which

10 While the babies are watching, the female monkeys floss their teeth very slowly.

11 just a story

12 the water level was low

13 dropped stones into the jar

01 'What does ~ look like?'는 '~는 어떻게 생겼니?'라는 의미로 주어의 외모나 생김새를 묻는 질문이다. 비슷한 표현으로 'How does ~ look?', 'How do you describe ~?', 'Tell me what ~ looks like.' 등이 있다.

02 규칙적으로 반복되는 일련의 선, 모양, 색깔: pattern (무늬, 도안)

03 (1) sign: 몸짓, 신호, 표시 / teach 목적어+to 대상: ~에게 ~을 가르치다 (2) stripe: 줄무늬

04 조건절에서는 현재시제로 미래시제를 대신한다.

05 (1), (2) 선행사가 사람이면 that이나 who를, 사물이나 동물이면 that이나 which를 쓴다. (3) who를 목적격 whom 대신 쓸 수 있지만 whom을 who 대신 쓰지는 않는다.

06 (1), (2) 선행사가 사람이면 that이나 who를, 사물이나 동물이면 that이나 which를 쓴다. (3) 주절이 앞에 나와도 되고 종속절이 앞에 나와도 된다.

07 (1) 'unless = if ~ not'이므로 if로 고쳐야 한다. 보통 unless가 이끄는 절에는 부정어가 나오지 않는다. (2), (3) 조건절에서는 현재시제로 미래시제를 대신한다.

08 마카크 원숭이들이 이빨을 치실질하기 위해서 사람의 머리카락을 사용하기 때문에, 사람들에게 와서 머리카락을 뽑을지도 모른다.

09 선행사가 동물이므로, 주격 관계대명사 which로 바꿔 쓸 수 있다.

10 While 다음에는 보통 진행형이 나오는 경우가 많다.

11 당신은 이것이 그저 이야기라고 생각할지도 모르지만, 그렇지 않다('단지 이야기가 아니다')

12 '물 높이가 낮아서' 까마귀는 물 위에 떠 있는 벌레를 먹을 수 없었다.

13 다른 까마귀들도 모두 '항아리 안으로 돌을 떨어뜨렸다'는 뜻이다.

🐰 창의사고력 서술형문제   p.108

|모범답안|

01 cat, grey, long
I'm looking for my cat., It's small and it has grey, has a long tail, Where, I lost it near the library.

02 (1) who flies an airplane
(2) who paints pictures
(3) who drives a car

01 그림을 보면, 잃어버린 동물의 종류는 고양이(cat)이고, 이 고양이는 회색 털(grey hair)을 가지고 있다. 이외의 특징으로는 긴 꼬리 (long tail)를 가지고 있다.

단원별 모의고사
p.109~112

01 ④　　　　02 ②

03 (1) out　(2) at　(3) on, of　(4) to

04 (1) record, during　(2) while
　　(3) the first female　(4) told, fables

05 (A) coin purse (B) a key chain

06 smiley　　07 Can you tell me more about it?

08 (1) long brown → short yellow
　　(2) a racket → a book
　　(3) her → him

09 ⓐ help　ⓑ is　ⓒ look　ⓓ has　ⓔ has

10 I lost him near the main gate.　　11 ④

12 lost, umbrella / yellow / a white flower pattern

13 (1) I have a dog which[that] is eleven years old.
　　(2) I like the car which[that] won the race.
　　(3) The boy who[that] has blond hair is my little brother.
　　(4) If it snows, we won't go to the park.

14 ⑤　　　　15 ①

16 (1) It worked really well.
　　(2) He drove me to school.

17 ②　　　18 ④　　　19 that are　　20 ②

21 hide　　22 ⑤　　　23 ⑤

24 항아리에 들어 있는 물 위에 벌레 한 마리가 떠 있지만 물 높이가 낮아서 까마귀가 그 벌레를 먹을 수 없는 것

01 유의어 관계 ① pattern: 무늬, 도안 design: 디자인, 무늬 ② way: 방법 method: 방법, 방식 ③ photograph: 사진 picture: 그림, 사진 ⑤ record: 기록하다, 등록하다; 기록 document: 기록하다; 기록 (물)) ④ 반의어 관계 slowly: 천천히 fast: 빨리

02 try to find: 찾으려고 노력하다 ② look for: ~을 찾다 ③ talk with: ~와 이야기하다 ④ look like: ~처럼 보이다, ~ 와 닮다

03 (1) find out: 알아내다 (2) be good at: ~을 잘하다, ~에 능숙하다 (3) on top of: ~ 위에 (4) dance to music: 음악에 맞춰 춤추다

04 (1) record: 기록하다, 등록하다 / during+기간 명사: ~ 동안
　(2) while+주어+동사: ~하는 동안에 (3) female: 여성의, 암

컷의 (4) fable: 우화, 동화

05 그림에서 표시된 물건은 동전지갑이다. coin purse: 동전 지갑 / key chain: 열쇠고리

06 smiley: 동그라미 속에 눈 두 개와 웃는 입 모양을 그려 넣은 단순한 얼굴 그림 ☺

07 tell(4형식 동사)+me(간접목적어)+more about it(직접목적어): 그것에 대해 더 많은 것을 나에게 말하다

08 그림을 보면, Steve는 짧고 노란색 머리카락을 가지고 있다. 또한 그는 안경을 쓰고, 책 한 권을 들고 있다. short: 짧은 / yellow: 노란색 / glasses: 안경 / hold: 잡고 있다

09 May I help you? 도와드릴까요?, 외모를 묘사할 때에는 'be 동사+형용사' 혹은 'have+형용사+명사'의 표현을 사용할 수 있다. look like: ~처럼 보이다, ~와 닮다

10 lose–lost–lost: 잃어버리다 / near: ~ 근처에서

11 ④ announcement: 발표, 소식 / make an announcement: 방송을 하다

12 umbrella: 우산 / yellow: 노란색 / pattern: 무늬 / white: 하얀색

14 a girl이 선행사이고 주격이므로 who나 that을 써야 한다. ③번은 관계대명사나 접속사와 주어가 없어서 잘못되었으며 관계대명사는 접속사와 대명사의 역할을 하므로 ④번에서는 who 다음의 she를 생략해야 한다.

15 조건의 부사절을 이끄는 if가 적절하다.

17 주어진 문장과 ②번은 부사절을 이끌고 있으나 나머지는 명사절을 이끌고 있다.

18 ④ 수컷 원숭이들이 새끼 원숭이들에게 무엇을 가르치는지는 대답할 수 없다. ① Because they may come to you and pull out your hair. ② They use human hair. ③ No. ⑤ By flossing their teeth very slowly while the babies are watching.

19 주격 관계대명사와 be동사를 같이 생략할 수 있다.

20 ⓑ와 ②번은 명사적 용법, ① 형용사적 용법, ③ 부사적 용법(이유), ④ 형용사적 용법, ⑤ 부사적 용법(목적)

21 문어들은 '숨기에' 좋은 장소를 찾을 수 없을 때, 보호를 위해 코코넛 껍데기 아래에 '숨는다'

22 ⓐ와 ⑤ 저장하다, ① 상점, ② 비축[저장]량, ③ 「형용사적으로」 기성품인, store clothes: 기성복, ④ (특정한 종류의 상품) 저장고[창고], a grain store: 곡물 저장

23 앞에 나오는 내용과 상반되는 내용이 뒤에 이어지므로 However가 가장 적절하다. ① 예를 들면, ② 게다가, 더욱이, ③ 즉, 다시 말해, ④ 그 결과

24 과학자들이 실험에서 설정한 상황을 가리킨다.

Lesson 5

Living Healthily and Safely

사가 적절하므로 regularly가 적절하다. (3) 명사 problems를 수식하는 형용사 형태가 적절하므로 동사 vary를 various로 고친다. (4) 문자를 보내다는 의미로 동사 text를 현재분사인 texting으로 바꾸는 것이 적절하다.

시험대비 실력평가   p.116

01 instead of   02 ①   03 blink   04 ③
05 ③   06 ⑤   07 nervous   08 ④

01 한 가지가 또 다른 것을 대체하거나 다른 것을 할 때 사용하는. 식사나 회의 중에는 스마트폰을 꺼라. 문자를 보내는 대신에 사람들과 직접 대화를 나눌 수 있다.

02 take medicine: '약을 복용하다', take a rest: '휴식을 취하다'

04 스마트폰을 확인했을 때 아무런 문자 메시지가 없다면 슬픈 기분이 드는가? 만약 당신의 대답이 '그렇다'이면, 당신은 스마트폰 중독일지 모른다.

05 신체의 일부가 아플 때 가지는 느낌 – 고통

05 매일, 매주 등의 같은 시간에 – 규칙적으로

07 유의어 관계이다. 건강한 = 초조한, 불안한

08 '스마트폰을 현명하지 않게 또는 과도하게 사용하면 다양한 문제가 일어날 수 있다.', '스마트폰을 내려다볼 때, 목에 가해지는 압박이 증가한다.'

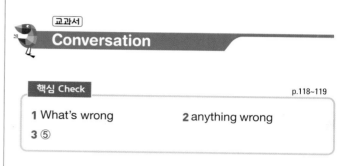

교과서 **Conversation**

핵심 Check   p.118~119

1 What's wrong   2 anything wrong
3 ⑤

교과서 대화문 익히기

Check(√) True or False   p.120

1 T   2 T   3 T   4 F

서술형 시험대비   p.117

01 (1) has   (2) well   (3) smombie   (4) nervous
02 (1) prevent, 방지하다, 막다   (2) medicine, 약, 약물
(3) addiction, 중독   03 (t)ext / (c)ause
04 (1) without   (2) such   (3) From now on   (4) fall
asleep   05 (1) addiction   (2) regularly
(3) various   (4) texting

01 (1) '머리가 아프다'는 표현으로 동사 have를 사용한다. (2) '건강해 보이다'는 look well을 사용한다. (3) 글의 흐름상 단어 '스몸비'가 적절하다. (4) 나는 스마트폰이 곁에 없을 때 초조해진다.

03 • 많은 사람들은 전화를 하기 보다는 문자 메시지를 보내기를 좋아한다. • 스마트폰을 과도하게 사용하면 눈이 건조해질 수 있다.

04 (1) without: ~ 없이 (2) such: 그러한 (3) from now on: 지금부터 (4) fall asleep: 잠들다

05 (1) 스마트폰 중독의 의미로 동사 addict를 명사 addiction으로 바꾸어야 한다. (2) 빈칸에는 동사 exercise를 수식하는 부

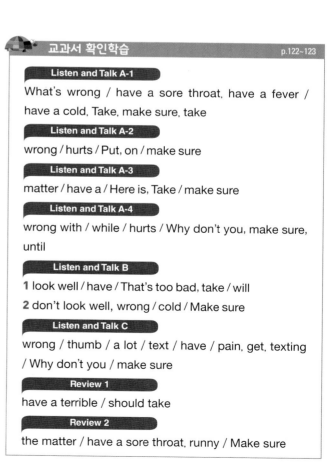

교과서 확인학습   p.122~123

Listen and Talk A-1
What's wrong / have a sore throat, have a fever / have a cold. Take, make sure, take

Listen and Talk A-2
wrong / hurts / Put, on / make sure

Listen and Talk A-3
matter / have a / Here is, Take / make sure

Listen and Talk A-4
wrong with / while / hurts / Why don't you, make sure, until

Listen and Talk B
1 look well / have / That's too bad, take / will
2 don't look well, wrong / cold / Make sure

Listen and Talk C
wrong / thumb / a lot / text / have / pain, get, texting / Why don't you / make sure

Review 1
have a terrible / should take

Review 2
the matter / have a sore throat, runny / Make sure

01 Make sure   02 ④   03 ③   04 have a

01 상대방에게 당부하는 표현으로 '반드시 ~하도록 해라, ~을 확실히 해라'라는 의미의 'make sure ~'를 사용한다.

02 빈칸에는 상대방이 어딘가 아파 보일 때 묻는 말이 적절하다..

03 감기에 걸린 것 같다는 말 다음에 이어질 말로 치과에 가라는 말은 어색하다.

04 '~가 아프다'는 표현은 'have a/an+명사' 형태로 쓴다. 명사 자리에 아픈 증상이나 병명을 써서 어디가 아픈지 표현한다.

01 ④   02 ⑤   03 ④   04 ⑤
05 the [problem]matter, happened   06 ⑤
07 ④   08 pain   09 Here is   10 ③
11 What's the matter with you   12 ④
13 ⑤   14 ④

01 B의 대답으로 보아 빈칸에는 문제점이나 증상을 묻는 말이 오는 것이 적절하다.

02 빈칸 뒤의 this는 medicine을 가리키므로 '약을 먹다'는 표현으로 동사 take를 사용한다.

03 (D) 상대방의 증상을 묻는 표현 → (A) 증상 말하기 → (B) 상대방에게 당부하는 표현 말하기 → (C) 알았다고 대답하기

04 '~가 아프다'는 표현은 'have a/an+명사' 형태로 쓴다.

06 (B)는 상대방에게 당부하는 표현이다.

07 '반드시 ~하도록 하다, ~을 확실히 하다'라는 의미의 'make sure ~'는 상대방에게 당부할 때 사용하는 표현이다.

08 toothache는 '치통'이기 때문에 '아픔, 통증'을 나타내는 pain이 적절하다.

09 '여기에 ~가 있다'는 표현으로 'Here is+단수 명사'를 사용한다.

10 이가 아프다고 했기 때문에 치과에 가라는 충고가 적절하다.

11 문제점이나 증상을 묻는 표현이다.

12 It은 texting thumb을 가리키는 대명사로 'What's texting thumb?'에 대한 대답으로 ④에 들어가는 것이 적절하다.

13 Ms. Kim이 문자 메시지를 많이 보내지 않는다는 것은 본문에 언급되어 있지 않다.

14 ④번은 '몸이 안 좋아 보여. 무슨 일 있니?'라는 물음에 '아무 문제없다.'는 대답 다음에 머리가 아프다고 말하는 것은 어색하다.

01 ⓐ wrong ⓑ have ⓒ have
02 Take this medicine and make sure you take a good rest.

03 (A) What's wrong with your leg
 (B) while I was playing soccer
 (C) make sure you don't play socce
04 pain, thumb   05 make sure, don't text
06 I get tired easily.

01 ⓐ 아파 보인다는 말 다음에 상대방의 증상을 묻는 표현이 적절하다. ⓑ와 ⓒ는 '~가 아프다'는 의미로 동사 have를 사용한다.

02 '이 약을 먹어'라는 명령문으로 동사 Take로 문장을 시작한다. 그리고 '꼭 ~하도록 해라'는 당부의 표현으로 'make sure+주어+동사' 어순이 적절하다.

03 (B)의 while은 접속사로 '~하는 동안'의 의미를 가지고 뒤에는 '주어+동사'가 와야 한다. be동사와 함께 사용이 되어 축구를 하다는 표현은 진행형으로 나타내는 것이 적절하다. (C)는 상대방에게 당부하는 표현으로 'make sure+주어+동사'의 어순이 적절하다.

04 Andy가 엄지손가락이 아프다는 말을 한 것으로 보아 texting thumb은 엄지손가락에 있는 통증을 말한다는 것을 알 수 있다.

05 texting thumb은 문자 메시지를 너무 많이 보내서 생기는 통증이므로 Ms. Kim의 충고는 '문자 메시지를 너무 많이 보내지 말라'는 것이 적절하다.

06 get+형용사: ~하게 되다 / tire를 tired로 바꾸어 '피로한, 피곤하게 된'을 의미하도록 한다.

교과서
Grammar

1 (1) who/whom/that   (2) which/that
2 (1) call, text neck   (2) made, rich man

01 ②, ⑤
02 (1) who → which[that]
 (2) which → who[whom/that]
 (3) to be the king of beasts → the king of beasts
03 (1) These are the shoes which I bought yesterday.
 (2) We called our fish Ernie.
04 ①

01 선행사가 The friend로 사람이며 met의 목적어 역할을 할 수 있는 목적격 관계대명사 who나 whom 또는 that이 적절하다.

02 (1) 선행사가 사물이므로 who를 which나 that으로 고쳐야 한

다. (2) 선행사가 사람이므로 which를 who나 whom 또는 that으로 고쳐야 한다. (3) call은 목적격 보어로 to부정사를 취하지 않는다.

03 (1) which는 관계대명사 목적격이다. (2) 'call+목적어+목적격 보어'의 어순을 취한다.

04 call A B: A를 B라고 부르다 the arrow on the screen: 화면의 화살표

01 ②   02 ④   03 ⑤

04 (1) that   (2) which   (3) which   (4) which

(5) consider   05 I still remember the stories (which[that]) my grandfather told me.   06 ⑤

07 ④   08 ①   09 ③

10 (1) that   (2) whom   (3) who is   11 ⑤

12 ②

13 (1) New York is a big city which[that] many people visit every year.

  (2) My favorite subject is math which[that] I'm good at.

  (3) The man who[whom/that] I saw at the mall was my math teacher.

  (4) She is a famous movie star who[whom/that] many people like.

  (5) I was surprised at the speed with which he learned to speak. 또는 I was surprised at the speed which[that] he learned to speak with.

  (6) Do you know the girl to whom Anne is talking? 또는 Do you know the girl who[whom/that] Anne is talking to?

14 ①   15 ④

16 (1) We call Shakespeare England's national poet.

  (2) I consider him to be a coward.

17 ②, ④

01 <보기>와 나머지는 목적격 관계대명사이지만, ②번은 주격 관계대명사이다.

02 모두 주격이나 목적격으로 사용된 관계대명사 that이 들어갈 수 있지만 ④번은 소유격 관계대명사 whose가 들어가야 한다.

03 take는 보통 to부정사나 as와 함께 쓰이며 take A(명사) B(명사)의 형태로 쓰이지 않는다.

04 (1) 선행사가 사람이므로 that, (2) 선행사가 사물이므로 which, (3) 전치사 in이 있으므로 that은 쓸 수 없다. (4) 선행사가 사물이므로 which, (5) to부정사를 목적격 보어로 쓸 수 있는 것은 consider이다.

05 '이야기들을 아직 기억한다'에서 목적격 관계대명사를 이용하여

'이야기들'을 '할아버지께서 내게 해 주신'이 수식하는 구조로 만들어 준다.

06 call은 동사 다음에 두 개의 명사(구)가 목적어, 목적격 보어로 쓰이므로 'as hip hop'이 아니라 as 없이 'hip hop'이 되어야 한다.

07 관계대명사의 선행사가 사람이면 who, whom이나 that을 쓰고 사물이면 which나 that을 쓴다. ③ This is the house which she lives in.

08 ①번은 접속사이지만 나머지는 모두 관계대명사이다.

09 ③번은 4형식이지만 <보기>와 나머지는 모두 목적어와 목적격 보어가 있는 5형식이다. call A B는 목적격 보어 자리에 to부정사나 형용사를 쓰지 않지만 to부정사나 형용사를 목적격 보어로 취하는 많은 동사들이 있다.

10 목적격 관계대명사와 '주격 관계대명사+be 동사'는 생략할 수 있다.

11 선행사가 사람이므로 who, whom이나 that을 이용하고 목적격이므로 목적어로 쓰인 him은 쓰지 말아야 한다.

12 call은 동사 다음에 두 개의 명사(구)가 목적어와 목적격 보어로 쓰인다. 형용사나 to부정사가 목적격 보어로 올 수 없다. call A B: A를 B라고 부르다

13 목적격 관계대명사는 수식하는 선행사가 사람이면 who나 whom, that을, 사람이 아니면 which나 that을 쓴다. 일반적으로 목적격 관계대명사는 생략될 수 있다. 목적격 관계대명사가 전치사의 목적어인 경우 전치사는 관계대명사절의 끝에 오거나 관계대명사 앞에 올 수 있다. 전치사가 관계대명사절의 끝에 올 경우에는 관계대명사를 생략할 수 있다. 전치사가 관계대명사 앞에 올 경우에는 관계대명사 that을 쓸 수 없으며, 관계대명사를 생략하지 않는다.

14 call은 동사 다음에 두 개의 명사(구)가 목적어와 목적격 보어로 쓰인다. regard가 'A를 B로 여기다'의 뜻으로 쓰이는 경우 보통 'regard A as B'의 형태를 취한다.

15 ④ 관계대명사 that은 전치사 다음에는 쓸 수 없다. that → whom

16 call A B: A를 B라고 부르다 (2) consider는 call과는 다르게 목적격 보어로 to부정사를 취할 수 있다.

17 주어진 문장과 ②, ④번은 목적격 관계대명사이다. ① 동격절을 이끄는 접속사, ③번은 의문사, ⑤번은 주격 관계대명사이다. swallow: 제비

01 (1) I bought the snack which[that] everyone likes.

  (2) Romeo and Juliet is the movie which[that] Helen saw.

  (3) The person who[whom/that] I love the most is my sister.

  (4) The author who[whom/that] I like the most is C.S. Lewis.

23

(5) Look at the boy to whom Mary is talking. 또는 Look at the boy who[whom/that] Mary is talking to.

(6) Look at Chris and his dog that Bella is playing with.

02 (1) People call New York City the Big Apple.

(2) Some people may not consider him as a hero.

(3) They named her the Boxer of the Year.

(4) His ability made him a famous person.

(5) We elected him to be a leader.

(6) His followers believed him to be a genius.

(7) They regard Mike as a fool.

03 call the rooftop garden the park in the sky

04 (1) Andy is the boy (who/whom/that) Hajun met in Canada.

(2) The table (which/that) my dad made for me is sturdy.

(3) Hemingway is the author whom I like the most.

(4) The book which he wrote is fun.

(5) Can I borrow the book (which/that) you told me about? 또는 Can I borrow the book about which you told me?

05 (1) My grandmother made the chocolate cake.

(2) We met the people on the plane.

(3) He wants to rent a car.

(4) Do you have a friend?

06 (1) They called him Mr. Long.

(2) They regarded him as their leader.

07 (1) We call Chicago the Windy City because it is very windy there.

(2) I like the cookies (which/that) my mother made for me.

(3) The country (which/that) I want to visit the most is France.

(4) Harry was the partner that I worked with last year.

01 (1), (2) 선행사가 사물이므로 관계대명사 which나 that, (3), (4) 선행사가 사람이므로 관계대명사 who, whom이나 that, (5) 목적격 관계대명사가 전치사의 목적어인 경우 전치사는 관계대명사절의 끝에 오거나 관계대명사 앞에 올 수 있으며 전치사가 관계대명사절의 끝에 올 경우에는 관계대명사를 생략할 수 있다. 전치사가 관계대명사 앞에 올 경우에는 관계대명사 that을 쓸 수 없다. (6) 선행사가 '사람+동물'이므로 관계대명사 that을 써야 한다. 목적격 관계대명사는 생략될 수 있다.

02 (1) call A B: A를 B라고 부르다 (2) consider는 consider A as B의 형태로도 쓰인다. (3) name A B: A를 B라고 이름 짓다 (4) make A B: A를 B로 만들다 (5) elect는 to부정사를

목적격 보어로 취할 수 있다. (6) believe는 to부정사를 목적격 보어로 취한다. (7) regard A as B: A를 B로 여기다

03 call A B: A를 B라고 부르다 rooftop: 지붕[옥상] / 우리는 옥상 정원을 하늘의 공원이라고 부른다.

04 (1) 선행사가 사람이므로 who, whom이나 that, (2) 선행사가 사물이므로 which나 that, (3) 관계대명사가 접속사와 대명사의 역할을 하므로 him을 삭제해야 한다. (4) 관계대명사가 접속사와 대명사의 역할을 하므로 it을 삭제해야 한다. (5) 전치사가 관계대명사 앞에 올 경우에는 관계대명사 that을 쓸 수 없으며, 관계대명사를 생략하지 않는다. sturdy: 억센, 튼튼한

05 목적격 관계대명사는 선행사가 사람이면 who나 whom, that, 사물이나 동물이면 which나 that을 쓰고 관계대명사절에서 목적어 역할을 한다. 목적격 관계대명사절에는 동사 뒤에 목적어가 없다는 것에 주의한다.

06 (1) call A B는 목적격 보어 자리에 to부정사나 형용사를 쓰지 않는다. (2) regard는 'regard A as B(A를 B로 여기다)' 형태로 쓰인다.

07 선행사가 사물이면 which나 that, 사람이면 who, whom이나 that을 쓴다. (4) 함께 일한 파트너이므로 전치사 with를 빠뜨리면 안 된다. 또한 that을 사용해야 하므로 전치사 with를 관계대명사절의 마지막에 위치시켜야 한다.

교과서
Reading

확인문제　　　　　　　　　　　　p.136

1 T　2 F　3 F　4 T

확인문제　　　　　　　　　　　　p.137

1 F　2 F　3 T　4 T　5 F　6 T

교과서 확인학습 A　　　　　　　p.138~139

01 Be Smart with　　02 Living without smartphones

03 unwise or too much use　　04 a smombie

05 like zombies　　06 on their smartphones

07 such people　　08 various safety problems

09 may not see, so　10 get into　11 to prevent

12 simple　　13 while, walking

14 dry eyes, text neck　　15 health problems

16 dry eyes　　17 look at, blink

18 feel dry　　19 Another problem

20 look down at, on

21 Too much use, too much texting

22 text neck　　　23 some tips

24 try to blink　　　25 up to your eye level

26 neck stretching exercises

27 How do you feel　28 feel nervous, around

29 feel sad, no text message

30 smartphone addiction　　　31 to prevent this

32 turn off, during　33 instead of texting

교과서 확인학습 B p.140~141

1 Be Smart with Your Smartphones!

2 Living without smartphones is difficult for many of us these days.

3 However, unwise or too much use of smartphones can cause various problems.

4 Are you a smombie?

5 All over the world, people are walking around like zombies.

6 Their heads are down, and their eyes are on their smartphones.

7 We call such people smombies, smartphone zombies.

8 If you are a smombie, you can have various safety problems.

9 You may not see a hole in the street, so you may fall and get hurt.

10 You may get into a car accident, too.

11 So what can you do to prevent these problems?

12 It's simple.

13 Do not look at your smartphone while you are walking!

14 Do you have dry eyes or text neck?

15 Smartphones can cause various health problems.

16 One example is dry eyes.

17 When you look at your smartphone, you do not blink often.

18 Then your eyes will feel dry.

19 Another problem you can have is neck pain.

20 When you look down at your smartphone, the stress on your neck increases.

21 Too much use of your smartphone, for example, too much texting, can cause neck pain.

22 We call this text neck.

23 Here are some tips for these problems.

24 For dry eyes, try to blink often.

25 For text neck, move your smartphone up to your eye level.

26 You can also do some neck stretching exercises.

27 How do you feel when you don't have your smartphone with you?

28 Do you feel nervous when your smartphone is not around?

29 Do you feel sad when you check your smartphone and there is no text message?

30 If your answers are "yes," you may have smartphone addiction.

31 There are various things you can do to prevent this.

32 For example, turn off your smartphone during meals or meetings.

33 You can talk to people instead of texting them.

시험대비 실력평가 p.142~147

01 ②　　　02 ①, ④　　　03 ⑤　　　04 ③

05 Other → Another　　　06 ④　　　07 ②

08 (A) nervous　(B) sad　(C) to prevent addiction　　　09

10 people　　11 ③, ④　　12 ②

13 (A) smartphone　(B) safety　　14 ⑤

15 ②　　　16 Another problem that[which] you can have is neck pain.　　17 ③

18 is around → is not around

19 smartphone addiction

20 (1) I can turn off my smartphone during meals or meetings.

　(2) I can talk to people instead of texting them.

21 ④　　　22 he was texting and (he) didn't see a hole　　23 ①, ③　　24 ④　　25 ③

26 ①　　27 (A) addiction　(B) off　(C) instead of

28 ④　　29 ③　　30 ⑤

01 ② 앞에 나오는 내용과 상반되는 내용이 뒤에 이어지므로 However가 가장 적절하다. ① 그러므로, ③ 게다가, ⑤ 즉, 다시 말해

02 ⓑ와 ①, ④번은 5형식, call A B는 'A를 B라고 부르다'라는 의미이며, smombies와 smartphone zombies는 동격이다. call A B와 유사하게 목적격 보어 자리에 명사가 올 수 있는 동사로는 make, name, elect, consider 등이 있다. ② 3형식, ③, ⑤ 4형식

03 안전 관련 문제들을 예방하는 것은 '간단하다.'

04 주어진 문장의 these problems에 주목한다. ③번 앞 문장의 내용들을 받고 있으므로 ③번이 적절하다.

05 other 뒤에는 복수명사, another 뒤에는 단수명사가 온다.

06 ② 부사적 용법(목적), ⓑ와 나머지는 명사적 용법

25

07 ② 위 글은 '스마트폰으로 인한 건강상의 문제들과 이런 문제들을 방지하기 위한 몇 가지 조언'에 관한 글이다.

08 (A) feel은 감각동사로 '형용사'를 보어로 써야 하므로 nervous가 적절하다. (B) feel은 감각동사로 '형용사'를 보어로 써야 하므로 sad가 적절하다. (C) 이것을 '예방하기 위해' 할 수 있는 일이라고 해야 하므로 to prevent가 적절하다.

09 addiction: 중독, 1. 해로운 약을 복용하거나 그것의 복용을 중단할 수 없는 상태, 2. 어떤 것에 대한 매우 강한 소망이나 그것에 대한 욕구

10 '사람들'을 가리킨다.

11 ⓐ와 ③, ④번은 동명사, 나머지는 모두 현재분사

12 위 글은 스몸비들이 스마트폰을 보며 걷다가 일어날 수 있는 안전 관련 문제들에 관한 글이므로, '당신은 스몸비인가요?'가 적절하다. ⑤ troublemaker: 말썽꾸러기

13 다양한 '안전' 관련 문제들을 예방하기 위해 걷고 있는 동안에는 '스마트폰'을 보지 말아야 한다.

14 ⑤ 스몸비들이 가질 수 있는 가장 위험한 문제가 무엇인지는 대답할 수 없다. ① No. ② Yes. ③ It means a smartphone zombie. ④ They can have various safety problems.

15 ⓐ look at: ~을 보다, look down at: ~을 내려다보다 ⓑ For dry eyes[text neck]: 안구 건조증[거북목 증후군]에는

16 목적격 관계대명사 'that'이나 'which'가 생략되어 있다.

17 ⓓ와 ③번: (특정한 수·정도)까지, up to your eye level: 당신의 눈높이까지, ① (육체적·정신적으로) ~할 수 있는, ② ~에게 달려 있는, ~의 의무[책임]인, ④ (특히 나쁜 짓을) 하고 있는, ⑤ look up to: ~을 우러러보다, 존경하다

18 스마트폰이 주위에 '없을' 때 당신은 초조한 기분이 드는가?라고 하는 것이 흐름상 적절하다.

19 '스마트폰 중독'을 가리킨다.

20 (1) 식사나 회의 중에는 스마트폰을 끌 수 있다. (2) 문자를 보내는 대신에 사람들과 이야기를 할 수 있다.

21 이 글은 '스마트폰 중독과 예방'에 관한 글이다.

22 '문자를 보내고 있었고 구덩이를 보지 못했기 때문'이다.

23 ⓐ와 ①, ③번은 접속사(때), ②, ④, ⑤번은 의문부사(언제)

24 ④ 스마트폰을 눈높이까지 들고, 목 스트레칭 운동을 해야 하는 사람은 '수지'이다.

25 주어진 문장의 this에 주목한다. ③번 앞 문장의 smartphone addiction을 받고 있으므로 ③번이 적절하다.

26 앞의 내용의 예가 나오고 있으므로 For example이 가장 적절하다. ② 그러므로, ③ 게다가, 더욱이, ④ 그러나, ⑤ 다른 한편으로는, 반면에

27 (A) 스마트폰 '중독'이라고 해야 하므로 addiction이 적절하다. addition: 덧셈, 추가(된 것), (B) 식사나 회의 중에는 스마트폰을 '끄라'고 해야 하므로 off가 적절하다. turn on: 켜다, (C) 문자를 보내는 '대신에'라고 해야 하므로 instead of가 적절하다.

28 빈칸 뒤에 이어지는 예들(거리에 있는 구덩이를 보지 못해서 넘어져서 다칠지도 모르고, 또한 교통사고를 당할지도 모르는 것)은 다양한 '안전' 관련 문제들에 해당한다. ② 정신적인, ③ 경제적인, ⑤ 신체적인

29 ⓐ와 ①, ④: 현재분사, ②, ③, ⑤: 동명사

30 이 글은 '현명하지 않은 스마트폰 사용으로 인한 다양한 안전 관련 문제들'에 관한 글이다.

서술형 시험대비
p.148~149

01 (A) is   (B) like   (C) It's
02 (A) zombies   (B) heads   (C) eyes
03 (1) 당신은 거리에 있는 구덩이를 보지 못할 수도 있고, 그래서 넘어져서 다칠지도 모른다.
　 (2) 당신은 또한 교통사고를 당할지도 모른다.
04 blink
05 When you look down at your smartphone, the stress on your neck increases.
06 (A) too much use   (B) texting
07 머리는 아래를 향하고 눈은 스마트폰을 향한 채로 스마트폰을 보며 걷는 것
08 We call such people smombies, smartphone zombies.　　　09 As[Because]
10 원인: 스마트폰을 볼 때, 눈을 자주 깜박거리지 않기 때문이다.
　 원인: 눈을 자주 깜박이려고 노력해라.
11 for instance

01 (A) 동명사 'Living'이 주어이므로 is가 적절하다. (B) 좀비'처럼'이라고 해야 하므로 like가 적절하다. alike는 명사 앞에는 쓸 수 없다. (C) '주어+동사'가 와야 하므로 소유격 Its가 아니라 It's가 적절하다.

02 그들은 '머리'를 숙이고, 그들의 '눈'은 스마트폰을 향한 채로 '좀비'처럼 걸어다니고 있는 사람들이다. walk with one's head hanging down: 머리를 숙이고 걷다

03 스마트폰을 보며 걷다가 일어날 수 있는 안전 관련 문제들이 ⓐ번 뒤에 설명되어 있다.

04 blink: 눈을[눈이] 깜박이다, 눈을 감고 아주 빨리 다시 눈을 뜨다

05 'on'을 보충하면 된다.

06 너무 많이 '문자'를 하는 것과 같이 스마트폰을 '너무 많이 사용하는 것'으로 인해 생기는 목 통증을 의미한다.

07 스몸비의 모습이 스마트폰을 현명하지 않게 사용하거나 너무 과도하게 사용하는 것의 예에 해당한다.

08 smombies와 smartphone zombies는 동격이므로 사이에 콤마를 찍는 것이 적절하다.

09 'so' 대신에, 이유를 나타내는 접속사 'As'나 'Because'를 맨 앞에 쓰는 것이 적절하다.

10 '스마트폰을 볼 때, 당신은 눈을 자주 깜박거리지 않기 때문에' 눈이 건조하다고 느낄 것이라고 했다. 안구 건조증에는, '눈을 자주 깜박이려고 노력하라'는 조언을 하고 있다.

11 for example = for instance: 예를 들어

01 (i)ntelligent   02 ④   03 ③
04 ①   05 cause   06 ③   07 ④
08 ③   09 문자를 너무 많이 하면 texting thumb
이 생길 수 있다는 것   10 ⑤   11 ⑤
12 ④   13 ③   14 ⑤   15 ③
16 ④   17 ①   18 ④
19 (1) *Jane Eyre* is the book (which) Yumi read yesterday.
    (2) The jacket (which) I'm wearing is a present from my grandmother.
    (3) People call such food fajitas.
    (4) The festival made the city a popular place to visit.
20 ①   21 ③   22 ②, ⑤   23 ④
24 ②   25 (A) Another   (B) increases   (C) tips
26 Do you feel nervous when your smartphone is not around?   27 while → during
28 ④   29 Emma / feel dry
30 (1) 스마트폰이 주위에 없을 때 초조한 기분이 드는 경우
    (2) 스마트폰을 확인했을 때 아무런 문자 메시지가 없으면 슬픈 기분이 드는 경우
31 texting

01 반의어 관계이다. 비싼 : 싼 = 어리석은 : 똑똑한

02 스마트폰 없이 사는 것은 요즘 많은 사람들에게 어려울 수 있다. 하지만 스마트폰을 현명하지 않게 또는 과도하게 사용하면 다양한 문제를 야기할 수 있다.

03 팔, 다리, 몸을 가능한 멀리 펴다. '뻗다, 기지개를 켜다'

04 잠이 든; 자고 있는

05 • 그 사고의 원인은 분명하지 않다. 경찰은 여전히 그것을 조사 중이다. • 스마트폰을 과도하게 사용하는 것은 건조한 눈을 야기할 수 있다. look into: 조사하다

06 blink는 '눈을 깜박거리다'는 뜻이다.

07 상대방의 증상을 묻는 표현이 아닌 것을 찾는다.

08 texting thumb이 무엇이냐는 물음에 'It's pain in your thumb.'이라고 답하는 것이 적절하다.

09 that은 앞의 문장을 가리키는 대명사로 사용되었다.

10 Texting thumb은 문자를 너무 많이 해서 생길 수 있는 아픔이기 때문에 마지막 문장은 'you don't text too much'가 되어야 적절하다.

11 make sure는 뒤에 '주어+동사'가 나와야 한다. 그래서 'make sure you don't play soccer'로 바꾸는 것이 적절하다.

12 ④ A의 '축구하다 넘어져 다쳤다'는 말에 B가 '그거 좋겠다'고 답하는 것은 적절하지 않다.

13 ⓒ의 take는 '먹다, 복용하다'는 의미로 사용되었다.   this는 'some medicine'을 가리킨다.

14 call A B는 목적격 보어 자리에 to부정사나 형용사를 쓰지 않는다.

15 ③ The card (which/that) I bought yesterday was sent to Sue.

16 ④번은 주격 관계대명사이고 나머지는 모두 목적격 관계대명사이다.

17 call을 제외하고 모두 to be를 목적격 보어로 받을 수 있는 동사들이다. call은 동사 다음에 두 개의 명사(구)가 목적어와 목적격 보어로 쓰인다.

18 ④번은 목적격 관계대명사로 생략할 수 있다. ① 주격 관계대명사, ② 지시형용사, ③ 접속사, ⑤ 지시대명사이다.

19 (1) Jane Eyre는 책이름으로 사물이므로 which를 사용한다. (2) '입고 있는'은 진행형으로 나타내는 것이 적절하다. (3) call A B: A를 B라고 부르다 (4) The festival made the city to visit이 a popular place를 수식하도록 만든다.

20 주어진 문장의 various safety problems에 주목한다. ①번 뒤 문장에서 안전 관련 문제들의 예가 나오고 있으므로 ①번이 적절하다.

21 ⓐ their eyes are on their smartphones: 그들의 눈은 스마트폰을 향하고 있다, ⓑ get into a car accident: 교통사고를 당하다

22 ⓒ와 ①, ③, ④는 부사적 용법, ② 형용사적 용법, ⑤ 명사적 용법

23 위 글은 스마트폰이 일으킬 수 있는 건강상의 문제들 중에서 안구 건조증과 목 통증에 대해 설명하는 글이므로, '당신은 안구 건조증이나 거북목 증후군이 있나요?'가 적절하다.

24 앞의 내용의 예가 나오고 있으므로 for example이 가장 적절하다. ① 게다가, ④ 사실은, ⑤ 그 결과

25 (A) various health problems 중에서 일어날 수 있는 '또 다른 문제'이므로 Another가 적절하다. another: 셋 이상 중에서 두 번째, the other: 둘 중에서 나머지 하나, (B) 스마트폰을 내려다볼 때, 목에 가해지는 압박이 '증가한다'고 해야 하므로 increases가 적절하다. decrease: 줄다[감소하다], (C) advice는 셀 수 없는 명사이므로 복수 형태로 쓸 수 없다. some pieces of advice로 쓸 수 있다.

26 when 이하는 시간의 부사절로 '~할 때'라는 의미이다. around는 부사로 쓰였다.

27 during+특정한 때를 나타내는 명사, while+주어+동사

28 식사나 회의 중에는 스마트폰을 끄고 '문자를 보내는 대신에' 사람들과 이야기하라고 하는 것이 적절하다.

29 Q1: ‘Emma’가 눈을 자주 깜박이도록 노력해야 한다. Q2: 스마트폰을 사용할 때 눈이 ‘건조하다고 느끼기’ 때문이다.

30 본문 앞부분의 질문에 대한 대답이 ‘그렇다’이면, 당신은 스마트폰 중독일지도 모른다고 했다.

31 전치사 다음에 동명사로 쓰는 것이 적절하다.

단원별 예상문제   p.156~159

01 various   02 ③   03 (A) Here are
(B) (n)ervous   04 look well   05 ②, ④   06 ④
07 ④   08 (A) What's wrong   (B) It's pain in
your thumb   (C) make sure you don't text too much
09 Why don't you do some finger stretching
exercises?   10 ③
11 (1) The pizza (which/that) my dad made was really
      delicious.
    (2) I know the girl (whom/who/that) you are talking
      about.
    (3) We elected Chris class president.
    (4) The game that we saw was very boring.
    (5) He called me Queen.
12 ①, ③, ⑤   13 ④
14 (1) We call such a dance Salsa.
    (2) Nobody liked the spaghetti which Nicole made.
    (3) We elected Alex president of our club.
    (4) She is the singer who[whom] I like most.
15 ②   16 ③
17 various safety problems   18 ⑤
19 ③   20 healthier
21 (1) 운동을 많이 하지 않는다.
      → 매일 30분 동안 걸으려고 노력할 것이다.
    (2) 너무 많은 패스트푸드를 먹는다.
      → 일주일에 한 번만 패스트푸드를 먹을 것이다.
    (3) 종종 밤에 먹는다.
      → 10시 이후에 먹지 않을 것이다.
22 ②

01 유의어 관계이다. 아픈 = 다양한

02 유명한 사람: 유명 인사

03 ‘여기에 ~가 있다’는 표현은 Here is[are] ~를 사용한다. some tips라는 복수명사가 있으므로 Here are가 적절하다.

04 ‘look+형용사’를 이용하여 ‘~처럼 보이다’를 쓰고, well은 형용사로 ‘건강한’의 의미를 가지고 있다.

05 머리가 아프다는 말에 ‘안 됐구나’라는 표현이 적절하다.

06 스마트폰이 야기할 수 있는 여러 문제를 언급하고 있기 때문에 (A)는 various가 적절하고, (B)는 눈을 자주 깜박거리지 않기 때문에 눈이 건조해진다는 dry가 적절하고, (C)는 목에 가해지는 압박이 증가한다는 increases가 적절하다.

07 ⓓ ‘have + a/an+병명/증상’ 형태로 ‘어디가 아프다’는 표현이다. have cold → have a cold

08 (A)는 상대방의 증상을 묻는 표현이 적절하다. (B)는 texting thumb이 무엇이냐는 물음에 대한 답으로 적절한 것을 고르면 된다. (C)는 texting thumb을 예방하기 위한 조언으로 적절한 표현을 찾는다.

09 ‘Why don't you+동사원형 ~?’ 형태를 이용하여 영작한다.

10 등이 아프다는 증상에 대해 스트레칭 운동을 하라는 조언이 적절하다.

11 (1) 선행사가 사물이므로 which나 that, (2) 선행사가 사람이므로 who, whom이나 that, (3) ‘목적어+목적격 보어’의 어순이 되어야 한다. (4) 관계대명사가 접속사와 대명사의 역할을 하므로 it을 삭제해야 한다. (5) call은 동사 다음에 두 개의 명사(구)가 목적어와 목적격 보어로 쓰인다. as를 삭제해야 한다.

12 선행사가 사람이므로 목적격 관계대명사로 who나 whom 또는 that을 써야 한다.

13 ④ They called the ship Titanic. call은 동사 다음에 두 개의 명사(구)가 목적어와 목적격 보어로 쓰인다. 목적격 보어 자리에 to부정사나 형용사를 쓰지 않는다는 것에 주의한다.

14 (1) call A B: A를 B라고 부르다 (2) 선행사가 사물이므로 목적격 관계대명사로 which를 쓴다. (3) elect A B: A를 B로 선출하다 (4) 선행사가 사람이므로 목적격 관계대명사로 who나 whom을 쓴다.

15 these problems는 스마트폰을 보며 ‘걷다가’ 일어날 수 있는 안전 관련 문제들이므로, ‘걷고 있는’ 동안에는 스마트폰을 보지 마라고 하는 것이 적절하다.

16 ③번: 비슷한(형용사), ⓐ와 나머지: ~와 같이[마찬가지로], ~처럼(전치사)

17 these problems는 ‘various safety problems’를 가리킨다.

18 글의 흐름으로 보아 ‘건강’ 문제가 알맞다.

19 스마트폰을 내려다볼 때, 목에 가해지는 압박이 ‘증가한다’.

20 healthy-healthier-healthiest

21 First, Second, Third 다음의 내용을 쓰면 된다.

22 ⓑ는 부사적 용법(목적), ① 부사적 용법(형용사 수식), ④ 부사적 용법(원인), ⑤ 부사적 용법(이유), ② 형용사적 용법, ③ 명사적 용법(진목적어), persuade: 설득하다

서술형 실전문제   p.160~161

01 wrong / have a, headache / should take / will
02 texting thumb, pain / (1) finger stretching
     exercises   (2) tex
03 (A) What's the matter   (B) have a sore throat
    (C) Make sure you get some rest
04 (1) The book which/that I'm reading is about
     nature.

(2) Kenya is the country which/that John wants to visit.

(3) J. K. Rowling is a famous novelist who/whom/that many people like.

(4) I want to know the name of the girl who/whom/that I met at the party.

(5) Start by identifying the people with whom you want to work. 또는 Start by identifying the people that/who/whom you want to work with.

(6) The rate at which hair grows can be very slow. 또는 The rate which/that hair grows at can be very slow.

05 (A) without   (B) hole   (C) prevent

06 Their heads are down, and their eyes are on their smartphones.

07 (A) smartphones   (B) hole

08 (A) dry eyes   (B) neck pain   09 up → down

10 원인: 스마트폰을 너무 많이 사용하는 것, 예를 들어 너무 많이 문자를 하는 것

조언: (1) 당신의 눈높이까지 스마트폰을 위로 올려라.
(2) 목 스트레칭 운동을 할 수 있다.

01 그림으로 보아 Mike는 두통이 심하다.

03 (A)는 B의 대답으로 보아 어디가 아파 보일 때 증상을 묻는 표현이 적절하다. (B)는 아픈 증상을 이야기하는 표현으로 동사 have를 이용한다. (C)는 Mina에게 당부를 하는 표현으로 'make sure+주어+동사'의 어순을 이용한다.

04 목적격 관계대명사는 선행사가 사람이면 who나 whom, that을, 사람이 아니면 which나 that을 쓴다. 보통 목적격 관계대명사는 생략할 수 있다. 목적격 관계대명사가 전치사의 목적어일 때 전치사는 관계사절의 끝에 오거나 관계대명사 앞에 올 수 있다. 전치사가 관계사절의 끝에 올 경우에는 관계대명사를 생략할 수 있다. 전치사가 관계대명사 앞에 올 경우에는 관계대명사 that을 쓸 수 없으며, 관계대명사를 생략하지 않는다.

05 (A) 글의 흐름상 스마트폰 '없이' 사는 것이 어렵다고 하는 것이 적절하다. (B) 거리에 있는 '구덩이'를 보지 못할 수도 있다고 해야 하므로 hole이 적절하다. whole: 전체[전부]의, (C) 이런 문제들을 '예방하기' 위해라고 해야 하므로 prevent가 적절하다. protect: 보호하다

06 'down'을 보충하면 된다.

07 그들은 걷고 있는 동안에 '스마트폰'을 보고 거리에 있는 '구덩이'를 보지 못할 수도 있기 때문이다.

08 스마트폰이 일으킬 수 있는 건강상의 문제들 중의 하나는 '안구 건조증'이고 또 다른 문제는 '목 통증'이다.

09 거북목 증후군에는 당신의 눈높이까지 스마트폰을 위로 올리라고 조언하고 있기 때문에 스마트폰을 '내려다'볼 때, 목에 가해지는 압박이 증가한다고 하는 것이 적절하다.

10 스마트폰을 내려다볼 때, 목에 가해지는 압박이 증가하므로 '스마트폰을 너무 많이 사용하는 것'이 목 통증을 일으킬 수 있다. text neck에는 '당신의 눈높이까지 스마트폰을 위로 올리고 목 스트레칭 운동 또한 할 수 있다'는 조언을 하고 있다.

|모범답안|

01 (1) A: You don't look well. What's wrong? B: I have a toothache.
A: That's too bad. Make sure you go to the dentist. B: OK, I will.

(2) A: You don't look well. What's wrong? B: I have a sore throat.
A: That's too bad. Make sure you drink a lot of water. B: OK, I will.

02 call the clock tower Big Ben

03 (A) to change   (B) From now on
(C) once a week   (D) after   (E) my best

02 call A B: A를 B라고 부르다 the clock tower: 시계탑

01 ③	02 pain	03 ①	04 ⑤
05 ④	06 ②	07 ⑤	
08 your back		09 ①	10 ④
11 ②	12 texting thumb		

13 (1) Cameron is the director (who/whom/that) Gillian likes best.

(2) We liked the story Jason told us.

(3) His business made him a millionaire.

(4) We call Bali the island of gods.

14 ②

15 (1) Every student respects him.

(2) You can do various things to prevent this.

16 ⑤

17 (1) He is a gentleman (who/whom/that) I built a good trust on.

(2) These are the pants (which/that) I bought yesterday.

(3) She doesn't consider him an artist.

(4) This is the issue about which we need to express our opinion. 또는 This is the issue (which/that) we need to express our opinion about.

(5) Ella received some flowers that her boy friend had sent to her.

(6) They call it 'Non La.'

01 ③의 prevent는 '예방하다, 막다'는 의미로 'to stop something from happening, or stop someone from doing'이 되어야 한다.

02 유의어 관계이다. 건강한 = 고통

03 빨리 배우고 이해할 수 있는: 똑똑한

04 빈칸에는 모두 아픈 증상을 나타내는 표현으로 'have a+증상/병명' 형태가 적절하다.

05 (D)의 증상을 묻는 질문에 (A)의 답이 적절하고, 이어서 (C)의 걸을 수 있는지에 대한 물음에 (B)가 적절하다.

06 ② A의 몸이 안 좋아 보인다는 말에 노래 경연대회에서 일등을 했다는 말은 어색하다.

07 ⑤ 문제점을 묻는 질문에 대해 상대에게 당부하는 표현은 자연스럽지 않다.

08 Peter의 등이 아픈 것에 대해 처방을 해주는 문장으로 it은 Peter의 등을 가리킨다.

10 ④ 콧물이 난다는 말에 치과에 가라는 말은 어색하다.

11 ② Andy가 Ms. Kim을 찾아간 이유는 오른손 엄지손가락이 아파서이다.

13 선행사가 사람이면 who나 whom, that을 쓰고, 사물이나 동물이면 which나 that을 쓴다. 보통 목적격 관계대명사는 생략될 수 있다. call A B: A를 B라고 부르다 make A B: A를 B로 만들다

14 목적격 보어로 명사와 동사원형을 취할 수 있는 동사로는 make가 적절하다.

15 선행사가 사람이면 who나 that을 쓰고, 사물이나 동물이면 which나 that을 쓴다.

16 call은 동사 다음에 두 개의 명사(구)가 목적어, 목적격 보어로 쓰이므로 'as Cookie Eater'가 아니라 as 없이 'Cookie Eater'가 되어야 한다.

17 (1) 선행사가 사람이므로 who, whom이나 that, (2) 선행사가 사물이므로 which나 that, (3) '목적어+목적격 보어'의 어순이 되어야 한다. (4) 전치사가 관계대명사 앞에 올 경우에는 관계대명사 that을 쓸 수 없으며, 관계대명사를 생략하지 않는다. (5) 관계대명사가 접속사와 대명사의 역할을 하므로 them을 삭제해야 한다. (6) call은 동사 다음에 두 개의 명사(구)가 목적어와 목적격 보어로 쓰인다. as를 삭제해야 한다.

18 (A) feel은 감각동사로 '형용사'를 보어로 써야 하므로 dry가 적절하다. (B) Another problem이 주어이므로 is가 적절하다. (C) '목 스트레칭' 운동 또한 할 수 있다고 해야 하므로 stretching이 적절하다.

19 ②번과 ⑤번은 4형식, ③번은 3형식, ⓐ와 ①, ④번은 5형식이다.

20 스마트폰을 볼 때, 당신은 눈을 자주 '깜박거리지 않기' 때문에 눈이 건조하다고 느낄 것이라고 했기 때문에 눈을 자주깜박거리는 것은 스마트폰으로 인한 다양한 건강상의 문제에 해당하지 않는다.

21 목적격 관계대명사 which 또는 that이 생략되어 있다.

22 ③ 스마트폰 중독을 예방하기 위해 할 수 있는 일은 '여러 가지가 있다.'

교과서 파헤치기

Lesson 3

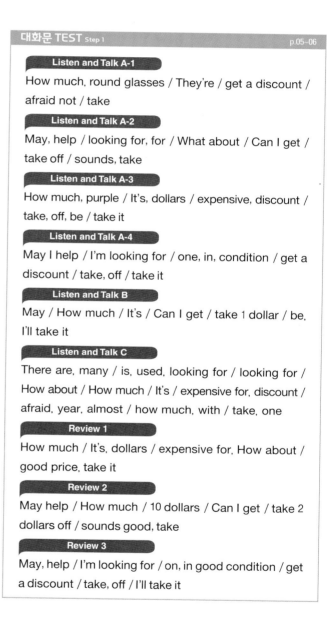

단어 TEST Step 1　　　　　　　　　　p.02

01 둥근　　　　　02 할인
03 두려워하는, 걱정하는　　　04 자주색의; 자주색
05 비싼　　　06 상태, 조건　　　07 중고의
08 거의　　　09 큰　　　10 가격
11 던지다　　　12 양동이　　　13 가죽 끈
14 악기　　　15 고무 밴드, 고무줄　　　16 업사이클링
17 칼　　　18 환경　　　19 각각의, 각각
20 이해하다　　　21 의미　　　22 누군가, 누가
23 설명하다　　　24 조합, 결합
25 항상, 개선; 개선하다　　　26 재활용
27 업사이클하다　　　28 개최하다, 열다　　　29 쓰레기
30 옷, 의복　　　31 ～를 통해　　　32 창의적인
33 바느질　　　34 장식하다　　　35 할인을 받다
36 ～을 할인하다, 깎다　　　37 버리다
38 잠깐 생각해 볼게　　　39 ～에 좋다　　　40 ～에 관한 것이다
41 ～로부터 이야기[소식]을 듣다　　　42 예를 들어
43 ～을 자르다

단어 TEST Step 2　　　　　　　　　　p.03

01 glasses　　　02 backpack　　　03 interesting
04 musical　　　05 blue jeans　　　06 event
07 like　　　08 thing　　　09 nursing home
10 kit　　　11 sew　　　12 bottom
13 shoulder　　　14 lastly　　　15 through
16 combination　　　17 strap　　　18 understand
19 bucket　　　20 trash　　　21 discount
22 expensive　　　23 throw　　　24 environment
25 decorate　　　26 recycling　　　27 instrument
28 meaning　　　29 knife　　　30 almost
31 used　　　32 price　　　33 explain
34 hold　　　35 be made by　　　36 look for
37 sound like+명사　　　38 cut off
39 be good for　　　40 for example　　　41 throw away
42 get a discount　43 talk about

단어 TEST Step 3　　　　　　　　　　p.04

1 discount, 할인　　2 clothes, 옷　　3 meaning, 의미
4 environment, 환경　　5 combination, 조합, 결합
6 interested, 관심 있는　　7 instrument, 악기
8 explain, 설명하다　　9 creative, 창의적인
10 decorate, 장식하다　　11 backpack, 가방
12 trash, 쓰레기　　13 round, 둥근　　14 bucket, 양동이
15 purple, 자주색의　　16 recycling, 재활용

대화문 TEST Step 1　　　　　　　　　　p.05~06

Listen and Talk A-1

How much, round glasses / They're / get a discount /
afraid not / take

Listen and Talk A-2

May, help / looking for, for / What about / Can I get /
take off / sounds, take

Listen and Talk A-3

How much, purple / It's, dollars / expensive, discount /
take, off, be / take it

Listen and Talk A-4

May I help / I'm looking for / one, in, condition / get a
discount / take, off / take it

Listen and Talk B

May / How much / It's / Can I get / take 1 dollar / be,
I'll take it

Listen and Talk C

There are, many / is, used, looking for / looking for /
How about / How much / It's / expensive for, discount /
afraid, year, almost / how much, with / take, one

Review 1

How much / It's, dollars / expensive for, How about /
good price, take it

Review 2

May help / How much / 10 dollars / Can I get / take 2
dollars off / sounds good, take

Review 3

May, help / I'm looking for / on, in good condition / get
a discount / take, off / I'll take it

대화문 TEST Step 2　　　　　　　　　　p.07~08

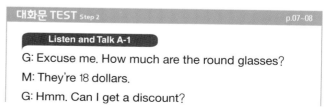

Listen and Talk A-1

G: Excuse me. How much are the round glasses?
M: They're 18 dollars.
G: Hmm. Can I get a discount?

M: No, I'm afraid not. Sorry.

G: That's OK. I'll take them.

Listen and Talk A-2

M: Hello. May I help you?

G: Yes. I'm looking for a backpack for school.

M: What about this red one? It's 12 dollars.

G: Can I get a discount?

M: OK. I'll take 2 dollars off.

G: That sounds good. I'll take it.

Listen and Talk A-3

G: Excuse me. How much is this purple T-shirt?

M: It's 10 dollars.

G: That's expensive. Can I get a discount?

M: OK. I'll take 1 dollar off. That'll be 9 dollars.

G: I'll take it, then. Thank you!

Listen and Talk A-4

M: Hello. May I help you?

G: I'm looking for a baseball glove.

M: This one is 15 dollars and it's in good condition.

G: Can I get a discount?

M: OK. I'll take 2 dollars off.

G: Then it's 13 dollars. I'll take it.

Listen and Talk B

A: May I help you?

B: Yes. How much is this soccer ball?

A: It's 6 dollars.

B: Can I get a discount?

A: OK. I'll take 1 dollar off.

Listen and Talk C

B: Wow! There are so many interesting things here.

W: Everything here is old or used. What are you looking for?

B: I'm looking for a clock.

W: How about this red clock?

B: How much is it?

W: It's 15 dollars.

B: That's too expensive for me. Can I get a discount?

W: No, I'm afraid not. It's only one year old. It's almost new.

B: Then, how much is this blue clock with the large numbers?

W: It's 10 dollars.

B: Then, I'll take the blue one. Thank you.

Review 1

G: Excuse me. How much is this yellow backpack?

M: It's 18 dollars.

G: Hmm. That's expensive for me. How about this red one?

M: It's 15 dollars.

G: That's a good price. I'll take it.

Review 2

W: May I help you?

B: Yes. How much is this blue T-shirt?

W: It's 10 dollars.

B: Can I get a discount?

W: OK. I'll take 2 dollars off.

B: That sounds good. I'll take it.

Review 3

M: Hello. May I help you?

G: I'm looking for a clock.

M: This one is 15 dollars and it's in good condition.

G: Can I get a discount?

M: OK. I'll take 2 dollars off.

G: Then it's 13 dollars. I'll take it.

본문 TEST Step 1   p.09~10

01 Let's about   02 club members

03 As, year's, about

04 each, to understand, meaning   05 Can, explain

06 upcycling, combination, recycling

07 Like, good, environment

08 When, better, from old   09 let's talk, each

10 Let's, with   11 My, to hold

12 combination, trash, fashion   13 trash, clothes

14 other, interested, through   15 sounds like

16 about, group   17 going, make, instruments

18 make, from, buckets

19 also, from, rubber   20 plan, the, in

21 let's hear from

22 will, from, clothes

23 For example, use   24 Look at

25 made by, of   26 Isn't it   27 more, sell, on

28 going, to, nursing   29 That's, great

30 Your, all, creative   31 want, to work

32 Cut off, of   33 Sew, together

34 Make, straps, of   35 sew, straps, top

36 Decorate, with, and

본문 TEST Step 2   p.11~12

01 Let's about   02 club members

03 As you know, about upcycling

04 Before, talk about, to understand, upcycling

05 explain upcycling
06 upcycling, combination
07 Like, is good for
08 When, upcycle, from old things
09 let's talk about
10 Let's start with   11 hold a, show
12 a combination of
13 to make clothes
14 become interested in, through
15 sounds like fun   16 What about
17 is going to, instruments   18 from, buckets
19 also, from, rubber bands
20 plan to play, instruments
21 let's hear from
22 make, from old clothes
23 For example, jeans   24 Look at
25 was made by, one of   26 Isn't it
27 more, on Environment Day
28 all the money, nursing home   29 great idea
30 Your, creative   31 want, to work hard
32 Cut off, blue jeans   33 Sew, together
34 shoulder straps, one   35 Sew, to
36 Decorate, with

16 너희 그룹은 어떠니, Eric?
17 저희 그룹은 낡은 물건으로 악기를 만들려고 합니다.
18 낡은 플라스틱 양동이로 드럼을 만들 겁니다.
19 또한 저희는 낡은 상자와 고무줄로 기타를 만들 겁니다.
20 저희는 소규모 음악회를 열어 그 악기들로 연주할 계획입니다.
21 고맙다, Eric. 그럼 이제 수미의 그룹 의견을 들어 보자.
22 저희 그룹은 낡은 옷으로 가방을 만들 거예요.
23 예를 들어 청바지를 이용할 거예요.
24 이 가방을 보세요.
25 이것은 저희 모둠원 중 한 명인 하준이가 만들었어요.
26 멋지지 않나요?
27 우리는 가방을 더 많이 만들어서 환경의 날에 팔 거예요.
28 번 돈을 모두 양로원에 줄 예정이에요.
29 훌륭한 생각이구나.
30 너희들의 발상은 모두 아주 창의적이구나.
31 너희들 모두 환경의 날을 위해 열심히 노력하길 바란다.
32 청바지의 다리 부분을 잘라낸다.
33 아래쪽을 붙여서 바느질한다.
34 다리 한 짝으로 어깨끈을 만든다.
35 청바지의 윗부분에 어깨끈을 바느질한다.
36 핀이나 단추로 가방을 장식한다.

1 Let's Talk about Upcycling
2 Hello, club members.
3 As you know, this year's Environment Day is about upcycling.
4 Before we talk about each group's event idea for that day, I want you to understand the meaning of "upcycling."
5 Can anyone explain upcycling?
6 Yes. The word "upcycling" is a combination of "upgrade" and "recycling."
7 Like recycling, upcycling is good for the environment.
8 When you upcycle, you make new and better things from old things.
9 Good. Now, let's talk about each group's idea for the event.
10 Let's start with Pei's group.
11 My group wants to hold a trashion show.
12 "Trashion" is a combination of "trash" and "fashion."
13 We'll use trash to make clothes.
14 We want other students to become interested in upcycling through the show.
15 A trashion show sounds like fun!
16 What about your group, Eric?

1 업사이클링에 대해 이야기해 봅시다
2 동아리 회원 여러분, 안녕하세요.
3 여러분도 알다시피 올해의 환경의 날은 업사이클링에 관한 것입니다.
4 각 그룹이 그날에 할 행사 아이디어를 이야기하기 전에 여러분이 '업사이클링'의 의미를 이해하기를 바랍니다.
5 누가 업사이클링의 뜻을 설명해 줄 수 있나요?
6 네. '업사이클링'이란 단어는 "upgrade"와 "recycling"이 결합한 것입니다.
7 재활용과 마찬가지로 업사이클링도 환경에 좋아요.
8 업사이클링을 하면, 여러분은 오래된 것들로 새롭고 더 좋은 것을 만들어요.
9 좋아요. 이제 각 그룹의 행사 아이디어에 대해 이야기해 봅시다.
10 Pei의 그룹부터 시작하죠
11 저희 그룹은 트래션 쇼를 하고 싶습니다.
12 "트래션(Trashion)"은 "trash"와 "fashion"이 결합한 말입니다.
13 저희는 옷을 만들기 위해 쓰레기를 이용할 것입니다.
14 저희는 이 쇼를 통해서 다른 학생들이 업사이클링에 관심을 갖게 되기를 바랍니다.
15 트래션 쇼라니 멋지겠구나!

17 My group is going to make musical instruments from old things.

18 We'll make drums from old plastic buckets.

19 We'll also make a guitar from old boxes and rubber bands.

20 We plan to play the instruments in a mini-concert.

21 Thank you, Eric. Now, let's hear from Sumi's group.

22 My group will make bags from old clothes.

23 For example, we'll use blue jeans.

24 Look at this bag.

25 This was made by Hajun, one of our group members.

26 Isn't it nice?

27 We'll make more bags and sell them on Environment Day.

28 We're going to give all the money to a nursing home.

29 That's a great idea.

30 Your ideas are all so creative.

31 I want everyone to work hard for Environment Day.

32 Cut off the legs of the blue jeans.

33 Sew the bottom together.

34 Make shoulder straps from one of the legs.

35 Sew the straps to the top of the jeans.

36 Decorate the bag with pins and buttons.

구석구석지문 TEST Step 1

Around the World

1. to give, lessons to
2. don't, any
3. can help
4. have
5. thank
6. can make, from
7. sends us trash
8. send back
9. upcycling

Think and Write

1. Creative Upcycling
2. Need, jeans, sewing
3. Cut off
4. to, bottom of
5. sew, to
6. Decorate with

구석구석지문 TEST Step 2

Around the World

1. Kids, I want to give music lessons to you.
2. But we don't have any musical instruments.
3. I can help you.
4. I have a good idea.
5. Oh, thank you!
6. I can make musical instruments from trash.
7. The world sends us trash.
8. We send back music.
9. This is the power of upcycling.

Think and Write

1. Creative Upcycling Idea: Blue Jeans Basket
2. You Need: old blue jeans, sewing kit, scissors, buttons and pins
3. Step: 1 Cut off a leg of the old blue jeans.
4. 2 Cut out a piece to make the bottom of the basket.
5. 3 Sew the bottom to the leg.
6. 4 Decorate with buttons and pins.

10 experiment, 실험, 시험　11 floss, 치실질을 하다, 치실

12 announcement, 발표, 소식　13 pile, 쌓다, 포개다

14 record, 기록하다, 등록하다　15 tool, 도구, 수단

16 pattern, 무늬, 도안

단어 TEST Step 1　　p.21

01 뱀	02 남색	03 사진
04 화장실	05 고릴라	06 운이 좋은
07 성공하다	08 발표, 소식	09 절, 사원
10 ~하는 동안에	11 대개, 보통	12 벌레
13 해결하다, 풀다	14 보호	15 높이, 정도, 수준
16 앵무새	17 면	18 재능
19 천천히	20 기록하다, 등록하다; 기록	
21 문어	22 (딱딱한) 껍데기, 껍질	
23 남자의, 수컷의	24 상상하다	25 까마귀
26 무늬, 도안	27 놀라게 하다	28 한때, 한동안
29 실험, 시험	30 꼬리	31 또한
32 입다, 신다, 쓰다	33 가게; 저장하다	34 A가 아니고 B
35 ~을 잘하다, ~에 능숙하다		36 ~을 뽑다
37 ~처럼 보이다, ~와 닮다		38 음악에 맞춰 춤추다
39 ~에 대해 조심하다, 경계하다		40 휴식하다
41 그 밖에, 그 외에	42 알아내다	43 꼭 ~처럼

단어 TEST Step 2　　p.22

01 hide	02 way	03 pile
04 fable	05 floss	06 leave
07 carry	08 round-shaped	09 sign
10 tool	11 jar	12 float
13 stripe	14 example	15 also
16 coconut	17 drop	18 unique
19 experiment	20 protection	21 succeed
22 pattern	23 temple	24 slowly
25 photograph	26 imagine	27 cotton
28 usually	29 male	30 octopus
31 parrot	32 gorilla	33 worm
34 announcement		35 more than
36 find out	37 on top of	38 take a rest
39 not A but B	40 look for	41 be good at
42 pull out	43 look like	

단어 TEST Step 3　　p.23

1 fable, 우화, 동화　2 coconut, 코코넛 열매

3 surprise, 놀라게 하다　4 shell, (딱딱한) 껍데기, 껍질

5 level, 정도, 수준　6 navy, 남색　7 talent, 재능

8 photograph, 사진　9 cotton, 면

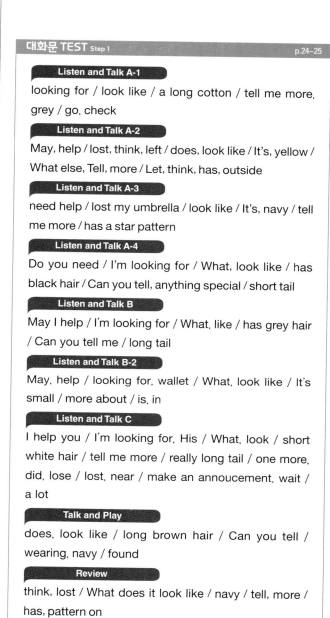

대화문 TEST Step 1　　p.24~25

Listen and Talk A-1

looking for / look like / a long cotton / tell me more,
grey / go, check

Listen and Talk A-2

May, help / lost, think, left / does, look like / It's, yellow /
What else, Tell, more / Let, think, has, outside

Listen and Talk A-3

need help / lost my umbrella / look like / It's, navy / tell
me more / has a star pattern

Listen and Talk A-4

Do you need / I'm looking for / What, look like / has
black hair / Can you tell, anything special / short tail

Listen and Talk B

May I help / I'm looking for / What, like / has grey hair
/ Can you tell me / long tail

Listen and Talk B-2

May, help / looking for, wallet / What, look like / It's
small / more about / is, in

Listen and Talk C

I help you / I'm looking for, His / What, look / short
white hair / tell me more / really long tail / one more,
did, lose / lost, near / make an annoucement, wait /
a lot

Talk and Play

does, look like / long brown hair / Can you tell /
wearing, navy / found

Review

think, lost / What does it look like / navy / tell, more /
has, pattern on

대화문 TEST Step 2　　p.26~27

Listen and Talk A-1

B: Excuse me. I'm looking for my scarf.

W: What does it look like?

B: It's a long cotton scarf.

W: Can you tell me more about it?

B: Well, it's grey.

W: OK. I'll go and check.

W: May I help you?

B: Yes. I lost my bag. I think I left it in the restroom.

W: OK. What does it look like?

B: It's small and yellow.

W: What else? Tell me more about it.

B: Let me think. Oh, it has two pockets outside.

W: Do you need help?

B: Yes. I lost my umbrella.

W: What does it look like?

B: It's long and navy.

W: Can you tell me more?

B: Yes. It has a star pattern on it.

B: Do you need help?

W: Yes. I'm looking for my cat.

B: What does it look like?

W: Well, she's not very big and she has black hair.

B: Can you tell me more? Is there anything special about her?

W: She has a short tail.

A: May I help you?

B: Yes. I'm looking for my cat.

A: What does it look like?

B: It's small and it has grey hair.

A: Can you tell me more about it?

B: It has a long tail.

A: May I help you?

B: Yes. I'm looking for my wallet.

A: What does it look like?

B: It's small and red.

A: Can you tell me more about it?

B: There is a card in it.

M: May I help you?

G: Yes. I'm looking for my dog. His name is Prince.

M: What does he look like?

G: He's very small and has short white hair.

M: Can you tell me more?

G: Well, he has a really long tail.

M: I see. And one more thing. Where did you lose him?

G: I lost him near the main gate.

M: OK. I'll go and make an announcement. Can you please wait here?

G: Sure. Thanks a lot.

A: What does Amy look like?

B: She's tall and has long brown hair.

A: Can you tell me more?

B: She's wearing short navy pants.

A: I found her.

G: Hi. I think I lost my umbrella.

M: What does it look like?

G: It's a big navy umbrella.

M: Can you tell me more?

G: It has a white flower pattern on it.

본문 TEST Step 1   p.28~29

01 That, Tools   02 once thought, only

03 finding out, also

04 in, watch out for   05 may, pull out

06 to floss, teeth 07 female, that are, flossing

08 While, watching, floss, teeth   09 way, to floss

10 don't usually think

11 However, can, use

12 use, shells, protection

13 can't find, hiding, hide   14 store, for, use

15 pile, carry, later   16 How smart

17 drops, into, to raise   18 may think, just

19 were studying, experiment   20 put, with, front

21 worm, floating, top

22 water level, low, could   23 solved, just as

24 dropped, into 25 special, wrong

26 experiment with, did, same

본문 TEST Step 2   p.30~31

01 That, Tools   02 once thought, can use

03 finding out, can also

04 go to, temple, watch out for

05 may come, pull out

06 to floss their teeth

07 female, are teaching flossing

08 While, are watching, floss their teeth

09 This way, learn to floss

10 usually think, octopuses

11 However, can also use

12 shells for protection

13 can't, hiding place, hide under

14 even store, for later use

15 pile, carry, to use later　　　16 How

17 fable, drops, jar to raise

18 may think, just, but

19 who were studying, experiment　20 put, in front of

21 worm, on top of

22 However, level, low, could not　23 solved, just as

24 dropped, into　25 If, special, wrong

26 same experiment, other, too

1 도구를 사용하는 동물들

2 사람들은 한때 인간만이 도구를 사용할 수 있다고 생각했다.

3 이제 과학자들은 많은 동물들 역시 도구를 사용할 수 있다는 것을 밝혀내고 있다.

4 당신이 태국의 롭부리의 절에 간다면, 마카크 원숭이들을 조심해야 한다.

5 그들이 당신에게 다가와 당신의 머리카락을 뽑을 수도 있다.

6 그들은 이빨을 치실질하기 위해서 사람의 머리카락을 사용한다.

7 만약 당신이 운이 좋으면, 당신은 새끼들에게 치실질하는 것을 가르치고 있는 암컷 원숭이들을 볼 수 있을 것이다.

8 새끼들이 지켜보고 있는 동안, 암컷 원숭이들은 아주 천천히 그들의 이빨을 치실질한다.

9 이런 방식으로, 새끼 원숭이들은 치실질을 배운다.

10 사람들은 대개 문어가 영리하다고 생각하지 않는다.

11 하지만, 문어는 매우 영리하고 또한 도구를 사용할 수 있다.

12 그들은 자신을 보호하기 위해 코코넛 껍데기를 사용한다.

13 그들이 숨을 만한 좋은 장소를 찾지 못했을 때, 그들은 코코넛 껍데기 아래로 숨는다.

14 어떤 문어들은 심지어 코코넛 껍데기를 나중에 쓰기 위해 모은다.

15 그들은 코코넛 껍데기를 쌓아두고 나중에 쓰기 위해서 가지고 다닌다.

16 얼마나 똑똑한가!

17 이솝 우화 속 '목마른 까마귀'에서 까마귀는 물 높이를 높이기 위해 항아리 안으로 돌을 떨어뜨린다.

18 당신은 이것이 그저 이야기라고 생각할 수 있지만, 그렇지 않다.

19 까마귀를 연구하던 과학자들이 실험을 했다.

20 그들은 까마귀 앞에 물이 든 항아리를 놓았다.

21 물 위에 벌레가 떠다니고 있었다.

22 하지만, 물 높이가 낮아서, 까마귀는 그 벌레를 먹을 수 없었다.

23 그 까마귀는 우화에서처럼 문제를 해결했다.

24 까마귀는 돌을 항아리 안으로 떨어뜨렸다.

25 만약 당신이 이 새가 특별하다고 생각한다면, 당신이 틀렸다.

26 과학자들은 다른 까마귀들에게도 똑같은 실험을 했고, 그들 모두가 똑같이 그렇게 했다.

1 Animals That Use Tools

2 People once thought that only humans can use tools.

3 Now, scientists are finding out that many animals can also use tools.

4 If you go to a Buddhist temple in Lop Buri, Thailand, watch out for the Macaque monkeys.

5 They may come to you and pull out your hair.

6 They use human hair to floss their teeth.

7 If you are lucky, you may see female monkeys that are teaching flossing to their babies.

8 While the babies are watching, the female monkeys floss their teeth very slowly.

9 This way, the baby monkeys learn to floss.

10 People don't usually think that octopuses are smart.

11 However, octopuses are very smart, and they can also use tools.

12 They use coconut shells for protection.

13 When they can't find a good hiding place, they hide under coconut shells.

14 Some octopuses even store coconut shells for later use.

15 They pile the coconut shells and carry them to use later.

16 How smart!

17 In Aesop's fable The Thirsty Crow , a crow drops stones into a jar to raise the level of water.

18 You may think this is just a story, but it is not.

19 Scientists who were studying crows did an experiment.

20 They put a jar with water in front of a crow.

21 A worm was floating on top of the water.

22 However, the water level was low, so the crow could not eat the worm.

23 The crow solved the problem just as in the fable.

24 It dropped stones into the jar.

25 If you think this bird is special, you are wrong.

26 Scientists did the same experiment with other crows, and they all did the same, too.

Around the World

1. longest, ever

2. long

3. recorded

4. record

5. The oldest

6. lived for

Think and Write

1. with

2. There are, have

3. example

4. which, to talk

5. can sing

6. are, that, talents

7. An example

8. female, lives

9. talk with, in

10. more than

구석구석지문 TEST Step 2 p.39

Around the World

1. The longest snake ever is Medusa.

2. She is 7.67 meters long.

3. Alley recorded the longest jump by a cat.

4. Her record was 1.83 meters.

5. The oldest pig ever is Ernestine.

6. He lived for 22 years and 359 days.

Think and Write

1. Animals with Special Talents

2. There are many animals that have special talents.

3. An example is Einstein.

4. He is an African Grey Parrot which can use 200 English words to talk with people.

5. He can sing the "Happy Birthday" song.

6. There are many animals that have special talents.

7. An example is Koko.

8. She is a female gorilla which lives in America.

9. She can talk with people in American Sign Language.

10. She knows more than 1,000 signs.

10 increase, 증가하다　11 medicine, 약, 약물
12 prevent, 막다, 예방하다　13 safety, 안전
14 thumb, 엄지손가락　15 exercise, 운동
16 addiction, 중독

단어 TEST Step 1　　　　　　p.40

01 충고　02 유명인사, 유명인　03 ~ 동안
04 현명하지 않은　05 아픈, 쓰린　06 열, 열병
07 단순한　08 눈을 깜박이다　09 엄지손가락
10 막다, 예방하다　11 목구멍　12 건강
13 피부　14 초조한, 불안한　15 다양한
16 구덩이, 구멍　17 과목　18 건조한, 마른
19 식사　20 약　21 규칙적으로
22 똑똑한, 지적인　23 어려운　24 다치다
25 약속　26 사고　27 안전
28 예, 사례　29 증가하다　30 작가, 저자
31 끔찍한, 무서운　32 중독　33 야기하다
34 아픔, 고통　35 지금부터　36 전 세계적으로
37 잠들다　38 ~ 대신에　39 (~한 상태에) 처하다
40 휴식을 취하다, 쉬다　41 목이 아프다
42 예를 들어　43 건강해 보이다

단어 TEST Step 2　　　　　　p.41

01 thumb　02 hole　03 health
04 difficult　05 promise　06 regularly
07 simple　08 nervous　09 advice
10 prevent　11 hurt　12 during
13 skin　14 blink　15 various
16 celebrity　17 sore　18 unwise
19 subject　20 medicine　21 fever
22 dry　23 intelligent　24 throat
25 meal　26 increase　27 dentist
28 smart　29 exercise　30 addiction
31 without　32 toothache　33 safety
34 author　35 instead of ~　36 a few
37 these days　38 have a runny nose
39 for example　40 take a rest　41 try to+동사원형
42 fall asleep　43 from now on

단어 TEST Step 3　　　　　　p.42

1 rest, 휴식　2 pad, 패드　3 cause, 야기하다
4 hole, 구덩이　5 blink, 눈을 깜박이다
6 regularly, 규칙적으로　7 pain, 고통
8 text, 문자를 보내다　9 throat, 목구멍

대화문 TEST Step 1　　　　　　p.43~44

Listen and Talk A-1
look sick, What's wrong / have a sore throat, have a fever / have a cold, Take, medicine, make sure, take, rest / Thank you

Listen and Talk A-2
wrong / back hurts a lot / Put, on / I will / make sure, stretching exercises

Listen and Talk A-3
matter / have a, toothache / Here is, medicine, Take / make sure, dentist / I will

Listen and Talk A-4
wrong with / fell, hurt, while / Can, walk / hurts / Why don't you, make sure, don't play, until

Listen and Talk B
1 don't look well, wrong / have a headache / That's too bad, Make sure, take / will
2 don't look well, wrong / have a cold / Make sure, doctor / I will

Listen and Talk C
wrong / thumb hurts / use, a lot / text a lot / have texting thumb / pain, your thumb, get, from texting / didn't know / Why don't you / make sure you don't text

Review 1
wrong / have a terrible headache / should take some medicine / I will

Review 2
the matter / have a sore throat, have a runny nose / cold, Make sure, get some rest / I will

대화문 TEST Step 2　　　　　　p.45~46

Listen and Talk A-1
W: You look sick. What's wrong, Inho?
B: I have a sore throat. I have a fever, too.
W: I think you have a cold. Take this medicine and make sure you take a good rest.
B: OK. Thank you.

W: What's wrong, Peter?

B: I don't know, Ms. Kim, but my back hurts a lot.

W: Put a heating pad on it.

B: OK, I will.

W: And make sure you do some stretching exercises.

Listen and Talk A-3

W: What's the matter, Chris?

B: I have a terrible toothache.

W: Here is some medicine. Take this.

B: Thank you.

W: And make sure you go to the dentist. B: OK, I will.

Listen and Talk A-4

W: What's wrong with your leg, Sam?

B: I fell and hurt my foot while I was playing soccer.

W: Can you walk?

B: Yes, but it hurts a lot.

W: Why don't you put some ice on it? And make sure you don't play soccer until next week.

Listen and Talk B

1 A: You don't look well. What's wrong?

B: I have a headache.

A: That's too bad. Make sure you take some medicine.

B: OK, I will.

2 A: You don't look well. What's wrong?

B: I have a cold.

A: That's too bad. Make sure you go see a doctor.

B: OK, I will.

Listen and Talk C

W: What's wrong, Andy?

B: Hello, Ms. Kim. My right thumb hurts.

W: Hmm. Do you use your smartphone a lot?

B: Yes, I text a lot. Why?

W: I think you have texting thumb.

B: Texting thumb? What's texting thumb?

W: It's pain in your thumb. You can get it from texting too much.

B: Oh, I didn't know that.

W: Why don't you do some finger stretching exercises?

B: OK, I will. W: And make sure you don't text too much.

Review 1

G: What's wrong, Mike?

B: I have a terrible headache.

G: I think you should take some medicine.

B: OK, I will.

Review 2

M: What's the matter, Mina?

G: I have a sore throat. I also have a runny nose.

M: I think you have a cold. Make sure you get some rest.

G: OK, I will.

본문TEST Step 1   p.47~48

01 Be Smart with 02 Living without, difficult, days

03 unwise, use, cause   04 Are, smombie

05 over, around like   06 down, eyes, on

07 call such people

08 If, various safety

09 may, so, fall, hurt   10 get into, too

11 what, to prevent   12 It's simple

13 at, while, walking   14 dry, text neck

15 cause, health problems

16 example, dry eyes

17 When, look at, blink   18 your, feel dry

19 Another, have, pain

20 down at, on, increases

21 use, for, texting, cause

22 call, text   23 Here, tips, problems

24 dry, try, blink 25 move, up, level

26 also, stretching exercises

27 How, feel, don't

28 feel nervous, around

29 feel sad, check, text

30 answers, may, addiction

31 There, various, prevent   32 turn off, during

33 instead of texting

본문TEST Step 2   p.49~50

01 Be Smart with

02 Living without smartphones, these days

03 unwise or too much use, can cause

04 Are, a smombie

05 All over the world, walking around like zombies

06 down, on their smartphones

07 call such people smombies

08 various safety problems

09 may not see, so, may fall, get hurt

10 may get into, too

11 to prevent these problems   12 simple

13 Do not look at, while, walking

14 dry eyes, text neck

15 various health problems

16 One example, dry eyes

17 look at, blink often   18 will feel dry

19 Another problem, is neck pain

20 look down at, stress on, increases

21 Too much use, too much texting, neck pain

22 call, text neck 23 Here are some tips

24 dry eyes, try to blink

25 move, up to, your eye level

26 can also, neck stretching exercises

27 How do you feel

28 feel nervous, around

29 feel sad, no text message

30 answers, smartphone addiction 31 to prevent this

32 For example, turn off, during

33 can, instead of texting

1 스마트폰을 현명하게 사용하라!

2 스마트폰 없이 사는 것은 요즘 많은 사람들에게 어렵다.

3 하지만 스마트폰을 현명하지 않게 사용하거나 너무 과도하게 사용하는 것은 다양한 문제를 야기할 수 있다.

4 당신은 스몸비인가요?

5 전 세계적으로 사람들이 좀비처럼 걸어다니고 있다.

6 그들의 머리는 아래를 향하고, 그들의 눈은 스마트폰을 향하고 있다.

7 우리는 그런 사람들을 스몸비, 즉 스마트폰 좀비라고 부른다.

8 만약 당신이 스몸비라면, 당신은 다양한 안전 관련 문제들을 겪을 수 있다.

9 당신은 거리에 있는 구덩이를 보지 못할 수도 있고, 그래서 넘어져서 다칠지도 모른다.

10 당신은 또한 교통사고를 당할지도 모른다.

11 그렇다면 이런 문제들을 방지하기 위해 무엇을 할 수 있을까?

12 간단하다.

13 걷고 있는 동안에는 스마트폰을 보지 마라!

14 당신은 안구 건조증이나 거북목 증후군이 있나요?

15 스마트폰은 다양한 건강상의 문제를 일으킬 수 있다.

16 한 가지 예가 안구 건조증이다.

17 스마트폰을 볼 때, 당신은 눈을 자주 깜박거리지 않는다.

18 그러면 눈이 건조하다고 느낄 것이다.

19 일어날 수 있는 또 다른 문제는 목 통증이다.

20 스마트폰을 내려다볼 때, 목에 가해지는 압박이 증가한다.

21 스마트폰을 너무 많이 사용하는 것은, 예를 들어, 너무 많이 문자를 하는 것은 목 통증을 일으킬 수 있다.

22 이런 증상을 거북목 증후군이라고 부른다.

23 여기에 이런 문제들을 위한 몇 가지 조언이 있다.

24 안구 건조증에는, 눈을 자주 깜박이려고 노력해라.

25 거북목 증후군에는 당신의 눈높이까지 스마트폰을 위로 올려라.

26 목 스트레칭 운동 또한 할 수 있다.

27 스마트폰이 없을 때 어떤 기분이 드나요?

28 스마트폰이 주위에 없을 때 당신은 초조한 기분이 드는가?

29 스마트폰을 확인했을 때 아무런 문자 메시지가 없으면 슬픈 기분이 드는가?

30 만약 당신의 대답이 '그렇다'이면, 당신은 스마트폰 중독일지도 모른다.

31 이것을 방지하기 위해 할 수 있는 일은 여러 가지가 있다.

32 예를 들어, 식사나 회의 중에는 스마트폰을 꺼라.

33 문자를 보내는 대신에 사람들과 이야기를 할 수 있다.

1 Be Smart with Your Smartphones!

2 Living without smartphones is difficult for many of us these days.

3 However, unwise or too much use of smartphones can cause various problems.

4 Are you a smombie?

5 All over the world, people are walking around like zombies.

6 Their heads are down, and their eyes are on their smartphones.

7 We call such people smombies, smartphone zombies.

8 If you are a smombie, you can have various safety problems.

9 You may not see a hole in the street, so you may fall and get hurt.

10 You may get into a car accident, too.

11 So what can you do to prevent these problems?

12 It's simple.

13 Do not look at your smartphone while you are walking!

14 Do you have dry eyes or text neck?

15 Smartphones can cause various health problems.

16 One example is dry eyes.

17 When you look at your smartphone, you do not blink often.

18 Then your eyes will feel dry.

19 Another problem you can have is neck pain.

20 When you look down at your smartphone, the

stress on your neck increases.

21 Too much use of your smartphone, for example, too much texting, can cause neck pain.

22 We call this text neck.

23 Here are some tips for these problems.

24 For dry eyes, try to blink often.

25 For text neck, move your smartphone up to your eye level.

26 You can also do some neck stretching exercises.

27 How do you feel when you don't have your smartphone with you?

28 Do you feel nervous when your smartphone is not around?

29 Do you feel sad when you check your smartphone and there is no text message?

30 If your answers are "yes," you may have smartphone addiction.

31 There are various things you can do to prevent this.

32 For example, turn off your smartphone during meals or meetings.

33 You can talk to people instead of texting them.

구석구석지문 TEST Step 1 — p.57

Talk and Play

1. wrong
2. have a fever
3. Make sure, some rest
4. I will

After You Read B

1. Be Smart with
2. fell, got hurt
3. was texting, didn't see
4. Do not, while, are walking
5. feel dry
6. Try to blink
7. when, text a lot
8. up to, eye level, stretching exercises
9. have smartphone addiction
10. Turn off, during, instead of texting

Around the World

1. Be careful, using, while
2. There are, so, while, are using
3. means, side, who are texting

구석구석지문 TEST Step 2 — p.58

Talk and Play

1. A: What's wrong?
2. B: I have a fever.
3. A: That's too bad. Make sure you get some rest.
4. B: OK, I will.

After You Read B

1. Be Smart with Your Smartphones!
2. Minho: Yesterday, I fell on the street and got hurt.
3. I was texting and I didn't see a hole.
4. Reply: Do not use your smartphone while you are walking.
5. Emma: My eyes feel dry when I use my smartphone.
6. Reply: Try to blink often.
7. Suji: I have neck pain when I text a lot.
8. Reply: Move your smartphone up to your eye level and do some neck stretching exercises .
9. Eric: I think I have smartphone addiction.
10. Reply: Turn off your smartphone during meals or meetings and talk to people instead of texting them.

Around the World

1. This sign says, "Be careful of using your smartphone while you are walking."
2. There are traffic lights on the ground, so people can see them while they are using their smartphones.
3. This sign on the ground means, "This side of the street is for people who are texting."

MEMO

MEMO

적중100

영어 기출 문제집

정답 및 해설

동아 | 윤정미